The FAUBOURG MARIGNY of NEW ORLEANS

The FAUBOURG MARIGNY of NEW ORLEANS

A HISTORY

SCOTT S. ELLIS

Louisiana State University Press
Baton Rouge

Published with the assistance of the V. Ray Cardozier Fund

Published by Louisiana State University Press

Manufactured in the United States of America
FIRST PRINTING

DESIGNER: *Mandy McDonald Scallan*
TYPEFACE: *Calluna*
PRINTER AND BINDER: *Sheridan Books, Inc.*

Library of Congress Cataloging-in-Publication Data

Names: Ellis, Scott S., author.
Title: The Faubourg Marigny of New Orleans : a history / Scott S. Ellis.
Description: Baton Rouge : Louisiana State University Press, [2018] | Includes bibliographical references and index.
Identifiers: LCCN 2018007291| ISBN 978-0-8071-6935-3 (cloth : alk. paper) | ISBN 978-0-8071-7004-5 (pdf) | ISBN 978-0-8071-7005-2 (epub)
Subjects: LCSH: Faubourg Marigny (New Orleans, La.)—History.
Classification: LCC F379.N56 F384 2018 | DDC 976.3/35—dc23
LC record available at https://lccn.loc.gov/2018007291

The paper in this book meets the guidelines for permanence and durability of the Committee on Production Guidelines for Book Longevity of the Council on Library Resources.

For Gene and Lloyd

CONTENTS

ILLUSTRATIONS

Maps

Photographs and Drawings

PREFACE

The original settlement of New Orleans, founded in 1718, became what we now call the French Quarter, or as the settlers fondly said, the Vieux Carré (old square). In 1788 the first suburb of New Orleans, Faubourg (false town, or suburb) St. Mary, was created, upriver from the Vieux Carré. In 1805 Bernard Marigny, heir to the largest fortune in Louisiana, divided his property just downriver from the Vieux Carré into lots and established the second suburb of New Orleans, naming it Faubourg Marigny.

While the Vieux Carré remained the legal, social, and commercial heart of the city for many years, the Faubourg Marigny was from the start a working-class residential district with corner stores, bars, and restaurants that catered to the neighborhood.

The Vieux Carré endured a long social and physical decline between the Civil War and the First World War. After 1919 a coalition of socialites, writers, and artists created a revival. That revival culminated in a 1936 state constitutional amendment that made most of the Vieux Carré a protected district, with a Vieux Carré Commission (VCC) to preserve the *tout ensemble*—the effect of the whole—of the district. Ever since, the VCC, its allies, and its antagonists have struggled with the balance between the tourist dollar and residential dignity. There have been wins and losses for each side.

The Vieux Carré, as the heart of New Orleans, with its old architecture and famous, worldly associations, has a unique celebrity cachet. Issues arising there receive attention that far outshines other areas of the town and attract interest on the national level. There is nothing in the city so valuable, so marketable, so commercial or potentially commercial as Quarter property. Major changes to property in the district usually involve lengthy controversy.

The Vieux Carré's younger sister, the Faubourg Marigny, has forever lived in the shadow of her famous older sibling. That shadow has usually been comfortable. The Marigny has been spared many—but not all—of the issues that have roiled the Quarter since the beginning of revival in 1919. Free, until recently, of the three-cornered conflict between tourism, vice, and residential life, the Faubourg Marigny has lived a quiet existence.

As the Quarter saw ethnic groups come and go, the Faubourg Marigny retained its legacy of Germans and Italians. While the Quarter's guardians fought demolition of irreplaceable properties, some Faubourg Marigny dwellers made modern upgrades to their historic homes, blissfully free of restraint or guidance. Urban pioneers saved Quarter buildings by dint of hard work and tight funds, while Faubourg Marigny buildings of equal pedigree collapsed in ruin. As the Quarter became more a refuge for single people, many families remained in the Faubourg Marigny. While organized crime, in league with compliant city administrations, offered debauchery in an increasing Quarter club scene, Faubourg Marigny residents tippled quietly with extended families in neighborhood bars. As apartments were manipulated to squeeze renters determined to remain in the Quarter at almost any cost, whole houses were available for less in the Faubourg Marigny. While gay life blossomed loudly in the lower Quarter—and not always to cheers—it became an important current in the Faubourg Marigny with almost no fanfare at all.

The neighborhood we recognize today as the Faubourg Marigny is a legal construct created in the 1970s. The original Faubourg Marigny was bounded by portions of the Marigny family holdings and over time became submerged in the Third District and the Seventh, Eighth, and Ninth Wards that it contains. Particularly after the Civil War, the residents drew their identities more from the boundaries of district and ward. Our narrative will expand its geographic scope as the Faubourg Marigny became absorbed into the Third Municipality and Third District and then refocus on the boundaries, concept, and identity of the current Faubourg Marigny, as crafted in the recent past.

No discussion of the Faubourg Marigny can omit its founder, the redoubtable and storied Antonio Xavier Bernardo de Marigny de Mandeville. Much tripe was written about Bernard in days past, and these legends and provable errors have been repeated unto the latest generation. Although this is not a biography, in this work I lay out the known facts of his life and address the frothy claptrap that is repeated about him.

A Note on Terminology

The Marigny and *Faubourg Marigny* are used interchangeably by residents, and I do the same when referring to the first settlement and the post-1970s enclave. Likewise, *the Quarter, French Quarter,* and *Vieux Carré* roll off the native tongue side by side.

Creole is a term that deserves special explanation. It originally meant a child born in the New World of parents who emigrated from France, Spain, or the Germanic states. Over time, it became associated with Louisianans of French descent who were not Acadians expelled from Canada (today's Cajuns). Eventually, through intermarriage and emigration from the Caribbean, *Creole* has also become associated with light-skinned people of mixed race. In this work these mixed-race people are referred to as *Modern Creoles* after the Civil War. The "original" Creoles, some of whom took concubines of color in the system called *plaçage* and produced some of today's Modern Creoles, are referred to here as *French Creoles* or *Spanish Creoles.* It is important to note that *Creole* is a cultural identification as well as an ethnic one and the concept is still evolving. As James Nolan explains in his memoir *Flight Risk,* "But New Orleans is too layered with nuances. Once the gumbo is cooked, you can't separate it back into the ingredients."

The streets of the Marigny "Triangle," between Esplanade and Elysian Fields Avenues, were originally named by Bernard Marigny to suit his fancy. Beginning in 1852, the city renamed many to coincide with their "mother" streets in the Vieux Carré. In later years others were renamed. Today only a few of Bernard's original choices remain. In this work, I list the original names on maps of that era, with current names in parentheses. The current street names are used in the text for modern familiarity.

The streets of the Quarter nearly all make a rectilinear grid. The streets of the Marigny that are extensions of Quarter avenues must conform to a bend in the Mississippi River. In this work, Marigny streets that run more or less parallel to the river's course are referred to as *riverwise*; streets running more or less from the river toward Lake Pontchartrain are referred to as *lakewise* streets.

Cardinal directions mean little in New Orleans. Directions toward the lake are called just that and those to the river, likewise. Locations upstream of the river are called upper and those downstream, lower.

Acknowledgments

Amanda Glenn produced the beautiful maps and certain illustrations. Serena Saye was once again my patient technical editor. Greg Beaman assisted me with research on the convoluted history of the original Marigny mansion. William Black, Elizabeth Elmwood, Howard Margot, Andrejz Raczynski, and Eric Smith were my translators. Jim Van Dorin helped with research. Dale Irvin and Dave Johnson; Matt Warner and Steve Blair; Matt Harring, and Lynn Stetzer sheltered and encouraged me. Rand Dotson at LSU Press believed in the project. Joy Margheim expertly copyedited.

Kenneth Aslakson, Jack Belsom, Dorian Bennett, Chuck Berg, Kevin Bozant and his family, Evelyn Broders, Kevin Brown, Judge Pascal Calogero, Richard Campanella, Dan Castoriano, Lorelei Cropley, Melissa Daggett, Jim Van Dorin, Dorenda Dupont, Matt Easley, Steve Fauré, Jim Grigsby, Lee Meitzen Grue, Ann, Laura, and Joan Guiccione, Nancy Gunn, Robyn Halvorsen, Dan Hammer, Chris and Marilyn Hankel, Dr. Kenneth Holditch, Christine Horn, Angela Hughes, Dave Hulbert, William de Marigny Hyland, Sonnet Ireland, Dr. Florence Jumonville, Pres Kabacoff, Steve Keith, Jim Kellogg, Paul Lachance, Robin Leckbee, James Lide, Dr. Brobson Lutz, Cosimo Matassa, Rev. Richard Meyer, Leon Cahill Miller, Rev. and Mrs. Johnnie Montgomery, Julian Doerr Mutter, James Nolan, Greg Osborne, Jason Patterson, Frank Perez, John Pope, Don Richmond, Pat O'Rourke, Eric Seiferth, Becky Smith, Mary Smith, Brice Sowell, Jamie Temple, Benn Trask, Alex Vialou, Irene Wainwright, Barnie Williams, and Steve Wilson all helped me along the way.

Finally, my greatest thanks to Eugene Cizek and Lloyd Sensat, who spread their lives' work before me and inspired me to press on.

In my gratitude to all who helped me, I must add that the conclusions and opinions expressed, unless otherwise attributed, are my own.

The FAUBOURG MARIGNY of NEW ORLEANS

1

The Father of Waters and the Fathers of the Marignys

About twenty-eight hundred years ago, the land on which Orleans Parish now floats was formed south of Lake Pontchartrain.[1] The restless Mississippi River, forever seeking its own path to the sea, attained its current course about AD 1000.[2] Eventually, human settlement took root, and the tribes of the area discovered that a strip of land between river and lake, a portage, was a valuable conduit for trade.

In the seventeenth century, French explorers arrived. The Le Moyne brothers, Sieurs Bienville and Iberville,[3] established the first French settlement on the Gulf Coast with a 1699 landing on what is now Biloxi Beach, Mississippi. This colony did not prosper. The land was sandy scrub and the colonists began to starve. One of the officers who served with the Le Moynes was François Philippe de Hautmesnil de Mandeville. Born in 1682 in Bayeux, Normandy, Mandeville came to the New World in 1702, serving in Montreal alongside his brother Gabriel before coming to the Gulf Coast. Mandeville returned to his homeland in 1708 and the next year wrote a complaint against Bienville, who had been named the colonial governor, contending that the colonists were enduring a famine, eating acorns to survive.[4] Every French colonial governor of Louisiana was a target of the most bitter criticism; Bienville was merely the first. After Mandeville returned to New France in 1711, Bienville repaid the criticisms by accusing him of deceiving the royal court by passing himself off as his brother Gabriel, who had died around 1705.[5]

In 1718 Bienville and a party journeyed to a point opposite a sharp bend in the Mississippi about one hundred miles from the river's mouth. This area featured the portage known to the indigenous tribes, which allowed canoes to be carried through the cypress swamp from the river to Lake Pontchartrain via Bayou St. John. Near the juncture of the bayou and the lake was a sometimes-occupied group of huts built by the Acolapissa Indians and known as Tchoutchouma.[6] On the natural levee overlooking the river, Bienville founded Nouvelle Orléans, named in honor of the French town of Orléans and Philippe II, Duke of Orléans, the regent of France.[7] The limits of the new town, roughly present-day Iberville to Barracks Streets and North Rampart to Decatur, were soon surrounded by rudimentary fortifications, with redoubts at each corner. These decayed, then were improved, and then allowed to decay again. On the downriver city line, a patch of land was dedicated to the king's ownership. This commons allowed the forts' cannon a free field of fire against invaders. In peacetime, animals grazed there and certain men were allowed to put up buildings, with the proviso that the structures must be dismantled if invaders drew nigh.[8]

In 1721 Mandeville ran into more trouble and was dismissed as an officer, only to be restored to his rank after a few months. In June of that year he arrived in present-day Mobile in the company of Charles d'Arensbourg, leading a group of German settlers. Mandeville now wore the high honor of the cross of St. Louis.[9] The year 1722 found him married and in command at Fort Condé near Mobile. His marriage produced a son, Antoine Philippe Marigny de Mandeville, who was born in 1722. By 1724 Mandeville was named *major de place,* the military commander of New Orleans.[10] He was granted land in St. Bernard Parish; a portion of this concession now forms the Chalmette Battlefield National Park.[11] His family lived at what is now 410 Chartres Street, home of the Williams Research Center of the Historic New Orleans Collection.[12]

François Mandeville set two important patterns that would be taken up by his male descendants. The first was protracted conflict with authority, as witnessed by his conflicts with Governor Bienville. The second was the fathering of children by nonwhite mistresses.[13] He died in 1728 and was interred beneath the floor of St. Louis Cathedral. Mandeville's son Antoine, like his father, was a soldier and an explorer in the service of France. On June 15, 1757, Antoine's son, Pierre, was born.

The Affair of Louisiana

Antoine Marigny de Mandeville became embroiled in the ten-year Affair of Louisiana, a complex tangle of allegations, libelous pamphlets, interrogations, depositions, and trials. This conflict pitted the governor of Louisiana, Louis Billouart, Chevalier de Kerlerec, against a group of fellow officers and came as close to mutiny as anything the colony had yet experienced. The affair began in 1759 when an English ship out of Jamaica, the *Texel,* captained by David Diaz Arias, a Jew, anchored in the Mississippi River. France's Code Noir forbade Jews from entering the colonies,[14] and thus Arias and his ship were seized by the colonial government on the orders of Vincent de Rochemore, *ordonnateur* (treasurer and comptroller) of the colony. Rochemore posted guards to secure the ship for the government. Kerlerec believed the provisions the ship carried were desperately needed by the colony and that Rochemore and his cronies planned to sell them for personal profit. Kerlerec sent troops to relieve the ship's guards and restored the vessel to Arias.[15]

A pamphlet, *A Letter from a Louisiana Officer to the Commissioner of the Marine,* was circulated in New Orleans and France in 1764, detailing allegations against the governor.[16] Kerlerec arrested Rochemore and his associates, including Antoine Marigny de Mandeville, and sent them to France to answer charges of insubordination. While their ship sheltered from a storm in the Spanish port of St. Sebastian, Monsieur Grandmaison, Kerlerec's escort for the prisoners, went to deposit Kerlerec's bill of indictment with the local French consul for safekeeping. He made the mistake of taking his prisoners with him, and while Grandmaison and the consul were distracted, the indictment conveniently vanished.[17] Antoine remained free in France until May 13, 1765, when he was rearrested and taken to the Bastille.[18] As gentlemen, Kerlerec's tormentors had a comfortable stay in that dreaded fortress, being allowed to walk on the grounds and to write and receive letters.[19] By May 30, due to lobbying by prominent courtiers, the men were freed.[20]

The affair dragged on, with more charges and countercharges, until the spring of 1769. The investigation produced an astounding 749-page report, which almost totally sided with Kerlerec's enemies. As a result, Kerlerec was sent into internal exile, being forbidden to come within seventy-five miles of Paris or any of the royal residences. However, Louis XV did temper this punishment by dismissing the extravagant claims for damages filed by Kerlerec's accusers.[21] The internal exile was lifted in February 1770, and

Kerlerec, impoverished and sickly, died in deep debt in September of that year.[22] Restored to their military ranks, Antoine Marigny de Mandeville and his fellow rebels returned to Louisiana. Marc de Villiers du Terrage, author of the comprehensive *The Last Years of French Louisiana,* argues that Antoine was a bold explorer and good-natured fellow who eventually became disenchanted with his fellow accusers.[23]

The use of an official position for personal gain is the eternal norm in Louisiana, and it is doubtful that any of the parties to the affair were completely innocent. In view of his accusers' sweeping allegations and their fantastic demands for damages, I have concluded that Kerlerec was, at least in this instance, guilty of nothing worse than not playing the usual Louisiana game and refusing to let other officers share in the booty. However, it is no credit to Kerlerec that he stripped the colony of most of its leadership and its governor for five years to pursue this vendetta.

The Spanish Dominion

By the time Antoine Marigny de Mandeville came home, a new controversy had arisen in New Orleans. At the end of the French and Indian War in 1763, France lost Louisiana to the Spanish Crown. In 1766 Antonio de Ulloa arrived as the first Spanish governor. The French and German Creole people of New Orleans were astounded at their handover to an alien realm and hatched plots against Ulloa, who had few soldiers to back him up. In 1768 Ulloa ended trade with France and attempted to suppress smuggling, which, despite its illegality, had been a vital part of the town's economy since its founding.[24] The sorrow the city felt over its abandonment by Paris was now compounded by economic woes, and a group of the most prominent Creole leaders decided that the "tyrannical" Ulloa must go.[25] After rioting broke out, Ulloa and his wife were forced to leave on November 1, 1768.[26] As the ship disappeared down the river towards the open sea, the Creoles felt satisfied that, having routed the Spanish governor, France would now take them back and this nightmare would be over. Antoine is not listed among the conspirators. Perhaps as a military man, he knew Spain's humorless approach to colonial discipline and had the prudence to stay out of this latest contretemps.

In July 1769 an Irish soldier of fortune in the service of Madrid, Alexander O'Reilly, arrived in New Orleans with two thousand Spanish troops.

Overawed by his might, the rebellion's ringleaders received him cordially and pledged fealty to Spain. O'Reilly invited them to dinner and then had them arrested. The chief conspirators were tried, five were shot, and others were imprisoned in the Moro Castle of Havana for two years.[27]

Antoine Marigny de Mandeville died November 6, 1779, and like his father, was buried under the floor of St. Louis Cathedral. Pierre Enguerrand Philippe de Marigny de Mandeville now bore the family banner and in his brief life raised it ever higher. As a youth, he served in the French army in Guyana and France, and in 1772 he married Jeanne d'Estrahan, daughter of the royal treasurer in New Orleans. Pierre was the commanding officer of garrisons around south Louisiana, including the Côte des Allemands (German Coast), upriver from the capital.[28] Spain retained colonial officials of many nationalities, as long as they were Catholic and loyal to Madrid. The Spanish governor Manuel Gayoso de Lemos esteemed Pierre as the "richest, most prominent and one of the persons most addicted to the Spanish cause in these provinces."[29] Pierre donated land lying downriver from New Orleans, originally purchased by his father Antoine, to the Spanish Crown,[30] and on this land in 1780 he was authorized to settle immigrants from the Canary Islands, the Isleños. The area was named St. Bernard,[31] and Pierre became the settlement's first commandant of troops.[32] On October 28, 1785, just as the infant United States was transitioning from its revolutionary days to a shaky confederation, Pierre's third son and fourth child, Antonio Xavier Bernardo, known as Bernard, was born. The much-loved Père Antoine baptized him in St. Louis Cathedral on February 2, 1786, over the bones of his ancestors.[33]

Pierre Marigny was appointed "ordinary alcalde," or chief magistrate, of New Orleans in 1791.[34] The year 1798 saw him promoted to command the troops of New Orleans with the rank of colonel.[35]

On December 18, 1798, Pierre swapped the future Chalmette plantation and battlefield with Lorenzo (Laurent) Sigur in return for the land that became the Faubourg Marigny.[36] The size of the property was about 1,161 acres.[37] This property's upper boundary was the downriver limit of the old commons, which had been fixed in 1797 by Governor Gayoso and was called Gayoso's Line.[38] The commons followed essentially the line of Barracks Street to the back of the blocks facing Esplanade. The downriver boundary was the property of Nicholas Daunoy, which began about where Franklin Avenue now runs. The lakeside boundary would have been approximately present-day North Derbigny Street. At Franklin, the Faubourg Daunoy was cut off from the Marigny by a ropewalk, a long shed for braiding rope.[39] For this reason, the future Faubourg Marigny stopped at Franklin, and in years to come, many would recognize Franklin, not Press, as the Marigny's downriver boundary.

The land Pierre Marigny acquired had an interesting history. As noted before, the plans for the town's rudimentary fortifications included a commons area. However, fortifications were not built until 1760. Below the commons, spanning downriver approximately between Franklin and Press Streets and lakeward to about St. Claude, was Pierre Dreux's brewery (La Brassier).[40] Claude Dubreil bought the land below the commons from Dreux's widow. By 1743 Dubreil had acquired most of the commons as well.[41] Dubreil created a thriving industrial park, with a brickyard and mills for sawing wood, husking rice, and grinding cement. These mills were powered by waterwheels dipping into the canal dug before 1758, which ran between the river and Bayou St. John.[42] Dubreil also raised sugarcane and successfully refined it into the coveted granulated form, although he died before he could start large-scale production.[43]

In 1753 Dubreil gave the old brewery land to his granddaughter, Mrs. Hypolite Amelot.[44] After Dubreil died, his remaining property was sold to Jacques Delachaise in 1758.[45] The property passed through a few more hands until it was bought by Lorenzo (Laurent) Sigur on August 12, 1789, and as we have noted, Pierre Marigny acquired the land in 1798.

Pierre erected the Marigny mansion, a two-story plantation house, on what is now the square bounded by Elysian Fields, Decatur, North Peters, and Marigny.[46] It was renowned for its rich furnishings, including carved rosewood furniture and costly objets d'art brought back from the family's many trips to France.[47]

In the late 1790s the Duke of Orléans, Louis-Philippe of France, and his two brothers lived in and toured North America in postrevolutionary exile. In 1798 they sojourned in New Orleans for over a month, staying with Governor Bernardo de Gálvez, who entertained them at considerable expense.[48] Even though New Orleans was a Spanish possession, sentiment for *la belle France* ran deep, and Pierre Marigny fêted the young noblemen with legendary lavishness.[49] Pierre is also reputed to have given the impecunious young men a loan to continue their travels, which was reportedly repaid in 1813.[50] Regardless, this visit was the opening chapter in the long book of Marigny legends.

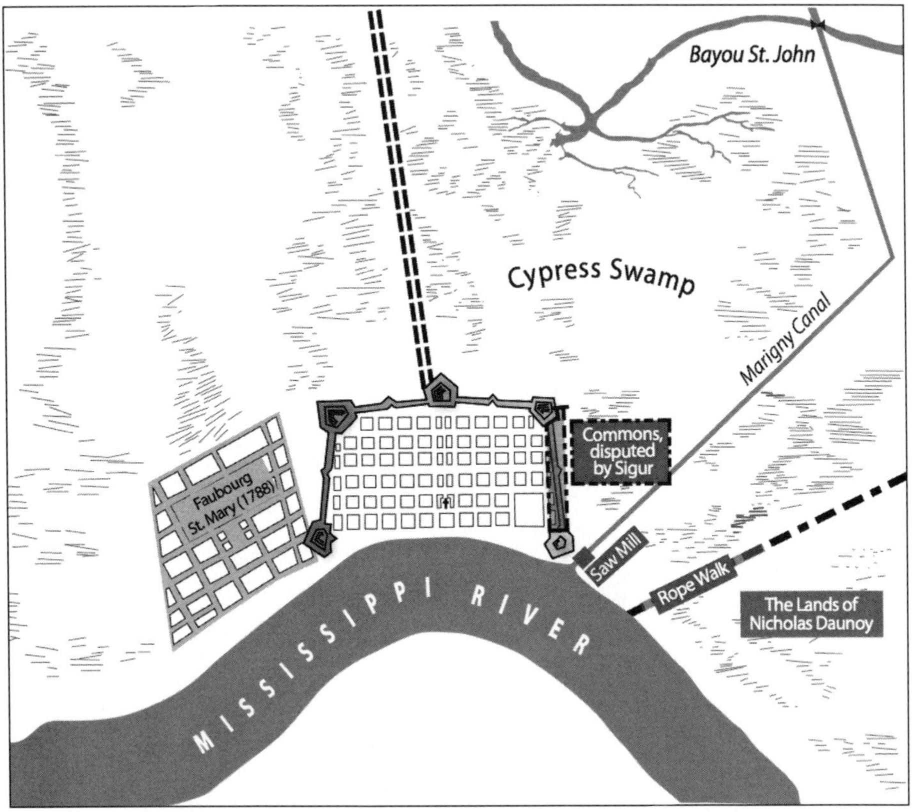

Colonial New Orleans in 1798. Map by Amanda Glenn.

Although Pierre and Jeanne had five children, neither fame nor power nor riches could extend eighteenth-century life spans. Their first child, Antoine, lived for only seven months. Their second, Jean Philippe, lived but twenty-five years. The third child, Marie, lived to a ripe seventy-eight but spent many of her later years in France, away from New Orleans' stew of hazards and disease. Daughter Antoine Maria saw only two years in the world. Like his grandfather, François, Pierre also fathered a mixed-race child, Eulalie, by a mistress in 1774. She was treated as a daughter and sister by the family.[51]

In 1800, at age fourteen, Bernard buried the forty-nine-year-old Pierre under the floor of the cathedral and inherited his share of his father's fortune, his land, and his slaves. At this point in history, there should have been a roll of drums to announce the ascendance of Bernard Marigny, whose actions would have profound consequences for the growth, character, and very existence of New Orleans. For much of his first fifty years, his life and the life of his city were wound about each other, and it is scarcely possible to separate them. Bernard's personality, embroidered by legend, became conflated with, and the epitome of, the character of French Creoles. Our story of the neighborhood that bears Bernard's surname really begins here.

2

Bernard and the Stars and Stripes Ascend

Following Pierre Marigny's death, Bernard's cousin, Ignace Delino de Chalmette, was appointed his first curator, that is, conservator and guardian ad litem.[1] Bernard's life from 1800 to the Louisiana Purchase in 1803 is well storied but not well documented. J. W. Cruzat and Grace King have maintained that he was first sent to Pensacola to learn business in the important trading firm of Panton, Leslie and Company.[2] It is also thought that he did not apply himself there and so was sent to the firm's home offices in London. In London, Bernard was to study business under the tutelage of John Leslie, managing partner of the firm.[3] In London and Paris, Bernard is supposed to have learned all about gambling and the charms of women who flock to wealthy men, even precocious teenage boys. Chalmette, supposedly believing the young heir to be too wild and endangered in the fleshpots of Europe, recalled the fledgling back to the nest sometime around the late summer of 1801.[4] The existing record of the handover shows Chalmette pleading that his own affairs needed his attention. He also arranged the sale of some of the Marigny mansion's household goods and provided an inventory of Bernard's possessions. Francisco Delille Dupard was assigned as the new curator.[5]

The enduring legend, parroted uncritically, is that Bernard gambled away most of his inherited fortune. These losses, it is averred, compelled him to carve up the old plantation into the infant Faubourg Marigny. That he named a street Craps (today's Burgundy) is considered additional corroboration. This notion, repeated down the years, is contradicted by known facts and logic. Bernard, as a legal minor, would never have been turned loose with full rights to draw on his father's estate. His brother Jean still lived and claimed his share. It is believed that Bernard had an allowance of two thousand dollars a year while in Europe.[6] Even this then-princely sum would not have drawn down the family fortune by much, and it seems that Bernard stayed in London for, at most, a little over a year. If he really needed cash upon returning to New Orleans, why did he wait another three years to start selling real estate?

Was Bernard a gambler at all? Well, it would be difficult to find a Louisiana man of wealth at the dawn of the nineteenth century who did not play games of chance. If Bernard had *not* gambled, it would be an astonishing departure from prevailing norms. If indeed gambling losses compelled Bernard to sell off the plantation, his decision was a bad counter-bet. The many foreclosure suits he had to bring in the first years of the faubourg's existence bear witness to that.[7] If he really wanted to recoup losses, he would have been better off to sell the property intact to an American speculator, take his profits, and invest elsewhere. As we will see, Bernard indeed had well-documented, terrific financial losses in his life, but the largest were not attributable to gambling.

In any event, the young Monsieur de Marigny was back at home by the beginning of 1802, just as the brief pause in the Napoleonic Wars was ending and his hometown was about to change, forever. Unbeknown to the people of New Orleans, they were French again, thanks to the secret Treaty of San Ildefonso, signed between Napoleon and Spain in October 1800. By the spring of 1801, President Thomas Jefferson knew all about it.[8] The treaty was not published by Spain until 1802. In that year, President Jefferson sent Robert Livingston and James Monroe to France to negotiate the purchase of New Orleans. Unexpectedly, Napoleon threw in the entire Louisiana territory, and the treaty was signed on April 30, 1803. On November 30, the retrocession from Spain to France was formalized and for the next twenty days, the French Tricolor flew over the Cabildo, seat of government. French commissioner Pierre Clément de Laussat had been delegated the delicate task of ensuring that both transfers went smoothly. He was a guest of the eighteen-year-old Bernard Marigny, who served as one of his aides-de-camp.[9] Bernard, now through with his abbreviated formal education, was master of the family manse, located a short distance from the eastern gate of the city at Fort St. Charles.[10] On December 20, with Bernard faithfully attending, Laussat watched the Tricolor come down and the Stars and Stripes go up. He handed the keys to the city's gates over to General James Wilkinson, and the city and a vast inland region became America's.[11]

Most of the Louisiana Purchase was the wild realm of many Indian nations. La Nouvelle Orléans, the original object of the venture and jewel of the piece, was the outlet for American goods from the Mississippi Valley and, instantly, the seventh-largest city in America.[12] New Orleans was also the American window onto the Caribbean, which was roiled by European exploitation, colonial revolts, and piracy. Americans were convinced that the city would be the fulcrum of leverage to the peoples and riches of emerging southward nations.

The high-spirited young heir Bernard Marigny quickly settled down following the change in power, at least domestically. On May 28, 1804, he married Mary Jones, daughter of the former American consul.[13] His inheritance, recorded in the marriage contract, was quite substantial.[14] The land, the mansion house, twenty-eight slaves, and other items were valued together at 100,000 *piastres.*[15] This record of wealth also contradicts the legend that Bernard gambled the better part of the family fortune away. About a year after their marriage, Bernard and Mary had their first child, Clementine, who lived less than two months, being baptized a week before her death.[16]

At the time of the Louisiana Purchase, much of the interior of Orleans Parish was occupied by a cypress swamp—*la cyprière,* home to many alligators and snakes. *La cyprière* meant that the initial growth of New Orleans would parallel the river along the old natural levee, as witness the upriver Faubourg St. Mary and the downriver Faubourg Marigny, as well as lesser faubourgs toward the St. Bernard Parish line. So the housing required for the town's growth would be along this "Sliver by the River," as it is now called.

Besides the influx of fortune-seekers from the eastern states, another wave of arrivals drove a demand for housing. The French colony of Saint-Domingue, present-day Haiti, shipped large amounts of sugar, coffee, and cotton to Europe, enriching the French economy toward the end of the eighteenth century.[17] These riches were wrung from the bodies of hundreds of thousands of slaves, who were treated with great brutality.[18] Brutality breeds revolution, and in 1791 the slaves rose in wrath. Over the next twenty years, thousands of whites and free people of color (the *gens de couleur libres*) fled the island, bringing some of their slaves along. The nearest Francophone port was, of course, New Orleans.

One of the more significant waves of fleeing Saint-Domingans lapped the levee of New Orleans in 1804. This group included two thousand free people of color, the single-largest contingent, more than doubling that group's numbers in town.[19] The largest wave of Saint-Domingue refugees arrived in New Orleans at the end of 1809. Over nine thousand refugees showed up, bringing the town's population to seventeen thousand people in 1810. The American governor, William Claiborne, already had his hands full trying to govern a population of pirates, American adventurers, and regretful former French and Spanish nationals. Claiborne feared that old-country partisanship would prevent the French Creoles from coming to the defense of New Orleans should the British attack.[20]

By the end of 1810, the white population of New Orleans was nearly half again as large as it had been in 1806; the number of slaves had increased by one-third, and the population of free people of color had more than doubled. Eventually, over twelve thousand former Saint-Domingans arrived in New Orleans.[21] The tide of Saint-Domingue refugees bolstered the Francophones of New Orleans. These refugees, often called the foreign French, were, in the main, better educated and had more taste for business than the established Creoles. In the antebellum era, the foreign French supplied two New Orleans mayors and a governor and their numbers were well represented in lesser offices, the bench, and the bar.[22]

The Founding of the Faubourg

In April 1805 Bernard Marigny and his last guardian, Solomon Prevost, applied to the *conseil de ville* (city council) and the territorial legislature for permission to subdivide most of the downriver Marigny plantation into a new faubourg of the city. In order for this to occur, three things had to happen. The first was permission for Prevost to act for Bernard, since Marigny was under the age of majority, twenty-five at that time.[23]

The second was to confirm the boundaries between the old commons or king's land, between present-day Barracks Street and the beginning of the Marigny property, a span of about 120 feet. Property holders, including the industrious Monsieur Dubreil, had been allowed to erect buildings on the king's land.[24] The now-American city council decided not to challenge the existing

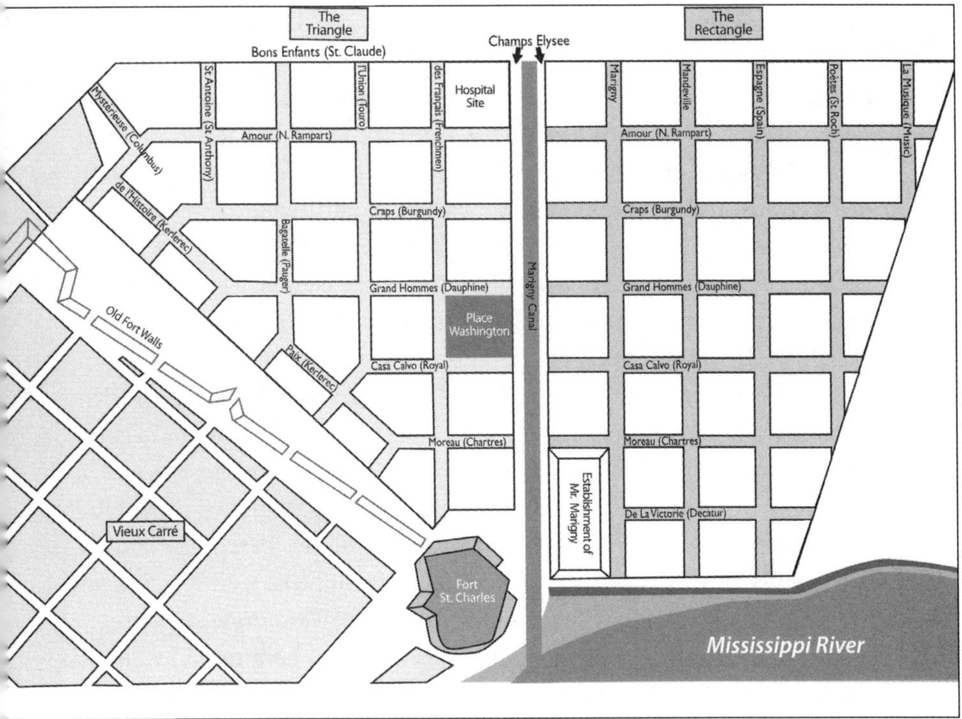

The Early Marigny. Map by Amanda Glenn.

understanding, and Bernard's land claims were confirmed.[25] The city maintained its claim based on Gayoso's Line and a few years after the founding of the Faubourg Marigny started dividing lots along Esplanade Avenue. In 1812 the city surveyor, Jacques Tanesse, laid out the entire street. Thus the land between Barracks Street and the downriver side of Esplanade was not owned by the Marignys and therefore not a part of the new faubourg.[26] Dr. Lewis Heerman built a naval hospital at the lower lake corner of Esplanade and Royal, which endured until 1821.[27]

The third action was for the city to approve Bernard's layout for the faubourg, as designed by Nicholas Finiels and physically delineated by Barthélémy Lafon. The riverwise streets were aligned with the corresponding streets of the Vieux Carré. The design included a public square later named Washington Park, a square reserved for a never-built hospital, and a double square on which the Marigny plantation house and dependencies stood.

Two strips of land, each fifty feet wide, flanked the Marigny Canal, which was itself fifty feet wide at that time. These strips formed the thoroughfare Champs-Élysées Rue et Promenade Publique, today called Elysian Fields Avenue. Bridges crossed the canal at the levee and Dauphine Street. Most of the remaining squares of land were initially divided into twelve lots apiece. Five lots were on each of the sides of the block paralleling the river, and two "key" lots faced the side streets. The irregular squares forming the "turn" from the Vieux Carré's original streets at the river's bend had other layouts, as did the squares butting up against the other properties in town.[28] The new faubourg was bounded downriver by the rope walk, running down Franklin from Dauphine to Chartres.[29] This marked the boundary with Faubourg Daunoy, a narrow suburb spanning present-day Franklin Avenue to St. Ferdinand Street.[30] Below the Faubourg Daunoy ran the one-street Faubourg Nott, and next to it the one-street Faubourg Delphine, named for Delphine Lalaurie, later infamous for abusing her slaves. Part of the land in these neighborhoods was owned by Daniel Warburg, who sold it in 1833 to the Company of Architects, from which Architect Street, an alley between Royal and Chartres, running between Port and St. Ferdinand, took its name. Faubourg Delphine would become the Cotton Press Street corridor, named after the huge Levee Steam Cotton Press.[31] The lakeside boundary, now North Rampart, was put through to coincide with St. Claude Avenue in Tremé. (The original Faubourg Marigny, bounded by Esplanade, Elysian Fields, St. Claude, and the river, is called the "Triangle"; the later portion, bounded by Elysian Fields, St. Claude, Press Street, and the river, is referred to as the "Rectangle.")

The legalities resolved, Bernard got busy. As early as September 1805, he appeared before notary Narcisse Broutin to record a sale. Throughout the autumn and winter of that year, twenty-eight lots were sold.[32] By June 1807, 182 out of the original 272 lots had been sold.[33] The legal fiction that Bernard Marigny was still a minor lost credibility as his empire grew, and so on June 7, 1806, the territorial legislature granted him emancipation and adulthood.[34]

Although few Saint-Domingue refugees were among the first buyers of Marigny lots,[35] eventually a number of them settled there, especially after the great wave of 1809. Unlike the Americans from "up north," Saint-Domingue refugees of different colors lived in close proximity to each other.[36] This pattern of settlement would persist in the Marigny for many decades.

A View of New Orleans Taken from the Plantation of Marigny, ca. 1803, by John de Woiseri. Courtesy of The Historic New Orleans Collection, acc. no. 1958.42.

Vue d'une Rue du Faubourg Marigny, Nouvelle Orléans, with the Marigny mansion in the background, ca. 1821, by Felix Saint-Aulaire. Courtesy of The Historic New Orleans Collection, acc. no. 1937.2.2.

The refugees from Saint-Domingue liked the affordability of the Faubourg Marigny. The first houses were usually small and were replaced after a decade or so by larger cottages, including those in the well-known Creole cottage style.[37] The Saint-Domingue influence is believed to be especially pronounced in this style of house.[38] The influx of refugees strained the housing market of the city, and Bernard Marigny, not one to miss an opportunity, quickly offered more real estate. In November 1809 he marketed 535 additional lots on the lake side of his property, calling it New Marigny.[39] The New Marigny was bounded by St. Claude, St. Bernard, Marigny, and North Derbigny Streets. A lakeward finger ran between Frenchmen and Marigny, on either side of the canal, to North Galvez Street.[40]

The free people of color from Saint-Domingue and their descendants would play prominent parts in the Marigny and the city in general. They were the most influential group in the Third District prior to the German and Irish migrations of the mid-1840s. Bringing business acumen and French-honed education and tastes, they formed the nucleus of the intelligentsia of New Orleans' free people of color throughout the nineteenth century.

Among them was Jean-Louis Dolliole, a designer and builder of several Marigny and Tremé houses, including those at 1436 and 1455 Pauger, 820 Elysian Fields, and 1227 St. Philip. Louis Nelson Fouché, another architect-builder, built the well-known three-story house at 2340 Chartres.[41] Charles Laveaux bought most of Square 264, bounded by Dauphine, Kerlerec, Pauger, and Burgundy, from Bernard Marigny in 1806 and ran a *victular,* a grocery and provisioner for ships, at 1801 Dauphine at the corner with Kerlerec.[42] Another early refugee buyer was Marie Couvent, who purchased a lot on the lakeside corner of Dauphine and Tour.[43]

Besides selling lots, Bernard and Mary were busy having more children. Prosper was born in March 1806, and then Gustave in June 1807.[44] At the start of 1808, Mary's health began to fail. Bernard resigned his military commission to deal with the crisis.[45] Mary traveled to Philadelphia for treatment, dying there in June. Bernard buried her near his old plantation chapel,[46] later the site of Annunciation Catholic Church on Mandeville, between Marais and Urquhart Streets.[47]

In 1807 Bernard and his family had two residences. One was the original plantation house built by Pierre. The other was built nearby somewhat later. In 1807 Bernard sold the newer house to Barthelme Bosque; after Bosque's death in 1818, his widow sold it back to Bernard. The older home was ap-

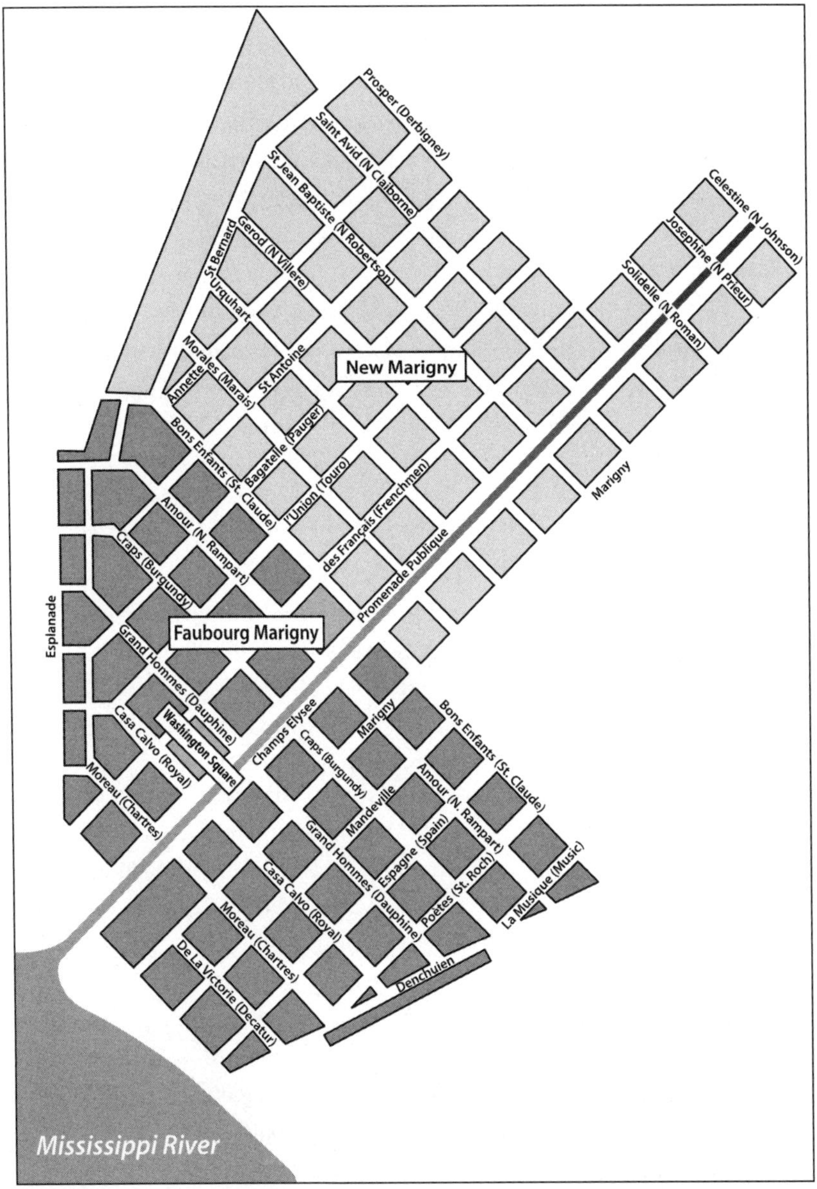

Original and New Marigny. Map by Amanda Glenn.

parently leased and may have been made into a hotel in the 1830s. The site today is occupied by a power substation, humming its perpetual mantra at sixty cycles per second.[48]

On March 21, 1809, Bernard married Anna Mathilde Morales in Pensacola.[49] In September, he was elected a delegate to the territorial legislature, starting a legislative career that would last until 1838.[50] Louisiana was admitted to the Union in 1812 and Marigny was a delegate to the constitutional convention.[51]

Bernard and Anna's first child, Antonio Santiago, was born in 1811.[52] The parents would go on to have four other children: another son and three daughters. However, it was this first son, always called Mandeville, who would carry the family banner through the last period of his family's prominence.

To the Ramparts of Chalmette

New Orleans had been American for a bare nine years when the United States went to war with Britain in 1812. Despite the distraction of the long-running Napoleonic Wars, Britain very nearly reconquered its old colonies. Although the war went badly for America in the East, most of the Gulf Coast held fast. A large British force sailed to seize New Orleans in late 1814.

When the British drew nigh, a Committee of Defense, with Bernard Marigny as president, was formed to marshal the town's resources. By his own account, Bernard turned to Jean Lafitte, a very successful gulf pirate or, as we might say now, "disruptive entrepreneur" who had been charged with violating American trade laws after his base of operations at Barataria Bay was destroyed by American forces.[53] Bernard convinced a judge to suspend the prosecution of Lafitte and his comrades, enabling the Baratarians to join General Andrew Jackson's forces.[54] Bernard himself did not fight in the battle but was at Jackson's headquarters at the rear of the American line at Chalmette plantation.[55] White Saint-Domingans made up over one-quarter of Jackson's forces, and a second battalion consisted of 256 free people of color from that island.[56] Among the American soldiers that day was the builder Jean-Louis Dolliole.[57]

The pirate cannoneers ably mowed down the orderly redcoat ranks as the soldiers proceeded in accordance with the set-piece engagements they had fought in Europe. The story has often been told of how Jackson led a disparate group of regular soldiers, Appalachian long riflemen, free men of color, and Jean Lafitte's pirates to victory against some of the finest soldiers of the Old World.

The battle was won and the town saved. The victory made Jackson a hero both to Americans and to the twenty-nine-year-old Bernard, who would ever after be Jackson's champion and never missed a chance to remind anyone who would listen of his friendship with the general.

3

Princes and Municipalities

After the War of 1812, finally free to bring goods, capital, and personal ambition to Louisiana, Americans arrived in droves. Louisiana was the first non-English colony to be folded into the nation. Whatever the differences between, say, New England Yankees and Carolinians, they were as nothing compared to the division between the *Américains* and the French Creoles. Louisiana had been a halfhearted French experiment, subjected to long periods of neglect and then transferred, like chattel, to Spain. The Spanish rule, initially hated, eventually melded with, and was moderated by, Gallic sensibilities, and Franco-Iberian marriages became common. The French, Spanish, and German Creoles were still smarting from being tossed between France and Spain as playthings of kings. The very fact that they called the arrivistes "Américains"—when they were now Americans as well—expressed their dismay at being divorced from the old country forever. Also, in colonial days Paris and Madrid had been far away, and despite occasional crackdowns, like that of O'Reilly in 1769, the colony had usually been left to decide its own fate. Now came a federal governor, General Wilkinson, along with a host of U.S. soldiers, tax collectors, and inspectors of customs, an alien constitution, alien laws, and above all, aliens speaking an alien language. The animosity many Creoles felt toward Americans did not vanish with the smoke of battle at Chalmette; it would persist to deeply wound the growing city.[1]

As the former colonials learned to be Americans, they were reluctant to give up the privileges and ways of the society they had created. Americans tended to be direct in speech, not elliptical, and to see profit as an end in itself, forswearing many other pleasures and diversions in its pursuit. They were also more geographically mobile than the Creoles and more egalitarian in their choice of wives. Worse yet, they wanted to speak only English and saw no reason to learn a "foreign tongue" within the United States. For the Americans, Creoles were baffling people with strange speech and confusing mores. For all their deep Catholicism, the Creoles maintained concubinage with mixed-race mistresses, gambled avidly, and drank wine in preference to whiskey. Although dueling was popular across America, the Creoles seemed especially fond of the "field of honor," even for trifles.[2]

The French Creoles clung to their vision of Gallic life, molded by the harshness of the frontier and isolation from the mother country. Creole pride created a self-reinforcing cultural identity, feeding on itself until, in the hearts of the French Creoles, New Orleans became more French than France itself. The old titles might still be uttered with respect in New Orleans. French Creole boys might be sent to France for superior education. Finery from Paris ateliers was still coveted. But as the nineteenth century rolled on, the New Orleans Creoles morphed into something not as ultra-French as they fancied; no, to their horror, they had become more typically American. The French Creoles of the early nineteenth century clung to clannishness, and their descendants would loudly defend their fantasy of racial purity for decades. In truth, they mixed the customs and traits of Iberville's Canadians, the imported girls of every grade, the Spaniards, the mixed-race mistresses, the Américains, and a handful of aristocrats.

One aspect of the old-country Creoles resonated all too well. The concept of the landed squire, who ruled the lives of his family and servants with a seemingly benevolent yet iron hand, was reproduced in stark tones in Louisiana. No one put it better than the novelist George Washington Cable: "The courteous manners of France were largely retained; but the habit of commanding a dull and abject slave class, over which a 'black code' gave every white man full powers of police, induced a certain fierce imperiousness of will and temper; while that proud love of freedom, so pervasive throughout the American wilderness, rose at times to an attitude of arrogant superiority over all constraint, and became the occasion of harsh comment in reports sent to France by officers of the king."[3] Before the Americans arrived, governing bodies were often too torpid to intervene in civil affairs.

Now, even if American law was flouted in some respects, constraint in the form of competition—for land, for commerce, for slaves, even for suitable wives—had arrived.

Despite all the differences, that unconquerable force, love, would eventually meld many Creole and "American" family lines. Bernard was an early adopter with his marriage to the daughter of the former American consul.[4]

New Orleans was a fertile field of dreams for young Americans of ambition. They could bring portable wealth from the East or float goods down from the valley and make money quickly. Perhaps they might buy fecund land and plant cotton or sugarcane. Maybe they would take work as a clerk, parlaying that humble beginning into their own brokerage or countinghouse. Bilingual lawyers versed in the "new American" legal system found ample employment. Above all, there was the chance of a fresh start. New identities and new notions could create new lives. In this city of easy gain, easy pleasures could be had. Farewell to frowning towns of New England that forbade any Sabbath activities other than churchgoing and folded-hands quietude. Hello to uproarious New Orleans Sundays of drinking, gambling, cockfighting, theater, hunting, and militia parades.[5]

The Perpetual Candidate

The 1820s seem to have been Bernard Marigny's peak decade. He was in one elected office or another the entire time. He went to France at least twice, when such a journey was measured in months. He was awarded the mantle of defender of the Creoles for his support of the use of French in legal proceedings. Minutes of meetings to settle family business or debts were recorded in a document called a *procès-verbal.* In 1822 the Louisiana Supreme Court ruled that *procès-verbaux* in French were invalid. The alarmed Francophones saw their legal scaffolding collapsing under the weight of English-language American law. Bernard pushed through a bill that explicitly allowed *procès-verbaux* to be in French.[6]

Bernard's outsize personality, his wealth, and his flaunting of friendships with elites rubbed some people the wrong way. He ran for governor in 1824, in a bitter race pitting him against another Creole, the former governor Jacques Villeré, and three Americans. Bernard accused Villeré of being too friendly to American interests, a tactic that endeared Bernard neither to

"Americans" nor to the French Creoles who were his usual base of support.[7] During the campaign the *Courrier de la Louisiane* spewed bile in response to a letter from Bernard in another paper[8]: "Bernard de Marigny, candidate *forever and ever* for the office of Governor, which he shall *never* get, notwithstanding all his journeys, and the handsome Spanish songs and Boleros with which he treated the voters of the upper Fourche; his promises to some, and his threats to others, in short those delicate means which excited a feeling of pity in the mind of everyone" (emphasis in original).[9]

He placed third in the race.[10] Perhaps frustrated by his lack of upward political progress, Bernard seriously considered leaving the land of his birth and resettling in Europe. At least that is what he told Duke Bernhard in 1826.[11] Why he decided to stay is another Marigny mystery. Perhaps he realized that even though he was not His Excellency, *Governor* Marigny, he was still a big fish in a small pond. In post-Napoleonic Europe he would be an American arriviste and might have been treated no better than the American arrivistes were in New Orleans.

Lakeward, Ho!

One of the original attractions of the site of New Orleans was the relatively easy transit from the river to Lake Pontchartrain via the portage that led to Bayou St. John, which connected with the lake. To reach the city from the Gulf of Mexico, people and goods had to brave the open sea, await high tide to pass over sandbars, and go against the current, up the river for one hundred miles. They might also ride smaller coastwise vessels from Lake Borgne and then to Lake Pontchartrain, landing on the south shore. This was the usual approach for passengers and freight from eastern cities such as Biloxi and Mobile.

In the eighteenth century a canal to power the mills of Claude Dubreil had been dug between Bayou St. John and the river.[12] It was too narrow for many larger boats, and so by the 1830s Marigny Canal, as it was then known, was used chiefly by fishermen.

In 1794 Spanish governor Carondelet ordered the digging of a shipping canal that ran from Bayou St. John to a turning basin just north of the Vieux Carré. This later inspired the naming of Basin Street, famed in the jazz era. In the early 1830s the Faubourg St. Mary decided it would have a canal to match or surpass the Carondelet Canal of the Creole First District.[13] The

New Basin Canal was finished in 1832, paralleling the Carondelet but westward by about a mile and a half. It too ended in a turning basin.

Canals were fine, but they required regular dredging and could be a source of flooding in bad weather. Their cost in human lives could be staggering; thousands of Irishmen died, mostly of cholera and fevers, digging the New Basin Canal.[14] As railroads came to America in the 1820s, it seemed logical to link the lake and river by rail. Railroads allowed for much faster travel than canals and wouldn't flood the surrounding land. They could be installed quickly and usually at lesser human cost.

The Pontchartrain Railroad Company was chartered in 1830 and swiftly bought a strip of land from Bernard Marigny running along the Marigny Canal, paralleling Elysian Fields, to the lake.[15] The depot was built at the foot of Elysian Fields, near the Marigny mansion. On April 23, 1831, the railroad made its inaugural run to the lake, pulled by horses since the steam engine had not yet arrived. By September of the next year, steam ran the railroad.[16] The train had ten cars; the last two or three were reserved for free people of color. The run from lake to river, a distance of about 5.5 miles, took about nineteen minutes at the breathtaking speed of nearly twenty miles per hour.[17] That amazing velocity depended on a lack of obstructions. Without fences or gates, cows frequently wandered onto the rails. A collision with even one bovine would derail the little engine.[18] Drunks were killed or dismembered after falling asleep on the tracks.[19]

Travelers remarked upon the wild beauty of the vine-covered trees, tall grasses, and many irises as the route passed through *la cyprière*.[20] The Pontchartrain Railroad also developed real estate acquired along the right-of-way. The swift and usually easy ride made the lakefront grow. Restaurants, dance halls, "bathing resorts" for swimming, and saloons sprang up. Eventually the area became known as Milneburg, after one of the original landowners.[21]

Bernard Marigny also had a keen interest in taking people swiftly from river to lake. In 1829 he bought a large tract of land along the north shore of Lake Pontchartrain in St. Tammany Parish.[22] This he named Fontainebleau Plantation and later subdivided part of it to create the town of Mandeville, named for his ancestral family. He started selling lots in 1834 and hired the steamboat *Black Hawk* to ferry prospective purchasers over the lake.[23] Doubtless, Marigny entertained, or tormented, his prospects with his well-known singing and comedy routines during the voyage.

The Milneburg Train, engraving by H. W. Wanderwall. *Louisiana Conservationist,* 11 (1959): 14.

The Marigny Riverfront at Elysian Fields, ca. 1836. Illustration by Amanda Glenn.

The Great Legend

We now come to the oft-retold central legend of Bernard's life and what is widely believed to be a pivotal moment in the life of the Faubourg Marigny. New Orleans folklore holds that this scene depicts a real turning point in the city's life. At this moment, many esteemed writers assure us, the old French New Orleans began a slow death and the new American New Orleans was born, like a phoenix that must arise from the ashes of its former self.

It is a scene worthy of Verdi or Puccini. On stage, three men of wealth and influence: The great impresario of the South, an actor at the height of

Bernard Marigny, ca. 1820. "Ialeské-Chata," *Mandeville: A Historical Compendium* (New Orleans: Eugene Joubert, 1918), in Louisiana Research Collection, Tulane University.

his dramatic power. The entrepreneur and urban pioneer, who dares greatly in a city that urges caution and conservatism. The grandee of all Creole grandees, friend of kings and presidents, heir to a once great but now somewhat dissipated fortune.

The three are close to sealing a deal that will transform much of the city to which all are devoted. The grandee will sell a part of his birthright in the faubourg that bears his proud surname. The actor and the businessman will draw this land from an eighteenth-century slumber into the bustle of the nineteenth-century industrial world.

The pens are in the stand, the document is on the table, the three are in concord; only one thing remains. The grandee's wife cannot be found to countersign for her spousal rights to the land. A violin strikes an urgent note. No report of her. The purchasers are stirred to fury at this seeming duplicity and arrogant betrayal. The grandee protests his ignorant innocence at this rupture.

The actor draws himself up as if on the boards of La Scala and raises a fist to heaven: "I shall live, by God, to see the day when rank grass shall choke up the streets of your old faubourg!"[24] The two frustrated buyers stalk out to build up the rest of the city as soap-opera organ chords swell and fade away. In one quick set change, the grandee is now a very old man, surrounded by that rank grass, speaking a nostalgic soliloquy on a stage now bare of both friends and enemies because he has outlived them all. *Curtain.*

In writing this history, I have been continually confronted with this story, repeated and embellished in books, magazines, and on websites. It seems, like many legends, to be a grain of truth surrounded by pearly nacre of deathless "accepted history."

But did it really happen? My search for the essence of this story has taken me through the lives of the trio involved: the redoubtable thespian James Caldwell, father of much of the theater in the antebellum South; Samuel Peters, a far-sighted businessman who established a great deal of the city's early infrastructure; and Bernard Marigny, the arch-Creole grandee we think we know so well.

James Caldwell arrived in New Orleans in 1819 with a troupe of actors. By 1823 he had built a theater and lit it with the novelty of gas supplied from his own works. After building other theaters and shepherding troupes around America, he retired from the stage in 1843 and occupied himself with various businesses in New Orleans. He died in New York in 1863.[25]

Samuel J. Peters landed in New Orleans in 1822 and took work in a countinghouse. He quickly became known as a man of integrity, enterprise, and energy. He was the mover and manager behind the Pontchartrain Railroad, which bought much of its rail bed from Bernard Marigny in 1830. He led the way, against tremendous resistance, to paved streets, a municipal waterworks, and public education in New Orleans.[26]

The three men certainly knew each other; everyone of prominence knew Bernard—whether they liked him or not. Caldwell apparently left no record of the legendary encounter. Noah Ludlow, who knew Caldwell well and wrote of him at length, is silent on this matter.[27] Fortunately for him, William Sparks dueled only poetically with Bernard and left an admiring portrait of his old legislative opponent. Yet he too says nothing of this incident, even as he emphasizes the touchy pride of his late adversary.[28] Grace King recites the incident in her own fashion, but the basic story is the same.[29] John S. Kendall also repeats the tale.[30] A 1947 biographical article on Peters also recounts the event.[31]

All the writers who record this incident quote from Henry Castellanos, and him alone. He published *New Orleans as It Was* in 1895, citing no sources. Of the contretemps, he assures us, "It is related and the story rests upon authenticated tradition."[32] Castellanos (1828–96) was a New Orleans lawyer and certainly knew of Bernard, although he was a lad of four years when this alleged drama unfolded.[33]

So where shall we look for the kernel of truth? The New Orleans Notarial Archives, a rich mine of local history, has established that Bernard and Anna sold the land and both the older mansion and the newer, or "Bosque," house to the Company of Architects (COA), a local development group, on April 12, 1832.[34] Anna renounced any interests, including two mortgages. Neither Caldwell's nor Peters's name appears on the acts; Toussaint Mossy represented COA. In fact, I found no evidence that Peters and Caldwell were involved with the COA at all. One interesting aspect is that one of these sales was contingent upon the Marignys satisfying an existing mortgage against the property in favor of a bank, the Consolidated Association of Louisiana Planters. The act of sale required the mortgage to be satisfied within two years. The legal and newspaper record recount none of the high drama and deceit that are supposed to have accompanied this sale.

There the matter might rest, except for two facts lurking in the archives. Jean Boze was the overseer of a plantation in the Gentilly neighborhood of New Orleans owned by Henri Ste-Gême, who had moved to France. Both men were Saint-Domingue refugees. Boze wrote his boss a series of letters detailing the news and gossip of the time.

At the end of May 1832 Boze wrote an intriguing letter to his employer, excerpted here:

> I already told you that Mr. de Marigny had recently sold his house, formerly belonging to the Bosque heirs, to the Company of Architects, as well as his old house facing the river, along with all the lands depending from these two properties, for a sum of around 90 thousand gourdes;[35] the acts of sale of which were passed publicly, and which he alone signed without his wife, but while promising that she would sign it, which convinced the Company to agree to the clauses and conditions demanded by the vendor, and in all confidence, in that neighborhood, they began preparations for opening a new street with structures for several big stores, useful to the commerce that would spring up around them once they'd reached completion.

But alas! The property owners, American and otherwise, of Faubourg Ste. Marie, jealous to see the beginnings of prosperity in the Faubourg Marigny—whose annihilation they desire, if it were possible!—made a proposition to this noble landowner (!) to pay him a greater sum for his two acquisitions if he would agree to annul the sale of them, by claiming the refusal of his wife to give her signature, and offer to the Company the restitution of its payments in both cash and loans, the Company, finding itself revolted by such a proposition, formally refused the arrangement, which gave rise to a law suit.

The architects thereafter named a committee of five director-shareholders to defend their cause, and Mr. Marigny, through his smooth-talking, and pressing of the flesh, and prostrations managed to get three of them to decide in favor of his wishes. Nevertheless, two of them, having a male character, maintain that the act [of sale] must be fully enforced! And as it is necessary to have a majority of four out of five, the opposition party still cannot win the day and [thus] allow the Marquis to sing of the victory he expects from his underhanded maneuver, for quite to the contrary, the two honest members hope, by the justice of their reasoning, to make the other three of weak character recognize their error in having let themselves be seduced by flattery, and doubtless they will come around to the side of the other party and precipitate the triumph of their cause—reclamation—, which they have a right to expect from the justice of the courts.

It is said after all that the architects are sufficiently satisfied with only having Mr. Marigny's signature, if his wife nevertheless persists in her refusal to approve the act of sale; for the reason that her husband, by virtue of his large private properties guarantee, at need and in all cases requiring their expenditures, that they need not worry about the future.

The law suit filed by the Company of Architects against the marquis of the Faubourg was decided in favor of the latter. But alas! He owes his success entirely to the numerous intrigues which he employed to get this result, which annulled the sale of several houses to the Company, even though they were ratified in a notarial act, by arguing that they had not been signed by Mme [de Marigny] his wife, in spite of the fact that her signature had not been insisted upon by the acquirers, who were satisfied with his alone.

Honor shrugged its shoulders over this!

The outcome of this affair has caused a great discontent among the members who were opposed! Who should reproach their comrades for having lacked the firmness of character to support their just cause, and for allowing themselves to be influenced by this crawling conniver who is now laughing over his victory, such that several [members] now have the intention of withdrawing from the Company.[36]

Boze's letters were acquired by the Historic New Orleans Collection in the early 1970s from the Ste-Gême family in France, and therefore Castellanos would have had no access to them during his lifetime.[37] However, since the life spans of Boze and Castellanos overlapped, there is a possibility that Castellanos heard this account directly from Boze. Yet Castellanos did not state that attribution, which would have bolstered the credibility of his "authenticated tradition."

The historian is now caught between the legal record, which should be unambiguous, and this juicy piece of "dish," that seems to provide a factual basis for at least part of Castellanos's oft-repeated narrative. A review of the acts of sale establishes that Boze was wrong about Anna's absence; she signed both acts. A search of New Orleans court records reveals no suits filed by the Company of Architects against Bernard.

Boze asserts that Bernard was paid by uptown "American" factions to "take a dive" and scuttle the sale. Although Boze does not mention them by name, Caldwell and Peters were both very much part of the uptown crowd, but again, we see no proof of their involvement. In fact, Caldwell was one of the members of the 1845 constitutional convention, thirteen years later, who voted Bernard a gold medal for his service.[38]

It is well documented that Caldwell and Peters were very much engaged in improving the infrastructure of New Orleans, and many French Creoles resisted them. It is also true that they concentrated their energies upon the Faubourg St. Mary, or the "American sector," and the Faubourg Marigny lagged behind its sister faubourgs as industrialization took hold in the antebellum years. In any event, Bernard had already sold most of the Elysian Fields strip and Marigny Canal to the Pontchartrain Railroad—of which Samuel Peters was a principal—in 1830.

How Caldwell and Peters became associated with Castellanos's tale is unknown. I can only conclude that Castellanos heard this story many years after the fact, and after many cycles of "improvement" by saloon and parlor gossip.

Grace King, that oft-cited source of the unsubstantiated and simply wrong, states that Anna's absence was confirmed by the filing of a suit, shortly thereafter, for restitution of her "paraphernal" rights; paraphernal meaning, in essence, "beyond the dowry."[39] In lay terms, she filed an action to reclaim her ownership of her individual property. Such an action would have sought a legal division of property, to the effect that Bernard would no longer have her property available for his disposal or to use as collateral. The extensive online records of Orleans parish courts show no suits at all filed by Anna Morales or Anna Marigny that went to trial. We know that Anna's fortunes were dragged down with her husband's reverses in the 1840s and 1850s.

What then to make of Boze's letter? It is possible that Boze was simply repeating gossip and did not bother to check its veracity. In other letters, Boze was sarcastic about Bernard.[40] We know Boze was wrong about Anna's absence and the lawsuit filed by the COA. We have further established that no lawsuit tax was collected in any suit between Bernard and the COA in the years 1830–36.[41]

The second lurking fact was revealed after I had a title search performed on the property in question. Bernard sold this same parcel to Louis Muh in 1864.[42] Each sale includes a recitation of all previous sales. Yet the sale to Muh says nothing of the 1832 sale to the COA. Bernard continued to occupy the property between 1832 and 1864. It is as if the 1832 sale never happened, yet there is no record of the sale being voided.

Therefore, the research yields just two core facts. Bernard sold the property to the COA in 1832, and he continued to occupy it for many years. My theory, which may one day be revised by more uncovered documentation, is this: Bernard consented to the sale but very soon thereafter changed his mind, for reasons unknown. The COA thought about suing but could never get a majority to agree and so simply took their refunded money and went on to other deals, including the purchase of a large tract north of St. Claude. Boze, although wrong about Anna's part, which was a matter of public record, was probably right about Bernard's "conniving." Bernard was nothing if not crafty, and it seems in character that he might pull a stunt like this—though for what end, we may never know.

The origins of New Orleans' civic vice, exceptionalism, are found in the tensions between the French Creoles and the Americans between the Louisiana Purchase and the late 1840s. The Creoles wanted an accommodation, an exception, with the Americans that left the Creoles free to do precisely as they wanted, with only minimal American, and especially governmental, intrusion. Had the French Creoles not chopped a city out of a cane thicket? Had they not created a colony from a wilderness? Had they not fought off the native tribes and then stood with Jackson at Chalmette? The Creoles—French, Spanish, and German—should have primacy, especially in New Orleans and south Louisiana. The plantations yielded crops; the river transported cotton to the city; the free people of color, although respected, could not vote or hold office. So all was well. Rather, it should have been well, except for meddling Americans and their strange notions. Paved streets were better than the usual filthy mire, but cart wheels on pavement might be too loud for Creole ears. Why did the city need gas light? Candles had been good enough for all the centuries before. The Creoles still dominated the city government, even as Americans settled the Louisiana prairies and asserted themselves in the statehouse.

Samuel Peters had some of these strange notions, but he tried to ingratiate himself with the Creoles by learning French to prepare himself before moving to New Orleans in 1822. By 1829 he was wealthy and on the city council. He was made head of the finance committee, assumed to be a rubber stamp for everyone whose hands were in the public till. He audited the books and found many irregularities. The Creole administrators—respectable gentlemen all—were offended. That someone could blow the whistle on the theft and mismanagement outraged their sense of honor, and Peters found himself challenged to duels and nearly killed. Yet he finally straightened out the city's accounts.[43]

The Creole-dominated city council directed most improvements, at least those they could bring themselves to approve, to the Vieux Carré and Marigny. The Faubourg St. Mary, or American Sector, usually got little or nothing since the Creoles always had a working majority in the council, anchored by mayors who could be counted on to veto American bills.[44] Worshiped by New Orleanians, the Mississippi River, like most deities, has its own agenda. The soil washed down from America's heartland was deposited heavily on the upper, or New Orleans side, of the bank. By 1835 the wharves of the Faubourg St. Mary stood inland on this deposited batture, where ships could not approach them. This diverted cargo to the lower, Creole parts of town, whose solons kept up their wharves.[45] In October 1835, Peters and others from the Faubourg St. Mary proposed to rebuild the uptown wharves and offered to front the city the funds, carrying bonds at 5 percent interest for ten or twenty years.[46]

Alderman James Caldwell—familiar from the alleged contretemps with Bernard Marigny—pitched the deal at a city council meeting later that month. The Creole councilmen dismissed it out of hand, preferring to spend the city's money on enlarging the levee at the Vieux Carré. One of them stated that "many of the oldest inhabitants"—that is, the French Creoles—were opposed.[47]

Faubourg St. Mary residents were furious and refused to let this Creole checkmate go on forever. In March 1836 the state legislature debated the partitioning of the city into three municipalities. Bernard Marigny mustered all his rhetorical powers against the measure.[48] But the bill passed, and the three municipalities were created, plus a weak overall city government. Each municipality was therefore a city in all but name, each having a chief executive called a recorder. The Faubourg St. Mary became the Second Municipality. The Creoles were divided between the First Municipality, which included the Vieux Carré and Faubourg Tremé, and the Third, which was the rest of the parish, including the Faubourg Marigny, from Esplanade Avenue and Bayou St. John eastward.[49]

The Third Municipality was divided into four wards. The First Ward included today's Seventh Ward and Marigny Triangle. The Second Ward spanned Elysian Fields and included most of the current Eighth Ward. The Third Ward ran from Franklin to the eastern limits of the parish and included most of today's Ninth Ward. The Fourth Ward was the balance of the parish up to the lake and to the eastern borders with Lake Borgne and St. Bernard Parish. This ward was mainly marsh and composes today's Gentilly and New Orleans East.[50] Although the municipalities were important, residents owed their allegiance and a fair part of their identity more to the ward they lived in. This would be true until the establishment of legally defined special subdistricts, like the Vieux Carré in the 1930s and the revived Faubourg Marigny in the 1970s.

The Third Municipality had, in 1840, approximately twenty-nine thou-

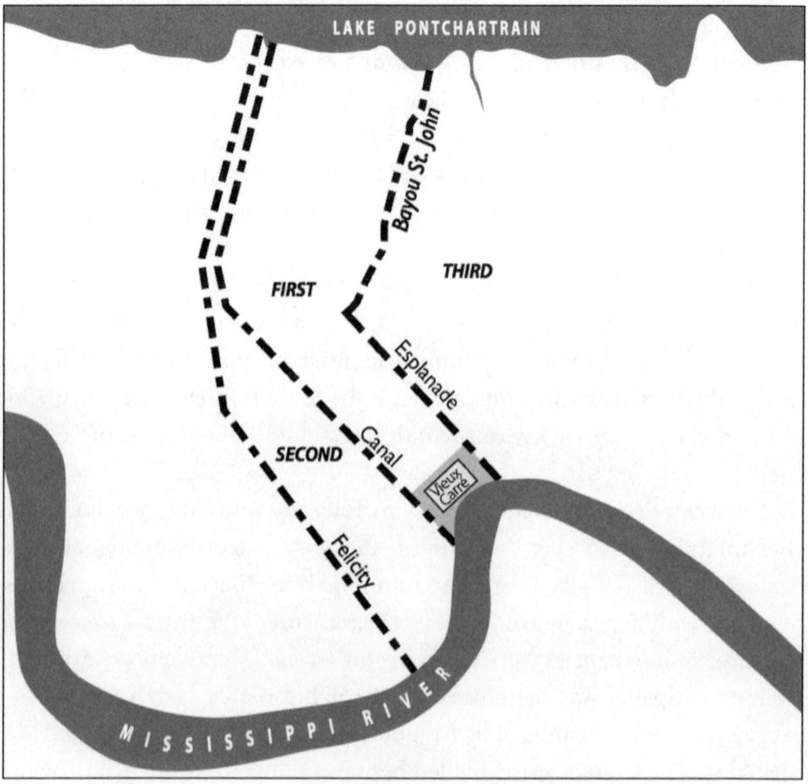

The Three Municipalities, 1836–1852. Map by Amanda Glenn.

sand residents, or about 29 percent of the city's population. The First Municipality was more populated by far, with about forty-eight thousand people, about 49 percent of the total, and the Second Municipality the smallest, with approximately twenty-one thousand dwellers, or about 21 percent of the city's population.[51]

Now each municipality was its own master, or so residents thought. They believed that, free of the never-ending American versus Creole conflicts, each part of the city might do as it wished for its own happiness. This was swiftly proved to be a dangerous delusion. The annual visit of yellow fever prompted calls for a citywide board of health.[52] Doing anything citywide was now almost impossible, thanks to the willful stances of the three municipalities. Fires, storms, plagues, and criminals jumped the borders

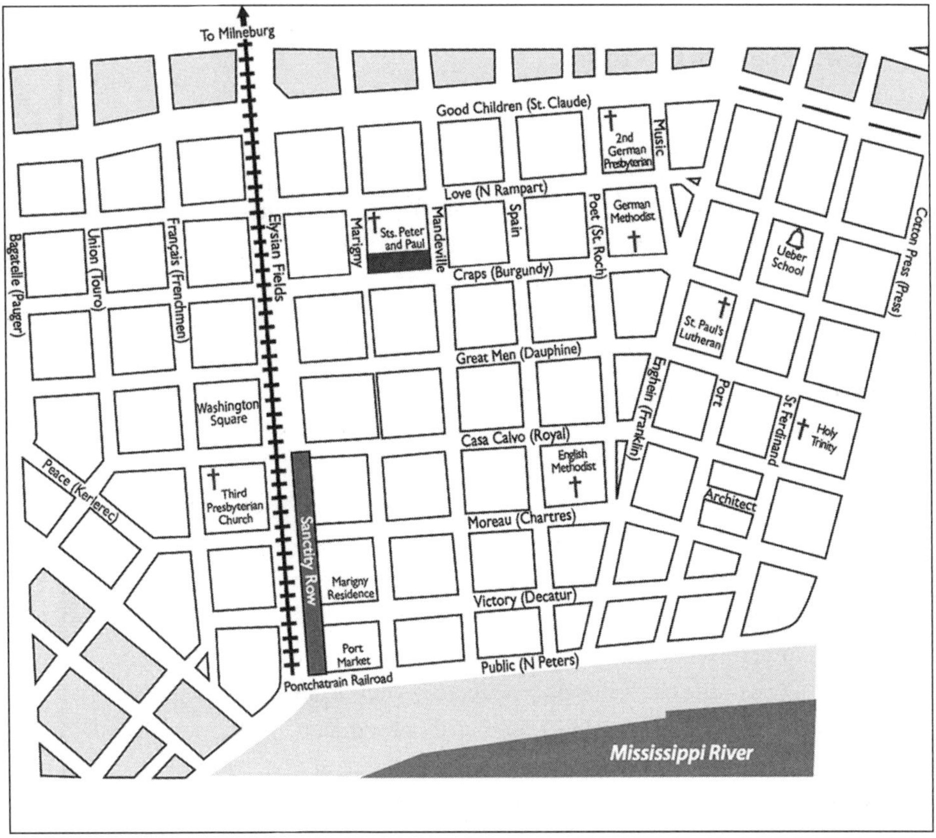

The Central Third Municipality, ca. 1850. Map by Amanda Glenn.

drawn by men. Yet coordination was deemed inexpedient and against the pride of the politicians who had precipitated the fissures. The men who occupied the wobbly throne of mayor of New Orleans pleaded and tut-tutted with the municipality councils to little avail. The three new quasi-cities also started life saddled by their shares of the old city debt and, over the sixteen years of the experiment, racked up much more obligation.

If the Third Municipality had a capitol, it was the Recorder's Office on the upper side of the corner of North Peters at Elysian Fields. The jail was on Levee between Louisa and Piety, and the District Bureau, which seems to have held miscellaneous offices, was at the corner of Marigny and Decatur. Two public markets served the Third's citizens: the Port Market between

Marigny and Elysian Fields and the Washington Market on Louisa between North Peters and Chartres.[53]

Free and Slave Working in the Old Third

The people of the Third Municipality, later the Third District, were labeled by various outsiders as poor, dirty, immoral, and un-American. But who were they? They were rather typically New Orleanian, in that many were immigrants. There were the eternal collection of transients, and many were workers in the primary industries of antebellum New Orleans: cotton processing, shipping, saloons, and prostitution. The practice of law and the breaking of laws each had their devotees. The religious life was well represented in Catholic and Protestant congregants.

Fortunately, New Orleans has had a series of city directories that cataloged people and their occupations prior to the Civil War.[54] The first that captured life in the bounds of the present Marigny was published in 1811, just six years after the first lots were sold in Bernard's faubourg. We can look across time to see the evolving neighborhood and especially the vivid contrasts between the last antebellum directory, of 1861, and the first postwar directory, of 1866. However, these directories obscure one vital view. Although free people of color were legally obliged to append *f.m.c.* or *f.w.c.* to their names on documents, they sometimes did not. They were also under no obligation to tell a directory canvasser what race they claimed, and so these directories do not accurately reflect their numbers in various occupations.

The 1811 directory has but thirty-six responses. The top five occupations were, in order, carpenter, butcher, cabinetmaker, blacksmith, and bricklayer. That the faubourg's population was very small is reflected in that just one doctor, one baker, and one sailor lived in its bounds. Carpenters would nearly always be in the top five occupations, and they were never out of work in a town where the subtropical clime and frequent fires devoured wooden houses.

The directory of 1822 reflects the expansion of river-borne trade brought by the steamboats. The top five occupations were now carpenters, grocers, sailors, ship carpenters, and thirteen "victualers." The latter assembled provisions for ships. Three "fowlers," hunters and trappers of birds, show the still-rural nature of the Third.

The 1832 list has carpenters again as number one, accountants as number two, and grocers, sailors, and traders rounding out the list. Tailors, cigar makers, blacksmiths, and tinsmiths were well represented. The directory of 1832 is also the first that notes the job of a free person of color, as a cordwainer (maker of fine shoes), along with twelve whites in the same profession.

The 1842 directory notes only a modest increase in the total number of professions, perhaps reflecting the Panic of 1837. Grocers, coffeehouse workers, clerks, clothing workers, and shoemakers made up the top five occupations. For some reason, the number of carpenters fell from forty-one in 1832 to a mere seventeen, barely in the top ten occupations. Free people of color had seven entries, barbers and shoemakers among them.

By 1850, despite the rapid growth of the rest of New Orleans' population and massive immigration, the Old Third had barely budged. Its population increased a tiny 2.8 percent over 1840, while the American Second Municipality had zoomed upward by 65 percent and the Creole First Municipality registered a slight loss over the decade.[55] Many northern European immigrants established long-enduring businesses during this period. Norwegian Andreas Hansen sold crockery at Dauphine and Mandeville for half a century,[56] Charles Burkenstock ran a saddlery for many years at Frenchmen and Royal,[57] and John Lange was the long-time lessee of the Washington Market.[58]

In 1861, on the cusp of the Civil War, the number of responses had nearly doubled again, with an important new inclusion. Laborers were the number-one occupation, outpacing the next profession, clerks, by nearly six to one. Grocers, carpenters, and shoemakers concluded the top five. Screwmen, who forced, or "screwed," cotton tightly into ship holds, were number six. Boardinghouses numbered thirty-five. The 1861 directory is also the last listing free people of color. Forty-two are listed, with carpenters and bricklayers the most numerous and a mere five laborers among them. So we see that the Old Third's share of the essential legitimate business of New Orleans—shipping, retail, and cotton—expanded but did not diversify much until the Civil War.

The Third Municipality's government exhibited a curious blend of progress, indolence, and corrupt incompetence. Under Alexander Dimitri's tutelage, the Third had the greatest number of public schools of all municipalities.[59] This included two high schools, one for boys at the corner of Elysian Fields and Burgundy and a girls' high school on Pauger.[60] Besides the public schools, scholars of the Old Third might attend the New Orleans Commercial Institute on Kerlerec between Chartres and Dauphine[61] or Thomas O'Brien's academy facing Washington Square.[62] The Catholic and Lutheran churches offered schooling for their congregants as well.

Before long, the economic folly of the municipality experiment was brought home. In 1847 the municipalities had public debt-to-income ratios as follows: the First, 2.4 to 1; the Second, 5.2 to 1; and the Third, a scandalous 7.3 to 1. These figures do not include the "old city" debt, a shared burden of just under $3 million. The Third's money woes did not stop there; nearly one-third of its debts were past due, the highest rate among all three municipalities by a wide margin.[63]

The Third's precarious position did not keep it from freely spending money not in the coffers. In 1847 the council gave a contractor a sweetheart deal to pave Royal between Esplanade and Elysian Fields and Elysian between Royal and North Peters. The mayor harrumphed but approved the contract anyway.[64]

Groaning under high debt and small revenues, the Third's council decided to see if blood really could be squeezed from a stone. During the 1840s and 1850s, various extra taxes were levied on a population that could ill afford them.[65] One of these duns was a 1 percent tax on real property and slaves in 1849; this was considered an unjust burden on working men.[66] In March 1852 the Third's tradespeople rebelled against an occupational license tax. So strong were their protests that the Third made no further attempt to collect these fees, yet did not repeal them either. This was a classic New Orleans government ploy of seeming to let citizens off the hook while holding a regulation over them for some future, "gotcha" time.[67]

Less financially interested observers could only wring their hands and moan about the Third's spendthrift ways. Of the three municipalities, the Third's wharves were in the worst shape. Even the Creole First Municipality, famed for its reluctance to change anything, was upgrading its port facilities to keep up with the American Second Municipality.[68]

In 1850 the uptown *Daily Crescent* opined, "Rents in the Third are not one third as high as in the Second and real estate meets with no sales. The Municipality is bankrupt—no improvements are going on, and the only thing that has any life is the indomitable [*Daily*] *Orleanian.*"[69]

The *Daily Orleanian* was the Third's official paper and Irishman J. C. Prendergast its editor. The paper had a French-language side, *L'Orléanais.*

This sister paper had its own editor and Prendergast allowed *L'Orléanais* some divergence in opinion from its Anglophone sibling.[70] Prendergast championed the "famine Irish" who arrived post-1847 and urged the formation of an Irish immigrant society. He bitterly accused the older, wealthier "lace-curtain" Irish who had made their fortunes before the 1840s of forgetting their roots and their suffering countrymen.[71] Unfortunately, the depressed economy of the Old Third and the loss of the municipal printing contract after the city's reconsolidation doomed the paper, and it folded in 1858.[72] Never again would the Marigny have a dedicated daily newspaper.

The lives of urban slaves, quartered in New Orleans, and plantation slaves were very different. Plantation slaves lived in the deep countryside and saw few outsiders, aside from visitors being fêted by their masters. Contact with poor whites was discouraged.[73] The slaves' social life was limited to Sundays and a few after-work hours on the plantation. They were usually forbidden to be outdoors after dark. Although they were permitted small plots for vegetables and chickens, they were utterly dependent on their owners for every necessity of life. The cabins that housed them were primitive and their clothing was the simplest that would do for modesty and protection from the elements. Plantation slaves had a distinct hierarchy of occupations. Those with artisanal skills, like blacksmiths, and those trusted as house servants, like cooks, had the easiest lot. Field hands labored hard on the crops. Sugarcane cultivation required an especially brutal effort.[74]

In the larger houses of the Quarter and uptown, slave quarters were often multistory attachments located across a courtyard from the "big house" and connected by covered balconies, forming an "ell."[75] In the Marigny, these quarters were often freestanding single-story buildings, sometimes attached to the main dwelling at an angle. The kitchen and washhouse were combined in these quarters. City slaves tended urban occupations, such as those of coachmen, butlers, valets, maids, nurses, gardeners, and cooks. Because these slaves were visible to other whites in town, their masters tended to give them better clothes, including some out-of-fashion castoffs from owners' wardrobes.[76] Coachmen and butlers wore dignified uniforms reflecting their masters' status. Some slave artisans were lodged in town as well. Factories used many slaves, among them cotton pickeries and the Levee Steam Cotton Press, which owned over one hundred slaves in 1850.[77]

Living in a city provided contacts with other people, slave and free. Some slaves were trusted to do marketing and run errands for their masters, which allowed them to also visit friends, grog shops, and sexual partners. The groggeries were especially noted as the resort of slaves who slipped out at night, throwing off supervision while the shop owner paid the police to stay away.[78] On Elysian Fields were found the "black rookeries," coffeehouses kept by free people of color, which also catered to slaves.[79] The most public and famous slave social opportunity was Congo Square, now part of Armstrong Park, where slaves were allowed to gather and dance on Sunday afternoons.[80] Legally, slaves could not work for themselves. However, some masters told their urban slaves to find work in town and commanded them to bring back at least part of their earnings. They could keep a portion, which enabled some to save up and buy their freedom.[81]

New Orleans was a major market for the buying and selling of human beings. Most of the human "livestock" came from slave farms in Virginia and elsewhere. Because slaves were used as security for loans and were heritable as chattel, they also went to auction when the loans defaulted or estates were liquidated. One of three primary clusters of the city's slave retailers, and one of the largest, was at Chartres and Esplanade, on the Marigny side.[82] Various dealers occupied this area in antebellum times.[83] Slaves stood on display from nine in the morning to four in the afternoon.[84] Solomon Northup, a free man of color kidnapped into slavery, was sold there to an upcountry master.[85] This event is now noted by a historic marker.[86] Despite slavery's institutional strength, to witness the actual buying and selling of humans was more than some could stomach. The smells and the spectacle of humans made to display themselves made even conservative citizens blanch. The city council tried to restrict slave sales without much success, and the Marigny was exempted from any restrictions at all.[87]

Between 1850 and 1860 the city acquired over fifty thousand new residents, swamping out the frightful tolls of epidemics.[88] Yet over that same decade, the city had about four thousand fewer slaves. The decrease in slaves may be attributed to several factors, but one seems especially pertinent here. Many urban masters decided to sell young male slaves to plantation owners. This removed the young men from the temptations of city life and eased urban whites' minds about insurrection.[89] The tide of German and Irish immigrants flowing into town provided many hands for labor formerly performed by slaves. The Irishmen dug canals and loaded ships, at an incredible cost of life, but they were deemed cheaper to replace than slaves. Irish girls were engaged as maids and cooks. Some Germans brought mechanical arts with them, but some gardened, drove drays, and performed other less-skilled labor. As families, free and slave, grew, urban dwellings got crowded, unlike rural farms where there was plenty of space to expand slave housing.

As we have noted, much of the interior of Orleans Parish was occupied by a cypress swamp. A few humans, a mixture of escaped slaves and white criminals, had taken up residence there. They felt secure in the dreaded cypress tangle where law-abiding citizens feared to go. The whites made a living by fencing stolen goods and illegally selling liquor to slaves who circulated between their owners' properties in town and *la cyprière.* These perambulating bondsmen were often caught and jailed; their owners would have to bail them out and pay a fine. The slave might receive a whipping as well.[90]

The Firemen

Before 1891, all New Orleans firefighters were volunteers. Firefighting was the most essential and consistent service enjoyed by citizens of the usually slouching and corrupt municipalities.

The nature of the city and its businesses meant that firemen had no end of work. Many buildings were wooden or had wooden interiors. There were stables full of hay, forges inside wooden shacks, warehouses brimming with oil, and above all, cotton presses, pickeries, and warehouses. Fires from cotton sources were especially dangerous. Once cotton caught fire, burning tufts borne on the wind set other buildings alight.

Besides the general hue and cry, firemen were alerted by the ringing of bells. Two minutes' worth of tolling was followed by one, two, or three "taps," signifying the district where the fire was underway.[91]

The irony of New Orleans firefighting was that, despite the advent of steam pumpers and the vast Mississippi just at hand, water to fight fires was often in short supply. Even on the wharves, if the river was low, the fire companies sometimes did not have enough suction hose to reach the water. In 1859 there were only sixteen hydrants in the entire city, and the firemen usually relied on the cisterns of homeowners and businesses.[92] These cisterns, in turn, were dependent upon the rain. In that year, water-short firemen fought a fire that devoured the Lower Cotton Press and associated businesses over four city blocks.[93] This shortage of water meant high fire insurance premiums.[94]

Besides ignorance about fire prevention, many fires were the work of arsonists. It was common at store and warehouse blazes to see crowds looting the buildings that the firemen were trying to save.

The Old Third had several fire companies, among them:

- Phoenix No. 8, chartered 1845, Decatur between Marigny and Mandeville
- Creole No. 9, chartered 1837, originally on Elysian Fields between Chartres and Decatur; it now occupies the triangular island formed by Esplanade, Decatur, and Frenchmen
- No. 24, chartered 1853, on Dauphine near Port
- Hope Hook and Ladder No. 3, chartered 1851, Royal between Frenchmen and Elysian Fields

The volunteer fire companies were a citywide fraternity of working-class white men.[95] The Firemen's Charitable Benevolent Association, founded in 1834, still provides medical care, funeral services, and stipends to widows and orphans. It founded and still owns Cypress Grove Cemetery, where generations of New Orleans firefighters repose.[96]

The life and work of the Old Third was not just the lot of the hardworking immigrants, the slaves, the free people of color, or the volunteers who fought the many blazes. It was also the avocation of the saloon keepers, the gamblers, the prostitutes, and the interrelated businesses that supported them. Far from composing an underworld, these avocations were a mainstream part and parcel of the city, and the Faubourg Marigny itself.

4

Disorder Is Our Order

In the decades before the Civil War, New Orleans was known as a bachelor's town. In 1840 adult white men outnumbered white women by more than two to one. By 1860 the ratio had balanced somewhat, but men still outweighed women on the scale of the census. This large population of unattached men with disposable income fueled four symbiotic industries; saloons, sports, gambling, and prostitution.[1] In New Orleans a man could bet on a sporting event, perhaps a contest like a cockfight conducted right before him. He could drink as much as he pleased. He could find a dance partner, who might solicit him for a paid encounter. All of these entertainments were common to saloons, ballrooms, and brothels alike.

The city had a well-deserved reputation for early mortality among young men from the North. As Joseph Ingraham observed in 1835, "Here the most promising of our northern young men have found an untimely grave, and, as she long has been, so New-Orleans continues, and will long continue to be, the charnel house of the pride and nobleness of New-England."[2]

It was not merely disease that felled young Yankees on the make. The giddy abandon of the town, the minor yet murderous quarrels, the constant tippling, the low dives where strangers were always separated from their money and sometimes their lives by hoodlums and hookers all created the "New Orleans effect," which persists in tripping up, and sometimes burying, careless visitors to this day.

Dr. J. S. MacFarlane had this view of the "New Orleans effect," sighing in 1853,

How often has it come within my knowledge in the course of a long residence in New Orleans, that men who were considered moral, orderly and virtuous, and who were even models of piety and religion at home having heard so much of the immorality of New Orleans and believing from what they have so often heard uncontradicted, that there is no such thing as law or propriety in New Orleans, so soon as they arrive here, being removed from the censorship of families and neighbors, have given the reign to all their depraved desires, appetites and passions, and as was to have been expected, the sudden change of habit has been at once productive of disease, too often terminating fatally, thus contributing to swell our bills of mortality, and to add to the opprobrium which common rumor has affixed to our name.[3]

Boozing It Up

Drinking and New Orleans have been intertwined from the first. The hardships of a remote, rude frontier town, lack of effective medicine, and fatalistic acceptance of a high chance of early death all made people consider the bottle an ever-reliable friend and comforter. Periodically, the city tried to restrict drinking and bars, without much effect. In the antebellum era, many saloons were called "coffeehouses," which may have sounded more high-toned than "tavern." Some of these observed the French tradition of serving coffee in the morning and wine and spirits in the afternoon and evening. Coffeehouses were for men, although some also admitted women who were there strictly on business without pretense of respectability. For men and women to drink together in public was considered scandalous, and the moral guardians ranted against it for years. Although not all "respectable" ladies were teetotalers, they were expected to sip their dinner wines, cordials, and "female elixirs" at home. The notion of coed drinking was not really accepted until the establishment of German beer gardens in the 1840s and 1850s, where husbands and wives, boyfriends and girlfriends might quaff a glass of beer together while children ran about. In 1850 New Orleans had one licensed bar for about every fifty persons, and there were many unlicensed saloons as well.[4]

The coffeehouses were not merely bars. They were centers of business and political activity, and many served as polling places on election days.

Drinking and voting coexisted, and alcohol sometimes turned political debates into brawls and riots. Some coffeehouses featured gaming tables, and some had prostitutes on tap. The proprietors of the coffeehouses were men of some stature in their neighborhoods. They cultivated contacts, made introductions, and put the right word in the right ear for a favorite. As we would say today, they were networkers and facilitators.

Constant drinking was not entirely universal in New Orleans. The temperance movement found adherents even in the soggy, sodden Crescent City. Temperance societies built halls, one of the best known of which was the 1858 Franklin Temperance Hall, at Spain and North Rampart. Like many lodge buildings, this hall was also rented out to organizations with no brick and mortar to call their own. The building, repurposed as a dwelling, survives to this day.[5]

The Sporting Life

New Orleanians played and watched many sports before the Civil War, and there was more mixing of classes and races at these events than in any other aspect of civic life. The Third District was famed for its *raquette* field, bounded by Galvez, St. Bernard, North Claiborne, and Elysian Fields. Raquette was similar to lacrosse and played on a huge field, somewhere between six hundred and twenty-five hundred feet long.[6] The best-known teams, the Bayous and the Lavilles, staffed by free men of color, played on Sunday afternoons for prize money.[7] Vendors of beer and snacks catered to huge numbers of racially mixed spectators. Members of the Choctaw tribe visited and played these teams.[8]

For some, sport was not really sport unless blood was drawn, and it flowed freely from several venues of the Old Third. Bare-knuckle boxing by flashily dressed young men was common on Sundays. Another sport, practiced to this hour in Louisiana, was cockfighting. In 1852 the *Daily Orleanian* reported that the "American and Spanish Cock-Pit" was newly opened at St. Claude and Kerlerec Streets.[9]

Place Your Bets

Gambling deserves special mention for two reasons. In the first instance, it may be thought of as almost as natural in New Orleans as the river building the batture or the hurricanes suddenly spinning up out of the gulf. In the second instance, it is the vice most identified with Bernard Marigny.

Gambling was not simply another vice, like drinking, smoking, and whoring. Those indulgences have the certainty of pleasure, at least in the short term. Wagering was an organic response to the daily chances of New Orleans life, warped unpredictably by disease, violence, storms, wholesale commercial collapse, and other causes of personal ruin. Like young athletes playing with pain, gamblers teased the dragon of fate, a play of defiance against the whims of Fortunata. A man's skill with cards, as much as his skill with swords, women, or business, was a measure of his manhood. The roll of dice, the spin of a wheel, might enrich or, far more often, ruin not merely a man but his family.[10] Some men who lost everything committed themselves to the river rather than face their creditors, wives, and children.

Wagers also took the form of commercial speculations, loans taken against slaves, crops, and political gambits. There were some notable winners and losers. If we hang the label of gambler on Bernard Marigny, we do it not for bad hands of cards but for his tangled finances, interdependent loans, trading of human chattel, and oft-shuffled real estate. The baize cloth of Marigny's gamesmanship was spread across four parishes, and on it he rolled the dice throughout much of his long life.

Crime Did Pay

The editors of the city's antebellum papers repeatedly demanded impartial courts, effective police, clean streets, efficient government, and the suppression of vice. They got none of it.

The line between the observance and breaking of the law has always been murky in New Orleans. The ten-year Affair of Louisiana proved that even the town's leadership was held to no fixed standards. Much of what would be called crime anywhere else was just tagged survival by New Orleanians. There was no reason for street kids to go hungry or penniless when they could help themselves to spills and unwatched goods at the levee. Slaves could earn real money from stolen goods thanks to white fences. Politicians close to the public till could rarely resist the urge to give themselves extra compensation. For muggers, there was always a steady supply of clueless drunks to supply cash. Street robbery was a mini-industry all its own, with artisans supplying tools of the trade. These included slung shots, small weights on chains or cords to stun victims; concealed knives to slit open pockets and purses; and brass knuckles.[11] The richest mugger feeding grounds were near the levee. Sailors flush with cash and alcohol were one target. Drunks visiting the whorehouses were another. All of the perpetrators would tell you that they were just doing what they needed to "get by." Honest folk carried arms of some sort, especially if they went out at night. These might be the gentleman's weapon of a sword cane or a pistol or two tucked into a coat or vest. Nighttime excursions were best made in groups, with each man, and perhaps some of the women, armed.

Assault and battery was not just visited on drunken revelers staggering home from the barrooms. On March 6, 1853, just after he had finished his valedictory tome *À ses concitoyens* (To the citizens), the sixty-seven-year-old Bernard Marigny, who once inspired existential fear on the dueling grounds, was beaten with an iron bar and robbed on Esplanade by George Stocks. Stocks attacked the officer who apprehended him with a slung shot, but the policeman prevailed.[12] Stocks was allowed to escape the Third District lockup; he and seven cohorts, charged as accomplices to the assault, were rearrested shortly thereafter.[13] He was sentenced to two years in prison.[14]

Violence was the most common method of settling disputes, real and fancied, and the formalities of the *code duello* were not observed when two antagonists fought it out in the streets.[15] In the years 1859–61, New Orleans officially registered 132 murder victims, a yearly rate of about 2.5 murders per thousand. This is nearly the same rate as in the year 2014, with a population about two and one-half times larger.[16] Of course, many murders went undiscovered, the river's mighty current serving as pallbearer.

Prostitution was the biggest of the big four industries of New Orleans leisure, and as an antebellum city business, may have been outranked only by the port itself.[17] Editors vied to create synonyms for the practitioners of the old occupation: fair damsels, frails, *nymphs de pavé,* and *belles de nuit* were common.

Although each municipality had its own share of vice, the Old Third bore the nickname Dirty Third for having the greatest amount of prostitution.[18] In the Dirty Third the primary red light area was the tailbone of Elysian Fields, roughly between Royal Street and the river, on the downriver side. Here, just across the Marigny Canal and Pontchartrain Railroad from the municipality's headquarters, was Sanctity Row.[19] The row contained not only bordellos but saloons, including the "black rookeries" that provided illegal gathering and drinking venues for slaves.[20] All of this went full blast in view of the Third's government. Another nearby neighbor was Bernard Marigny, who still owned the old family property bounded by Decatur, Elysian Fields, Marigny, and Chartres. Interestingly, Bernard's name never appears in connection with either the pro- or anti-vice crusades of the antebellum era. Yet he could hear and see all of it from his second-story gallery. Perhaps, like most New Orleanians, he simply accepted it as a normal part of his faubourg and city.

Another hot spot was the riverwise end of Esplanade, joined to the end of Elysian Fields by the ligament of Decatur Street. Bordellos also were scattered throughout the Third; a particularly well-known one was the Evening Star on Chartres.[21]

The ballrooms played a prominent part in less-than-respectable society. The *Daily Picayune* snorted that the ballrooms attracted "sailors who happen to be sots, professional pickpockets, blacklegs . . . the frailest of the frail and the vilest of the vile."[22]

These dance halls allowed men and women socialization facilitated by the lubrication of alcohol and unhindered by the controls of chaperonage. "Purchasable" women, and probably men, were available. The ballrooms were breeding grounds for disputes, over women and other flashpoints, aggravated by liquor. A slight between two people could escalate into a riot in a moment.[23] Con men and muggers preyed on patrons too naïve or drunk to defend themselves.[24] In the Third Municipality, the Louisiana Ballroom, on Esplanade at Decatur, was especially notorious.[25]

The debauchery and chaos surrounding ballrooms moved reformers of the Old Third in 1849 to petition the municipality's council to abolish the establishments. The reformers did not object just on moral grounds. They felt that drunkenness, prostitution, and associated violent crime prevented hardworking, honest families from moving in and that the incumbent Third leadership neglected infrastructure improvements.[26] Despite the urgent pleas and many signatures, the council declined to act.[27] Just a few weeks later, the council received another petition, this time from citizens who wanted the Louisiana Ballroom to continue undisturbed.[28]

Besides the bordello and saloon keepers, the reformers also faced the power of the city's large landowners. One of the largest was John McDonogh, whose legendary miserliness might have inspired the character of Scrooge. McDonogh owned sixteen hundred lots in the First and Third

Municipalities. He paid little taxes on the undeveloped lots and opposed taxes for any frivolities like infrastructure and railroads.[29] McDonogh, who ironically endowed many schools in New Orleans and Baltimore, was the arch-facilitator of the bordellos, since he rented houses to many of them. He engaged in block-busting, planting a bordello in a "nice" neighborhood and then scooping up houses for pittances when their owners fled the onslaught of hookers and pimps.[30]

Other men of high status also enabled the Third's vice industry. In an 1851 trial of the proprietor of the Lion's Den, one of the worst dives of the Third, a defense attorney blurted out that the actual owner and landlord of the place was none other than George Eustis Sr., the chief justice of the Louisiana Supreme Court.[31]

The vice industry was entrenched at city hall as well. In the mid-1840s Adbil Crossman was the chairman of the First Municipality police committee. He favored licensing ballrooms and discouraged the suppression of bordellos. He was elevated to the mayor's office in 1846, a position he held for nine years, catering to the larger ballroom operators with licenses that he usually denied to smaller firms. The city license only permitted the nominal operation of a ballroom and did not legalize any other hanky-panky. However, licensed ballrooms were rarely raided by the police.[32]

In 1850 the exasperated general council of New Orleans' weak central government asked Crossman to identify ballrooms frequented by "lewd and abandoned characters." In a few pithy paragraphs, Mayor Crossman made it clear that he would do no such thing and was faintly insulted by the request.[33]

The biggest obstacle to reformers seeking to clean up the Dirty Third was Recorder Peter Seuzeneau. He held this office from 1846 to 1856, when he accepted a diplomatic posting to Mexico. Besides being the executives of their municipalities, recorders were also the justices of the peace and could hold, forward to another court, or dismiss anyone brought before them.

In his judicial capacity, Seuzeneau gave a pass to most, but not all, strumpets brought before him, earning himself the nickname "Awful John." He had the authority to commit them to the workhouse, a crude sort of vocational and correctional institution, or fine them, or both. He could also order suspects bound over to the First District (parish) court.[34] Sending hookers to the First District court was a win-win for Seuzeneau. It showed that he was ostensibly doing "something" about vice. If the strumpets or their managers were well connected, it shifted the burden of prosecution and punishment onto other officials, who had to consider the wrath of the landlords who rented out the whorehouses. Many cases bound over to the First District court were dropped before trial. Between 1846 and 1861, only 13 percent of those brought to court for brothel keeping were convicted.[35] In many cases, the fines imposed were entirely trivial to the hookers but created a consistent revenue stream for the courts and the city. Individual prostitutes might pay five dollars, while madams might be fined as much as twenty-five dollars.[36] Whether fined or sent to the workhouse, the "public women" were back on the streets soon, and those who escaped the clutches of "the life," or drank themselves to death, were quickly replaced.

Those brothel keepers who actually went to trial faced Judge John Larue. Larue initially wanted to deal severely with the hookers and madams. In 1850 Larue, disgusted with Seuzeneau's revolving door for prostitutes, called for his impeachment.[37] Seuzeneau struck back by sending Larue three German men accused of running the Lion's Den on Elysian Fields.[38] They were duly tried, convicted, and sent to jail for two months.

In the 1850 election cycle, a group of Third District reformers, including *Daily Orleanian* editor J. C. Prendergast, nominated P. G. Collins for the office of recorder, hoping to unseat Seuzeneau. However, Seuzeneau was still the boss, and on election day he told the First (today's Seventh) Ward's police to leave the polling place while he sent a mob of Gallatin Street hoodlums to stuff the ballot box in his favor. Then he sent a police lieutenant to lead a mob in an attack on the offices of the *Daily Orleanian* itself.[39]

The canny Awful John then sent Larue the case of Salvador Viosca, accused of keeping a brothel. Viosca was no mere hustling poor immigrant; he operated two major ballrooms, the Whitehall and the Globe, whose owner was on the city council. Viosca borrowed money from a blacksmith firm and bought liquor on credit from a grocer. Thus "legitimate" businesses had a keen interest in letting ballrooms run on unchecked. Having political ambitions, and not wanting to alienate powerful Democrats, Larue declined to try Viosca, mumbling the outright lie that he had no law respecting brothel keepers.[40]

The Third District reformers succeeded in gaining control of the municipality council in 1851 and issued a noble-sounding ordinance to suppress vice. However, they fumbled their mandate badly. The reform council cut the district police force by more than half. The angry, laid-off policemen and their on-duty brethren preferred the certainty of bribes from the vice operators and refused to enforce the ordinance.[41]

The 1852 reconsolidation of the city and subsequent rise of the Know-Nothing Party to dominance in New Orleans changed the dynamics of antivice activities. At first, the Know-Nothings cracked down on brothels, especially those run by blacks and those accused of entertaining racially mixed clienteles. The outcry from the bordello landlords and their allies split the Know-Nothings, who regardless retained an iron grip on the city. In 1858 Know-Nothing mayor Gerald Stith reconciled with the vice lords by appointing some of their members to the police department.[42] The desperate city council tried licensing prostitutes and establishing districts where they could practice in peace. In the Third District, the restricted zone was bounded by the river, Esplanade, Elysian Fields, and Broad Street.[43] This ordinance was overturned by the courts in 1859, and the bordello industry returned to its accustomed minimal interference from the authorities.[44]

Old Man River kept a-flowin', and so did the movement of money through the ecosystem of entertainment. The sailors, the drunks, and the suckers spent money at the bordellos, ballrooms, and barrooms. Those firms bought supplies from "legitimate" stores and paid rent to "respectable," wealthy landowners. The little fish—the muggers and the pimps—got their cut and did touchbacks with the police for protection. The politicians got support, above and below the official table, from all concerned. It just had to be that way, you see, because *everybody* got *something.*

5

The Marquis Marigny in Midlife

Bernard Marigny had many resources, and the greatest was a boundless faith in himself. Frustrated in his quest for the governor's chair, he tried other gambits, and he would endeavor to keep himself relevant and at the forefront of society and politics. Bernard was a legend in his own lifetime and probably heard some of the mythology that followed him. One evergreen fable is that Marigny used hundred-dollar bills to light his cigars. In rebuttal to this tale, he is supposed to have remarked, "I may have thrown my money away, but I was never foolish enough to burn it."[1]

The other aspect of the fantasy surrounding Bernard was created in 1933 by Edward Larocque Tinker in a little book, *The Palingenesis of Craps.* Had the plural *s* been omitted, the reader would have a good indication of the true value of the book. Tinker apparently collected numerous free-floating legends about Bernard, and the focus of the book is Tinker's contention that Bernard brought the English dice game hazard, later called craps, to America. This is unprovable, but it fits all too neatly with the persistent canard that the Marigny fortune was gambled away. Tinker also avers that Bernard was a playboy with many mistresses, whom he installed on Love (North Rampart) Street, and he flaunted them before his second wife, Anna Mathilde. Like Castellanos, Tinker cited no sources. The durability of these legends is such that they are repeated verbatim, or sometimes "improved" in books and on websites. This Marigny tale, like most of them, is unprovable. Returning again to norms of the time and place, it would be difficult to find a man of similar means in New Orleans who did not have a woman on the side.

Jean Boze, who we already noted seemed to harbor animus toward Marigny, wrote his boss in late 1829 that Anna Marigny, "tired of his libertine conduct, which he doesn't blush to bring to the very bosom of his household," had left Bernard, taking their daughters with her. She returned several days later after extracting an oath from her husband that he would "conduct himself towards her and her daughters with all the regard and consideration that befits their rank, their birth, and her wifely fidelity in order to avoid a new scandal."[2]

What scandal this was is unknown, but surely Bernard's political ambitions influenced his desire to repent and square things with his family. Context for Bernard's possible extramarital frolics may be gleaned from the preceding and succeeding generations. His father, the renowned Pierre, had a mistress of color, and their daughter was received by the Marigny family as one of their own.[3] Bernard's second son, Gustave, saw other men's wives and girlfriends as fair game.[4] So, bracketed by these examples, it would be difficult and unwise to rule out Bernard as the keeper of a concubine or to deny that he had a roving eye. However, the notion that Marigny, as busy as he was and as complex as his finances were, could have entertained and supported several mistresses at once is not credible.

A menacing aspect of Bernard's nimbus was his skill as a duelist. It was said that he won a deadly duel for the hand of his second wife and would have fought six more had her other suitors not demurred.[5] Skill with the sword (épée) was a vital component of French Creole manhood, and Bernard crossed épées, and exchanged pistol shots, with several men over various affairs of honor. His adversary in the legislature, William Sparks, had some moments of anxiety when the two exchanged mocking poetry, but Marigny did not resort to swordplay to settle the dispute.[6] The legend says that he fought fifteen duels;[7] it is doubtful if even half were fatal to his adversaries. The French Creole tradition was that honor was satisfied at the first draw of blood; even a scratch from an épée would do. Combatants would bind their wounds, have wine, and sometimes strike up or resume friendships. Occasionally, for serious affronts like adultery, rage would take over, and despite the pleading of the seconds, the duel would be declared to the death.[8] However, the Creole *code duello* also prohibited duels between white men and free men of color. In the words of a contemporary writer, "It would have been deemed disgraceful and cowardly to insult one [a free man of color] who could not demand satisfaction."[9]

Bernard knew quite well the sorrow, as well as the glory, of dueling. His friend Judge Paul Preval was from Saint-Domingue[10] and is today remembered as the builder of the so-called Spanish Stables on Governor Nicholls Street.[11] In 1826 Preval's hotheaded teenage son was killed in a duel.[12] The boy was laid out at Bernard's house and from there borne to his final rest.[13]

It seems that Bernard had a great need for popular approval but at the same time an indifference to individual opinion. He cared not a whit that people were sometimes sarcastic when he sang in public or cracked his puns. Perhaps it was because he felt so secure in his privileged position, which became even more distinctive, if of less immediate import, as the years rolled on and his contemporaries took their last rides to one of the St. Louis Cemeteries.

In sum, he was a mirror of his city's character: proud, with history under his fingernails, quick in anger, laughter, and love, generous, unfazed by contradictions, and snug in his vision of his own greatness.

A Duel to Remember

Theoretically, the old titles meant nothing in America, but Bernard was still referred to—sarcastically by Boze—as the marquis. Just as Bernard had been emancipated, so he consented in 1827 to the legal advance to adulthood of his two eldest sons: Prosper, age twenty, and Gustave, nineteen.[14] As sons of the marquis, Prosper and Gustave were raised like their father—as spoiled, headstrong princelings, surrounded by luxury and expectant of privilege. Their birth mother dead, they could be disrespectful of their stepmother.[15] For the two sons, their notion of privilege also extended to other men's wives and girlfriends.[16]

Charles Lanusse was one of the men—and apparently there were several—whose wives were receiving undue attention from Gustave. Gustave was warned but persisted. On October 26, 1830, Charles, Gustave, and four friends acting as seconds went to Metairie to settle the issue.

The duel began with épées, which produced only minor wounds. Honor not being satisfied, the duelists resorted to two rounds of pistols, neither of which had any serious effect. At this point, the seconds lost their enthusiasm for the fight and urged conciliation. Charles would have none of it, and he and Gustave picked up the épées once more. All we know of this final combat is that in the end Gustave lay mortally wounded on the field of Metairie and was dead by the time he was borne back to his father.[17]

The marquis must have been wounded also by the awful example he had set for his sons. As the senior surviving son, Prosper must have felt compelled to carry on the fine old family tradition. In 1832 he fought a duel with an army officer, wounding that man seriously.

The toll of dueling finally moved Bernard and other prominent men to form an association against duels in 1834, with Marigny, naturally, as president. Many prestigious Creole names appear among signatures on the resolution condemning the practice.[18] The legislature tried to suppress dueling by force of law, but for many years to come the "fields of honor" continued to drink the blood of duelists.[19]

Rising of the Third Son

Antonio Santiago, better known as Mandeville de Marigny, was eighteen when his stepbrother fought his last duel.[20] The tradition, which seems corroborated by contemporary accounts, is that Louis-Philippe, having taken the throne of France in 1830, remembered his old benefactors from his days of exile. Bernard and Mandeville went to France shortly after the coronation, and there the king became the young man's patron.[21] It is alleged that the king appointed Mandeville to the French military academy of Saint-Cyr, from which he graduated about 1832 and then attended the cavalry school at Saumur.[22] It is also asserted that, following the examples of his fractious stepbrothers, Mandeville dueled in France and thereby made himself unwelcome in that country. He returned to Louisiana and joined the Orleans Lancers militia. Jean-Joseph Vaudechamp, perhaps the finest portraitist of the antebellum South, painted an exquisite picture of Mandeville in an elaborate uniform, radiating confidence and power, which hangs in the Cabildo today.[23]

The Marigny Imperium

Bernard presided over an empire that spanned four parishes. At various times he controlled plantations in Iberville, Plaquemines, and St. Tammany Parishes.[24] In Orleans Parish he owned various properties and there made his home.

Like other planters, Marigny mortgaged his lands, slaves, factories, and future crops to keep the entire show going. Notes were refinanced multiple times, and the entire web of interdependent loans was ultimately secured by whatever the land and slaves were worth at auction. In some cases, slaves were mortgaged twice over. In the seventeen years between 1834 and 1851, Bernard shuffled mortgages on land and slaves fourteen times.[25] Local banks held notes to the assets and sold bonds to the great commercial banks of Europe. Thus the fortunes of Louisiana businessmen were, in part, determined by bankers in London and Amsterdam.[26] The other Fates spinning destiny for the planters were the weather and the river. Droughts could spell disaster, and so could breaks in levees, called crevasses, that flooded the land.

In 1833 the Citizens Bank of Louisiana was established, with a brief to increase the credit supply to the state's planters and merchants. Marigny espoused the bank's charter. When it became obvious that no European banks would touch Citizens' bonds, Marigny and others secured Louisiana's commitment to back the notes.[27]

In 1839 Bernard had his accountants total up his wealth. It amounted to a sum of $915,000, more than half of which was shares in the Citizens Bank, drawing a handsome 18 percent interest. His debts amounted to about $320,000, most of which was owed to the bank. Off he sailed to France for another vacation and to park his feet again under the royal table of his old friend, King Louis-Philippe.[28] During his absence, the pyramid of loans forming the Citizens Bank began to crumble. The bank decided to cover itself by speculating in cotton futures, the output of the very process it was formed to support. The bank mistimed the market and lost money.[29] When Bernard landed back in New Orleans, he found his debt to the bank had increased by 24 percent and his share income was about zero.[30]

Bernard Observed

Two text portraits of Bernard at age sixty-two were published in 1847. Each gives fascinating views by men who knew him well. John Smith Whittaker wrote:

> Marigny is good looking, a little bent with years, about the middle height, his eyes piercing, black and restless. The man who eats with his fingers, discarding the luxury of knives and forks; who, in his ad-

dress, is hasty, forward, and regardless of ceremony; who sings, at all times, in and out of season, whether on the steamboat, at table, or in the counting house; has, in times past, been "the glass of fashion and the mould of form," a mirror in which our young men dressed themselves. In that day, when the Creole held the precedence in court and hall, young Marigny was among the first, the leader of the dance, the very soul of mirth and merriment. At our saturnalia, at the ball, the opera—none more distinguished than Marigny. . . . Marigny is active, restless, ever projecting, never finishing. He is ambitious of political sway, fond of applause, simple, unostentatious. It is surprising when one observes the career of this eccentric man, to see how many parts he has played upon life's theatre.[31]

Attorney and essayist Cyprien Dufour had this to say:

Today, he carries the weight of the years and some setbacks; he has such enthusiasm, and so friendly and cheerful that many young people tell him everything without reservation. However, he sometimes falls into excesses that seem to go against his character. Those seemingly opposite traits can be found everywhere. He always looks very busy, but as far as I know, hasn't much to do. Seeing him silently walk the street, we could mistake him for a Danube peasant, and the stranger would never know that this is one of the most friendly and brilliant men of our society.

Mr. Marigny has tried to drink from the source of all political honors and often succeeded. Member of the 1812 Convention, of the House and Senate for many years, and the last Convention of '44–'45, he is a master in laws and constitutions. I heard that when he had the energy of youth he was a great tactician in parliament. In those difficult times, where one must show skill and audacity, he showed boldness and bonhomie. I don't doubt he had lots of success.

Mr. Marigny is one of the most loved orators by the public. He has a voice particularly suited for it. We regret he has not more seriously applied himself. He is a natural at it, and if he studied things a little more, delve deeper into things, he would have an envious career.

Mr. Marigny . . . was often asking friends, "Have you heard my last joke?" He makes so many we are sometimes too embarrassed to answer him. With anyone else, this weakness would be annoying, but Mr. Marigny, long time a public servant, proved his seriousness and high intelligence, can allow himself some latitude, and say to the world, "*Honi soit qui mal y pense.*"[32]

Bernard's skill with his sword, his eloquence in council, and his oft-trumpeted friendships with men of power could not keep natural disasters at bay. Crevasses in 1849 and 1851 washed away his sugar crops. The price of sugar and bricks fell like an old cliché and his brickyard became unprofitable.[33] Bernard and Anna Marigny's cash flow was so poor in 1851 that they could not buy supplies to keep the slave-operated brickyard going. The Citizens Bank obtained a writ of seizure against the brickyard, which the couple managed to postpone for four months. In March 1852 the brickyard and slaves were finally sold.[34] In the early 1850s Bernard was appointed register of conveyances for Orleans Parish, a sinecure that kept the family afloat.[35]

Near the sunset of his public life, Bernard felt obliged to publish a pamphlet, *À ses concitoyens* (To the citizens), recounting his accomplishments and refuting the contention that he was an irrelevant "old fogy."[36] Among the many defenses he offers for his fall from wealth, perhaps the following is the most intriguing: "'But,' say certain loudmouths, 'why did Mr. Marigny have only $500,000 in 1839—he should have been in possession of a million?' Then these same loudmouths cite [as example] some [other] rich men, men who died as soon as they were born, because they never did live liberally. . . . My contemporaries . . . will tell you: 'Bernard Marigny did not know how to say "no" to the unfortunate; his forthrightness was unfailing.'"[37]

Anna Mathilde Marigny died in August 1859.[38] Bernard's home in 1860 included his son Mandeville; his wife, the former Sophronie Claiborne; and their son, also called Mandeville.[39]

Perhaps in 1860, at age seventy-five, Bernard Marigny thought that he and New Orleans had nothing else for each other and his task was now simply to endure. But he and his city were not through with each other, not at all.

6

The Wet Grave

New Orleans' original settlement clung to the old natural levee of the river, which was the highest ground in the parish, save for a few isolated ridges. Most of this occupied land was only four to five feet above the level of the river. In the Spanish period, aboveground tombs, with their ability to hold generations of family members, became popular.[1] Only the poorest, or victims of pandemics, were buried in the earth. These soggy sepulchers and the city's high mortality earned it the sad but accurate tag of the Wet Grave.

The very high water table and spongy soil meant that there could be no stone aquifers, as were found in many northern towns. Most people bought drinking water from street vendors. The prudent poured the water into tall jugs, added charcoal, and allowed the water to settle and hopefully become more pure.[2] This water's source was the river itself, which was the common slop chute of the town. Upstream detritus, garbage, dead animals, and occasionally dead people bobbed along, sometimes clinging to the wharves and levees. Yet this same river water might be used for swimming, drinking, cooking, and washing. In this era, bathing was infrequent and thought to tempt illness.

For men who could afford them, public bathhouses offered European-style ablutions. For working-class men and boys, swimming au naturel in the Mississippi River or Lake Pontchartrain counted as bath enough. The city council eventually passed an ordinance that forbade skinny-dipping during daylight hours.[3] Women bathed at home with water heated on the stove.

Some houses had a cistern, a large wooden barrel on stilts that collected rainwater, ostensibly more pure than *eau de Mississippi.* Most had no covering and so collected the droppings and bodies of birds. More significantly, they made excellent mosquito hatcheries.[4] Besides the cisterns, there were countless ruts, pits, and pools to collect rain and permit Madame de *Aedes aegypti,* the mosquito, to lay her eggs.

To sink a well was to draw even worse water from the high, contaminated water table. The city's privies were simply seats over a brick-lined pit. A bit of quicklime would be thrown in to hasten decomposition. From time to time the privy vault was supposed to be dug out and the waste hauled away. Collectors would dig out privies and empty the contents into a "honey wagon." Collection could be hit or miss; the contractors or city employees, as might be the case, were inconsistent.[5] The "night soil" was supposed to be taken to the "nuisance wharf," where it was loaded on a boat. The night soil was emptied a few miles below town in the middle of the river and washed along to downstream communities and eventually out to the gulf.[6] On those streets that were paved, gutters ran alongside, rarely cleaned except by hydrants at the head of lakewise streets and by torrential rain, which moved the filth along to the next waypoint of decay.[7] Many streets were not paved at all. In the Marigny in 1853, North Rampart, Burgundy, and Dauphine were hard surfaced only to Elysian Fields. Royal and Chartres were paved only to Franklin, and Decatur only to St. Ferdinand. Of course, the all-important Levee Street was paved. The others were dirt, graded from time to time with a horse-drawn wooden or iron bar.[8]

The doctors of the early nineteenth century knew nothing of germs, let alone viruses. Lister's discovery of antisepsis would not come until the mid-1860s. Many physicians suspected that the general filth encouraged disease, and when it came to cholera and other human-communicable diseases, they were right.[9] Cholera knew no season, unlike yellow fever. It could be contracted anytime. Between 1848 and 1855 alone, cholera carried off nine thousand New Orleanians.[10] Epidemic fevers were believed to be caused by "miasma," which meant the exhalations of rotting vegetable and animal matter. Cleared swamps were thought to generate miasma.[11] However, *la cyprière* was steadily cleared because the city needed room to grow.

Although cholera and other diseases were dangerous, the most notorious killer of the newly arrived was yellow fever, also called Bronze John.[12] From previous exposure, many longtime New Orleans residents were immune, or as was said then, "seasoned." This was especially true of the French Creoles, white and black. In the early 1850s a doctor surveyed the city's graveyards and calculated average ages at death. Catholic Creoles, of all colors, lived to be about forty-six, Protestants to between twenty-six and thirty years, and Jews in the Hebrew Cemetery and those consigned to Bayou Cemetery—the local potter's field—a mere twenty-seven years.[13]

Yellow fever was hardly confined to the South; outbreaks had been known as far north as Philadelphia. We now know that the *Aedes aegypti* mosquito carries the virus between human hosts. Although doctors of the nineteenth century suspected that the fever was contagious, they were unaware that only the mosquito could spread the virus from one human to another. Therefore, infected people can spread the illness, but this transmission is not affected by any attempts at disinfection. Many blacks seemed to have inborn resistance, so much so that whites assumed—falsely—that all blacks were immune to yellow fever.[14]

Dependent upon one species of mosquito, yellow fever rose and fell with that insect's life cycle. The long, wet southern summer produced a high tide of mosquitoes and thereby Bronze John from June until the weather finally began to cool in September and October. If only to escape the heat, even those "seasoned" New Orleanians who could usually closed up their houses and shops and fled to cooler climes from June until September. Some went as far as New England and Europe. For French Creoles of means, a summer's sojourn in *la belle France* was a pleasant vacation.

For lack of prior exposure, immigrants were especially prey to yellow fever and, for lack of sanitation, to cholera and dysentery.[15] The doctors among them were dependent entirely on the indigenous knowledge, such as it was, of treatment. "Unseasoned" doctors put their own lives in deadly peril to attend the sick, the raving, and the dying. Because the summer was a slow business time, many laborers were unemployed or barely employed until business picked up in the autumn, and their families lived on meager savings. Therefore Bronze John struck unseasoned working-class families when their resources were at their lowest.[16] It was especially cruel for the immigrants, tossed up on an alien shore with a glimmer of freedom from oppression and want at home, only to die delirious, lying in filth, in what was supposed to be a new refuge.

Whatever social support existed for immigrants came from social aid groups and churches, and from each family. Health insurance and "sick leave" did not exist. If a breadwinner became too ill to work, his family might starve, and some did. A malnourished family could not provide much help to sick parents. Families might be reduced to selling their furniture and clothing to get grocery money. If the breadwinner died, there might be no life insurance, either. The mother and children would have to find some work or ask relatives to take in some or all of the family. Teenage girls might be drawn into the clutches of prostitution simply to survive.

But the cruelty of epidemics did not stop there. Entire families might fall in a few days, leaving a house of corpses to greet visitors.[17] Those who lived alone often died alone and were discovered only by smell. Children too young to know their surnames were orphaned. They were adopted, but their tie to family history was irretrievably broken.[18]

New Orleans, both as three municipalities and as a city, had no enduring board of health. For fear of scaring away business, newspapers and civic authorities were reluctant to announce cases of yellow fever. The hospitals of the time were not large enough to deal with pandemics. As unseasoned immigrants crowded into New Orleans, the pool of potential victims increased. An 1837 epidemic prompted the editor of the *Picayune* newspaper to call for a city-wide board of health.[19] But the city had just split into three municipalities, and none of the four governing bodies could rouse themselves to action.

A group of very young men, mostly bachelor clerks, responded to the situation on September 15, 1837, by announcing the formation of the Young Men's Howard Association.[20] Named for a British philanthropist, the association's announced purpose was to minister to the sick and indigent during the yellow fever epidemic. The first president was twenty-two years old, the vice-president, seventeen.[21] Dividing the city into wards, members actively sought out the sick.[22] The Howards hired nurses and paid for doctors and medicine. With their own hands they medicated, washed, emptied chamber pots, and mopped fevered brows.[23] The stamina of youth was essential, as many of these men sat up all night with fever sufferers, stumbling home at dawn when relieved by another member or a nurse. In all too many cases, these newly minted adults closed the eyes of the dead and arranged for their funerals. Two of the senior and more prominent Howards were Reverend Charles Whithall and J. M. Vandegriff, a lawyer. Reverend Whithall was the pastor of St. Anna's Episcopal Church, 1313 Esplanade.[24]

The deadliest yellow fever season was that of 1853, coinciding with the peak of German arrivals in the city.[25] Perhaps because the proportion of unseasoned immigrants was very high, the number of casualties was horrendous. Early on, as usual, the notion of another epidemic was hushed by newspapers and officialdom, who had no board of health and a great fear of scaring away trade.[26]

Finally, after extended denial by the civic authorities, the Howards declared an epidemic emergency,[27] and soon a flood of donated money arrived from all parts of the Union.[28] The Howards supplied clean bed linens, medicine, cooking utensils, and groceries. Ice, expensive in summer but indispensable for rehydrating feverish patients, was also provided. For destitute families, the Howards handed out coupons, called *bons,* worth fifty cents to one dollar, which were accepted as cash money all over town. The German social group Deutsche Gesellschaft (which will be discussed in the next chapter) cooperated with the Howards to aid the stricken. In the Marigny the Deutsche Gesellschaft established a branch office, run by August Hoppe, at Chartres and Franklin Streets. Hoppe and three men at the other branch offices of the Deutsche Gesellschaft visited sick Germans, interpreted for them, and attempted to take them to a hospital. All of these subagents fell ill themselves.[29] The September meeting of the Deutsche Gesellschaft was attended by only four members. Usually two hundred showed up.[30]

At the epidemic's height on August 22, 315 people died in twenty-four hours.[31] The inrush of dead were buried in shallow mass graves, dug by laborers swilling whiskey to numb the horror.[32] The Howards rented out a building in each district as fever hospitals.[33] A hospital was established in the Third District, on Marigny between Chartres and Decatur Streets, with male patients on the first floor and females on the second. As of August 4, 1853, the Howards had received less than $200 from the Third District to support the hospital.[34] Of the patients in the Third District hospital, two-thirds were Germans, the remainder French and Irish. The *Daily Delta* reported on August 21, near the peak of the epidemic, "Not an American has applied for admission as yet."[35] The *Delta* went on to note, "As regards our own city, those quarters suffered the most which contain the largest number of recent and unacclimated inhabitants. Amongst these, the poorer classes, as usual, suffered the most, on account of their manner of living, exposure to the exciting causes, imprudence of living, etc. The Third Municipality, upper part of the Second, and back part of the city generally, having the largest number of small houses of cheap rent, necessarily contained the greatest portion of this class and consequently suffered most."[36]

The 1850 census ranked New Orleans as the fifth-largest American city, with a population of 116,375.[37] The official figures, which may be low, count 12,151 deaths that dreadful summer of 1853. The epidemic therefore killed about 10 percent of the city's total population. Of the victims, 29 percent were Irish and 19.2 percent German, representing about 15 percent of the German population.[38]

The next major yellow fever outbreak, in 1858, killed fewer people, but the ethnic mix of patients was similar. Of a total of 3,414 Howards patients that season, 43.4 percent were Irish, 31.3 percent were German, 11.9 percent were American, and other nationalities accounted for 13.4 percent. Of all these, 22.5 percent died while in the Howards' care.[39]

The Howards would go on to serve in other epidemics through 1878, at which time their organization was overwhelmed by the need to distribute welfare to the poor while simultaneously attending to another epidemic in a growing city.[40]

New Orleans' last outbreak of yellow fever was in 1905, and almost all the victims were in the crowded Italian section of the French Quarter. The knowledge about transmission of the disease by mosquitoes was disseminated, and cisterns and windows were screened. Mosquito eradication became a permanent concern, requiring vigilance lest mosquito-borne illness again ravage the town.[41]

7

The Germans and the Irish

The first Germans and Swiss arrived in the Louisiana colony in late 1720 via John Law's Company of the Indies.[1] Of the thirteen hundred who departed from Europe, about five hundred died at sea and, since no accommodations had been prepared for them, another five hundred perished on Biloxi Beach, where they had been dumped to starve. Their leader, D'Arensbourg, implored Governor Bienville for help. Bienville relocated the Germans about twenty-five miles above New Orleans at what is now called the German Coast, near present-day Hahnville. There, despite hurricanes and Indian attacks, they thrived and provided much of the foodstuff for the still-struggling colony of New Orleans.[2]

Some of the newly arrived Germans became indentured servants. An ancient practice, indentured servitude was common among many ethnic groups arriving in the New World. It had two objects: the provision of low-cost labor for masters and a way for indentured servants to learn a trade outside of a guild or being born into a profession. It was also useful in locales where slavery was illegal. Unlike slavery, indentured servitude had a definite end date. In the Germans, masters found people who already had some skills of the Western world and might be useful from day one, unlike African slaves, who required long periods of acclimation and training.[3] Unlike the Africans, children born to indentured servants did not acquire indentureship longer than that of their parents, so each servant would eventually have to be replaced. Like African slaves, indentured servants were not paid wages; they received only food, clothing, shelter, and a modicum of medical care. Legally, masters were also required to provide some education, perhaps in off-work hours at a night school.

Indentured servitude was already in place when Louisiana became an American territory. In its first session in 1806, the territorial legislature passed an act regulating the terms of indenture. A boy could be indentured until he was twenty-one, a girl until she was eighteen and presumably ready to be supported by a husband. People over the age of twenty-one could consent to indenture for seven years. The law attempted to protect the rights of both parties, citing that masters and mistresses had the right to file suit against indentured servants for absconding and servants had the same recourse for cruel treatment.[4]

After the Napoleonic Wars ended in 1815, many sections of Germany suffered severe famine. Religious upheaval followed. These were incentive enough for many Germans to leave their homeland.[5] Escaping the tumult of post-Napoleonic Europe was not easy, especially for those already reduced by hardship. If a prospective immigrant, or family, could not pay the fare for passage overseas, they could sign a contract agreeing to be indentured in the New World; these contracts could bind children as well as adults. Because these immigrants redeemed their transportation, they were called "redemptioners." Their contracts would be sold not only to tradesmen in America but also to families seeking house servants or, in some cases, replacements for their own children, lost to the very high mortality of the era.[6]

Immigrants might pay for passage up front and then be robbed by ships' crews, forcing the parents to sell all or part of the family into indenture in the New World. If a family member died of disease or starvation during the voyage, the rest of the family assumed the debt of the deceased.[7] Families might have no choice but to sell some or all of their children, who were rarely seen again by their parents, even if they were well treated by the purchasing adults.[8]

The immigrants' voyage across the deep, which by sailing ship took 70 to 120 days, might have been scripted by Dante.[9] Typhus, commonly called "ship fever," killed many immigrants at sea.[10] The ship's crews usually reserved the best food for themselves and doled out to their passengers provisions that a modern American would hastily feed to a garbage disposal. The crew would sometimes steal from the passengers' luggage. In one well-publicized case, which seems to have been more typical than not, the crew of three ships bound for New Orleans in 1818 charged the passengers for food and demanded to be paid a second time for passage. The casualty rate on these three ships was an astounding 45 percent, with people dying from disease and malnutrition, or in some cases being driven mad by fever and thirst and jumping overboard.[11]

The notoriety of this 1818 scandal moved the Louisiana legislature to pass an act to protect refugees. The act specified that the state would provide legal guardians for the redemptioners, who would inquire after their treatment and refer causes of action to the attorney general, and reiterated that no one might be indentured past the age of twenty-one, that no redemptioner would be forced to pay for another's passage, and that husbands, wives, and children would not be separated, except by spousal or parental consent. The act also forbade free people of color to take white people as indentured servants and provided that any whites in service to blacks would be immediately set free, leaving the legal door open for the free people of color to receive compensation.[12]

Redemptioners' experience varied widely. Some had kind masters who treated and taught them well. Others had masters who, as usual for authorities at the time, resorted to the whip.[13] While masters of slaves had incentive to take good care of them in view of their resale value, masters of redemptioners had no such inducement. Some redemptioners ran away, facing two extra days of indenture for each day they were absent, plus whatever punishment their master might dish out. Some runaways were easily apprehended; some with passable English and enough skills could vanish into the great American interior.

From Old Sod to New

The Irish of New Orleans came in two distinct waves. The first were those drawn by the possibilities of the newly American city after 1803, some of whom became comfortably prosperous. These were often called "lace-curtain Irish." The second wave, the "famine Irish," consisted of those driven out of Erin by the potato failures of the mid-1840s. Although the majority of Irish immigrants to New Orleans would settle toward the city's center, they formed a very large group in the Third Municipality. For many reasons, the incoming Irish had the worst experience of all non-African groups arriving in New Orleans.

Manual labor, as practiced on farms, was the only skill many Irishmen possessed. Consequently, in America they were often employed at the hardest tasks, such as digging canals, which cost thousands of Hibernian lives. It scandalized visitors to New Orleans to learn that Irishmen were often given tasks considered too dangerous for valuable slaves, Irish lives being deemed cheaper.[14]

Yellow fever epidemics slaughtered thousands of immigrants. The Rectangle was hit especially hard in the 1847 epidemic. The sickness emptied many Rectangle houses occupied by free people of color; these were promptly occupied by arriving famine Irish, who were now in the crosshairs of the disease and were also prey to cholera.[15] The Third Municipality's Third Ward, the modern Ninth Ward, which spanned the area between Franklin Avenue and the parish line, became overwhelmingly Irish.[16]

The tide of Irish Catholics moved the archdiocese in 1848 to found a new church, Sts. Peter and Paul, on Burgundy between Mandeville and Marigny. It would be a fulcrum of Catholic life in the Marigny for over 150 years.[17]

The censuses of 1850, 1860, and 1870 tell an interesting story about the Irish of New Orleans. In 1850 the Irish were recorded as 17 percent of the city's population, and in that decade about seventy thousand crossed the wharves. But the 1860 census reveals only 14 percent of the city to be Irish. Clearly there were horrendous casualties from disease, but these numbers also tell us that many Irish did not stay in the Crescent City but moved on to other towns. Besides the Union blockade and deaths in the Civil War, economic stagnation reduced the Irish population even further, and the 1870 figure shows the Irish as being but 7.6 percent of the city's residents.[18]

A Lamp beside the Golden Door

In May 1847 the consuls of the various German states in New Orleans set up the Deutsche Gesellschaft von New Orleans (German Company of New Orleans) to aid and protect new migrants from their country.[19] Deutsche Gesellschaft agents met the ships, advising the migrants on safe places to stay, filling out customs forms, arranging upriver passage if desired, and generally doing all they could to make the transition a smooth one. In 1849 the editor of the *Daily Orleanian,* J. C. Prendergast—himself an Irishman—praised Germans generally as "thrifty, prudent and patriotic" and contrasted the well-tended German migrants with other groups, such as the Irish, that were left to mill about looking for official welcome. The editor wondered why immigrant societies could not be established for each arriving nationality.[20] Later that year Prendergast and a handful of established Irishmen started the Irish Union Immigrant Society, but it failed for lack of investment in less than a year.[21] The operators of work crews and bordellos established employment agencies called "intelligence offices." These funneled young immigrant men, particularly the Irish, into work gangs. Their young female relations would be fortunate to get work as hotel or parlor maids. All too often, girls barely out of adolescence were directed to the whorehouses.[22]

The *Daily Orleanian* painted a dismal picture of immigrants who had no facilitators:

> The great bulk of the immigrants—Irish and German—land in this municipality, and stray around for hours engaged in useless inquiries—sometimes laughed at, rarely attended to and little regarded. An Intelligence office, if established here, by correct persons, and faithfully conducted, would be productive of much good. Not, however, such an Intelligence office as some we have knowledge of—where the last dollar is extracted from the pockets of the poor applicants—male and female—under the most plausible pretexts, and without furnishing any value in return therefor. Poor creatures are dispatched to various places, in quest of situations, which are not to be obtained, day after day, until tired and completely out of funds, they cease all further applications, knowing them to be fruitless. It is said too, that young girls, ignorant of the localities, are sent to the worst neighborhoods, to houses of questionable repute—where they are readily engaged! To guard against such frauds or rascality of any kind, a respectable person or persons—a man and wife for instance—should alone conduct such offices. If an intelligence office is established here, we shall soon ascertain who the parties are at the head of it.[23]

The *Daily Picayune* offers a contrasting, more favorable scene of German immigrant arrivals in early 1853:

> A large immigrant ship just arrived with a load of steerage passengers constituted one of the attractions that delayed our progress. Their

style of beauty proclaimed them German, and if that was not sufficient to ensure conviction, the grunting gutturals of their language, their meerschaums and picture-book clothing would have been conclusive. Little fraus and frauleins built on the six by five principle, waddled around the deck or climbed on the bulwarks and surveyed with prodigious leaden eyes the land of promise. Still smaller scions of the Germanic Confederation showed their hopeful heads over the railing and cried their joy in no doubtful terms, although somewhat indistinct to us. The masculines with an imperturbability of countenance that did them infinite credit, alternately smoked, jawed the women, and scolded the children. On the levee a large number of older emigrants from the fatherland assembled, who with stentorian lungs and beaming countenance called to the new comers. We left them at the height of their joy and wandered on.[24]

Migrant perils did not end when the ship docked. One of the best-known dangers was the boardinghouse runners, a persistent plague on the waterfronts of New Orleans and other ports. These men met incoming ships, sometimes boldly striding aboard in aggressive groups, to induce sailors and sometimes passengers into lodging at various boardinghouses.[25] Their main prey were sailors, who, after entering the boardinghouse, were told to fork over the advance they obtained for re-signing on the ship's return voyage. Sometimes runners would incite sailors to desert their original ship for a higher advance on another vessel, which meant greater profits for the house. Runners also might seek entry to passenger ships, claiming to have a relative aboard by using a name common for the nationality at hand.[26] They might grab passengers' luggage unbidden, so that the confused travelers followed them straight to the boardinghouse.[27] Travelers would usually be separated from their luggage, which was said to be "stored" for them. Men might be gotten drunk with "free" liquor so they could be easily robbed. The runners also recruited young women for bordellos.

Ship captains who were wise to these vermin would not permit them aboard. On land, however, anyone was fair game, and immigrants who spoke no English were at special risk. Runners might know a few foreign words and do their best to lead the unwary migrants straight to the clutches of their masters to be robbed and turned out into the alien streets.[28]

The Deutsche Gesellschaft also cared for children orphaned either by death at sea or death from epidemics on land. It also connected skilled workmen to the Work Referral Bureau, placing over fourteen hundred in the year 1847–48 alone.[29]

Some communities in Germany and Switzerland expelled "undesirables" and told them to go to America or starve. In one instance in 1855, 133 people, "crippled, infirm, unmarried and widowed women, and 42 minor children" were landed in the Third District with no funds to sustain them. After they were run out of the Faubourg Marigny, the Deutsche Gesellschaft stepped in and, "at the sight of the intense misery of these unfortunates, many of them almost naked and all of them destitute and without shelter against the bitter cold (they had left home in December) we determined to provide and care for them."[30]

Many Americans called the lower caste of German immigrants "Dutch," a corruption of "Deutsche," as a pejorative.[31]

To Work, Vote, and Pray

Once ashore and safely settled in work and lodging, Teutonic newcomers found a vibrant and well-organized community of their countrymen. There were German associations, groups, and lodges in New Orleans for every facet of their society; about fifty such organizations existed in 1859.[32] Of the antebellum ones, we may touch on only a very few: the turnverein, established in 1849, which promoted physical fitness and gymnastics for men;[33] the *Liederkranz,* organized in 1838, the first German singing society in America;[34] and the Baker's Benevolent Society, established in 1850, which held meetings at Dauphine Street and Elysian Fields Avenue.[35]

Some of the more prominent German immigrants in the Third District were:

- John Lange, who came to New Orleans in 1838. He operated a junk and rag business for over sixty years. A pillar of Holy Trinity Catholic Church, he founded St. Roch Cemetery.[36]
- Louis Leonhard, who was a child of three when he landed in New Orleans in 1844. He owned Leonhard & Sons department store at Louisa and Dauphine, where Bargain America is now. He was one of the founders of the Third District Building Association, an early savings and loan located at Royal and Franklin.[37]
- Henry Frantz, who arrived in New Orleans in 1857. He got to know

Jacob Schoen, another immigrant, who stepped ashore in New Orleans in 1859. By 1885 they had purchased a funeral home on Elysian Fields. A significant part of their business was the leasing of carriages. Frantz, a member of St. Paul's Lutheran, and Schoen, a parishioner of Holy Trinity, covered both major foci of German society in the Third District.[38]

Those Germans who settled in New Orleans lived all over the city, including Lafayette and Carrollton,[39] but there was a large concentration in the Faubourg Marigny. The neighborhood was close to the arrival wharf, had mills and factories, and was cheap.[40] Many present-day accounts say that the Marigny was referred to as Little Saxony for its Germanic concentration. However, this term was apparently not used before the Civil War; its first appearance is in J. Hanno Deiler's 1901 *Geschichte der New Orleanser Deutschen Presse* (History of the New Orleans German press).[41] A neighborhood north of Claiborne Avenue was later referred to as Soxonhaus, but of course this is outside the present-day Marigny.[42]

The waves of immigrants disturbed the fragile attempt at balance between the Creole and American factions of New Orleans. Bernard Marigny, a relic of the 1812 constitutional convention, was the champion of Creole interests when a new convention was called in 1845. Another delegate was also a man of Louisiana destiny, and himself a German immigrant. Christian Roselius (1803–73) had arrived in New Orleans from Bremen as a sixteen-year-old redemptioner. Admitted to the bar, he amassed a tidy, if not enormous, fortune.[43]

Bernard Marigny believed surviving yellow fever was "the baptism of citizenship" and wanted September elections so that those who fled New Orleans during peak plague months—high summer—could not vote. Christian Roselius responded that avoiding yellow fever could not be a disqualifier for citizenship and that suffrage must be extended to all who fit the legal requirements. Transients of the type labeled "birds of passage" by Marigny would not be qualified to vote in any event.[44] The convention settled on November as the month for elections.[45] The convention also rewrote the qualifications for voters. Free white men, age twenty-one and older, received the privilege after being a citizen of the United States for two years and residing two years in the state and one year in the parish in which they voted.[46]

Marigny did get his wish that the legislature could be addressed in either

French or English and that the secretary of the Senate and the clerk of the House had to speak both languages.[47] For this he was awarded a gold medal by grateful Francophones.[48]

The Forty-Eighters

A second wave of Germans came to New Orleans in the late 1840s and early 1850s. They were driven from their homes by several calamities. Competition from Britain had pushed home-woven cloth aside, overpopulation had increased competition for scarce land,[49] there had been back-to-back crop failures in 1845 and 1846,[50] and above all, the continental revolutions of 1848 had led to repression and a return to autocracy.

The German Forty-Eighters, as they were called, differed from the earlier redemptioners. Most were middle-class, some were intellectuals, and many were professionals with high ambitions.[51] According to Louis Voss, a German Presbyterian minister, they "had learned everything except that which was essential to success in this country—to work."[52] Some of them wanted to continue the revolutions of 1848 by remote control from America, raising money and developing bold plans to force petty monarchs from the thrones of Germania.[53] Those who arrived in New Orleans certainly found welcome from other Germans, but the Forty-Eighters pushed that welcome by presuming they would be the natural overlords of their established countrymen.[54] They also found a society already stressed by overheated local politics, anti-immigrant nativism, and *über alles,* southern fear of the abolition of slavery. The Forty-Eighters quickly learned not to publicly advocate abolition. Many, perhaps most, Germans of New Orleans considered slavery an alien and possibly un-Christian institution, but with a few notable exceptions, they kept their heads down and their opinions private. The most ardent revolutionaries seem to have gone upstream to the free states of the American Midwest, or to California in search of gold, or to any northern clime free from yellow fever.[55]

Not all of the Forty-Eighters were starry-eyed, presumptious rebels. In 1851 a teenaged Elizabeth Masset accompanied her parents to New Orleans. There she married Conrad Gross.[56] In time, the Gross family owned one of the largest bakeries in the Marigny, at 635 Elysian Fields on the corner of Royal, across from the present Teamsters Hall.[57] Her 1906 obituary cited her charity work and the headline awarded her the title of "Margaret of the

Lower District," a flattering reference to fellow baker Margaret Haughery (1813–82), whose generosity kept many orphans from starving in the aftermath of epidemics and the Civil War. The Gross family is remembered by a stained-glass window in the old Holy Trinity Church, now the Marigny Opera House.

The phenomenal growth of the city's population following the waves of Irish and German immigrants shows in the more than doubling of Faubourg Marigny responses in the 1851 directory. Grocers, carpenters, shoemakers, draymen, and coffeehouse owners held the top five occupational spots. The Germans drove a new category—beer brewer. Carpenters, masons, and cigar makers were represented in the trades of free people of color. Nine boardinghouses also appear.

German immigration to New Orleans peaked in 1853, and Irish arrivals seem to have peaked about 1855.[58] After this, it was possible to take a steamship from Europe to New York, get on a rail coach, and arrive at St. Louis in a journey of about twenty total days.[59] No longer was it necessary to arrive at New Orleans and board a riverboat, some as bad as the oceangoing vessels, to chug upriver.[60] By 1860, German-born New Orleanians hit their peak at about 11 percent of the city's population. The Civil War made immigration impossible, but the German-born residents would remain the single-largest foreign-born group in the city until they were displaced by the Italians in the 1910 census.[61]

Germanic talent contributed to the infrastructure of the Marigny. In partnership with Irishman Henry Howard, German architect Albert Diettel designed the Third Presbyterian Church, on the site of the present-day Christopher Inn, and Sts. Peter and Paul Catholic Church, on Burgundy between Marigny and Mandeville.[62] William Drews and Charles Hillger designed the second incarnation of St. Paul Lutheran at Port and Burgundy in 1860.[63]

Besides their craft skills, their penchant for organization, and their love of beer, Germans also brought their religious beliefs. Arriving in a town that was resolutely Catholic, Germans were primarily Lutheran, with some Catholicism, Presbyterianism, and Judaism in the mix. The German Jews seem to have settled first near the Vieux Carré and then in the town of Lafayette, now part of uptown New Orleans.[64] The first German Protestant congregation was established in what is now the Bywater in 1840.[65] In 1843 the church moved to Burgundy and Port.[66] It was the only German Protestant church below Canal Street. In 1858 it became a Lutheran church, eventually to take the name St. Paul. The church hosted a school, which was established on Chartres Street in 1840 even before the church itself was built.[67] The school was a reliable transmitter of German culture while simultaneously educating the children to be Americans. The Lutheran school was not without its own growing pains. In the mid-1850s brothers Jacob and John Ueber, the young principals of the school, had a contretemps with the church board of directors. After being kicked out, they promptly started their own institution at what is now 2718 North Rampart. Many St. Paul's congregants sent their children to the "Jake and John" school, which, with a high reputation, stayed in operation until 1901.[68] By 1865 there were eleven German schools across New Orleans.[69]

German Methodists started a church on Spain Street in 1840, then two years later moved it to Dauphine and Piety, in today's Bywater, and in 1854 built a church at Chartres and Franklin. This latter church was called the English Methodist or Moreau Street Church. Another congregation built a German Methodist Church on Burgundy near Franklin.

The German migration brought Catholics as well. They encountered churches that were almost always Francophone. The burgeoning German Catholic population of the Third Municipality moved the archbishop to commission a new church. In 1847 Father J. M. Masquelet bought property at the downriver corner of Port and St. Ferdinand. Holy Trinity was dedicated in 1848, burned down in 1851, and then was rebuilt.[70]

The Third Presbyterian Church was established on Royal opposite Washington Square in 1848, and a larger building was built in 1860. Its congregation had many Germans.[71] Fleeing war, famine, and resurgent autocracy, the Germans dreamt of a peaceful America with plenty of work, social harmony, and a democracy not achievable in the old country. Alas, in New Orleans their dream was brief, and the awakening rude.

8

Reconsolidation and Repression

In the life of the Marigny and of the city, 1852 would be an epic year. In retrospect, it looks like the high tide of antebellum New Orleans economic power, of a stable, if corrupt and unimaginative, civic body, and of the opportunities that brought wealth to some and left the hindmost to the metaphoric devils of stagnation and outright poverty. Yet in reality, the city was sliding downhill in many respects, faster and faster, as the decade wore on.

The most important event of the year was the long-awaited reconsolidation of the three municipalities. The triple municipality system had been created in the heat of anger in 1836, but it withered in the light of economics.

In 1846 the tightfisted solons of the Creole First Municipality had a surplus of revenue and a commendably small past-due debt. The "American" Second Municipality had a high debt, probably due to extensive infrastructure improvements, spent somewhat more than it took in, and had some debt past due. The "Poor Third" really was poor, with nearly a third of its debts past due and the highest ratio of debt to disbursement of the three. If each municipality had been an independent, isolated town, it is doubtful whether the Third could have stood on its own. The Second might have made it with well-rated bonds, and the First would have been stable, if stagnant.[1]

There had been proposals for reconsolidation for several years. The most common argument decried the multiplication of city bureaucracy and the ineffectual overall city administration. Four times the bureaucracy made for inefficiency and inaction. Another problem was the inability of the city to make uniform improvements. The wharves in one municipality rotted into the river while right next to them another's docks were well maintained. New Orleans was also falling chronically behind in the railroad game. "The River"—none other mattered—had been the Mississippi Valley's magic carpet. But railroads gave merchants of the South and Midwest the ability to ship goods swiftly across the continent and, most crucially, to other ports directly on the gulf, such as Mobile. These ports did not have the treacherous hundred-mile slog from New Orleans to the open sea, nor sandbars to hold up traffic. New Orleans' docking fees were three times those of Mobile.[2] Yet New Orleans held fast in its belief that it was the only gulf port that mattered and that all trade of the Mississippi Valley must pass through the city, and it alone, on its way to Latin America and points beyond. Besides the Pontchartrain Railroad, another Marigny-based short line was constructed in the 1840s. The Mexican Gulf Railroad started out on St. Claude at Elysian Fields and was mapped to run about eighty miles east, connecting with a deep harbor near the Isle of Pitre. Connecting the railroad to this port would eliminate the problems with the river route and allow the largest oceangoing vessels to unload directly into railcars.[3] The Mexican Gulf never reached that chosen harbor; due to inept engineering and bankruptcy, the line went only twenty-seven miles, to Proctorville, and after falling into decrepitude was finally liquidated in 1866.[4] So these short lines never displaced riverborne commerce. Even as late as the Civil War, New Orleans was connected to the national rail system only via Jackson, Mississippi, with no significant trackage west or east.[5] Banker James Robb, who had been the chairman of the consortium that built the line to Jackson, blamed the lack of further railroad progress on the divided authority, debt, and squabbling of the three-municipality system.[6]

The American opposition to reconsolidation was twofold. First, the Second (American) Municipality had often stood alone against the Creole First and Creole/immigrant Third Municipalities. Reunion would make the Creoles and immigrants the majority and masters again of American affairs in the Second Municipality. Second, the First and Third Municipalities were in fair to awful financial shape, and the prosperous Second did not want to take on their debts.[7]

The tipping point of the reconsolidation debate was the proposal of a community not even part of New Orleans. The city of Lafayette was then in

Jefferson Parish, on the upriver side of the Second Municipality, bounded downriver by Felicity and upriver by Harmony Street.[8] It proposed a union with the three Orleans parish municipalities. Lafayette leaned to the American point of view. Lafayette was also upriver of the three municipalities and could, if it chose to do so, absorb downriver trade, intercepting it before it could reach the wharves and countinghouses of New Orleans. Now the Americans liked this idea. With two American districts, there would be parity with the two Creole/immigrant districts. Yet the Americans, many of whom belonged to the tottering Whig Party, would soon find this parity an illusion.

On February 24, 1852, the three old municipalities, plus Lafayette, now absorbed by Orleans Parish, reconsolidated into a united city of New Orleans.[9] The absorption of the Third into the larger city had an effect not told by dollars and percentages. Within the Old Third, free people of color made up the most prosperous single class, and despite the legal and social strictures, exerted considerable influence on that municipality. Before reconsolidation, the laws repressing free people of color seem to have been enforced lightly or not at all in the Third.[10] The consolidation diluted the power of the free people of color as well as that of white Creoles, who were more sympathetic to the interests of the free blacks than those of the arriviste Américains.[11]

The recongealed city redrew its internal boundaries. The former First (French) Municipality became the Second District. The old American Second Municipality was now the First District. The Third Municipality became the Third District. The wards of the Old Third were redrawn to the configuration they bear today: the Seventh Ward, Esplanade to Elysian Fields, including the Marigny Triangle; the Eighth Ward, Elysian Fields to Franklin; and the Ninth Ward, Franklin to the border of St. Bernard Parish.

In that year, another state constitutional convention was called. The result watered down the voter registration requirements. Now every free white male age twenty-one or older who had been a resident of the state for one year (formerly two), had resided six months in his home parish (instead of a year), and had held U.S. citizenship as recently as that morning (vs. two years) could vote.[12] This was a tremendous enabler for the New Orleans Creole Democrats, who could more quickly register the post-1845 masses of immigrants. In particular, the Third Municipality had become much more German and Irish since the last constitution, and the voting provisions must have been attractive to those groups.[13] However, since the new constitution was ratified in the same balloting as the national elections, this liberalized voting would not be in play until the next state elections, in December 1852.

New Street Names for Old

In an era when street signs were uncommon, it was easy for strangers to get lost, sometimes fatally so, in the town's narrow, muddy, and refuse-strewn streets. That the riverwise streets of the First Municipality changed names when they crossed Esplanade into the Third Municipality did not help matters. Bernard Marigny's whimsical street name assignments had, for the most part, outlived their usefulness. In November 1852 the council of the reunited city changed the names of a number of streets.[14] Most of the names of the riverwise streets in the Marigny now conformed to their "mother" streets in the Vieux Carré. Farewell, Moreau, hello Chartres. *Au revoir* to Amour/Love, now North Rampart. Bons Enfants/Good Children became the more austere St. Claude. Some of the lakewise streets changed as well, to suit popular personalities of the day. However, many residents continued to use the old names for generations, just as New Orleanians of a certain age today still reflexively say "Moisant" when they think of the present Louis Armstrong International Airport.

The first year of reconsolidation yielded few of the promised benefits. Some of this is attributable to the economic conditions of the intervening seven years, and some can only be attributed to extravagance by the Democratic administration.[15] By 1855 things were not much better, with more complaints about high taxes. People felt that reconsolidation had brought them no benefits.

The *Daily Orleanian* observed, "Property in the Third District is of little value, and is mostly possessed by industrious and struggling working men who have not the ability to pay one dollar and fifty-five cents on every hundred dollars owned."[16]

The Know-Nothings

In the early 1850s New Orleans politics increasingly was the province of parties. Before this era, men ran on their names, with their own personalities and views as their platforms. Men from the native aristocracy of the town, like Macarty, Prieur, Roffignac, and our patron, Marigny, rotated between city hall, the state house, and sometimes the governor's chair. National politics meant little, unless there was a question of tariffs or, as time went on, the radioactive topic of slavery. The national Whig Party, the mainstays of which had been conservative businessmen, began to disintegrate about this time, and the Southern Democrats began to coalesce around their common fear, abolition.[17]

The other politic force majeure was the post-1847 tide of immigrants. The Irish potato famine and the post-1848 turmoil in Germany created a bumper crop of new arrivals in New Orleans. They were hungry, sick of travel, and eager for work and stability, and they believed in all the promises made in the name of America. The peak of post-1848 emigration from Ireland and Germany came in 1852–53, the years surrounding reconsolidation. Many of these immigrants settled in the Third Municipality, now encompassing the Faubourg Marigny, and the Germans and Irish overwhelmed the former Creole majority there.[18]

The immigrant vote, as expanded by the 1852 Constitution, was a key prize for whatever faction could command it. The American faction, mainly veterans of the dissolving Whig Party, seems to have been slow to grasp this concept. The Democratic Party, following a pattern in other cities with immigrant influxes, had already embraced the new arrivals as natural allies of the older Creole population. Converting immigrants into citizens and then, as quickly as possible, into Democratic voters, was the main order of business. Under the consolidation charter, the mayor had the power to appoint election commissioners, and these commissioners had unqualified power over who could and could not vote.[19] In the era of paper balloting, where every man's vote was witnessed by partisan and sometimes unfriendly eyes, many voters were created illegally.

By 1853 Americans knew that Irish and German voters, if aligned with Creoles, would swamp out American power, and the balance of two American and two Creole districts that enabled reconsolidation would vanish.[20] In that year, a familiar Creole name was on the ballot. Democrat Mandeville Marigny was elected as Orleans Parish sheriff. Since the Democratic city machine ran the polls, it is not surprising that the Democrats swept all the city offices.[21]

The 1840s saw the birth of a minor national party, the Native American Party, which stressed anti-immigrant, "all-American" origins and Protestant religion. By the early 1850s it rebranded itself as the American Party. Its detractors called it the Know-Nothing Party, since its members used the phrase as a password.[22] The national Know-Nothing Party had some successes in the 1854 congressional elections. Waves of immigrants, many Irish Catholics, voting reliably Democratic made the Know-Nothing Party attractive to the former Whig Americans of New Orleans who were looking to balance the political scale that was tilted so badly against them.[23] There was a strong element of ethnic and religious disdain in this. The Irish were often labeled second-best immigrants and stereotyped as ignorant, superstitious, brutish drunks, who owed allegiance to the Catholic Church above their adopted country. Even the most conservative pundits gave the Germans credit for industry, tidiness, education, and organization.[24] The majority of German immigrants were Protestants and so did not inflame anti-Catholic feelings in the Know-Nothings, though a few Germans stirred up animosity for espousing abolition along with other revolutionary ideas brought from the struggles of 1848. The New Orleans Know-Nothings, hoping to make headway in the 1854 elections, labeled themselves the Independent Reform Party. No one was fooled; the German press saw through the mask and warned Germans to vote only for Democrats.[25]

The election of 1854 marked the start of six years of violent repression of New Orleans' immigrant voters. In March a riot occurred at a ballroom serving as a polling station when a group of Democrats openly repeat voted. The Know-Nothing poll watchers protested, and after a melee between members of their party and neighborhood Democrats, in which several men were hurt, the ballot boxes were broken open and strewn in the street. In cases where ballot boxes were smashed, new elections were held, resulting in Know-Nothing victories.

Early in the week of September 10, the situation degenerated as a spat over a slain dog touched off bloody chaos between Know-Nothings and Irishmen in the American First District.[26] At night, armed, intoxicated bands of Know-Nothings, including career criminals and thrill-seeking teenage boys, roamed the streets looking for fights, shooting indiscriminately, and burning houses.[27] The brawling was made worse by the notable absence of the chief of police and the police captain of the First District.[28]

Mayor Lewis, a Democrat, tried to restore order by deputizing a special police force, the regulars having participated in the week of mayhem. This temporarily brought the violence down to New Orleans' usual baseline level. The election of March 1855 was another complete triumph for the Know-Nothings.[29]

In April 1855 the Know-Nothings impeached Third District recorder Peter "Awful John" Seuzeneau.[30] However, he escaped conviction, was reelected, and continued to serve in office until he accepted a diplomatic posting to Mexico in early 1856.[31]

Even in their hour of triumph, the New Orleans Know-Nothings had one acute local problem. The national party was vociferously anti-Catholic. In a heavily Catholic town, that party plank was poison. The Archdiocese of New Orleans sternly warned its congregants not to vote for the party.[32] The New Orleans Know-Nothings tried to distance themselves from this contagion by recruiting some well-known Catholic Creoles into their ranks. The most astonishing such celebrity was Bernard Marigny himself. At an August 1855 mass meeting in Thibodaux, Marigny defended the party from charges of anti-Catholicism, and six days later was elected, with great fanfare, president of a party convention held in New Orleans.[33] At this later meeting, a very xenophobic southern chord was sounded. Immigrants—and Germans were singled out—were described as abolitionist.[34]

We may never really know Bernard's motives in forsaking the Democratic Party of his hero Jackson, but two educated guesses may be allowed. First, his appetite for public acclaim and high office was never stilled, even as he began his seventieth year. The huzzahs offered him at these meetings must have warmed his old heart. Perhaps the New Orleans Know-Nothing Party might think him a safe choice for its electoral slate and he would ride to glory once again, confounding those who had written him off as an "old fogy" just a few years before.[35] Second, identifying immigrants as antislavery was more powerful than any lingering bad feeling about the Know-Nothings' national anti-Catholic plank. That was enough to unite both the target Protestant Know-Nothing audience and a few straying Democratic Catholics. This was an interesting ploy, since the Democratic Party of the South, and of course, New Orleans, was stridently proslavery and would never allow any doubters, native or otherwise, to sully that message. Perhaps Marigny and the other "American Creoles" felt that the Know-Nothing Party, untainted by immigrants from lands where slavery was unknown, was a better guardian of the "peculiar institution."

The Democrats fought back as best they could. On November 1, All Saints' Day, 1855, a major holiday in a very Catholic city, the courts stayed open to register as many immigrant voters as possible.[36] Some voted in more than one district, sometimes using names of the dead.

The election of November 1855 saw Know-Nothing violence raised to a new level. Immigrants were harassed and beaten before and after the day of voting, especially in the Second and Third Districts. The Know-Nothing election commissioners did their best to challenge any voters they did not recognize as their own, and often the cry was heard, "Clear the polls, you damned Dutch and Irish sons of bitches!"[37] An Irishman was shot dead at the corner of Decatur and Franklin by a Know-Nothing patrol.[38]

The worst violence originated from a terrorist cell within the Know-Nothings called the Red Warriors.[39] The Red Warriors did not simply keep immigrants away from the polls but beat, slashed, and killed Irish, Germans, and Italians on dark streets while they were going about their business. The police, controlled and staffed by Know-Nothings, lifted not a finger.[40]

Violence escalated in subsequent elections. The polls of 1856 witnessed the Red Warriors clubbing and slashing anyone not of their group attempting to vote.[41] The election of 1857 saw only 43 percent of registered voters mustering the courage to cast ballots, and again the Know-Nothings swept the field.[42] The Third District turnout in the 1857 election was very low, thanks to Know-Nothing intimidation.[43]

By 1858 the good people of New Orleans had had enough, and during the night of June 2, a vigilance committee seized the state arsenal and occupied Jackson Square and the surrounding streets. The committee's forces were under the command of U.S. Army captain J. K. Duncan. After several tense days and skirmishes between Duncan's men and the Know-Nothing mob surrounding Gallier Hall (city hall), the election was held as scheduled. The Know-Nothings triumphed again, defeating the Democratic mayoral candidate, Pierre Gustave Toutant Beauregard. The vigilance committee, seeing no mass of supporting citizenry behind them, disbanded and left Jackson Square early in the morning of June 8. Although there were rumblings of legal action against the committee and some fled town, no repercussions took form.

The election of 1859 was also a triumph for the Know-Nothings, but popular enthusiasm for its crude methods was waning. Its original leadership—moneyed merchants from above Canal Street—withdrew, leaving the party in the hands of laborers like former stevedore John T. Monroe.[44] Toward the end of that year, two Red Warriors were convicted of murder, an event that surprised ally and enemy alike. Both men were poisoned in their death-row cells to foil any incriminating confessions.[45]

John T. Monroe was elected mayor in 1860.[46] Although the Know-Nothings had effectively pushed all opposition aside, Monroe continued the tactics of intimidation, which would serve his cause well in the two years before the Civil War came home to New Orleans.

The cocktail of hope, horror, and mayhem that was New Orleans' bitter toast to the 1850s was drunk, and all eyes turned toward the consuming national drama of 1860. Before we follow our Third District over the edge of secession, we first examine that quietly influential yet nearly forgotten society—New Orleans' free people of color.

9

The *Gens de Couleur Libres*

Prior to the Civil War, New Orleans had the largest number of free people of color of any American city. Some of the *gens de couleur libres* had fled the bloody slave uprisings in Saint-Domingue. By 1810 a majority of the city's free colored population hailed from the West Indies. Some came from France and other Mediterranean lands. Some had bought their freedom from slavery, and others had been emancipated by their owners.[1] Some of the free people of color were slaveholders, in both urban and plantation settings. By 1830 one of every three free black families owned slaves.[2]

Compared to the British American colonials, French and Spanish colonials had a more relaxed attitude about nonwhites who were not slaves. Intermarriage between various nationalities and ethnic groups was common in colonial New Orleans. It was also common for white men to have liaisons with women of color, whether they were slave or free. These liaisons sprang from the earliest days of the colony, when French men far outnumbered French women and thus sought Indian women as sexual partners and wives. Although the church and French government clucked indignantly about this intercourse, they could do little to stop it. Many priests simply gave up and started officiating at weddings of whites and Indians.[3]

The American purchase of Louisiana brought Protestant British Americans to power over a population that was largely Catholic and Mediterranean. The new government approved of the strict regulation of slaves. It was ambivalent at best about the free people of color, whose numbers in 1805 stood at 1,566, about 19 percent of the city's population.[4]

From colonial times, New Orleans' free people of color faced exclusions and restrictions that, while giving them a status above that of slaves, set them apart from whites. They were not allowed to vote, run for office, or sit on juries. They were expected to show deference to whites. They were assigned separate seats at the opera, long the fulcrum of French Creole life in the Quarter,[5] and occupied separate cars on the Pontchartrain Railroad.[6] Because their admittance to or exclusion from these places was based on the shade of their skin, some free people of color were "passed" into "whites only" venues. Any white person could challenge the status of any African-appearing person, demanding to see either a slave pass or proof of freedom. In many cases, legally free people of color were jailed and forced to prove their free status. Even if they proved it immediately, the court often assessed them costs. Without proof, they could languish in jail for long periods of time.[7] Worse yet, free people of color were kidnapped, in slave states and free, and sold into slavery, often far from home.[8]

Free men and women of color were required to append the initials *f.m.c.* or *f.w.c.* after their names on legal documents.[9] However, this requirement was sometimes ignored. That some free people of color were able to amass large fortunes in the antebellum era is testimony that these restrictions did not always hamper the making of money.

Paul Francis de Gournay lived in New Orleans before the Civil War. He observed:

> In their business intercourse with the whites the F. M. C.'s were treated with the courtesy due to equals. No respectable white man would have insulted or ill-treated a colored man, unless under extraordinary provocation. . . . A [white] gentleman did not think he demeaned himself by shaking hands with a colored man, inviting him to sit down in his office, and chatting pleasantly with him about business and the news. He might find his conversation interesting and take pleasure in meeting him often, but there ended their social intercourse; he could not eat or drink with him. As to inviting him to his house, he would not dream of committing such a breach of the proprieties.[10]

Three of the best-known free entrepreneurs of color living or having holdings in the Marigny were Rosette Rochon, Marie Couvent, and François Lacroix.

Marie Louis Rose "Rosette" Rochon was born in Mobile to a white French father and a mulatto mother. Her father freed her at age three. Following his death, her family moved to New Orleans in 1771, and as a young woman, she lived in Saint-Domingue. The upheavals of that colony caused her to return to New Orleans, where she became a grocer. The 1822 directory finds her living in the 1900 block of Dauphine. Sometime before 1842, she moved near the intersection of Touro and Burgundy. One of the houses she built is still extant at 1515 Pauger.[11]

Marie Couvent was born in the vicinity of present-day Benin on the west coast of Africa, about 1757. At the age of seven she was captured and sent to Saint-Domingue.[12] Around 1804 her white masters fled the upheavals in Saint-Domingue, bringing Couvent with them, and settled in New Orleans.[13] Sometime in the next two years she obtained her freedom.[14] She was a *marchande,* a seller of local foods, and expanded her business with her slaves as sellers.[15] On May 13, 1806, she bought a lot from Bernard Marigny on the lake side of the 1900 block of Dauphine.[16] In her lifetime, at least twenty-three slaves passed through her hands.[17] She died in 1837.[18]

François Lacroix was born in 1806 in Cuba, probably to parents who had fled Saint-Domingue.[19] During the 1830s and 1840s, Lacroix was a partner of Etienne Cordeviolle in a men's clothing store, at 150 Chartres near Bienville,[20] creating haute couture men's clothing admired on both sides of the Atlantic.[21] Lacroix lived on North Rampart Street at first.[22] After the partnership dissolved in 1848, Lacroix continued his tailoring business at a new store on St. Charles Avenue.[23] He, together with his brother Julien, owned numerous properties in the Marigny and other parts of town.[24] Just a few of the Marigny properties owned by the brothers were 501 and 700–706 Frenchmen Street and 2105 and 2109 Decatur.[25] Julien Lacroix owned a gourmet grocery at 506 Frenchmen[26] and entertained in high style in his apartment above the store.[27] His rental income for 1860 was $130,000.[28] In 1861 François Lacroix's properties were valued at $250,000.[29] In the current New Orleans real estate market, the worth of Lacroix's holdings would be high indeed.

In the landmark study *New Orleans Architecture,* volume 4, *The Creole Faubourgs,* the authors aver that before the Civil War, 75 percent of the properties in the Faubourg Marigny had been owned at one time or another by free people of color.[30]

By 1830, 27 percent of New Orleanians were free people of color. Louisiana's paranoia about northern abolitionist agents expressed itself that year in a law criminalizing speech, acts, or writing that tended to "produce discontent among the free colored population of the state, or insubordination among the slaves." Death was a possible punishment.[31] Yet with all these obstacles, the free people of color thrived, prospered, and made important contributions to New Orleans culture.

The legal restrictions on free people of color tightened and took new forms as the antebellum era neared its end. The clinching of the legal binder stemmed from fear that free blacks might induce slaves to seek their freedom through revolt. Although this was never the case, whites still feared the influence of free people of color over the slaves. This was especially true in New Orleans, where people of color, free and enslaved, worked and traded on the same streets as whites.[32]

The years 1840–60 saw a drastic fall in the number of free people of color in New Orleans, as recorded by the census. Between 1840 and 1850, the number of free people of color in the city dropped over 50 percent.[33] The Third Municipality's free black population dropped 60 percent in the same decade, and their families were only half the size of those of 1840.[34] This decline in the Old Third cannot all be laid to changes in the laws, which, true to form, were often ignored. It is possible that some free people of color counted in 1840 were recorded as white in 1850.[35] The decade 1840–50 saw enormous numbers of Irish and Germans arriving in New Orleans. Particularly in the Old Third, some free blacks were displaced by Germans, especially after casualties among free blacks in various epidemics. It is also likely that some free people of color moved to nicer digs uptown and rented their old family houses to the arriving Teutons. The decline between 1850 and 1860 was also quite marked. The worst of the anti–free black laws were passed in this time. Secession and civil war were openly discussed, and the immigration of New Orleans' free people of color to places of possible equality also reduced their numbers. By 1860 most free blacks lived in the Fifth and Sixth Wards of the Second District and the Seventh Ward of the Third District. These wards encompassed Faubourg Tremé, most of the Vieux Carré, and the Faubourg Marigny Triangle.[36]

Despite their thinning ranks, the legal climate, and the threat of war, the *gens de couleur libres* were still economically strong. Between 1850 and 1860, the number of real property owners of color decreased 10 percent, yet the average value of their holdings increased 16 percent.[37]

By the middle antebellum years, some of the city's free people of color had already fled America for Francophone lands, Cuba, and Mexico.[38] Some went to the free American states and some to Europe. Some had been educated in France and found the original Champs-Élysées more enjoyable than Elysian Fields Avenue.

Free people of color in the New World were recruited to emigrate by two gambits. In 1858 Emperor Faustin I of Haiti engaged Emile Desdunes as his agent to recruit free blacks to emigrate from New Orleans.[39] Unsettled conditions following the revolt that displaced Faustin caused many émigrés to return from Haiti within a year.[40] However, Faustin's successor, President Fabre Geffrard, continued to encourage émigrés.[41] The Union blockade and subsequent conquest of Louisiana put an end to this movement. Temporarily, Mexico was also a land of dreams, and starting in 1855, free people of color from New Orleans migrated there. In 1857 the Mexican government and Louis Nelson Fouché, a supporter of the Marigny's Catholic Institution for Indigent Orphans, signed an agreement to found a colony near Tampico. This settlement, the Eureka Colony, was not successful due to the French intervention in Mexico and subsequent warfare.[42]

Meanwhile, even free blacks working on ships arriving in Louisiana ports were restricted by various laws crafted to keep them onboard, subject to a posted bond, and ordering their departure within thirty days of arrival.[43] An 1850 law revoked the state-issued charters of religious groups of free people of color and forbade the incorporation of new ones.[44] The Louisiana legislature of 1859 finally acknowledged that the state's purpose all along was to extinguish any free existence for blacks. This act extended the generous privilege to "any free person of African descent . . . to select his or her master or owner, and to become a slave for life."[45] At least seventeen free people of color took up this offer. Most seem to have been motivated by a desire not to be expelled from Louisiana and separated from friends and family.[46]

This offer contrasts with the *Daily Picayune*'s opinion of the same year, offered while discussing the Haitian emigration:

> Our free colored population form a distinct class from those elsewhere in the United States. . . . Some of our best mechanics and

> artisans are to be found among the free colored men. They form the majority of our regular, settled masons, bricklayers, builders, carpenters, tailors, shoemakers . . . whilst we count among them excellent musicians, jewelers, goldsmiths, tradesmen and merchants. As a general rule, the free colored people of Louisiana and especially New Orleans—the "creole colored people" as they style themselves—are a sober, industrious, and moral class far advanced in education and civilization.[47]

As early as 1842, free people of color had their own school, run by journalist J. L. Marciacq at North Rampart and Touro.[48] After her purchase of the lot from Bernard Marigny, Marie Couvent went on to amass a tidy fortune. Upon her death in 1837, her will provided "for the establishment of a free school for the orphans of color of the Faubourg Marigny." She desired that Father Constantine Maenhaut supervise the school.[49]

Ten years passed before her bequest was fulfilled. The reasons for the delay are cloudy now. It may be due in part to the Panic of 1837–43 that hit New Orleans' financial sector hard. Infighting between Father Maenhaut and the archdiocese may have slowed the process.[50] Whatever the reasons, a group of free black leaders, including businessman François Lacroix and poet Armand Lanusse, brought the bequest to fulfillment in 1847. Through fundraising and donations, they acquired enough money to found L'Institution Catholique des Orphelins Indigents (Catholic Institution for Indigent Orphans).[51] Initially housed on St. Anthony between St. Claude and Marais, the school moved to its permanent home at Dauphine and Touro in 1852.[52] Lacroix became the school's first president.

The Catholic Institution admitted parented children as paying students as well as orphans and provided a six-year instruction track. Classes were taught in English and French, boys on one floor and girls on another. Besides the expected academics, drawing, music, and logic were taught. The higher grades were taught bookkeeping and geometry as applied to carpentry and machines.[53]

The Catholic Institution became the intellectual core of free black life in New Orleans and an important social nexus of that community.[54] Félicie Cailloux, wife of cigar maker André, served as the first director. She was succeeded by Armand Lanusse.[55] Interestingly, besides donations from the community, the Catholic Institution also received funds from the state of

Louisiana. The state may have given with one hand, but it took away with another, as the effects of anti–free black legislation reduced student numbers from 1,008 in 1850 to 275 in 1860.[56]

The Catholic Institution's supporters also founded other civic venues for free people of color. Notable was the Friends of Order and Mutual Assistance, incorporated February 5, 1857, with André Cailloux as its first secretary. This was one of several mutual aid societies that provided a degree of support, including burial insurance, for its members and made donations to the Catholic Institution. Its hall was on Urquhart Street.[57]

Most free blacks espoused Catholicism and, in antebellum years, some worshiped at the neighborhood churches alongside whites, although sometimes in separate pews.[58] To suppress gatherings of free people of color, an 1858 city ordinance required all free black congregations to be sponsored and supervised by a white church.[59]

Besides Catholicism, two other belief systems, Voodoo and Spiritualism, were closely identified with the free blacks of the Third District. As part of the objectification of blacks as exotic and forbidden yet convenient sexual objects, whites were both titillated and repelled by the ecstatic ceremonies of Voodoo and its overlap with Catholicism. As far back as 1820, New Orleans newspaper reports of "voudou"[60] gatherings emphasized the skimpy clothing, erotic motions, and parareligious iconography.[61] As with every aspect of black life in the antebellum South, Voodoo became a question of control by white authority. These gatherings violated laws that forbade gatherings of slaves, and they were frequently broken up by police raids. Adherents maintained that Voodoo was a legitimate religion, an argument that provoked mirth in the newspapers of the day.[62] The Third Municipality offered Voodoo an audience of free blacks, slaves, and curious whites, as well as houses that were more private than those of the old French Quarter. In July 1850 some Voodoo practitioners attempted to sue the Third Municipality for illegal interruptions of religious ceremonies, false imprisonment, "extortion" of fines, and "general ill-treatment."[63] My research indicates this suit went nowhere.

The Spiritualist belief system found a home in the Third District for nearly eighty years. Spiritualism was popular throughout the United States in the 1840s and 1850s. In New Orleans, it especially resonated with Creoles of color who may have participated in, or were influenced by, Voodoo.

Melissa Daggett's definition of Spiritualist practices is the most precise found to date: "Beginning in the 1850s, the elite free people of color gathered around séance tables to commune with the departed and meticulously recorded their messages in voluminous registers, as the words of these revered spirits were deemed to be sacred. The medium occupied a particularly significant dual role: first, to convey messages from the departed; and secondly, to be a poet guiding his séance participants with his visionary powers to a better earthly world and celestial happiness in the spiritual world."[64]

Henry Louis Rey was a free man of color whose parents were part of the Saint-Domingue emigration of 1809. His father was on the first board of the Catholic Institution.[65] After his first spiritualist séance in 1858, he became a popular medium at gatherings in New Marigny and Tremé.[66] He was also a friend of André Cailloux.

The free people of color looked warily at the electoral contest of 1860. Although they could not vote, they realized that between abolition and secession, their collective fortunes and place in society, as free people and as slave owners, were in play on the national table. The roulette wheel turned, and the ball began to skip.

10

Waiting for Farragut

The choice of Lincoln and the Republican Party was not offered to Louisiana's voters in 1860. Three candidates were allowed on the ballot: John Bell of the Constitutional Union Party, which favored the status quo over secession; Stephen A. Douglas of the national, or northern, moderate Democratic party; and John Breckenridge of the southern proslavery, pro-secession Democrats.[1] Each of these parties was supported by clubs in New Orleans. Political clubs had existed in the city for years, but the crisis of 1860 spawned more. The city's love of pageantry showed in the quasi-military aspect of the clubs, which included flashy uniforms and elaborate parades. The Third District's Eighth and Ninth Wards each had a Douglas club.[2] The Union Club of the Ninth Ward supported Bell.[3] Washington Square hosted many club rallies.[4]

Despite widespread secessionist rhetoric, not everyone in New Orleans was rabid to pull out of the Union. Considerations of trade and the cosmopolitan attitudes of the city tempered the appeals of secessionist "fire-eaters" such as William Yancey, who visited New Orleans on the eve of the 1860 election.[5] However, Lincoln's election welded squabbling Democrats, Know-Nothings, and leftover Whigs into one party determined to pull the South out of the Union, and a war of revolution was on.[6]

It is often said that wealthy men start wars and poor men fight them. It is hard to find a truer, more cynical example than the Confederate rebellion. The cotton planters, the fire-eaters, the self-interested rich men, and the anti-immigrant Know-Nothings pushed the mass of New Orleans citizenry before them. Uniformed Germans and Irish prodded by bayonets; poor wives and mothers, missing the wages of breadwinners; free blacks, with mixed feelings; and slaves, secretly hoping for the breeze of freedom, were herded to the edge. Then all went over the event horizon, leaving just a stray brass button, some tear-soaked handkerchiefs, and streaks of blood leading into the abyss. In the air, a wispy echo of a marching song, like the thin, high wail of a dying animal.

In January 1861, even before the state left the Union, Louisiana militias seized federal arsenals and forts.[7] On January 26, Louisiana formally seceded.[8]

In April 1861 the *New Orleans Bee* remarked: "There is no mistaking it, the martial spirit is paramount in our city now, and the military excitement is 'all the go.' Every evening the sound of fife and drum, or the stirring strains from brass instruments tell of volunteer companies drilling and parading in every direction. . . . Everywhere on the street can be seen the blue uniforms of the State or Confederate State troop, and the picturesque red and blue uniform of the Zouaves."[9]

The Third District had many such militias. The Jackson Guards were an Irish outfit from the Eighth Ward, headquartered at the corner of Spain and Decatur.[10] Hibernians, recently scorned and chased from polls, were now prized for their ferocity in battle. One Third District Irish family sent all three sons and the father into service.[11] The Blücher Guards, drawn from the district's German population, mustered on North Rampart Street, and the *Daily Picayune* noted that "most . . . officers have served in the regular armies of Germany."[12]

The Third's free men of color answered the call as well. On April 22, 1861, a meeting was held at the Catholic Institution to organize the Native Guards militia.[13] Recalling their forefathers' 1815 stand at Chalmette, fifteen hundred free black men joined up and offered their services to defend New Orleans. Company E of the Native Guards, captained by André Cailloux, was largely drawn from the Third District.[14] His friend Henry Rey also served as a captain.[15] Despite the desperate condition of the city's defenses, the Confederate authorities never called on the Native Guards to fight.

The Third's fire companies supplied many troops to the cause. Hope Hook and Ladder had its firehouse near the site of the present-day Christopher Inn. In early 1861, the firehouse organized the Hope Guards, who in October of that year were melded with other district firehouse militias to become the Third District Fire Rangers,[16] who in turn were consolidated citywide into the Orleans Fire Battalion (later a regiment).[17]

The women of the Old Third were not content to just flutter handkerchiefs and cheer on the marching men. They organized fairs to raise money for the units, selling drinks, pastries, and small handicrafts. In July 1861 a "military fair" was held at the Desoto School on Mandeville Street, between St. Claude and North Rampart.[18] The Ladies' Aid Society, captained by Mrs. P. G. Laidlaw of the 2700 block of Chartres Street, gathered clothing and medical supplies for "the boys."[19]

Mandeville de Marigny was one of the early commanders of New Orleans' Confederate troops. On the basis of his military credentials, he was selected as the first colonel of the Tenth Louisiana Infantry regiment. In April 1861 his regiment was said to be a "lively mixture of French, Italian and Spanish members," with the commands given in French.[20] The first flashpoints between the old Union and the infant Confederacy would be in the East, and the Tenth Regiment, like many other Louisiana outfits, hurried to the battlefields of Virginia.[21]

By June 1861, twelve thousand Louisiana men had left to join the new Confederate army. This number only increased as time went on, and by February 1862 few regular troops were left in town. As the militia companies were amalgamated into Confederate units, a home guard was formed of foreign residents, including the French Volunteers, the Spanish Legion, the Italian Guards, the British Guards, and the German Hansa Guards, becoming known as the European Brigade.[22]

The elite of the city's older white men formed the Confederate Guards. The guards' uniforms were tailored, immaculate, and glittering.[23] The guards' home bivouac was in Lafayette Square, near city hall, where they drank champagne and received their families in style. The men got alternate days off to visit home and check up on business. Their enlistment contracts stipulated that they were not to leave Orleans Parish. The guards' only known action was to force an unwilling group of Italian American Confederate militiamen to the expected line of battle.[24]

The young men—husbands, fathers, and breadwinners—rushed off to war far from home to fight the early battles. George Washington Cable was then an office boy of fourteen and wrote a telling memoir of the anxious time between the departure of the troops and the Union conquest. He explained, "There had come a great silence upon trade." The Union blockade meant less food and fewer consumer goods coming over the once-bustling but now almost idle levee. Hard currency had nearly vanished and was replaced first by bank-issued "shinplasters" and finally by streetcar tickets.[25] Food prices were often marked up by "patriotic" speculators hoping to reap fortunes from the war.[26] Even coffee vanished from the shelf.[27] Wives and children of Confederate soldiers began to feel privation and outright hunger, and some were turned out of their homes for lack of rent money.

In June 1861 the city offered each Confederate wife a five-dollar stipend twice a month. In late July the city council neglected to appropriate the funds. Three hundred desperate women stormed Mayor Monroe's office. Tap dancing quickly, Monroe expressed his sympathy and said that he would ask the council to act that evening. When he explained that, with his own eight children, he could not fund the stipend personally, one buxom Irish mother bellowed, "Long life to yer Honor, but it's ten little humanities I've presented to the land of America meself!" Monroe gave fifty cents to each mother with a babe in arms.[28] This episode moved concerned citizens to found a free market to supply families of soldiers with the essentials of life. About fifteen hundred families a day were supplied in the first five months of operation.[29]

From his time as a chief of the Know-Nothings, Mayor Monroe had developed a network of domestic spies.[30] Monroe's experience in suppressing German and Irish voters was now put to use punishing dissent. Anyone foolish enough to denounce secession or question the Confederacy's eventual victory was arrested, tried by Monroe sitting as a court of one, and sentenced to jail.[31] Others were detained merely for being suspicious.[32]

Three circumstances gave New Orleans hope that it would remain Confederate. The first was the proximity of Forts St. Philip and Jackson, located on opposite sides of the Mississippi about sixty-five miles below the city. Their crossfire would shred any wooden ship attempting to ascend the river.[33] These forts were commanded by Confederate general Johnson Duncan, whom we last saw leading an unsuccessful rebellion against Know-Nothing mobocracy in New Orleans. The second was the construction of the *Mississippi* and the *Louisiana,* heavily armed ironclad warships being built in Algiers. These ironclads would destroy any wooden warships that survived the fire from the forts.[34] The *Mississippi* and *Louisiana,* if completed, would be dangerous indeed, as the ironclads *Monitor* and *Virginia* had already demonstrated at Hampton Roads. Progress on the ships was slow, and as April 1862 arrived they were still not finished.[35] The third reassurance was the swampy surrounding area, which would force a land attack across the well-known terrain of Chalmette, where a few cannons had been mounted near the present battlefield cemetery.[36]

But these defenses were inadequate against either a modern, boldly commanded fleet or a large land force. New Orleans' prime fighting men had all marched away, leaving the city's inner defenses manned by a few thousand old men, boys, and "foreigners" armed mainly with shotguns. There was not enough artillery at Chalmette to engage one enemy battalion, let alone a naval task force bristling with guns. Moreover, the river was at a record height, which flooded the lower parts of the forts and elevated the Union fleet above the levees, allowing them to look, and fire, down on the land.[37]

Many foreign-born residents hurried to their consulates to certify their nationalities and thus avoid the Confederate draft.[38] As the Federals approached, these residents took their money and valuables to consulates for safekeeping, hoping to put them beyond the reach of either American government.[39]

At this hour, the large numbers of Germans in the Third District and New Orleans itself deserve our special attention. Of the foreign born in town, Germans were second in number only to the Irish. Germans accounted for just under 13 percent of the city's population, which was about 42 percent foreign born.[40] The Germans were the most successful immigrant group in antebellum New Orleans. Their industry and love of organization were cited with admiration and a bit of envy by the town's newspapers. Considering how badly the city treated Germans, it is surprisingly that not all left for upriver cities free from yellow fever and the Know-Nothing regime of terror.

Now, as the infant Confederacy called for troops, it expected every able-bodied white man, regardless of nativity or enfranchisement, to march to the drum. Some Germans served the Confederacy with enthusiasm, but many of their countrymen in New Orleans had other ideas. Consider their perspective. They had fled their beloved *Vaterland* due to hunger, revolution, and repression. They endured hell ships across the Atlantic, and on arrival many became indentured servants. Escaping feudalism at home, the Teutons found an economy dependent on the enslavement of human beings. Slavery was, to many Germans, shockingly un-Christian in a society that loudly declared its faith and love of church. The Know-Nothings had almost pushed the Germans and other "un-Americans" out of participatory democracy in New Orleans and hung the most hateful label of the era on them. All the Germans craved was peace and stability to exercise their legendary work ethic and their religious beliefs. Now they were being required, not just asked, to fight for the very system that denied them the rights of citizens and slaves the rights of humans. Some of the soldiers in Forts Jackson and St. Philip were Germans. Regardless of nationality, these soldiers endured soggy, miserable living conditions, isolation from society, and discipline harsh even by nineteenth-century standards.[41] But the conscripted soldiers were not going to take it forever.

On April 18, 1862, the Union fleet led by Captain David Farragut and Commander David Porter sailed up to the forts and opened fire. Day after day, thousands of rounds were fired by both sides. The forts were damaged but could still fire back. Farragut's warships passed the forts, which still held the wooden troop transports at bay. After exchanging a few shots with the Confederate battery at Chalmette, the Union task force anchored at New Orleans on the twenty-fifth.[42]

At midnight on the twenty-seventh, most of the soldiers in Fort Jackson mutinied, and the soldiers of Fort St. Philip also rebelled. The forts were surrendered to the newly arrived Union army on the morning of April 28.[43] The surrender meant that wooden Union troop ships were now safe from Rebel guns. Troops could be brought upriver quickly and not have to slog through the one hundred miles of swamp between the mouth of the river and the gates of New Orleans. Farragut's fleet, for all its power, depended on supplies and safe ports, and these were now secured. For the mutineers, their surrender meant food, dry feet, eventual reunion with their families, and freedom from heavy-handed Confederate rule at home.[44] Some of the mutineers joined the Union army. Mutiny is traditionally punished with death. In September 1862, a Union outfit was overrun at Bayou des Allemands, about 150 miles north of New Orleans. The Confederates recognized ten of the men in blue as former Rebels—some of them Fort Jackson mutineers—and summarily shot them.[45]

After the city's recapture by the Union, a Confederate officer testified that "a large portion of the German population was disloyal."[46] German participation in the mutiny and subsequent conduct by New Orleans Teutons after the Union occupation seem to vindicate that opinion. Even without the abuses dealt the Germans and Irish by the Know-Nothings, slavery was never a cause the immigrants from free lands could espouse, especially at the cost of their suffrage, their livelihood, and their lives.

The seal of Louisiana features a pelican tearing strips from her breast to feed hungry chicks. Now New Orleans began to tear strips from its breast as well, but authorities despoiled them without any thought for the sustenance of the population, already pinched by blockade. To keep it out of Federal hands, all the cotton was pulled from the warehouses and set on fire. Ships not requisitioned by the fleeing Confederate authorities were torched. The levees were wreathed in smoke and flames. Pilfering from the levee was a customary means of support for the poor, and now mobs broke into the warehouses and helped themselves. Bacon, sugar, anything and everything was seized by hungry, desperate thousands. The gutters ran with molasses.[47] The European Brigade finally managed to restore order, but the looting probably ceased only when there was nothing left to take.[48]

Governor Thomas Moore and other officials commandeered two steamboats to skedaddle out of town, leaving behind a bitter populace. Six million dollars of scarce gold and silver currency were pulled out of the banks and sent north to Confederate coffers.[49] The Confederate authorities made sure the city was left impoverished and hungry, with less than three weeks' worth of food.[50] General Mansfield Lovell ordered a military evacuation of what few fighting troops and supplies were left to Camp Moore.

Among the troops ordered to Camp Moore were the well-to-do Confederate Guards. Many refused to leave town. Those that did arrive at the camp were unhappy about the illegality of their removal and complained bitterly to Lovell, who, after some hemming and hawing, let the guards go home on May 1, when Union troops began marching down New Orleans' streets.[51]

Farragut's fleet was now anchored in the river, covering the city's entire waterfront. On the levee, a stunned crowd gaped at the many ships, their gun ports open and cannons aimed squarely at the town. A few foolish observers applauded, and about seventy-five people were shot down by mounted thugs on the spot.[52] It is believed that about twenty of the casualties were Germans.[53]

Farragut demanded surrender. The mayor replied that he was just a civil officer and deferred to General Lovell. Lovell refused, adding that he would evacuate his troops and then the city government could decide. To his credit, Lovell refused to fight a hopeless battle in the streets under the guns of the Union fleet.

The city council put off the decision—after all, tomorrow is always another day in New Orleans—and notified Farragut to that effect. Farragut replied that he was not an occupier but would "speedily and severely punish" anyone who mistreated Union sympathizers.

Farragut's forces raised the U.S. flag on the U.S. Mint, and shortly thereafter a mob, led by middle-aged professional gambler William Mumford, tore it down. A Union ship fired a cannon shot over the heads of the throng, which did nothing to chasten them. Meanwhile, Mayor Monroe insisted that the Union forces would have to conquer the city; it would not be surrendered. Farragut's patience was wearing thin as he waited for the Union army's occupying forces. He told Monroe to evacuate women and children because in forty-eight hours he intended to start bombarding New Orleans. Monroe replied that such an evacuation was impossible, and in any event the city would take the Union shells without flinching rather than submit. Farragut desisted and deferred to the arriving Union general Benjamin Butler.[54] In the tense week between Farragut's arrival and the entry of Union army troops, Monroe used his old reliable method—a rampaging mob of thugs—to control the population.[55]

Dixie to a Different Drum

In times of crisis, New Orleans has needed, and sometimes had the luck to receive, stern taskmasters who could break through the walls of denial, civic fantasy, and the double-edge sword of exceptionalism. In 1769 it was O'Reilly, who, after shooting the most recalcitrant rebels against Spanish rule, installed a government much better than the French regime it succeeded. In 1815 it had been Andrew Jackson. Now another taskmaster arrived, also destined to be more hated for his methods than praised for his results.

General Benjamin Franklin Butler was a man of so many contradictions that New Orleans should have embraced him as one of its own. He had been a labor rights attorney in Massachusetts. He was an egocentric self-promoter with a melodramatic temperament.[56] He showed mercy toward men he might have hanged out of hand.[57] He kept the city from starving while he allowed his brother, and others, to loot the property of wealthy Rebels. Just like his nemesis Mayor Monroe, he relied on a network of spies who, seeking revenge and rewards, carried anti-Union gossip to his eager ears. Not much as a field commander, he was a master of the psychology of governance, even if most New Orleanians despised him heartily. The elite among his conquered subjects wanted to be coddled, soothed, and allowed to pretend they were still Confederates. That fantasy Butler would not indulge.

New Orleans women continued to resist, assaulting the Federals with saliva and the contents of chamber pots. Butler resolved that this aggressive humiliation would not continue. Butler's General Order No. 28 of May 15, 1862, the infamous "Woman Order," compelled the women of New Orleans to be ladies in their conduct toward the Union troops: "It is ordered that hereafter when any female shall, by word, gesture, or movement, insult or show contempt for any officer or soldier of the United States, she shall be regarded and held liable to be treated as a woman of the town plying her avocation." The "ladies" did not desire to be treated as prostitutes, and the prostitutes desired to be treated as ladies. As Butler noted, it was an order "that would execute itself."[58]

This edict caused Mayor Monroe, and numerous other Confederates, to puff up with indignation at this insult to southern womanhood. Monroe danced through two cycles of protests and apologies.[59] Butler lost patience and sent the Know-Nothing mobster to prison, where he stayed until just before Christmas 1862.[60] The general swept aside the thuggish, obstructionist city government and replaced it with military rule.

The Union administration had to walk a fine line. Fifteen thousand men occupied a city ten times that size. New Orleans was swarming with angry ex-Confederate soldiers and longtime Know-Nothings who formed drunken and armed mobs. Nevertheless, Butler was determined to show that he, not the mob, ruled New Orleans. William Mumford was caught, judged guilty by Butler, and hanged at the U.S. Mint, where he had pulled down the Stars and Stripes. Although Mumford's hanging is well remembered, it is less well known that Butler also hanged four men, some northerners, who were ransacking houses and stealing valuables while wearing Union uniforms.[61]

Butler required every adult to take an oath of loyalty to the Union. Those demurring were listed as enemies and their property confiscated. Many citizens chose not to renew their loyalty to the old Union, thinking that, by some miracle, "their country"—perhaps in the person of favorite son General Pierre Beauregard—would return and rout the odious Federals. This hope was not all Rebel fantasy. In 1862 Union forces held only a small part of Louisiana. New Orleans was only lightly secured by Federal troops and a well-equipped land and naval force could have wrenched it back. However, the Confederates never made the attempt.

The requirement for Union loyalty extended to the churches. Butler discovered that some clergy were still publicly praying for Jefferson Davis and the Confederacy. He decreed that political prayers would be offered only for Abraham Lincoln and the Union and sent his officers to monitor divine services.[62] Openly Rebel clergy and lay leaders were replaced with either Union officers or "reliable" civilians. Lists were made of loyal and disloyal clergy, the latter being just as subject to arrest as anyone else. In the Third District, the pastor and staff of the Third Presbyterian Church, on what is now the site of the Christopher Inn, were reported as known secessionists or as having fled to the Confederacy.[63]

Nor did schools escape Butler's doleful eye. We have seen how the Germans of New Orleans were nearly all for the Union. The Lutheran schools, including St. Paul's at Port and Burgundy, were pronounced loyal by the Butler administration.[64] However, the brothers Ueber flatly told the Union officers that they were Rebels to the core but only religious songs, not political ones, would be taught to the *kinder* in their school. For whatever reason, the brothers were allowed to continue their famous school at 2718 North Rampart without interference.[65]

One group of citizens successfully evaded Butler's loyalty edict. The city's remaining firemen, who had so eagerly joined the Confederate cause just a year before, now found themselves protecting a conquered city. They did not want to take the oath, but they feared Butler's network of informants. The firemen asked Butler if they could be exempt from the oath by declaring their neutrality. To the surprise of all, Butler agreed.[66] Among the loyalty oath takers we find Bernard Marigny.[67] Colonel Mandeville Marigny resigned his commission in July 1862, came home, and also took the oath.[68]

Butler considered himself a proconsul with a seemingly unlimited portfolio of authority. He decided to practice income redistribution by assessing those who had made donations to the Confederate Committee of Public Safety. This money would be used to relieve the wants of the city's poor. He also assessed the cotton brokers who, in October 1861, had urged planters not to send their product to the city, causing more hardship. Having already taken the oath, Bernard and Mandeville Marigny do not appear on the list of those Butler mulcted to relieve poverty.[69]

Like visitors before him, Butler found New Orleans dirty; the canals and French Market were especially filthy.[70] He put otherwise idle men to work cleaning the streets, canals, and markets. Butler also instituted a strict quarantine and inspection of incoming vessels.[71] It was later proved that Havana was the source of most yellow fever epidemics in New Orleans and the Mississippi Valley. During the Union occupation, the quarantine prevented another disastrous outbreak like the horror of 1853.[72]

The Native Guards offered themselves to the Union after Butler's arrival. Butler initially resisted converting them to U.S. troops but changed his mind after he realized how short he was on manpower.[73] The new Federal unit, the First Louisiana Native Guard Regiment, was not just a renaming of the old one; less than 20 percent of former Native Guards were mustered into blue.[74] Among them were Captains André Cailloux and Henry Rey and Henry's brother Lieutenant Octave Rey. Despite their fervor, the new First Louisiana's men were initially used only for menial labor in the deep countryside.[75]

New Orleans Germans, who had halfheartedly supported the Confederate cause, now enlisted in Federal ranks. One such enlistee was a twenty-three-year-old John George "Garret" Schwegmann, who had arrived in town just two years earlier. Wounded in battle, Schwegmann was honorably discharged in September 1865 and went to work in a grocery store.[76] With that choice he embarked on a career that would employ generations of Schwegmanns and leave a distinct stamp on the Marigny.

Being a political general, Butler was careful to bolster his support with important allies like Secretary of War William Stanton. Despite the bad press received from the Woman Order and the allegations of corruption—later proven true—Washington officials were inclined to keep Butler on the job in New Orleans. However, in his arrogance, Butler created several diplomatic crises by interfering with foreign consuls.[77] Secretary of State William Seward, though sometimes bellicose, wished to give no pretext for other nations to recognize the Confederacy as a sovereign state. When Butler was relieved of his command in December 1862, he blamed Seward's caving to French emperor Napoleon III's demands.[78]

Butler's relief was General Nathaniel Banks. Like Butler, Banks was an ambitious political general. Unlike Butler, who resembled a tired walrus, Banks was handsome and dashing. Banks, like Butler, disappointed on the battlefield. In support of Grant's assault on Vicksburg, Banks was charged with capturing Port Hudson, Louisiana. Banks's favorite tactic, the frontal assault, generated horrific Union casualties. In one sortie, the First Louisiana was hurled against the well-fortified Confederate line. Captain Cailloux, shouting, "*Avant, mes enfants!*" was killed leading his Company E.[79] He was given a large military funeral, to the astonishment of white New Orleanians.[80]

New Orleans' free people of color believed that with Union victory in Louisiana, their privileged status would not only be assured but elevated to the same plane as that of antebellum whites. In 1863 they sent a petition to Banks and President Lincoln asking for the vote; they were refused.[81]

To establish Union-loyal governments in reconquered states, President Lincoln established the so-called Ten-Percent Plan in 1863. If 10 percent of a state's voters, as enumerated in 1860, would take the oath of loyalty, then they could petition the Federal government for readmission to the Union. Slavery had to be outlawed first, but there was no requirement to give blacks the vote.[82]

New Orleans' early capture meant that Louisiana would be the first state to undergo this wartime reconstruction, and it was duly readmitted in 1864. However, as noted, the Union grasp on the state was shaky at best, and the population of New Orleans furnished the majority of the requisite 10 percent. Some of the conservative Unionists, thinking the Emancipation Proclamation only a wartime expedient, hoped to regain their slaves and so hedged their bets by throwing in with the occupiers.[83] However, Lincoln's hopes for a reliably pro-Union sentiment in Louisiana and other newly re-admitted states were shaken by the reinstatement of the old Black Codes to control and ultimately oppress freedmen and the former free people of color (who from this point I call Modern Creoles).[84]

New Orleans, briefly the Confederacy's largest metropolis, did not suffer the destruction visited on other southern cities. Yet the end of the war found it impoverished. At secession, the city had eleven banks; ten years later, it had four. These banks had less than half the capital held in 1861.[85] The loss of cotton from upriver markets greatly reduced that once-thriving industry. Thousands of freed slaves made their way to the Crescent City, living on Union army rations.[86] Many found homes in the Old Third, especially in parts of the Seventh and Eighth Wards nearest the river. One well-known neighborhood of freedmen was Shinbone Alley, just behind the levee on North Peters between Port and Franklin Streets.[87]

The war had not impoverished everyone of means. Some had shrewdly stashed their assets in Europe, beyond the reach of either Union or Confederate hands. Some had held on to U.S. dollars and lost little when Confederate money became worthless early in the war. The Modern Creoles who added to their wealth did so largely by urban real estate speculation, which was unscathed by emancipation and the ruin of the plantation system. However, several of the most notable Modern Creoles of New Orleans had substantial losses.[88] François Lacroix was still wealthy at war's end, although he complained about Union soldiers owing him back rent.[89]

Five years of civil war and occupation are apparent in the Faubourg Marigny's portion of the 1866 directory. Even as the total number of responses fell significantly, the diversity in occupations increased tremendously, reflecting an influx of workers with more specialized skill sets. For the first time, such specialties as lithographers, paint dealers, photographers, and telegraphers appeared. Laborers, grocers, clerks, carpenters, and shoemakers filled the top five occupations. A mere five boardinghouses are noted. Only nine individuals are identified as "Negroes"; the two leading trades among them are shoemakers and vessel stewards.[90]

John T. Monroe, whom we last saw released from prison whence General Butler had sent him, was reelected mayor in March 1866.[91] He resumed his Know-Nothing modus operandi, firing nearly all the city's policemen and teachers and replacing them with former Confederates.[92]

In 1866 a group of Radical Republicans decided to reconvene the state's constitutional convention, last held in 1864. The express purpose of this new conclave was to enfranchise all blacks and disenfranchise former Confederates.[93] Because it was not called by the legislature, the legality of this convention was dubious, but Governor James Wells issued a call for election of delegates.[94] The conventioneers decided to proceed and gathered at Mechanics Hall, now the site of the Roosevelt Hotel, on July 30, 1866. To protect the convention, a group of freedmen marched up Burgundy Street from the Third District. A mob of white civilians, Monroe's police, and whites deputized as "special police" clashed with the marchers. The white mob burst into Mechanics Hall and slew many of the delegates, black and white. The mob then rampaged through central New Orleans, killing and wounding many more blacks.[95] At day's end, about fifty people lay dead and about six times that number were wounded.[96] One of the dead was François Lacroix's son, Victor.[97] The ensuing investigation moved Congress to pass the acts of congressional Reconstruction, which emphasized federal supervision of southern politics and the ascendancy of Republican politicians throughout the South. The acts enabled General Philip Sheridan to remove Governor Wells and Mayor Monroe from office once and for all.[98]

The Modern Creole population showed a tremendous decline in numbers between 1861 and 1868, as many with the means to do so fled New Orleans for northern states and some migrated farther, to Latin America or France.[99] It was not just their loss of social status that perturbed this group. The increasingly binary view of race, so at odds with the multiple layers and nuances of the city's realities, forced separation between the Modern Creoles and their white Creole relations.[100] The Modern Creole anguish may be gauged in their attendance at Spiritualist séances. Many in Henry Rey's séance circle were associated with the Catholic Institution. Rey heard the voice of the dead Victor Lacroix offering encouragement for black rights in the future. These séances would provide consolation of an otherworldly sort as the lot of the former *gens de couleur libres* descended after Reconstruction.[101]

The increase in the black population of the Old Third meant that more houses of worship were needed. In 1867 the Second German Presbyterian Church sold its building on St. Roch between St. Claude and North Rampart to an African American Methodist congregation, which retains it to this day.[102]

Twilight by the Park

Few, if any, of his contemporaries saw such momentous events as Bernard Marigny, who had lived under four flags. Incredible changes had been wrought by war, revolution, and reconquest, but he was still standing. He was usually described as "venerable," which then, as now, meant honorable, albeit old and obsolete. If he no longer wheeled and dealed in vast properties, cash, and slaves, neither was he poor. Marigny, who had transacted so much in his long life, had one more real estate card to play.

Louis Muh, German immigrant, goldsmith, and aesthete, was friends with Bernard and many other prominent people. In 1864 Bernard sold Muh the old Bosque/Marigny mansion. Bernard moved to a smaller house on Frenchmen at Royal.

On any fair morning after the Civil War, on that corner, looking out at Washington Park, early risers might see a leonine old man sitting on the banquette in his dressing gown, writing at a small table. Little children might gawk before they skipped on; men would tip their hats, and women would giggle behind their hands. In this era of heavy, multilayered clothing, to see anyone outside in their dressing gown was faintly scandalous.

Bernard Marigny, late 1860s. Courtesy of The Historic New Orleans Collection, Gift of Mr. G. William Nott, acc. no. 1974.61.1.

On one such day a horse clopped up and the rider, looking much like his noble grandfather, dismounted. Pulling off his hat, he shook his head.

"*Mon père,* look at you, in the middle of the banquette in the morning, and in your nightclothes, no less." The patriarch tilted his head back, giving solemn regard to his middle-aged son. "Well, you know, I can't see very well anymore in that place, so the best light for me is now in the morning, and that's why I put my writing desk out. Besides, this is a cashmere robe, and there's nothing wrong with it. Finally, no matter what anyone thinks, I am *Bernard de Marigny.* Now you can go."[103]

Mandeville Marigny smiled and shrugged. That was a title no one else could claim, and it had a patent of nobility all its own. If Bernard was beyond accruing further glory, he was also immune to approbation from anyone, even his own combat-veteran son. As he sat outside his door, Bernard was surrounded by the shades of his mighty friends of old: Claiborne, Wilkinson, Jackson, Lafitte, and Louis-Philippe.

Bernard was fond of strolling up from his faubourg to the Vieux Carré, walking through the history in which he had played such a part. Sometimes whispers followed him, expressing curiosity about the old man with the cane or surprise that he still walked the earth. If he heard music, particularly a girl singing to a piano, he would knock at the door and tell the servant, "Tell them it is Monsieur de Marigny." Inevitably, he would be admitted and given a comfortable seat to listen, perhaps thinking of other Euterpes living only in memory.[104]

Monday morning, February 3, 1868, as he walked up the 1200 block of Royal Street, the eighty-two-year-old Bernard fell dead, possibly of a stroke.[105] On a cold and rainy afternoon, the hearse with many carriages in procession started from his house on Royal. Some thought he would be buried in St. Louis Cathedral like his famous foresires, but the procession turned toward St. Louis Cemetery No. 1. Bernard Marigny is buried there in the same whitewashed tomb as his son, Mandeville de Marigny, and his family.[106]

Bernard certainly did not die in poverty. Inventories of his estate showed a worth of a little over $15,000. He must have felt secure in his money, since six IOUs were found for loans he made in the last years of his life.[107]

Although Bernard had taken his last curtain call on the ever-dilapidated stage of New Orleans life, and his faubourg was now better known as the Third District, his story would be enlarged down the years. Bernard, whose life was the stuff of legend, became part of the larger legend that is New Orleans' image of itself. Now he is another actor in the tableau, alongside friends like Lafitte, Jackson, and other flamboyant people he never knew but would have certainly understood.

11

A Restless Sleep

The tensions of Reconstruction played themselves out as the 1860s turned to the 1870s. Carpetbaggers, northerners who followed the Union army south in search of profit and power, and scalawags, southerners who openly avowed the cause of the Union, controlled the Louisiana and New Orleans governments between 1867 and 1877.

These administrations rang up enormous debts and levied heavy taxes during this period. Parish sheriffs kept busy with seizures and public auctions of tax-delinquent properties.[1] New Orleans' civic debt more than doubled between 1867 and 1877.[2] The depressed local economy was reflected in metrics of the Old Third, whose alternate title, the Poor Third, was now all too accurate. An 1877 audit of the city's districts showed that the Third was poorer, in both relative and absolute terms, than the Second District, which included the Vieux Carré.[3] Many newspaper articles depicted the Third as dusty, muddy, poor, and decrepit.[4] Washington Square remained a perpetual problem as cycles of dishabille and cleanup continued.[5]

The Radical Republican carpetbagger state government was temporarily overthrown by the White League Democrats in the Battle of Liberty Place in 1874. President Grant ordered federal troops to suppress the insurrection and restore the Republican regime under Governor William Kellogg. Later that year, Democrats resumed control of New Orleans.[6] In 1876 Democrat and former Confederate general Francis T. Nicholls was elected governor.

In return for a promise to end Reconstruction backed by federal bayonets, Louisiana and other southern states cast their electoral votes for Republican Rutherford B. Hayes, giving him the presidency.[7]

The Old Third lost about 8 percent of its population between 1860 and 1870. There was a distinct racial shift. Free blacks had constituted about 16 percent of the Third in 1860. In 1870, their ranks swelled by the freedmen crowding into town, blacks amounted to 39 percent of the district's numbers. There were about 24 percent fewer whites in the district. This was especially marked in the Seventh Ward, where the black population tripled against a loss of about 4 percent of white residents. In fact, the Eighth and Ninth Wards showed dramatic losses of whites, while the only ward declining in black numbers was the Ninth.[8] Neighborhoods continued to be racially mixed, although schools and churches were segregated after the end of Reconstruction.[9]

Garret Schwegmann took work in a grocery store run by two German brothers and in 1869 married their sister at Holy Trinity Catholic Church. Despite the lousy economy, Schwegmann opened his own grocery store that year at the corner of Piety and Burgundy Street in the Ninth Ward.[10]

A Muddy Gilded Age

The Third District had led the way in the establishment of public schools just a generation before; now there were an average of forty-nine pupils per teacher.[11] The district's streets were still poorly lit and only partially paved, so that they turned to quagmires after heavy rain. The city's "drainage machines" were antiquated and did nothing to relieve heavy rains that frequently flooded families out of their homes.[12]

The Third had several textile mills during the final three decades of the nineteenth century. One was the Louisiana Cotton Manufactory, near the Jackson Barracks, which offered on-site housing for employees, a necessity in the hinterlands of the Lower Ninth.[13] Unfortunately for those workers, the mill went under in 1877.[14]

The Third's population slowly rebounded, with the 1880 census revealing a gain of nearly 17 percent. Only the Eighth Ward showed a loss of residents, including 20 percent fewer blacks. The Old Third continued to grow for the rest of the nineteenth century, with the Seventh, Ninth, and Eighth Wards experiencing the most growth, in that order. Well into the twentieth century, between one in five and one in four New Orleanians would call the Third District home.

The district certainly had some resources. One was the Third District Building Association, a homestead savings and loan cooperative founded in 1887. Its first headquarters, at 2601 Royal, was damaged by the 1915 hurricane and rebuilt as the brown brick structure seen today.[15] One of the founders was the German immigrant Louis Leonhard, one of the Teutons of the Third District who had gone to war for the Confederacy. His dry goods store at Louisa and Dauphine, in today's Bywater neighborhood, is now the Bargain Center.

The Germans were still a large group in 1880, and the geographic center of their population in the Third District seems to have been Holy Trinity Church.[16] Holy Trinity was the home church of the wealthiest Germans and also operated St. Roch Cemetery. Although it would always have a smaller congregation, for many years it would have more material wealth than its cousin, Sts. Peter and Paul.[17]

The Germans continued to brew beer in the Old Third. In 1867 Joseph Armbriuster opened a plant at 2837 Chartres that brewed for twenty years. Sebastian Soulé started brewing at North Peters and Port Street in 1871; after his firm folded in 1891, World Bottling took over the plant to produce soft drinks. Albert Erath moved Pelican Brewing to Chartres between Louisa and Clouet in 1888, closing its doors in 1910. Other, smaller brewers blinked in and out over time.[18] The largest and best-known Marigny brewery was Columbia on Elysian Fields at Chartres. In a sign of New Orleans' diversity, the Columbia had multiethnic management. Charles Karst was president; Gustave Paul, vice president; a Mr. Monteleone, treasurer; and one of the directors was a Mr. Pizzati.[19]

Besides the breweries, the Third continued to feature textile mills. In 1890 the Crescent City Yarn and Knitting Mills, on lower St. Ferdinand, took in cotton bales and shipped out socks, employing about 150, mainly women.[20]

When Reverend G. J. Wegener was called to St. Paul's Lutheran Church at Port and Burgundy in 1887, he took charge of the largest Protestant congregation in Louisiana. From the 1850s through the early 1880s, St. Paul's pastors baptized over two hundred children per year. Pastor Wegener discovered that much of the Third District still had no paved streets. The streets were lit, dimly, by gas, but oil lamps were more common at home. No water lines reached the Rectangle, and no sewers either. In short, conditions

Columbia Brewery, ca. 1910. Illustration by Amanda Glenn.

had barely changed in the Old Third since the days of the municipality some fifty years before.[21]

The Americanization of the German immigrants and their New Orleans–born children was signaled by language splits in the churches. In 1888 an English-speaking group of St. Paul's Lutherans formed their own congregation, eventually holding church at St. Claude and Port Street.

The German Methodists experienced an even earlier schism. In 1854, the Anglophones built a church at Chartres and Franklin, while the Germanophones built their church on Burgundy near Franklin. The two congregations merged in 1899 in a Burgundy Street church. A crenelated neo-Gothic structure was built on the site in 1907.[22]

In the mid-1880s, the Marigny we know today received its closing boundary. The New Orleans and Northeastern Railroad laid tracks paralleling Press Street to the wharf.[23] Over the years, the old notion of Franklin Street being the eastern limit fell away, being retained only in the artifices of census and planning districts. The tracks at Press now bounded what people considered the old Marigny, even as that term fell out of use for decades, and the Third District and its wards remained the primary identifiers of the larger area.

Before the Civil War, the Third's wharves swarmed with cotton and other goods. After the war, the river eroded the banks and the wharves fell in, reducing the Third's river traffic to almost nothing. In 1897 the banks were strengthened and new wharves were constructed to the Lower Ninth, linking the Third's waterfront with the rest of the east bank of New Orleans.[24] The riverfront remained a major employer for generations; citywide, about ten thousand men were on the docks in 1900,[25] with screwmen as elites commanding the highest wages. The work was seasonal, and many on the docks worked at the breweries in the off times. Despite strike turbulence at the end of the nineteenth century, the dockworkers maintained racial parity in the workplace[26] and had an integrated central union council, even in the teeth of Jim Crow legislation.[27]

An echo of the old Marigny sounded for the last time on June 4, 1890, as Mandeville de Marigny was laid to rest in the family tomb in St. Louis Cemetery No. 1, alongside his father.[28]

Many of the streets of the Third had been renamed in 1852 but still bore two-digit house numbers. Three- and four-digit numbers were adopted citywide in 1893, and odd- and even-numbered sides of the streets were established.[29]

The Panic of 1893, which lasted until the late 1890s, hit New Orleans hard. In the Faubourg Marigny, four bellwether types of businesses—bakeries, breweries, groceries, and saloons—had all increased in number since 1870 but suffered dramatic declines between 1890 and 1900. Bakeries and breweries were traditionally German establishments. The number of bakeries dropped from twenty-two in 1890 to eight in 1900 and breweries from three to one, the brand-new Columbia on Elysian Fields. That the number of saloons fell by about 42 percent in a hard-drinking town meant the depression was serious indeed.[30]

The 1890s were not all gloom in the Old Third. In 1891 the Alden Mill hosiery factory set up shop at 511 Marigny, with two large buildings erected in 1895 and 1916. Typical of the era, it recruited workers as young as age fourteen.[31] Small businesses, with owners living over the shop, predominated. The river side of Dauphine Street featured, among other firms, groceries combined with bars, barber shops, fruit stands, stables, dealers of oysters and charcoal, Chinese laundries, dry goods stores, cotton pickeries, dance halls, and blacksmiths.[32] About 20 percent of the city's workers were women, many sewing piecework at home, assisted by their children.[33]

Between 1895 and 1909, New Orleans finally established the water supply, sewer, and drainage systems as city services, run according to national standards.[34] However, many streets, particularly in the Ninth Ward, remained unpaved well into the twentieth century.[35]

As the nineteenth century drew to a close, the Germans of New Orleans were increasingly assimilated, and many second- and third-generation offspring spoke only the New Orleans dialect of English picked up on the streets. The old language was spoken now mainly by grandparents, preachers, and teachers, who found it useful to encrypt discussions *nacht für kinder.* By 1900 many churches either conducted services only in English or reserved German for special events.[36]

As the twentieth century rolled around, some of the Germans who had arrived in the antebellum tide and made it big began to die off. Among these were John Lange, Charles Burkenstock, and Louis Leonhard, of the Third District Building Association.[37] In another passage, John Ueber called an end to his career in 1901, and the famous "Jake and John" school on North Rampart closed.[38]

Although the big theaters and the French Opera House were on the other side of Esplanade, the Third hosted some places of amusement. One was the Elysium Theater at the upper corner of Burgundy and Elysian Fields. Founded as a vaudeville house in 1903,[39] the Elysium was leased as a "colored" theater in 1906.[40] It also hosted community events such as boys' boxing matches.[41] After a serious fire in 1919,[42] it was rebuilt as the Dreamland, which showed movies until at least 1945.[43]

Two Tickets to Destiny

On a quiet corner of a vacant lot on Press Street stands a historical marker. The marker looks out on the lonely postindustrial railroad corridor that today separates the Marigny and Bywater neighborhoods.

Cars crunch gravel and the bellows of train engines echo off graffiti-covered sheds. The peals of church bells still chase across the landscape like ghosts looking for haunts. It is a calm strip of an old New Orleans almost, but not quite, gone. Yet near this spot, events happened affecting the lives of millions.

Since 1865 the Modern Creoles had fought the long decline of their place in society. Laws cementing segregation of the races were passed in the 1890s, dictating that members of different races had to be seated separately in Louisiana's railroad cars and waiting rooms. In 1891 some Modern Creoles associated with the Catholic Institution, including Rodolphe Desdunes, decided to test the law in hopes that federal courts would kill it. Desdunes's son traveled from New Orleans to Mobile in the whites-only car, triggering legal action. In a separate case, the Louisiana Supreme Court ruled that the application of the law to interstate commerce was unconstitutional.

In the second case, the Catholic Institution team decided to test the law's action within the state. Homer Plessy boarded the white car bound for Covington, Louisiana, at a stop on Press Street. His refusal to move to the "colored" car and his subsequent arrest started a test case. The U.S. Supreme Court eventually upheld the state law in *Plessy v. Ferguson* in 1896, devastating Modern Creole hopes for a better season.

The Archdiocese of New Orleans established a black-only church in 1895, carving a path of segregation followed by other churches across the city. The Louisiana Constitutional Convention of 1898 was called primarily for the aim of disenfranchising blacks, which it did through a series of voter qualification laws that made it all but impossible for blacks to vote within the state. It would be nearly seventy years before the Louisiana restrictions, and similar ones across the South, would be voided by the federal Voting Rights Act of 1965.[44]

Today no passenger trains rumble down those tracks, and the most frequent visitors are dog walkers and joggers. The historical marker stands as a mute reminder of the momentous nearby events, which began with an overture of hope and ended with a coda of sorrow.

12

The Workers' Paradise

To understand what the Marigny became in the 1970s and after, we must understand what it was before. Nostalgia is an unreliable paintbrush that sepia-tints the messy, chaotic past and makes the present appear bleaker than it really is. Much of what was later marketed as "N'awlins nostalgia" has its roots in the Old Third District. No one who really examines life in the Third between 1900 and 1970 can deny that there was a secure sense of place in that society. That security had almost vanished from New Orleans even before Hurricane Katrina and is usually seen today only in rural, small-town America. If this sense of place was stifling to some, they needed only to cross Esplanade and take refuge in Our Mother of Outcasts, the French Quarter. It is this Marigny culture that the gay renovators of later decades inherited, absorbing some parts and troping others.

On my first adult visit to New Orleans, in 1982, I had the distinct sense of being transported in many ways back to the 1950s. It took years for me to realize that the culture I perceived as "fifties" was in fact much older and quite persistent in the Vieux Carré and Marigny. It is this old backstory that we now explore.

Children of the Storms

The immigrant tide of the nineteenth and early twentieth centuries left the white Marigny with, in the main, a mix of Irish, Germans, and Italians. The neighborhood also included other European populations, Hispanics, and Chinese. In some blocks, one group would predominate, in others, another. Some third-generation children of the Marigny were mixtures of all three of the major groups.[1]

Italians, mostly from northern Italy, were part of the European settlement of southern Louisiana from the start. By 1860 an Italian opera was established at the old Théâtre d'Orléans in the Vieux Carré.[2] Despite this long-time presence, it would be about fifty years before Italians were as prominent as the Irish and Germans were in the antebellum years.

About 106,000 Italian immigrants, chiefly from Sicily, arrived in New Orleans from 1880 to 1929. The busiest period, 1902–1909, accounted for about 30 percent of that total.[3] Some went inland to labor on plantations, but many stayed in town. The French Quarter absorbed most of those Italians, who found low-rent, crowded lodging near the fruit and vegetable trade of the wharf and French Market.[4] In the Quarter, Italians clustered between St. Philip Street and Esplanade and especially in the blocks between Bourbon and Decatur.[5] This enclave was known as Little Palermo.[6] Some Italians also went to the Third District, particularly along St. Claude Avenue; of these, some were truck farmers in the still-rural areas of the Third.[7] By 1910, 31 percent of the foreign-born population of the city was Italian.[8]

Although Jim Crow was an entrenched system, it did not keep the races apart completely. On the street, children of all ethnicities played, and their parents chatted at the stoop.[9] The real divisions came at church, school, movie theater, and streetcar, which all had "white" and "colored" sections. Certain jobs were reserved for whites, and to hire a black person for these positions was unthinkable.

Gulf Coast residents habitually approach the end of summer with dread, for that is when the most powerful hurricanes form. It has been New Orleans' fate to be in the path of several destructive storms, one of which occurred in 1915. With the advent of wireless telegraphy, the region got plenty of early warning, but apparently only a few people, chiefly those in low-lying coastal parishes, chose to get out.

On September 29, 1915, the city was hit head-on by a Category Four storm that came ashore at Grand Isle, about fifty miles south. The damage and loss of life in the coastal areas was awful; in total, at least 275 people were killed and much of Plaquemines Parish was destroyed. As the storm approached New Orleans, it made the river an accomplice in its fury, churning a swirling, foggy mist and slamming great waves against the docks and buildings. All exposed commodities on the wharves were ruined, and many sheds were torn apart. Flying glass shards and metal roofing imperiled the few people not under cover. Steeples, utility poles, and smokestacks toppled. Incredibly, only about twenty people lost their lives in the city limits, chiefly from collapsing brick walls.[10]

In the Old Third, many houses lost shingles and windows; a few crumpled before the winds. The Poland Avenue streetcar barn collapsed and the men inside, ducking into parked streetcars, barely escaped with their lives.[11] Washington Square, like the other parks, was greatly torn up.[12] The worst cultural damage in the Third was the loss of the Catholic Institution at Dauphine and Touro. This was the second building on that site; the first had been replaced about 1900.[13] Lacking funds to replace the building, the board of directors accepted an offer by Mother (later Saint) Katharine Drexel for a Catholic religious community to rebuild and operate the school. Renamed the St. Louis School, it has been operated by different religious societies, under different names, serving different groups of students, to the present.[14] Another building lost was the home of the Third District Building Association at 2601 Royal. By 1917 the brown brick structure seen today was up and running.[15]

The Industrial Canal and Other Transitions

New Orleans' chosen location between river and lake cried out for a canal between the two. The old Marigny Canal in its heyday was no wider than fifty feet and connected to the lake via Bayou St. John, making it useful only for small barges or fishing vessels. Due to the level differences between lake and river, all other canals had stopped short of the Mississippi. In the early twentieth century, shipping and business interests agitated for a canal for deep-draft vessels, and work commenced in June 1918. The "Industrial Canal" cut the Ninth Ward in two as it linked lake and river, opening in January 1923.[16] Besides offering the ability to move vessels between the two bodies of water, the canal provided dock space along its length and a turning basin that attracted new industry to employ men in the Third District and St. Bernard Parish.

The Lower Ninth Ward had been very rural all along and was regarded as a hunting and fishing reserve within the city limits. Cleaved by the canal, the "lower 9" became even more the civic stepchild of New Orleans, out of sight and mind of most leadership for decades.[17]

The 1920 census tells us that 1,691 Italians were the predominant group of foreign-born residents in the Old Third, with the bulk living in the Seventh Ward. Despite the animosities stirred up by the recent world war, 707 of German birth also lived in the Third, and true to the Marigny's roots, 736 born in *la belle France* called Bernard's old faubourg home. In total, the Third was home to 80,948 residents, or about 21 percent of the city's population in 1920.

The old Third Presbyterian Church facing Washington Square was bought by the Catholic Archdiocese and rededicated in 1920 as Holy Redeemer Catholic Church, serving the black Catholics of the Seventh Ward.[18]

In late 1923 it was decided to widen North Rampart below Esplanade to the same width as above that boundary and extend it to St. Claude. St. Claude became a four-lane boulevard with a neutral ground as the lakeside boundary of the Marigny. North Rampart, branching off just before St. Anthony, would now assume more of a residential character.[19]

From antebellum times, citizens of each ward had formed groups to protect or promote their neighborhoods. The wards of the Old Third often felt they were ignored or slighted by city hall. In the first quarter of the twentieth century, civic associations and leagues were organized in each ward. The earliest of these were formed by housewives to improve sanitation in a town that was traditionally the dirtiest in America.[20] Subsequent incarnations included men and worked for better lighting, drainage, police presence, and general upkeep. These leagues were, like so many parts of southern life, divided by race. Notable in the Old Third was the Seventh Ward Civic League, which, although chaired by blacks, welcomed white speakers. One of the founding members was the noted civil rights attorney A. P. Tureaud, later a mentor of Ernest "Dutch" Morial, New Orleans' first mayor of color. Civic leagues were organized in the Eighth and Ninth Wards as well. The leaders of the black leagues formed a Federation of Civic Leagues in 1928 to represent their interests before a white and usually uninterested city government.[21]

The onset of the Great Depression certainly affected New Orleans, although all indications point to fewer hardships than other cities suffered. No banks failed.[22] The unemployed joined the city's perennial tide of drifters. By 1931 the Baptist Rescue Mission at 740 Esplanade was helping men who were down on their luck. Its sister, the Baptist Rescue Mission for unwed mothers, opened in 1940 at 732 Frenchmen.[23] Just up the block from where Bernard Marigny had answered letters in his cashmere dressing gown, expectant mothers swung on the porch and counted down the days.[24]

Foreshadowing similar struggles a few decades ahead, the New Deal Federal Housing Administration (FHA) used an underwriting manual to determine which neighborhoods would qualify for FHA loans. The manual disapproved of older neighborhoods like the Marigny, where homes were cheek by jowl with other buildings. Among the "nuisances" the manual abhorred were "liquor dispensing establishments, rooming houses . . . public playgrounds, schools, churches, mercantile and industrial establishments."[25] Since almost every Marigny dwelling was near one or many of these, it is not surprising that the neighborhood was redlined as "hazardous" on the 1935 Home Ownership Loan Corporation map.[26] The influence of this judgment on Marigny housing is uncertain; New Orleans' savings and loans took their own counsel on loan decisions.

The 1930 census reveals a major increase in blacks in the Seventh Ward, against a modest increase in whites, and a moderate white decline in the Eighth Ward. In the Ninth Ward, the black population more than doubled.

Workin'

The Third District, even in the depths of the Depression, had a stable base of employment. The docks along the river and the shipyards lining the Industrial Canal employed thousands of men, many of whom could ride the streetcar to work. Just across the St. Bernard Parish line, the Domino Sugar refinery,[27] an oil refinery,[28] and a Ford assembly plant[29] provided employment for decades. Kaiser Aluminum operated a plant nearby from 1951 to 1983.[30] There were still a few textile mills, like the Alden on Marigny Street toward the river.

An iconic Marigny firm fired up its ovens and fryers in 1921. Simon Hubig opened a branch of his pie empire at 2419 Dauphine, offering his signature Honey Fruit creations.[31] In that era, nearly every business of any size had a sports team, and Hubig's baseball team at first called themselves the Hubig Honey Fruits.[32] Within a few snickering months, they renamed themselves the Hubig Pies.[33]

To have a wife employed outside the home raised questions about the ability of a man to provide for his family. Some unmarried young women worked to support their households but were expected to give their notice before heading down the aisle on their fathers' arms.[34]

While the men were at work, their wives were busy with homemaking. In the first third of the twentieth century, electric refrigerators were a luxury. Most Marigny families used the same old zinc-lined, oak iceboxes of previous generations, and the iceman made daily deliveries of the essential commodity.[35] This meant that most food was cooked and eaten the same day it was bought. For this, housewives patronized many small neighborhood groceries. Among these were Schiro's at Royal and St. Roch, Addison Bird's at Mandeville and Royal, Lapicola's at Port and Dauphine,[36] and Ferrara's at Spain and Chartres.[37]

If a mother had a small child to tend, she might telephone her grocer for a delivery. At one time, a call to Schiro's might have been fulfilled by delivery boy Pascal Calogero, future chief justice of the Louisiana Supreme Court.[38] If the children were around and old enough, they would be sent to the store to fetch the foodstuffs for the day. Most of these groceries operated on credit, keeping a ledger book behind the counter, awaiting patrons' paydays. The child couriers would receive lagniappe, Creole for "a little something extra," usually a piece of candy. If a housewife came in, her lagniappe might be a packet of spice to enliven the evening meal. Some of the groceries also contained small bars. These groceries operated on the full-service system. A customer would place an order and wait, gossiping with other patrons as the order was filled. The grocers were perhaps the best-informed people in the neighborhood. They knew each credit customer's financial standing, which children belonged to which family, who the teenagers were dating, and myriad other facts about the families they served.

Besides the corner groceries, there were public markets for meat and produce. The St. Roch Market at St. Roch and St. Claude started serving the neighborhood in 1875. In the late 1930s the Works Progress Administration (WPA) enclosed it and raised it to modern sanitary standards.[39] Lautenschlaeger Market at Burgundy and Touro, built in 1901, was also renovated by the WPA.[40]

Drugstores operated in much the same ways as groceries. A call to the

Schroeder's Grocery, Port at Chartres, 1904. Courtesy of Edwin Schroeder.

pharmacy would soon be answered by a boy at the door delivering the prescription, hot-water bottle, or aspirin. One well-known drugstore was Lividaus, at the corner of Dauphine and St. Ferdinand.[41]

If a housewife needed fruits or vegetables, she need only wait for a street vendor, most still in horse- or mule-drawn wagons. In these days before air conditioning, open windows let women hear the vendors' chants:

> I have watermelon, red to the rind
> I have onions and bananas
> I have straw-berr-ees
> I have plums

The watermelon vendor would cut a conical plug from a sample and offer it to the prospective purchaser, who, if she liked it, would buy the plugged melon; if not, she would try another.[42]

When it was time to go shopping for goods other than foods, there were a number of stores along St. Claude Avenue and, most importantly, Frenchmen Street. For working-class families, Canal Street was the highest of high streets. Women and girls dressed up to go to flagship stores like Godchaux's and D. H. Holmes. Many Third District families visited Canal Street most often for Carnival parades.[43]

The German influence on Third District business persisted, with such familiar names as Stumpf, insurance agent; Opperman, plumber; Duckert, baker; Sporl, shoe dealer; Eicke, grocer; and Leonhard, department store proprietor.[44]

When children walked to school in the morning, they probably headed to a parochial school, such as those of Sts. Peter and Paul, Holy Trinity, or St. Paul's Lutheran. If their parents chose a public school, it might well be Colton on St. Claude, between Spain and Mandeville. After 1939, if they were in high school, they might attend Francis T. Nicholls at 3820 St. Claude, between Pauline and Alvar, the city's first coed secondary school.[45]

Besides street games, kids' recreation revolved around church activities, such as the Catholic Youth Organization (CYO), which provided sports leagues and picnics. Sts. Peter and Paul hosted dances in the second-floor gymnasium of the school building on the corner of Marigny and Burgundy.[46] In 1946 the city created the New Orleans Recreation Department (NORD) and used some of the old firehouses, such as the one at 720 Mandeville, as community centers where kids could check out athletic gear.[47] NORD hosted a scouts-like group called the NORD Rangers, which offered supervised play for children until it was time to go home in the early evenings.[48] The public squares of the Third District, such as Piety (now Markey Park), Bunny Friend on Desire Street, and of course Washington Square, hosted many ball games.

Washington Square had certainly seen its ups and downs, as it ranged from a genteel promenade to a bushy expanse overrun, like most of New Orleans' public parks, by goats.[49] In the 1930s it had a bandstand and a concrete pavilion. When not hosting concerts, the bandstand had a reputation as a hangout for drinkers and dopers.[50] The park also hosted gang fights between rival groups of boys. In 1951 the bandstand and concrete were torn out and full-time management took over, transforming the park into a ball field under adult supervision.[51] A wading pool let small children cool off while their fathers and big brothers played baseball.[52] Wiltz Gymnasium, on North Rampart between Montegut and Clouet, offered a swimming pool, welcome in the long, sweltering summers.[53]

If a house had the luxury of a screened porch, that is where the family usually slept in the hottest summer months, and a home listed with a "sleeping porch" commanded a premium.[54]

One interviewee recalled his Marigny boyhood of the late 1940s and early 1950s: "like it was when I was a kid six, seven, eight, nine, ten, growing up here. You could walk from here [the 2600 block of Dauphine] all the way to Poland Avenue. . . . If you got in a fist fight, it was a kid your same age. Nobody would try and steal your bike. Nobody would try and steal your sneakers or anything like that. You knew everybody."[55]

Bars close to the waterfront catered to the dockworkers getting off their shifts.[56] The fathers would come home from the refineries, the docks, and the mills, wash up, have supper, and catch up on domestic and school events. Then the men would saunter down to the local bar to man talk, listen to prize fights on the radio, meet with their bookie, and perhaps to bend the ear of their ward leader. Before the 1960s, the ward leaders were the average man's connection to the city bureaucracy. The ward leader worked for the political machine in power, lining up reliable votes and tasking the voters of his ward to put out signs, organize rallies, and so forth in support of the chosen slate of candidates. In return, the ward leader was the intercessor for myriad problems, ranging from finding city jobs to restoring streetlights and fixing traffic tickets.[57]

New Orleanians love their recreation, and the Old Third certainly provided venues close to home. An observer in 1925 noted that "down in Marigny at night they enjoy life. One will go far and look closely to find as many dance halls in as little territory."[58] One well-known terpsichorean palace was the Circle, at 2222 St. Claude, between Elysian Fields and Marigny. Another was Luthjen's, first at 1200 Franklin Avenue at Marais and then, after 1960, at the corner of Marigny and Chartres. Luthjen's catered to an older clientele and featured a No Jitterbugging sign.[59] Neighborhood movie theaters connected the Third with Hollywood and newsreels. The Dreamland at Elysian Fields and Burgundy,[60] the Piety at Piety and North Rampart,[61] and the Bijou at Burgundy and Poland[62] all served the lower Third District. On warm summer nights, the Dreamland left its doors open, allowing people across the street to enjoy a long-distance view of the features for free.[63]

The Third District loved the revelry of Carnival as much as any other part of town and desired a krewe of its own. In 1939 the Krewe of Thirdist (later Nemo) debuted, with Congressman Joachim Fernández, political boss of the Ninth Ward, as king. Leading ten floats, he greeted a krewe queen in each of the three wards.[64] The next year the courts were united as one, and Thirdist/Nemo made a final appearance at Carnival in 1941.[65] After the entry of America into war that December, parades and balls were called off until the next peacetime Carnival season of 1946.[66]

Gambling has been a popular New Orleans pastime since the city's founding. The administration of Mayor Robert Maestri (1936–46) let gambling and other illegal vices run unchecked. It was widely believed that when New York mayor Fiorello La Guardia ran slot machines out of his town, they found their way to the Crescent City. Soon slots and other gambling devices were everywhere. The largest operator, with ties to New York mob boss Frank Costello, was the Louisiana Mint Company, which, under various names, had operated pinballs and slots in the city since at least 1939.[67] The machines operated by this company dispensed a small candy mint in return for a coin and a pull of the handle. Since the customer was getting something of value, he was not gambling per se, and the company thought it was cleverly evading the law.

The Marigny of the 1930s was, in the main, a quiet residential area off the tourist track. Perhaps that is why the Louisiana Mint Company chose 2601 Chartres, at the corner of Franklin, as its headquarters, where gambling machines were stored, serviced, and dispatched to bars, restaurants, and pool halls.

Despite loud squawks from religious groups, the Maestri administration ignored the existence of the machines. In February 1946 Maestri was defeated for reelection by deLesseps "Chep" Morrison, who had campaigned as a reformer. After taking office, Morrison had the Mint Company raided, destroying a number of slot machines and throwing the remains into deep water.[68]

In this period not every family had their own car, and besides walking, the extensive streetcar system was the magic carpet around town, whether for work, school, or play. The old Pontchartrain Railroad made its last trip in 1932,[69] and then the Louisville and Nashville (L&N) Railroad took over its tracks. Many students and travelers between 1932 and 1935 used the L&N Railroad for commuting to the Marigny from points east, like the Rigolets, Lake Catherine, and Chef Menteur. The L&N trains followed the old Pontchartrain roadbed on Elysian Fields and then, with a stop on St. Claude, chugged on up to Florida Avenue on the way to eastern Gulf Coast towns.[70] After 1935, L&N took up its tracks north of Florida Avenue and only operated freight trains toward the river.[71]

Although we have surveyed a mainly white, working-class swath of Marigny life, it is important to note that abject poverty also existed. Images

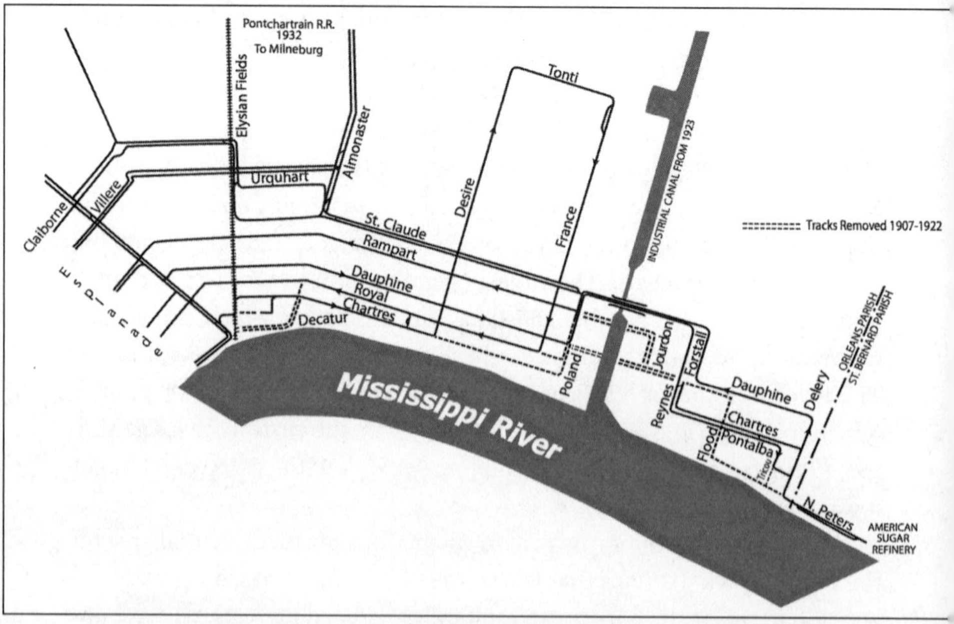

Passenger Railroads in the Third District, 1907–1948 (not to scale). Map by Amanda Glenn, adapted from 1922 New Orleans Public Service map reproduced in Hennick and Charlton, *The Streetcars of New Orleans*, 66–67.

by photographer Clarence John Laughlin, the famous "Haunter of Ruins," testify to this destitution. The poorest people were often found in the dilapidated commercial buildings dating from the antebellum years below Royal, toward the river, most now long demolished.[72]

Zooming In

Starting with 1940, we draw our focus more sharply on the once and future Faubourg Marigny. The census used two tracts whose bounds closely fit the Marigny we know today. One tract covers the Triangle and one the Rectangle up to Franklin Avenue. Most people who lived in the neighborhood from the 1930s to the 1960s did not call it Marigny in their youth.[73] That name and the original faubourg concept were consigned to the past. Yet as the decades rolled on, the neighborhood, like any evolving life form, began to develop a consciousness that slowly distanced itself from the larger Third

The Lonely House, Number Three, by Clarence John Laughlin, Architect at Port Street, 1949. Courtesy of the Clarence John Laughlin Archive at The Historic New Orleans Collection, acc. no. 1983.47.1.4088.

District. In part, it was due to a sense of boundary with the French Quarter up the river and the rest of the Third across the tracks, especially that portion now called Bywater, with St. Claude toward the lake.

The entry of the United States into World War II brought large defense industries to the city. Near the Old Third on the Industrial Canal were the Andrew J. Higgins and Delta Shipyards. Patrol torpedo (PT) boats were produced at Higgins, while Delta launched Liberty ships.[74] Thousands of people were employed at these and the other war plants in Orleans and St. Bernard Parishes. The Higgins yard survived the advent of peace, while most of the other war plants closed, returning their workers to the city's traditional industries or to the road out of town.

Down by Schwegmann's

In 1946 John G. and Paul Schwegmann left their family's old store at Piety and Burgundy to open the first Schwegmann Brothers Giant Supermarket at

Under the Deathly Fronds, by Clarence John Laughlin. Courtesy of the Clarence John Laughlin Archive at The Historic New Orleans Collection, acc. no. 1981.247.1.293.

the site of the former Circle dance hall at 2222 St. Claude.[75] Although the city had supermarkets before, they were out-of-town chains like A&P or Piggly Wiggly and did not enjoy wide popularity. The new store soon became the secular hub of the Marigny. The cheapness of the food, the convenience of the location, and the hometown persona all made the store indispensable to neighborhood life. Beyond the food and drink, the store became an important social nexus for housewives and later a rather different meeting place, beyond 1946 imaginations.

New Orleans revels in flamboyant personalities, and John G. Schwegmann soon took his place alongside Bernard Marigny, Pierre Beauregard, Louis Armstrong, and Andrew J. Higgins. He entered politics and became head of the state Public Service Commission. Schwegmann broke the legalized price fixing of milk and whiskey, enabling children and their elders to tipple for less. His opinions adorned the stores' paper grocery sacks. Eventually, eighteen Schwegmanns served the New Orleans area, and the larger ones were destination stores, offering gas pumps, opticians, florists, shoe stores, and banks.[76] Generations of college students cherished the cut-rate store brands of liquor. Day trippers from surrounding parishes and the Mississippi Gulf Coast went home with trunks heaped with cheap food, clinking beverage bottles, and gas gauges straining past the full mark.

"Making groceries down by Schwegmann's" became a way of life for the Old Third, and although the corner groceries held on for decades, the advent of Schwegmann's began their long sunset.[77] A few, like Ferrara's on Chartres at Spain, hung on until the 1970s.[78] For most, as the owners' children grew up, went to college, and perhaps moved out to one of the postwar suburbs or moved away completely, running a small corner store for a few elderly patrons lost its appeal. Some stores then became private homes or bars.

Where Did Everybody Go?

The 1940 census counted just over nine thousand people in the Marigny. Of these, about 6 percent were black. Most Marigny blacks lived in the Rectangle, which would hold true through 2010. The Triangle held a slight edge in population over the Rectangle. Every succeeding decade until 1990 showed steep losses in the overall Marigny, at which time the population leveled off.

The wholesale exodus of white people from central cities following school integration beginning in 1960—white flight—has been accepted as a truism, an "of course" assumption. The Marigny's population shifts tell a different version of this story that belies the handy "of course" axiom.

Between 1940 and 1950 the Marigny lost about 11 percent of its population, and between 1950 and 1960 it lost about 25 percent compared to the 1940 total. Yet integration was not a factor in those decades. So why did the neighborhood lose residents in these twenty years?

We begin by looking at the housing stock. Most were shotguns, Creole cottages, or variations on those styles. There were some two-story houses, but most of those held stores on the ground floor with living quarters above. A few houses were leftovers from antebellum prosperity, with servants' quarters and cookhouses in the back. Some of these outbuildings sheltered bachelor sons, elderly grandparents, or other relatives. Some were rented out for a little extra income. There were few vacant lots, most of which were former industrial sites and not suitable for houses. There was not much turnover in homes. So a young couple looking to buy a

Marigny house would be limited to a small stock of vacant old houses. These had been retrofitted with indoor plumbing and electric service around the turn of the twentieth century, and those utilities were already antiquated. Most houses were small, especially the shotguns. Life in a shotgun required a durable tolerance for family coming and going through each room in succession. Any privacy was fleeting and would vanish when someone wanted to go to the bathroom or kitchen at the back of the house. This situation suited turn-of-the-century working-class families with small children. However, as modern times and amenities came to New Orleans, brides—and husbands—wanted something better. If newlyweds had to live at first with in-laws in a shotgun or Creole cottage, they were eager to get out quickly and have privacy under their own roof. In the new suburbs, modern American floor plans offered compartmented rooms and utilities up to contemporary norms. A car of one's own put the downtown and other suburbs easily in reach.

The postwar GI Bill offered, among other things, low-interest loans for buying homes.[79] Although the loans could be used for an existing dwelling, the housing industry, after sixteen years of depression and war, wanted to put veterans into brand-new tract houses. So, many returning servicemen, now grown up and wanting to nest, left the old neighborhood.

Now we consider the first decade of integration in New Orleans, 1960–70. In 1960 the William Frantz and McDonogh No. 19 schools in the Upper and Lower Ninth Ward, respectively, were the first New Orleans schools to be integrated. The effort became a nightmare after white parents withdrew their children and housewives screamed obscenities at six-year-old black girls escorted by burly federal marshals.[80] The archdiocese integrated its schools after the autumn of 1962,[81] so those were eliminated as refuges of mono-racial education. Some whites who didn't like integration moved out to suburbs that dragged out integration for years. All this certainly had an effect on those Marigny whites with school-age children. The 1970 census reflected a loss of a quarter of the Marigny's population since 1960, and compared to 1940, 43 percent fewer people called the neighborhood home. The white population declined by a third, and the number of black residents more than doubled. Yet the Marigny was always majority white. Even at the peak of black residency, in 1980, there were more than three times as many whites as blacks.

Besides integration, the city's economy was changing. The Old Third had always had a big share of dockworkers, but as years went by the port trade slowly declined. Containerized cargo debuted in New Orleans in 1973. Most of the men who used to move crates, cotton bales, and bulk goods slowly became superfluous as the "conex boxes" of global trade took over.[82]

The Awakening

Long before *gentrification* was a contentious word in the New Orleans lexicon, properties were being bought, renovated, and resold throughout the city's historic old heart. The French Quarter pioneers of the 1920s had given way to second and third waves of renovators in the 1930s through the 1950s. These waves moved beyond saving old buildings to bringing them up to midcentury American standards. These later renovators brought aesthetic influences from other cultures and created comfortable and even elegant apartments and houses. The renovated properties then commanded a premium in the Quarter. Cheaper apartments were still offered by the old, mainly Italian families, who had owned their buildings outright for years. They were content with tenants who remained in place for decades or transients who were not too demanding about upkeep and amenities.

In the New Orleans of the 1950s, gay men with money, taste, and courage created a culture of renovation in the Quarter that would spill over Esplanade and slowly seep into the Marigny. Clay Shaw, manager of the International Trade Mart, renovated several Vieux Carré properties, setting new standards in rehabilitation, including that of the so-called Spanish Stables at Bourbon and Governor Nicholls.[83] One of the Quarter buildings forever labeled as haunted is the LePrete House, also called the Sultan's Palace, at 716 Dauphine. In 1959 it was bought by professional and personal partners Jack Fricks and Bob Hines,[84] who at one time or another owned twelve properties in the Quarter and Marigny, including the three-story Nelson Fouché house at 2340 Chartres.[85] A house from the 1830s, on Royal just past Franklin, was renovated by a male couple from 1957 to 1964. What they discovered was staggering: "On the street level there was a dirt floor. Some owner had sold the floor boards. Wood mantles were termite-eaten, plaster walls were sagging and cracked. . . . Many loads of trash had to be taken out of the house before renovation could commence." Once the couple completed their renovations, real estate agent and preservationist Martha Ann Samuel praised the resulting showplace in a 1964 two-page spread in the *Times-Picayune*'s Sunday magazine.[86]

Finding money for renovations of older buildings was a challenge. The savings and loans of New Orleans were reluctant to fund anything but first mortgage loans for primary residences and catered to old, established members, not "newcomers."[87] However, with the right connections, funding could be had. John Dodt was a director of American General Savings and Loan, which made some of the first historic renovation loans below the Quarter. The First National Bank of Commerce also would make loans for renovation.[88]

In the 1950s and 1960s, new neighborhood improvement associations sprang up in the old parts of the city. Like their predecessors, they wanted to preserve their domains from the decay of slumlordism, keep the streets fixed and the streetlights on. The Marigny was represented by, among others, the Elysian Fields Citizens Committee, the Elysian Fields Civic and Improvement Association, the Seventh Ward Civic Association, and the Washington Square Improvement Association. Another group was the Esplanade Avenue Improvement Association, seeking to bridge the lower Quarter and Marigny Triangle neighborhoods with common interests.[89]

Since 1936, most of the French Quarter's architectural stock has been monitored and, to a degree, regulated by the Vieux Carré Commission (VCC). The Marigny had no such governmental watchdog. Therefore, it was difficult for Marigny groups to gain the same traction as their Quarter residential counterparts, who, of course, recognized the Marigny's interests as being their own.

In the late 1960s these Marigny groups became most prominent in their opposition to the proposed Riverfront Expressway, which would have lofted an elevated road over the neutral ground of Elysian Fields, connecting with an elevated highway right in front of Jackson Square.[90] The proposed defilement of the square gathered flocks of well-placed defenders, near and far. The Marigny groups had to make their case that an elevated expressway down Elysian Fields would harm their neighborhood, too, making that road even more of a boundary than it was. The unbuilt Riverfront Expressway was ultimately killed by the federal government in 1969.[91]

In late 1958 a branch of Louisiana State University was established on the lakefront of New Orleans, close to the lakeside end of Elysian Fields Avenue. Envisioned as a commuter college for New Orleanians who could not go to Tulane or Loyola,[92] LSU New Orleans drew in faculty who needed places to live. The Gentilly neighborhood was nearby to the east, and the larger

Lakeview district to the west. But the once—and future—Marigny was just a short drive, a "straight shot," down four-lane Elysian Fields Avenue. It had cheap housing stock and rubbed elbows with its older sister, the French Quarter, at Esplanade. Professors could thus rent an old house, frolic in the Quarter, and have a swift commute to the college. So from miles away, the new school exerted a powerful gravitational influence on the old faubourg.

Some of the LSU New Orleans teachers were gay men. The Quarter was still the epicenter of gay life, and if not exactly an oasis of tolerance, offered recreational opportunities not found in the suburbs. In some ironic measure due to the gay renovators, the Quarter was getting more expensive, and the logistics of living there—the creaky infrastructure, the scarce parking, and the tourist intrusions—made many gay men look elsewhere. Their gaze strayed across Esplanade, most of whose mansions had been converted to cheap rooming houses years before, to the neighborhood beyond. Houses could be found there that actually had yards, some degree of parking, and few, if any, tourists. This was the closest intersection of 1950s American suburban ideals with the watering holes and sexual opportunities of the Quarter a gay man could hope for.[93]

In 1965 the City Planning Commission chartered a survey captained by Tulane professor of architecture Bernard Lemann. The study determined which areas of the city, apart from the Quarter, warranted controls for historic preservation. Among other neighborhoods, the study identified the Faubourg Marigny, but only the Triangle as we understand it now. The commercial properties along St. Claude and North Peters were excluded, just as the working riverfront of the Quarter had been ruled out of bounds by the 1936 amendment establishing the VCC.[94]

The Beat Moved On

The counterculture of 1950s and early 1960s America, usually called the beat or beatnik culture, had tendrils in New Orleans. The Ryder Coffeehouse on North Rampart flourished from 1962 to 1963.[95] After the building was condemned, Ryder's nucleus moved to 611 Esplanade and established a coffeehouse called the Quorum, sponsored in part by the local Methodist Church.[96] Reverend Robert Shirley was the first president of the private club. He was also a chaplain for the police department.[97]

At the Quorum, blacks, whites, straights, gays, the well-and not-so-well-educated listened to poetry readings and folk singers, played chess, and mostly importantly, conversed without the barriers society imposed. Aspiring painters and sculptors could meet established artists.[98] This interaction thrilled the patrons and worried officialdom. "Race mixing" of blacks and whites on equal terms, and possibly registering blacks to vote, was a flashpoint with southern officials. The New Orleans Police Department (NOPD) surveilled the Quorum for some time. Undercover agents bought memberships and recited poetry, to the appreciation of the audience.[99] Sargent Frederick Soulé was known as dedicated vice squad officer who in 1962 brought the long career of the celebrated madam Norma Wallace to an end.[100] To Sargent Soulé, the Quorum "seemed a melting pot of everybody with a beef against society. He said the site was the scene of Communist propaganda, homosexual parties, and integration agitation."[101] Soulé would later plead guilty to taking bribes from pinball machine companies in return for advance warnings of police raids.[102] The Quorum was also targeted by vigilantes who threw a dummy grenade inside and left a note stating that the Ku Klux Klan was watching the club.[103]

The Quorum was harassed throughout its run.[104] On July 29, 1964, artist George Dureau hosted a birthday party in his apartment above the Quorum. The police raided the party, netting seventy-three arrests for "disturbing the peace." Most of those arrested were bailed out by civil rights attorney and future mayor Ernest "Dutch" Morial.[105] The vast majority of the charges were dropped.[106] The Quorum continued on until early 1967, when it seems to have dissolved.[107]

Another powerful storm hit New Orleans in 1965. Hurricane Betsy flooded much of the Lower Ninth Ward. Although there was no flooding in the Marigny, several buildings, including Holy Redeemer Church and the Carnegie library, were badly damaged. This opened a new era at the corner of Frenchmen and Royal, which we more fully explore in chapter 14.

Declining or Reclining?

As the 1960s came to an end, the Marigny had lost jobs and population. The children of the first immigrant waves were nearly all gone, and their children were passing out of work life into old age.

Toward the end of the 1960s, the next phase of the counterculture came to New Orleans. A city that had usually welcomed adventurers, ne'er-do-wells, and scapegraces was no happier about these youngsters than it had been about the beatniks. Their appearance and their opposition to the Vietnam War and nuclear power grated the conservative sensibilities of the city's establishment, especially the police. The city did its best to harass these young people out of town. It especially annoyed the civic powers that "hippies" were so prominent in the Quarter. They might distract tourists from the b-drinking, gambling, prostitution, and strip clubs that enjoyed official protection.[108]

The counterculture kids quickly discovered that the adjacent neighborhood, just across Esplanade, was "cooler" in many respects than the Quarter. It had no tourist trade and therefore was less visible to police and self-appointed public morals minders. The rents were cheaper and the flats bigger.

To the old residents of the Marigny, this was unsettling. The new kids on the block didn't fit the rigid categories 1960s America assigned to young adults. They often stuffed many roommates into apartments or houses and smoked lots of weed. Some of them also dealt it.

One person's decadence is another's salad days, and the survivors of the counterculture era of the Marigny remember it mostly through the sweet haze of youth, close to the entertainments of Decatur Street but at a comfortable distance from the Quarter's hassles.

The sixties may have shuddered to their end on the calendar, but that horological conceit and New Orleans have rarely been close friends, and much of the older culture remained entrenched in the Marigny. The civic powers looked at the decade of the 1970s as a debutante looks to her presentation: as a page turning, a milestone passing. The seventies were opening, and a new Marigny cotillion was about to begin.

13

Rebirth and Reclaiming

January 1, 1970, was cold in New Orleans as the city prepared to host the Sugar Bowl. New Orleans still thought itself a great and growing city, in the same league with its archrival, Houston. Expanding the port, building a giant domed stadium, and growing New Orleans East were all on boosters' minds. *Their* New Orleans would be more like a "typical American" city and trump its regional rivals in every conventional measure while holding on to its ever-marketable "charm."

The Third District and the Marigny within were not really included in these plans. The Marigny was a declining working-class neighborhood of old families, old houses, and old ways. Unlike New Orleans East, it had little vacant land. Unlike the Central Business District (CBD), it hosted no skyscrapers. There were still neighborhood businesses, but little industry, aside from the port operations, remained.

In 1970 the Marigny had 5,249 people, and of these 81 percent were white and 19 percent were black.[1] Between 1960 and 1970 the Marigny had lost about 24 percent of its population; the city at large had lost about 20 percent of its residents in that decade. The Marigny was poorer than New Orleans, having a per capita income of only 82 percent of the city's. The neighborhood's income was a mere 54 percent of the national per capita income.[2] It was much less educated, with only 4.9 percent of its residents college graduates, a mere 46 percent of the city's rate.[3] Only a little more than one resident in five owned his or her dwelling.[4] Single men made up

40 percent of the Marigny's population, as compared to New Orleans' rate of 32 percent.[5]

The Triangle had a slight majority of the population, about 53 percent. About three times as many blacks lived in the Rectangle as in the Triangle. The largest black concentrations in the Triangle were north of Royal, along St. Claude to Elysian Fields, and in the Rectangle they were concentrated below Royal toward the river.[6] In 1970 there were slightly more census-defined families (related people under one roof) than nonfamilies in the Marigny, at 59 and 41 percent, respectively.[7] The Triangle had nearly twice as many nonfamily residents as the Rectangle.[8]

Rents were cheap. A one-bedroom unfurnished apartment in the Rectangle might be had for between $56 and $95 a month; in the Quarter, they ran $80–$180.[9] It was also possible to rent half of a double shotgun house in the Marigny for about the same amount as a Quarter apartment. In 1971 houses selling in the Triangle cost an average of $20,000, while those in the Rectangle averaged about $15,000.[10] Multiplexes with apartments for additional income were also offered.[11] In the Quarter, single-family houses were almost unknown except among the long-entrenched or wealthy, but they were common in the Marigny. As early as 1970, the displacement of the poor, old, and black by white-collar whites in the Triangle was noted by Bill Rushton, gay editor of the *Vieux Carré Courier,* who also remarked on a possible "hippie" influx: "When and if the hippies do move in they will have the company of homosexuals, prostitutes, Cuban refugees and members of the local intelligentsia—all of whom seem to find the area capable of accommodating their respective life styles."[12]

At 601 Esplanade at Chartres, a former church was the home of the Place, an experimental theater, which garnered favorable mention in the *Times-Picayune.*[13] The Dream Castle bar on Frenchmen was one of the few meeting grounds of black residents, bluesmen, and "hip" whites.[14] The old Dreamland theater at Burgundy and Elysian Fields was converted to an adult film house and rechristened the Paris in 1965.[15]

A Clarion Calls

In 1970 a young architect and University of New Orleans professor, Eugene Cizek, moved to a Triangle apartment in a former German bakery at Pauger and Dauphine. The lower Quarter was just a block away. His rent was fifty-four dollars a month. Although there were still old people living in the neighborhood, there were also the grandchildren of the old Italian and German families. They had taken over the long-paid-for family manses, and their elders had moved out to the new suburbs or passed on.

In Cizek's first years in the Triangle, he began to evangelize the Marigny, hosting parties to spread the word that the neighborhood was an interesting and inexpensive place to live. These parties included Cizek's students and friends, as well as old residents of the Marigny. Cizek explained, "These older people that lived in the neighborhood, it's like all of these grandmas and grandpas were so happy to have a son or a new grandson or granddaughter and they just would open up and were all very, you know, were talking about old Sicilian families, old German families, and old Creole; basically they'd all been creolized along the way and they were very vivacious, they all usually liked to drink and eat."[16]

Not content to merely show the neighborhood, Cizek made lists of interesting properties, determined their ownership, and encouraged their often-absentee owners to put them on the market so a renovator might buy them.[17] Under the auspices of the Preservation Resource Center, he guided Building Watchers Tours of various historic areas of town.[18] These urban tourists were, in the main, college students and middle-class professionals, and some—not all—were gay. These tours often ended at Cizek's house for wine and snacks.[19]

Lubricated by wine, infused with Cizek's expert knowledge, and energized by a shared notion of what had been and what could be, the mostly gay audience—who had the resources—wanted to pursue the gauzy Marigny dream. Over the next two decades, a drama of renovation, tribal community building, establishment reaction, deceit, corruption, and tragedy would be played out in the old faubourg. In the midst of these melodramatic themes, there was also quiet individual fulfillment and a new sense of what coupledom and community could mean for gay people.

In August 1972 the parties and tours coalesced into the Faubourg Marigny Improvement Association (FMIA).[20] Like similar groups in the Quarter, the FMIA sought not only to "improve" the Marigny but, as time went on, to defend the hard-won gains in quality of life from vandals of all sorts.[21]

The dream of official recognition was realized in 1974 as the FMIA succeeded in placing the Faubourg Marigny on the National Register of Historic Places.[22] Federal legislation in a 1976 tax act incentivized all rehabilitators of certified historic properties. A 1981 act enhanced the tax credits, including those for rehabilitation of nonhistoric buildings thirty or more years of age and commercial buildings of forty years of age or greater.[23]

After years of discussion, New Orleans created the Historic District Landmarks Commission (HDLC) in 1975,[24] giving it powers in designated districts over the streetscape portions of buildings, including the authority to issue stop-work orders against violators and to initiate the "demolition by neglect" process. Thus the HDLC has powers similar to, but not as sweeping as, those of the VCC in the Quarter.[25]

Even for men who could not buy a house, the Marigny had charms the Quarter had lost. Half of a shotgun double in the Marigny was usually more appealing than a tiny third-floor flat in the Quarter for the same price. The ease of street parking, the lack of tourists, and the opportunity to have a bit of garden all appealed.

Some of these early renovators lived on-site during the renovation. A shotgun double was especially convenient for this purpose, as one side could be a residence while the other was under renovation; then the process would reverse, and eventually both sides would be done. One half could now be rented and the other occupied by the owner.[26] From years of deferred maintenance and the native climate, many Marigny properties on the market were in bad shape. Plumbing and wiring were far out of date.

However, there were significant obstacles beyond the material decrepitude. The largest barrier was the difficulty in obtaining financing for purchases and renovations in the Marigny and other urban frontier zones. Another hurdle was obtaining insurance for a property. Cizek recounted:

> They would not give me insurance on this house because of the cars that were parked out front. It looked like the house was really pretty ratty looking but I mean, and the argument they gave was—after I painted the front of the house to make it look presentable—they then said now it didn't look that bad but they didn't want to give me insurance because he said, "Oh, the cars on the street are all beat up and raggedy." Well they were and they belong to some of the people that lived right in here and all around the area and so I said, "Okay you're gonna have to come out and take that picture again." And so I had friends of mine that had very nice cars like Mercedes-Benzes,

Cadillacs and Lincolns and we filled the street out there with those automobiles and they came and took pictures.[27]

A CAB to Nowhere

In the 1920s, New Orleans, like other cities, had an overheated real estate market. There was a cool comeuppance in the depressed thirties, as bad, overvalued loans were written off and owners lost hard-earned equity. In 1936 New Orleans' homestead associations formed a Central Appraisal Bureau (CAB). The purpose of the CAB was to control all appraisals, and it mandated that no loans in excess of 80 percent of the valuation of a property would be offered. Homesteads could offer less, but not more. This would prevent prospective buyers from shopping between homesteads and saving and loans to obtain a larger loan or a better valuation. The operation was touted as a "scientific" one. The appraisal process was to be "blind"; cases were assigned code numbers, and appraisers would not know the desired value, financial institution, or prospective buyer.[28]

In the years before the Veterans Housing Administration guaranteed loans, when much of New Orleans' existing housing stock stayed in family hands for generations and new construction was of paramount importance, the CAB may have worked as intended. However, as would-be buyers of older residential properties in the 1960s and later found out, the CAB monopoly was not their friend. The CAB's policies especially discriminated against renovators. Complaints about the CAB eventually reached the desk of Moon Landrieu, mayor from 1970 to 1978, who pressured the CAB to reform. In a 1976 editorial, the *Times-Picayune,* usually a defender of the city's fortress-like establishments, wrote, "The CAB has traditionally appraised at a 'loan' level rather than 'fair market' value so that the lending institution could sell the property quickly for the loan value in the event that a buyer defaulted on a loan soon after the sale. Young buyers especially complain they cannot bear the huge down payment required by this method and also sink $5,000 or $10,000 into renovations. Worse yet, a buyer who does invest in substantial renovations may find later appraisal is influenced less by the amount of investment than by the surrounding unrenovated houses."[29]

Under siege, the CAB fought back. It averred that some would-be renovators fell in love with a property's historic nimbus. Sellers, of course, were delighted to accept a higher price from an enraptured buyer. Buyers and sellers were not adequately nor equally informed about the real estate market and were often unaware of comparable sales—"comps." In pre-Internet days, finding comps involved tedious looking through back issues of the *Times-Picayune* and then visiting recently sold properties to see how closely they compared with the desired house. The CAB's defenders conceded that appraisers might not be considering "intangibles" that preservationists thought added value, since it was difficult to assign dollar values to these. The appraisers' adding machines did not have keys for "historic provenance" or "hopes and dreams."[30] The CAB's attitudes were not entirely based on cold figures. Preservationists had a perception that the CAB was controlled by wealthy uptown elites and staffed by people who did not live in, or care about, the old historic core.[31]

The CAB felt obliged to study the issue for three years, and in 1976 it decided to have its appraisers trained to national standards and to institute an appeals process. Simultaneously, it sniffed that the complainers were a "small group."[32] The CAB's next move was to cement its monopoly by state fiat. The state Commissioner of Financial Institutions attempted to ramrod a state law through, ultimately defeated, requiring financial institutions in Orleans, Jefferson, and St. Bernard Parishes to use the CAB. After three more years of fighting, the CAB conceded its monopoly.[33]

New Orleans civic institutions garb themselves in quasi-governmental power and defend their castles with medieval tenacity, but most are amenable to "grease." The right amount of cash or other type of gift lowers the drawbridge and opens the gates so that favorable results may be had. The ways the appraisal system could be gamed were not unique to the Marigny, or for that matter, New Orleans, where the practice seems to have gone on at least since the 1960s. There were at least two versions of the corruption.

In the first instance, an investor would obtain interim financing from a bank, not a homestead or savings and loan. The interim loan would cover the purchase and cost of the renovation. After renovation, the investor needed a "good" appraisal. This "good" appraisal would be taken to a homestead for a long-term loan that, of necessity, would pay off the interim note. If the appraisal was more than the interim note, the owner could pay it off and pocket the difference. The owner also now had a piece of paper stating that the property was worth more than before renovation, which would legitimize a higher price if it was to be resold quickly—that is, "flipped." If the renovated property had, by accepted standards, really increased in value, this process was, and is, perfectly legal. If the owner paid an assessor to inflate the value of the property just before shopping for a long-term mortgage, the process turned corrupt.

The second gambit required collusion between seller and buyer. The buyer would convince the seller to sign an agreement for a given price. Privately, they agreed on a lower figure, and the seller was given some lagniappe, as in cash, to keep mum. An appraiser would then be bribed to appraise the property at the documented, faux price. If the homestead or savings and loan agreed, the buyer obtained 100 percent of his or her financing, but the records would show only the mandated 80 percent. The buyer now had the difference in hand, to save or reinvest. As in the first ploy, a higher value was now documented on paper, and the property could command a higher price at resale.[34]

Although these practices sound victimless, they really harmed the Marigny and other reemerging neighborhoods. Neighborhood prices were artificially raised, shutting out other would-be renovators. Of course, the practitioners of these tricks put themselves in legal jeopardy.

The end of the CAB's monopoly meant that individual appraisers had more or less an open field. Some appraisers became more inclined to let their judgments be swayed by cash.

Enter Robert Hudson

Robert F. Hudson, a native of Florida, arrived in New Orleans in 1962, making his first recorded real estate sale in 1968.[35] By 1972 he was vice president of the Blackshear & Kornhaus firm.[36] In early 1973 he set up his own company at 314 North Rampart Street, in the upper Quarter.[37] Hudson's firm specialized in the Quarter and Marigny. His staff included a number of gay men, some of whom had been waiting tables before obtaining their real estate licenses.[38] Hudson aggressively promoted the Marigny as a community for gay men who wanted better choices than what the Quarter offered. At that time, gays and lesbians, having been rejected and marginalized for years, approached institutions with caution. Hudson's approach let them be frank about their lives, relationships, and real estate aspirations.

By all accounts Hudson's office was extremely successful in tapping this market. It seems that there was no deliberate coordination between the social promotion of the Marigny by Cizek and his friends and the real estate furnace stoked by Hudson and his competitors. That there was synergy was inevitable given the size of the neighborhood and the common audience, gay men.[39]

Hudson's candidness with his gay agents and clientele did not prevent some sharp dealing, however. The intoxicating hoopla led some men to get in over their heads. As a contemporary explained, "One particular trick of theirs was to get two gay men who were living together, talk them into buying a house with a high interest rate, and then wait for the couple to break up, and the one left couldn't handle all the mortgage payments, so they would reclaim the property; I mean, they were famous for that."[40] Hudson was certainly not the only real estate agent who gamed the appraisal system, but his prominence in the Marigny and the exposure of his misdeeds make his story highly germane to an understanding of the Marigny's development.

In May 1979 an appraiser was tried for accepting bribes from property owners. He mentioned Hudson as one of his correspondents.[41] Hudson's property manager testified that she saw the appraiser pick up several envelopes of cash from Hudson's office on the day appraisals were conducted.[42] Later that year, Hudson was convicted of "making false statements to a savings institution," fined $10,000, and given two years' probation.[43] Hudson continued his real estate business at least through 1987. By then, other events were eclipsing this state of affairs and eroding some of the hard-won gains of the first round of gentrification. Some blocks were renovated early on, and some languished for many years. One house might be renovated while its flanking neighbors decayed.

The gentrification of the Marigny in the 1970s was a movement largely of gay men, yet it was not a gay movement per se. Rather, it was a consequence of four interrelated factors. First, the French Quarter was getting too expensive, and properties that might be affordable to a middle-class, two-income couple tended to be small and usually in need of considerable updating. Second, the gay men who formed the vanguard in renovating the Marigny were in or approaching early middle age and had achieved a level of stability and income. They were also at the point in life to want a traditional home and not simply an apartment as a bachelor pad. Third, the real estate stock in the Marigny was just the right type to appeal to this group: freestanding houses, some with yards or portions that could be rented out, that were relatively inexpensive. Fourth, the Marigny real estate community made unprecedented opportunities for purchase and rental available to gay people. Thus we can visualize this migration being propelled by a push from the beloved but costly Quarter and a pull from its younger, poorer sister, the Marigny, with fuel for the trip provided by way of middle-age, middle-class incomes, and real estate agents performing very specific facilitation.

The credibility of this gentrification with the city's mostly straight establishment was cemented by emphasizing the "preservation" aspect of this movement rather than selling it as a "gay" trend.[44] As a longtime Third District resident remarked, "Then, a lot of new people moved in. Thank God for the gay community, I think, because they stayed with the neighborhood because they got kicked out of the French Quarter. They came into these two neighborhoods [the Marigny and Bywater]. I think they really did do a lot of good for the neighborhood here. They really did wonders with the houses. They were very good neighbors. They kept very good care of the neighborhood."[45]

Seeing other gay men happily engaged in the adventure of renovation, and their pride of place, made many men consider the Marigny as a new home. Safety in the evolving Marigny was a paramount concern, but it could be elusive. As a Quarter guy in the mid-1980s, I thought nothing of a twelve-block walk to visit friends in the Rectangle. After nightfall, my pals insisted I call United Cab to whisk me back; the shadowy nighttime Marigny streets, with many ghostly abandoned houses, were not convivial to casual, after-dark strolling. Many gay men felt at ease there—at least in daylight—due to the proximity of men like themselves and the comfortable distance from the tourist scene of the Quarter, with its outbursts of homophobia and gay bashing. Also, men carnally contemplated on the banquettes of the Quarter might or might not be gay, and they could be violently unfriendly to even discreet advances. In the Marigny, the chance of one's overtures being returned favorably were much higher. As one early 1980s resident of the 2400 block of Dauphine Street remarked at the time, "I can't walk out my front door without being cruised."

To many whites, the declining number of blacks in the Marigny indicated increasing safety. This attitude was not merely a superficial, racially polarized gloss; it was misleading. The blacks being forced out were largely longtime, older residents and their extended families. Within a decade, the Marigny's black population would largely be residents using the Housing Choice Voucher Program, commonly called Section 8. In brief, Section 8 was intended to move poor families away from the city's notorious housing projects and into small-scale housing scattered across town. Absentee landlords got a subsidy for having their houses in the program, and residents paid below-market rents. Section 8 was universally despised by Marigny whites, who would have welcomed middle-class blacks as fellow investors in the neighborhood. The presence of a Section 8 property on a block made the values of nearby houses go down. Neither can it have been comfortable for the Section 8 residents, who might very well be the only blacks on the block and did not necessarily have an attachment to the neighborhood or an incentive to participate in its social life.

New Orleans has forgotten the value of steady industrial paychecks for the working class, and the Orleans Parish school system, prior to Katrina, was a trough of corruption and despair. These factors, and others, gave rise to decayed and desperate parts of town close to the Quarter and the Marigny. As these neighborhoods gentrified, they furnished a bank for burglars and robbers to tap at will.

The 1980 census showed yet another decline in the Marigny's population, nearly 19 percent from 1970 and over 50 percent from 1940. The Triangle lost almost a quarter of its population between 1970 and 1980, and the Rectangle about 13 percent. The black population of the Triangle more than doubled during this decade, but in the Rectangle, that group shrank by 30 percent.

The Marigny, which a generation before had seemed so homogeneous as the grandchildren of Italians and Germans creolized, was now perceived as having distinct subneighborhoods, much like the French Quarter. The upper Triangle had a remnant of the old French Creoles; the lower Triangle, below Dauphine, had more early gay gentrifiers. The Rectangle had its own enclaves. By the late eighties, the stretch of Port and St. Ferdinand from the river to St. Claude was known for prostitution and drug dealing.[46]

Making the Leap

The final load of stuff from a buddy's pickup was inside, and the air conditioner was on. Maybe a joint smoked, maybe some beer opened by sweaty young men in cut-off jeans. To work, then, to hook up the stereo—always the first thing when moving in—and then to set up real adult housekeeping in a house with one's own mortgage. Life now revolved around the house and the yard. Initiation into the tribal mysteries of faux marble, the intricacies of cast-iron plumbing and knob-and-tube wiring. Consulting with old men at hardware stores, who might have known the house's former owners. Choices, hotly debated, of colors for the gingerbread, the columns, and the walls. Lamps tucked inside the soffit vents to cast a webby light at night over the elephant ears. Gardens blooming in the rich muck and puppies trained to obey and protect. Getting to know the neighbors and finding new sexual opportunities at Schwegmann's on St. Claude.

Bar life became a distant echo, a once-in-a-while thing, at least until the nest was settled. Then a new pattern became established. Friday and Saturday evenings might be spent not in a dark, smoky space reeking of spilled beer and testosterone but having potluck dinner parties with other house-poor male couples and sharing the mutual real estate adventure. Sunday was more for the endless home projects and less for recovering from Saturday night. The spare bedroom became a waystation for visiting friends, the relations who cared, or dared, to visit, the guests from the big cities, the refugees from the little towns, and the occasional stray of hot looks and good demeanor who might be found on the streets.

Break-ins were the downside. Hiding grass, porn, and sex toys before the police arrived with their usually indifferent attitude; the consequent alarm systems, pistol in the nightstand, and more fearsome canines. The feeling of being an unwilling bank for the larcenous from the other side of St. Claude, and the occasional twinge of regret when squaring New Orleans realities with youthful idealism.

One surfer of the Marigny gay wave of the eighties recalled the neighborhood as "one-third old original residents, living alone in quiet poverty; one-third 'Section 8' families, crammed into split doubles and living in noisy poverty; one-third gay couples, painting over termite-infested rotted shotguns and making them ephemeral showplaces."[47]

The male urban pioneers of the Marigny, the Bywater, and other New Orleans frontiers were part of the epoch of gay homesteading as seen in the Castro of San Francisco and in other cities. New Orleans had always sheltered outcasts, who usually lived on the margins in neighborhoods like the Quarter, where "bohemianism" was expected and, to a degree, accepted. However, the new residents were not living in the shadows of anyone else's culture. A new culture was aborning in the rich compost of a much older one, founded by immigrants and outcasts, once marginalized themselves. Yet it also owed much to American suburban bourgeois notions of detached houses, tended yards, and the flag flying from the porch pillar.

The Downriver Scene

The French Quarter had been the traditional center of gay life in New Orleans since the founding years, as the city, to varying degrees, tolerated gays and lesbians. We may think of it as the upriver scene of the city's gay life. In the 1970s and the 1980s, two other nexuses of gay life were established in the Marigny, and we may consider those the downriver scene of wider, gayer spaces. One was the intersection of North Rampart and Elysian Fields.

The corner building at 940 Elysian Fields was a drugstore for many decades and in the late 1960s hosted taverns. In 1977 Charlene Schneider opened her eponymous bar there. Other lesbian bars had been around, most notably the Key Club at Chartres and Piety in the 1950s, Brady's in the Quarter, and the Cuckoo's Nest and Tony's Garage in the Marigny.[48] Charlene's had a different vibe. Schneider was not merely the proprietor but a very public activist as well. Previous lesbian bars had stressed discretion, discouraging dancing and public displays of affection. Charlene's encouraged these things and often had live bands to get the customers swinging.[49] Charlene's was rarely open before late afternoon.[50] The passage along North Rampart between the lower Quarter and Elysian Fields looks deceptively short at six blocks, but it can be perilous. Aside from the uproar of lower Frenchmen Street, there are no nighttime waystations. With its apartment-style door buzzer and remote-control lock, Charlene's was widely considered an outpost of safety along the trails of North Rampart and Elysian Fields.

Across Elysian Fields, 941, like 940, was occupied by many different businesses over the years. In 1946 it hosted a grocery store that quickly withered in the presence of Schwegmann's across the street. It held a TV repair shop and then a hardware store in the 1950s. Two bars briefly occupied the space at the end of the 1970s and the beginning of the 1980s. Jamie Temple and George Kozik founded the Phoenix Bar there in 1982. It began life as a country-and-western tavern, evolving over time to become New Orleans' first and premier leather bar.

Off the tourist rabbit-trails of the Quarter and inside the gay-ifying Marigny, Charlene's and the Phoenix were perfectly situated. At the time, lesbians were subject to frequent harassment by straight men, and even some gay men considered leathermen outré. At this intersection of North Rampart, Elysian Fields, time, and space, these clienteles created their own havens. It was rare for tourists to mistakenly stumble into either bar, since this part of New Orleans was not yet on the tourism radar. Although the patrons of the two bars rarely mixed, Temple and Schneider were close friends, cooperating in activism and making the nexus work. The Phoenix hosted many yard sales for various organizations, including the Louisiana Gay Political Action Caucus (LAGPAC).

In another era, the residents of the 2200 block of North Rampart, around the corner from the Phoenix, might have been diffident about a nearby homosexual hangout. Now, with the neighborhood hollowing out with decay and the uneasy boundary of St. Claude just a block away, the many elderly ladies welcomed the vigorous male staff and patrons. One afternoon, an elderly neighbor fell through the rotting floor of her camelback house; a call to the Phoenix dispatched two strong lesbians to extricate her. Schwegmann's was closed at night, so the Phoenix patrons parked in its large lot. The bar reciprocated the favor by picking up the parking lot trash.[51] Just a few doors away, there was an echo of Sanctity Row in a high-class bordello.[52]

The second gay intersection in the Marigny was at the crossroads of Franklin and Royal, a commercial center for many years. The building at 2601 Royal was the original home of the Third District Savings and Loan, a hub of German American commercial power in the nineteenth century. In 1937 the institution moved into a Moderne building on St. Claude.[53] After that, 2601 was a clothing factory and then home to various bars.[54] In the mideighties, 2601 Royal, or "Twenty Six" to its denizens, became a watering hole for the lower Rectangle's gay population. Eventually it spawned a small back bar, Boots, catering to leathermen and urban cowboys, some of whom actually rodeoed. That bar migrated upstairs to become the short-lived Boots and Bears. The new name reflected the congregation at 2601 of gay men self-identified as "bears." The bears had a ritualistic gathering outside the bar during the annual Southern Decadence event to record a "mass mooning" picture, sometimes entertaining a passing city bus. Across Franklin, Big Daddy's, a former restaurant, also served neighborhood drinkers and offered drag shows on weekend nights. One door up on Franklin, a small bar was leased out to various operators. It was best known as the Copper Top, after the bar's original, but now removed, metallic surface.

Although all these bars were very openly gay, they welcomed everyone from the neighborhood, including straight residents who missed the comradery of their former haunts and long-gone friends. A few times a week, and for holidays and memorial services, all the bars hosted buffets where, for the price of a drink or two, patrons could eat red beans and rice, gumbo, or other traditional fare. Occasionally bars would fire up a charcoal grill and invite patrons to "bring their own meat" to be cooked; the diners could avail themselves of house-provided salads and potatoes. These dinners were important to many older people living in reduced circumstances, and not just for nutrition. At the gay bars they were entertained by the more flamboyant customers. They had bartenders who took an interest in them and let them bring their dogs inside and genial patrons who buffered the loneliness from dead spouses and faraway children. The bars in turn appreciated the dependability and good manners of their older neighborhood regulars. A younger bar patron might be assigned to walk one of his elder fellow celebrants home if too much drink was involved. A regular not showing up at the expected time might trigger a search party to check on him or her, and sometimes a drive to Charity Hospital. Occasionally bar denizens would accompany one of the old regulars to the cemetery for that last call that never happens in New Orleans' living moments.

Besides the bars, the Marigny hosted the Gay Service Center at 2004 Burgundy. The service center operated a telephone line offering listening, advice, and information for those who were just coming out or needed the name of a gay-friendly professional.[55]

A significant moment in the gay life of the Marigny was the city's first Gay Fest, held in July 1979. Organizers had originally asked to use Jackson Square or Armstrong Park; denied those, they turned to Washington Park. Charlene Schneider was co-chair of the fest. Thanks to a sympathetic District C city councilman, Mike Early, the fest was given an exemption by the city council to sell beer onsite.[56]

Although most police harassment of gays and lesbians—typically with the all-purpose charge of "blocking the sidewalk"—occurred in the Quarter, it happened in the Marigny as well. In 1983 patrons outside of Charlene's were roughed up, arrested, and transported to the city's notorious central lockup despite the intervention of the district councilman.[57] Across the street, the Phoenix was occasionally subject to raids based on reports of sexual activity. Typically these raids happened just before the weekends of Mardi Gras or Southern Decadence.

In New Orleans the illusions are always there; it is the realities that vanish like soap bubbles, just as they are about to be grasped. Louisiana's booming oil economy protected it against much of the general national economic malaise of the 1970s and early 1980s. Drivers elsewhere may have cursed the rising price of oil, but it made cash registers ring all over the Pelican State. New Orleans saw flush times exemplified by rising skyscrapers in the CBD.

In the Quarter, landlords looking to cash in on the expected tide of visitors to the 1984 World's Fair jacked up rents and subdivided buildings yet again to squeeze in overnight guests. The fair imploded, declaring bankruptcy while still open, leaving $120 million in debt and many stiffed contractors, some irrevocably ruined.[58] Some people who had been priced out of the Quarter moved on to the Marigny, much of which was still unredeemed from decrepitude.

Oil prices tumbled in the early to mid-1980s, and the state's petro miracle went *poof.* As the good-paying oil jobs vanished—often to Houston—the losses rippled throughout the city's economy, hitting service jobs as restaurant meals and bar nights suddenly became luxuries for those grimly hanging on. For the fortunate whose livelihoods did not depend on oil and service jobs, things were rosier. Vieux Carré rents came down from the stratosphere as units emptied. A real estate professional related that in 1984, one-third to one-half of all houses in the Marigny were boarded up, which squares with my recollection of those times.[59] In March 1985 I went apartment hunting in the Quarter, finding landlords eager to rent their flats to me. The man who became my landlord informed me that about one-third of all Quarter rental units were then vacant, which I subsequently confirmed.[60]

The bad news continued. The 1986 Tax Reform Act reduced historic rehabilitation tax credits and reduced the tax sheltering the credits allowed for investment income.[61] The act devastated the historic renovation industry. In New Orleans and elsewhere, both wealthy syndicate investors and individual homeowners who were already stretched incurred serious losses.[62] Very high interest rates on mortgages and consumer loans meant that some properties sank quickly underwater. Foreclosed buildings were being sold at low prices, further depressing the real estate market.

The progress of the Marigny had now been buffeted by the oil bust and the loss of tax credits, although the latter probably hit the multi-unit investors harder than individual home owners. These blows were quickly eclipsed by the arrival of AIDS. New Orleans recorded its first confirmed fatality in October 1982, although it is believed that there were earlier, undiagnosed cases.[63]

For many reasons, the disease made a slow march into the city.[64] New Orleans was not a cosmopolitan destination like New York or San Francisco. Many Crescent City gay men could not afford to travel widely and so stayed home, waiting for visitors—and the sexual opportunities they brought—to show up. New Orleans also had the advantage of early warning from the hubs of the plague. By 1983 the New Orleans AIDS Task Force (later called NOAIDS) was providing counseling for the worried well, support for the sick, and advocacy for government funding.[65] For many years, NOAIDS' offices were near the foot of Frenchmen Street.

The city's experience with the epidemic got worse in the mid- and late 1980s. Some men perished quickly, hale and apparently healthy one day and dead two or three weeks later. Others lost jobs, homes, and independent living as the dying process dragged on. For many who could not or would not return to their origins, the sixth floor of Charity Hospital became their last address. Like the Creole nurses of the yellow fever era, Charity's staff mopped brows and tried to comfort prematurely aged young men, some sightless and paralyzed.[66] Some patients found friends to take them in, passing away on their couches or spare beds. Those who could return to their relatives would disappear, families often cutting off their sons' friends with accusatory silence. Before effective therapy became available, some men took the diagnosis as a signal to take their own lives before the suffering began. Two were bartenders at the Phoenix; one all of nineteen years.[67]

The Archdiocese of New Orleans set up an AIDS hospice, Lazarus House, in 1985. At first the location was kept secret to shield the staff and patients from homophobic cranks.[68] Eventually, it became common knowledge that the house was in the Marigny, on Dauphine Street between St. Ferdinand and Press, in back of Holy Trinity Church. St. Paul's Lutheran stepped up to help, cooperating with the archdiocese in setting up Lazarus House and forming a task force in 1987 to assist AIDS patients.[69]

The gay Carnival krewes were devastated. At the high tide in the mid-eighties, there were about twelve gay krewes; by 1993 there were four.[70] It is not possible to parse out just how many Marigny men died, but individuals

AIDS Memorial, Washington Park. Photo by author.

are remembered. José Quintanilla was well known in the Triangle for riding his unicycle swiftly around the neighborhood. Dairy technician Tim Nettles had many friends along Dauphine Street. Accountant Benny Hebert once lived close to Hubig's bakery.

On the Dauphine Street side of Washington Park stands the New Orleans AIDS Memorial, also named the Guardian Wall, sculpted by Tim Tate. Thirty-four molded glass faces refract and reflect the ever-changing light, peering from the well of memory to let no one forget, that nothing may be forgotten.

More Departures

The oil bust, mortgage finance woes, and the toll of AIDS made themselves known in the 1990 census. That count revealed a profound drop in the Marigny's population, about 31 percent less than 1980s figure. Whites were down by a third and blacks by about 24 percent. The Triangle and the

Rectangle each lost about 30 percent of their residents. Just as the French Quarter got lonely in the mideighties, the Marigny began to feel hollow.

Some of the hard-won gains of the seventies and eighties were reversed as owners unable to pay mortgages walked away from their homes. New Orleans had the highest residential vacancy rate of any major American city. The vacant houses were targets of theft, vandalism, and squatters. The corruption-wracked New Orleans Police Department became disengaged from property crimes, and response and follow-up were the exception. The forlorn properties induced neighbors to move away, creating more blight. The state's cumbersome process for condemning and demolishing abandoned properties meant that they sat rotting for years.[71] One decaying Rectangle house on the downriver side of Elysian Fields became a "shooting gallery" for IV drug users; I could hear them whisper and moan as I walked by at night.

It was around this time that theft of architectural elements became a problem. The city had a long-standing legitimate trade in planters, statues, stained glass, trim, and other parts of demolished buildings. This was now augmented by thieves who offered to sell pieces they had "found," leaving another homeowner angry as his renovated house was chipped away, item by item.[72] One theft occurred while the family breakfasted; thieves attached a chain to their iron fence and pulled it up with a pickup truck, dragging it down the street. When the price of copper spiked, copper gutters, plumbing, and wiring were targets of theft. Addicts would steal anything. A friend of mine on Port Street bought a piece of inexpensive molding from a home improvement store to hold small houseplants in an external stairwell. One day someone scaled the patio wall and took this molding, leaving the plants sitting neatly on the stair landing.

Like the Carnival beads hanging from the trees, Schwegmann's on St. Claude seemed an organic part of the Marigny. By the 1980s the store, a relic of the chain's youth, was tired and dilapidated. John G. Schwegmann died in 1995, and his funeral mass was held at Holy Trinity, itself fading away.[73]

John F. Schwegmann took the chain's reins in 1979. In 1995 he bought the twenty-eight New Orleans stores of the National Tea Company and stores of three other competitors. The acquisition's debt started the old chain on the downhill slide, with an avalanche of competition thundering right behind it.[74] In 1997 Schwegmann's was sold to a holding company, which went bankrupt two years later.[75] The chain's competitors swooped in to divvy up the remains, and many longtime employees were thrown out on the street.

At 2222 St. Claude, the story was better. A small local chain, Robert's Fresh Market, leased the old Schwegmann's store, cleaned it up, and continued to sell groceries to the neighborhood. Although this Schwegmann's was missed, the long neglect of the store and the chain's expansion to explosion had eroded the old customers' affections, so the spruced-up Robert's was welcomed.

The Borderlands

The two rigid boundaries of the Marigny—the river and the railroad—changed slowly in the twentieth century. Warehouses continued to line North Peters Street by the river. The railroad corridor of Press Street got lonelier as the railroad shops and warehouses emptied. The once-elegant mansions of Esplanade, the border with the Vieux Carré, had become rooming houses years before but were being converted into condos and a few revived single-family dwellings. The lakeside boundary of St. Claude, like North Rampart in the Quarter, became a dividing line between the white Marigny and the mostly black New Marigny, sometimes called St. Roch. Businesses fled the old strip. Between 1978 and 2000, every Marigny block of St. Claude—on both sides—showed significant declines in residential and retail presence. Elysian Fields showed some loss in residences but less erosion in retail.[76]

The boosters' optimism of the early seventies now seemed like a dream of high school civics class, but the books had slammed shut, the bell had rung, and the city was now concentrating on survival.

The Big Parades Go On for Years

While the Marigny was leading the way in gay gentrification, it was also the vessel of old traditions. In 1873 the Comus Carnival parade depicted such unloved personalities as Benjamin Butler as a hyena, carpetbagger Governor Warmoth as a snake, and President Grant as a tobacco grub worm. The parade's lèse-majesté evoked public mirth but official consternation.[77] After that, Carnival krewes steered well clear of satire, choosing such inoffensive themes as flowers, classic mythology, and abstract ideas.

In 1987 the Krewe du Vieux Carré formed as a collective of subkrewes and returned satirical traditions to Mardi Gras. From their den on Architect Street, the Krewe du Vieux and assorted subkrewes parade before Fat Tuesday through the Marigny at night, featuring mule- and human-drawn floats. These floats sharply lampoon personalities and events of the day, taking liberties and flaunting graphic innuendos unimaginable to the Comus krewe of the 1870s.

The desire to recapture Carnival as a community-driven event moved Henri Schindler, Paul Poché, and Jon Newlin to found the Society of St. Anne in 1969.[78] St. Anne is a loosely affiliated group without formal membership. Someone pays for a band each year. On Fat Tuesday morning, beginning in the Bywater, the parade leaders step off, holding beribboned hoops called "crab nets" on poles. The band—at least at first—is immediately behind the crab nets, and the rest of the parade falls in.

St. Anne's revelers are a wide-ranging mix of Bywater and Marigny residents, New Orleanians, and out-of-towners who make annual pilgrimages. The costumes range from the simple, conjured up that morning with cardboard and bubble wrap, to elaborate and fanciful creations. Given the narrow, uncleared streets, the floats are small and usually foot-powered by walkers and bicyclists. Such steampunk creations as dirigibles and fire-breathing metal horses have appeared in recent years. Hewing to its roots as a community-centered happening, there may be suggestive costumes, but there is no nudity. Some young men may be just drunk enough to take off their shirts and not feel the seasonal chill. The battle cry of the Carnival bead economy—"Show yer tits!"—is never uttered. The mellow atmosphere brings families with small children, some riding in wagons, looking up wide-eyed at the forest of vividly garbed adults.

Royal Street toward the Quarter is the usual route, although Burgundy has been followed as well. Hundreds of costumed people fall in from side streets, and the parade usually stops at each Marigny bar. Resumption of the parade is signaled by the trumpet blast of the opening notes of "Second Line."[79] The parade winds its way past the Christopher Inn, handing throws to residents in wheelchairs and walkers on the banquette. Entering the Quarter, St. Anne arrives at Canal Street to watch part of the Rex parade. Then the parade—that part that has not been distracted by the barrooms, restrooms, and antics in the Vieux Carré—goes to the Moon Walk. Members who have died, and expressed the wish, are given a St. Anne funeral. Their ashes are scattered into the river while the band plays "Down by the Riverside." The glittery gray flakes float on the current out to the gulf, returning another Marigny or Bywater denizen to Mother Ocean.

As the Triangle had been the bellwether of gay gentrification, so lower Frenchmen Street condensed all the controversies and contradictions about entertainment venues in residential areas and the city's struggle with the human *tout ensemble.* We now go for a stroll up that storied street.

14

The Many Lives of Frenchmen Street

Frenchmen Street began its life as rue des Français (Street of the French), Bernard's homage to the Frenchmen who rebelled against the Spanish in 1769 and, for the most part, paid with their lives.[1] As the Américains arrived in New Orleans and anglicized French names, the street became simply Frenchmen.

Frenchmen Street was in an advantageous position within the new faubourg. Proceeding downriver from Esplanade, Frenchmen was the first full-length, straight-through lakewise street and intersected Esplanade just behind the site of Fort St. Charles, now the old U.S. Mint. It offered immediate access to the levee, the city's doorstep to the world. Frenchmen ran alongside Place Washington, making it a convenient thoroughfare for rallies and parades in the park. That it should become the "high street" of the original Faubourg Marigny—the Triangle—was only logical.

In 1805 ten of the fifteen new lots fronting Frenchmen between North Peters and Dauphine were quickly sold.[2] Whether the lots were bought for sheer speculation or for other reasons, only three of the original owners were still at those addresses in 1811.[3]

The street was much more populated in 1822, with three cordwainers—makers of fine footwear—there, along with carpenters, gunsmiths, and sailors. Besides these usual Marigny occupations, three blacksmiths inhabited this section in 1832. This number rose to five in 1842.[4]

By the 1850s, lower Frenchmen was sandwiched between two ballrooms, the Louisiana on Esplanade and Decatur[5] and Beaumi's at Frenchmen and Decatur,[6] and close to a third at Elysian Fields and Decatur.[7] The ballrooms, as we noted earlier, were one small step up from the murderous dives of Gallatin Street in the Quarter. Lower Frenchmen was also close by the brothels and ballrooms of Sanctity Row on lower Elysian Fields. So the river end of Frenchmen saw the drunken, quarreling traffic lurching between these establishments. This traffic was lucrative to the businesses of the street, which included brothels.[8]

By 1851, occupations had diversified, with the notable inclusion of three "coffeehouses"—in reality, saloons—and two "oyster houses," which doubled as taverns. Four grocery stores served the neighborhood. The beginnings of commercial specialization were evident: two printers, two watchmakers, and two "fancy stores" were in business. One of these, Laborde's, also offered undertaking services, conveniently close to the riverfront with its many boiler explosions, drownings, and industrial mishaps.[9] A confectionary at Frenchmen and Decatur was a neighborhood fixture for decades,[10] and the street would feature confectionaries from then on. Seven households of free people of color were recorded on Frenchmen, with two carpenters and two shoemakers among them. The city directories did not record every household head who was a free person of color, so these numbers are known to be low.

On the eve of the Civil War, an assortment of people called Frenchmen Street home, including laborers, grocers, teachers, and shoemakers. A confectioner and a hardware store were among the street's retail offerings. The Boys' High School held class on Frenchmen between Dauphine and Royal.[11]

In 1862 the city took charge of the triangular island in the 400 block between Frenchmen and Esplanade, building a firehouse for the Creole No. 9 company. This was replaced by another in 1881 and in turn by the contemporary structure in 1961.[12]

After the Civil War, like the rest of the Marigny, Frenchmen hosted a diverse retail scene, with a drugstore, hardware store, shoe store, oyster saloon, groceries, and a dry goods store. At the corner of Frenchmen and Royal, Charles Burkenstock sold saddles for many decades.[13] Bernard Marigny's last home was in the 700 block of Frenchmen, and in the later mornings of his life after the Civil War, he might be seen sitting at a small table on the sidewalk, reading and answering his correspondence.[14]

In 1870 the *Daily Picayune* observed that Frenchmen Street was then more entitled to be called "Irishmen" or "German" for its ethnic mix.[15] By

1880, of the 150 people enumerated on Frenchmen between Decatur and Royal, 80 were Germans.[16] By that time all people of color were technically free, and some of the old Modern Creole elite still clung to Frenchmen Street, including the Lacroix family, who ran a grocery at Decatur and Frenchmen.[17] At the corner of Decatur and Esplanade, Rougelot's *rabais* (discount) department store thrived for fifty-seven years.[18]

In 1907 the Carnegie endowment funded the establishment of a branch of the city library at the lower corner of Royal and Frenchmen, next to the Third Presbyterian Church.[19] French must still have been important in the district, since the library's opening was delayed until books in that language were delivered.[20]

Although New Orleans was a city of enduring local chain stores, the Great Atlantic and Pacific Tea Company occupied 624 Frenchmen between 1905 and 1915, being replaced by a local tea store that year. Frenchmen was a recognized retail hub in the teens of the twentieth century and had its own Frenchmen Street Merchants Association. The strip also was known for its Fat Tuesday celebration, featuring costume contests, which drew thousands of revelers to the street.[21] As the teens became the twenties, furniture stores and financial institutions were featured, as well as another national supermarket, Piggly Wiggly, at 606 Frenchmen, which lasted until the early 1930s. A local favorite was Reboul's grocery at 531 on the lower corner of Chartres, which roasted its own coffee, wafting a distinctive aroma over the neighborhood.[22]

In the years just before World War II, the Third District was composed of many small enclaves, each with its own retail venues.[23] Numerous corner grocery stores, running tabs for the neighborhood families, satisfied most daily food needs. For dry goods and specialties the little groceries didn't carry, the Old Third turned to Frenchmen Street, and to a certain extent the stores of St. Claude. Frenchmen Street was convenient via the Desire and St. Claude streetcars[24] and was much handier than the more upscale stores of Canal Street. Frenchmen Street was also convenient for people who lived in the lower Quarter and was described as a "miniature Canal street."[25]

Starting at Esplanade, a shopper of 1938 would pass Rougelot's discount store at the curving corner of Esplanade and Decatur, the long-established Firehouse No. 9, and Abadie's machine shop. Crossing Decatur, our buyer would find May's Dry Goods, Hirsch caterer's supplies, Popovich Millinery, Laborde Printing, and Homeseekers Savings and Loan. Crossing Chartres, there would be Gagliano Dry Goods, the Mocklin confectionary, Grunewald jewelers, Serio shoes, Zangara's barbershop, and Aimee-Bessec hardware. Strolling across Royal, shoppers found Ygnacio Drugs, Revolta used furniture, a branch of the public library, and opposite Washington Park, the Baptist Emergency Home for unwed mothers.[26] The H. G. Hill grocery store on the lower, lakeside corner of Frenchmen and Dauphine was the bookend to this retail district. As A&P and Piggly Wiggly discovered, New Orleans was not a good place for national chains, and so the H. G. Hill store went out in the late 1940s. The span of the street beyond, on up to St. Claude, was mainly a residential area. Of course, shopping was not confined to Frenchmen Street alone; many retailers could be found on the branching side streets of Decatur, Chartres, and Royal.[27]

Rougelot's at the corner of Esplanade and Decatur closed in 1948. The store had been an anchor since 1891, but the managing generation was leaving the frame, the rising generation did not care to take it on, and competition from the "destination stores" of Canal Street could not be overcome.

The retail life of Frenchmen Street peaked in the early 1950s, as did the presence of warehouses. Retail then began a downturn that would last until the early 1970s. Interestingly, residential life saw a marked upswing from the mid-1950s through the early 1970s, and the number of apartments peaked in 1975. Some of the wholesalers also offered minor retail sales, such as the confectionary and Jumawid oysters.[28]

If we were to repeat our prewar stroll up Frenchmen in 1960, we would encounter Mumphrey's garage, the wholesale Nu-Lite Electric, and Bauer Storage and Moving. Crossing Decatur, we would find the Salvation Army Bargain Store, Popovich Millinery, Ray's Liquors, Holtzmann's Furniture, Laborde Printing, Sparacino's gas station, the Dream Castle bar, and G&J wholesale candy. Crossing Chartres, we would come to the Fairway bar and restaurant, the Swiss Confectionary, Caravella Meat Packers, Grunewald Jewelry in its final two years, Cremo Chemical warehouse, Pontecarvo & Henry cabinet and leather shop, Degruise the barber, Jumawid Oyster Company, Aimee-Bessec hardware, Bond cleaners, and the Three Star vending machine company. Sauntering across Royal, we would find Batiste Restaurant, the Cunningham & Kincaid piano service, and Home Beverage Service. The H. G. Hill grocery store had departed in the early 1950s. So we see that the Frenchmen retail strip now catered less to neighborhood residents and more to commercial entities looking for roosts away from the high rents and heavy traffic of the Quarter or Canal Street.

The mid-1960s found Frenchmen Street a sleepy neighborhood, where the remaining businesses were mostly locked up at night and the sparse bar traffic was mainly college kids, "bohemians," and stray sailors from the dives of Decatur Street. Street crime was almost unknown.[29]

Established around 1960, the Dream Castle at 532 Frenchmen was a distinct overture to what the strip would eventually become. The upstairs of the building was occupied by a brothel,[30] honoring the traditional relationship between sexual commerce and musical innovation in Storyville. Although it was nominally a black bar run by a Modern Creole, it welcomed adventurous whites as well. Whites had to be adventurous indeed, since Louisiana law forbade the races from drinking or playing music together. In the mid-1960s the Dream Castle was harassed by police for this reason, as was the "beatnik" Quorum club, nearby on Esplanade, which shared some patrons with the Dream Castle.

As the author James Nolan recalled Frenchmen:

> There was only one club there and it was called The Dream Castle. It was run by an old Creole man of color and it was a black bar, and it was actually the first integrated bar in the city of New Orleans. We would go there with some friends of ours in the Bozo Band, who were some dropped-out kids from across the country who had a little sort of jug band. They were white. Babe Stovall, who was a black Mississippi Delta blues player, would sometimes play there, so he took us there. I remember very vividly that they [the police] were trying to bust the bar because it was integrated. When the police would come to the door, of course I was underage, so I would run to the bathroom and sit there for about half an hour and do my chemistry homework and wait for the police to leave.[31]

Whites performed at the Castle as well, including folksinger Steve Keith, who met Stovall at a party in the Quarter and performed with him at such Quarter clubs as the Seven Seas on St. Philip, the Intellect on Bourbon, and the Sphinx on Decatur.[32] As the 1960s wore on, after the Civil Rights Act of 1964, the NOPD ceased hassling the Dream Castle but still made life hard for "beatnik" joints where the races might mingle, blacks might be registered to vote, and somebody—anybody—just might be stoned.

By 1964 the strip hit a low point in activity, with every category of use

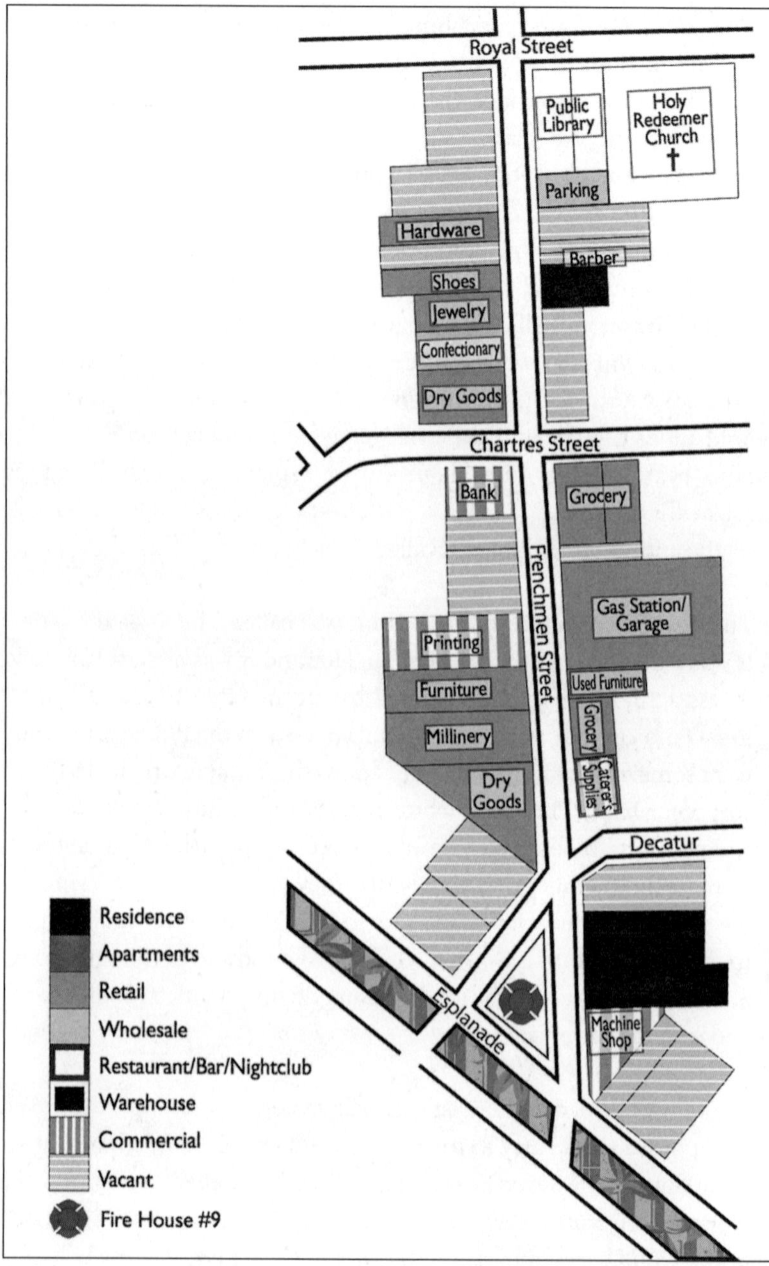

The Frenchmen Strip, 1938. Illustration by Amanda Glenn.

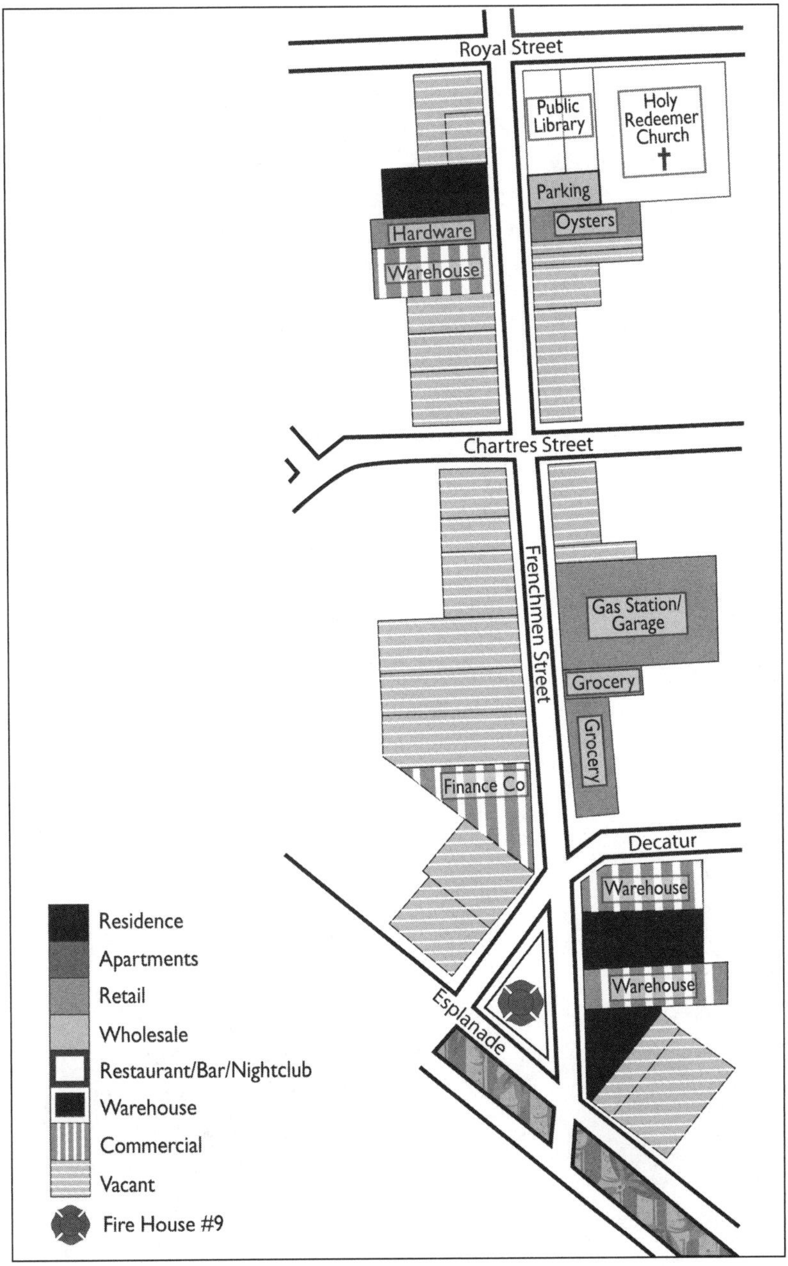

The Frenchmen Strip, 1952. Illustration by Amanda Glenn.

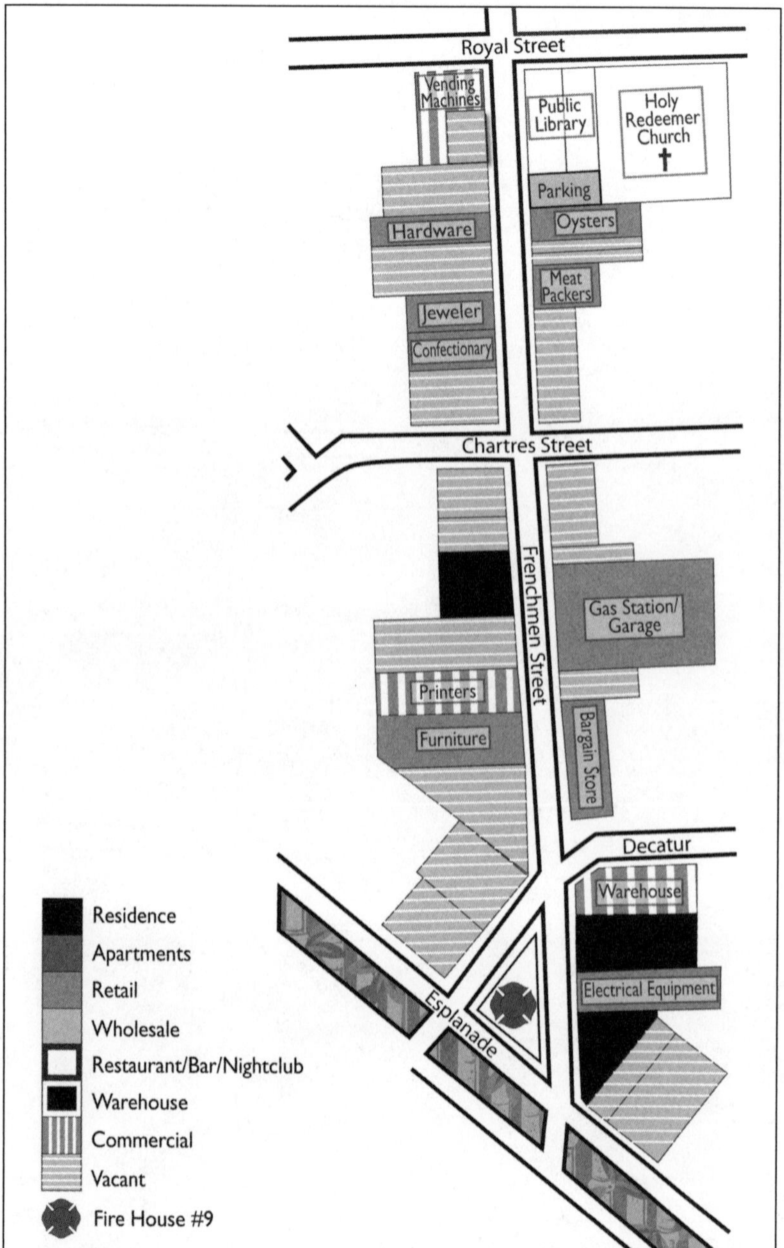

The Frenchmen Strip, 1960. Illustration by Amanda Glenn.

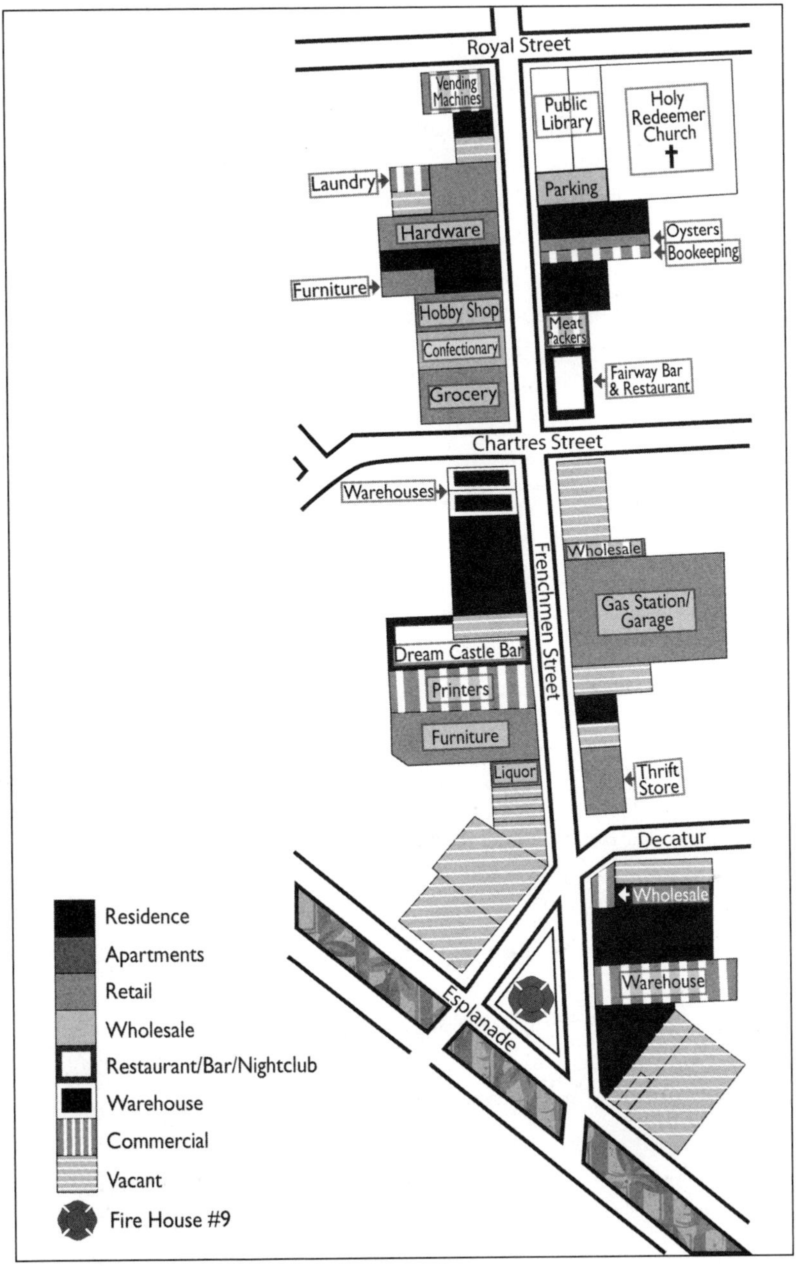

The Frenchmen Strip, 1964. Illustration by Amanda Glenn.

down. The arrival of the so-called counterculture, along with the cheap rents and proximity to downtown, prodded a slow, erratic revival through the early 1970s. Hurricane Betsy struck in 1965, causing destruction that would be exceeded only by Hurricanes Katrina and Rita in 2005. The Royal Street library facing Washington Park was so badly damaged that the city tore it down.[33] Its neighbor, the former Third Presbyterian Church and then the African American Holy Redeemer Catholic Church, was also beyond repair.[34] In 1972 the Archdiocese of New Orleans built the nine-story Christopher Inn retirement home on the old church and library lots.[35]

Although the strip is close to the mainly residential middle-class subneighborhood of the lower Quarter, for many years it has shared identity more directly with Decatur Street. Bourbon Street had the fame, the shame, the boozing college kids, and the well-established clubs. Discerning locals who wanted to walk on the wild side shunned touristy Bourbon and favored Decatur. In the late 1960s and early 1970s Decatur was a heady mix of sailors, students, "hippies," "bohemians," and the bars, prostitutes, and drug dealers that served them. From Jackson Square on down to the junction with Frenchmen at the firehouse, the dilapidated street had lost most of its old commercial occupants, and it became the canvas on which much of the Quarter's counterculture was displayed. The adult bookstore Sidney's News Stand at Decatur and Ursulines served extra helpings of naughtiness, especially to slumming out-of-small-towners. "Father" Mike Stark's ABBA foundation and its HEAD emergency health clinic were at 1212 Royal, and their flea market was at 1100 Decatur.[36] They served the "travelers" that the city's hospitals often turned away or reported to the police.[37] At 1107 Decatur, Molly's at the Market was an intelligentsia hangout. Down the block was the Abbey, an outpost of lawyers, reporters, and writers savoring libations and the passing parade.[38] As the first commercial street off Decatur, near the tailbone of Elysian Fields, Frenchmen was the natural estuary for the stream of party people flowing down Decatur. The Frenchmen strip was often referred to as the "fringe of the Quarter." So the legal and preservation boundary between the two neighborhoods meant nothing to the people strolling, staggering, and tripping along Decatur and Frenchmen.

As the late sixties wore on to the early seventies, fewer and fewer properties on Frenchmen were occupied by businesses of any sort, and the strip was described by a contemporary businessman as a "slum."[39] The Dream

Castle closed about 1970. The Cabaret Bar and Pool Room at 600 and the Fairway Bar and Restaurant at 601 were the only places to drink and eat on the strip for a while. The Fairway was noted for go-go girls[40] and prostitution busts.[41] After the Fairway went out, the address was occupied by Cord's Underground. On June 20, 1976, Cord's exploded, shaking up neighbors for blocks and bringing one hundred firemen to control the flames.[42] The bar owner was indicted for arson and insurance fraud; the site was not rebuilt until 2014.[43] In 1976 the Dream Palace, with considerable enlargement, opened in the old Dream Castle space.[44] Even before its official opening, the police stopped by to ask about "noise"—in this case a workman playing his drum set. The Dream Palace and the neighborhood slowly got used to each other.[45] The native music scene quickly blossomed there, with favorites like Lil Queenie and the Percolators, the Radiators, the Meters, and the Neville Brothers on stage. The "DP" was noted for legendary parties spilling into the street and surrounding neighborhood.[46] From 1980 to 1997, Theatre Marigny offered a mix of classic and unconventional plays at 616 Frenchmen.[47]

One of the modern Frenchmen strip's landmarks opened in 1982 at 626. Jason Patterson had been the director of the ABBA foundation. He bought the building at 626, and his lessee, George Brumat, established the Snug Harbor, with Patterson booking the acts.[48] Unique to the strip, Snug Harbor featured modern jazz. Among the Snug's early artists was the son of the parish district attorney. The novelty of "the D.A.'s kid" drew a curious local crowd, later evolving to a worldwide fan following, for Harry Connick Jr.[49]

The Frenchmen strip gathered momentum. In 1985 Brazilian Adgenor "Adé" Salgado moved his Quarter coffee shop to the corner of Frenchmen and Chartres, the old site of Reboul's grocery. Salgado painted the building lively yellow and blue, a bright beacon at the crossroads. Poetry, improv comedy, plays, and chess were offered. Eventually, Café Brasil got a liquor license and morphed from coffee shop to nightclub.[50]

In 1990 the former Dream Palace became the Café Istanbul, across the street from Café Brasil. Café Istanbul featured Middle Eastern food, belly dancing upstairs, and Latin music downstairs.[51] The two clubs hosted international bands and along with the other venues created a synergy up and down the strip.[52] The street became *the* late-night/wee hours/until daybreak entertainment venue.[53] Now music fans strolling up and down the three blocks were assured they would find at least one set to their liking, whether the performers were well-established favorites or brand-new talent. The last wholesaler left the strip in 1999.

Stores and restaurants were also part of the strip's ambience. Just two doors down from Café Brasil was Judy's Collage. It featured vintage clothing, such as old band uniforms, cheerleader outfits, hats, accessories, and an indescribable mix of other things. It was a prime resource for costuming, and its closure was another tear in the retail landscape.

On the other side of Chartres, at 600 Frenchmen, was Faubourg Marigny Art and Books, founded in 1978 by Episcopalian minister Tom Horner. FAB was the first openly gay bookstore in town. In its narrow aisles, hours could be passed rummaging through an eclectic mixture of the obscure, the academic, and the titillating.

Doctors and lawyers still had offices on the street. The New Orleans AIDS Task Force (NOAIDS) was at one end, and at the other end, in the same space as Bernard Marigny's last home, Boys' Town offered shelter for runaways. Retail experiments came and went as the kaleidoscope spun.[54] In 1990 black entrepreneurs Cecil Kaigler and Curtis Moore opened the Praline Connection at 542, offering the eponymous delicacy as well as classic New Orleans dishes like red beans and rice.[55]

Into this rollicking scene clomped the heavy, unsteady boots of the city. The strip was not zoned for live music, but, as is true with so many other city laws, clubs could be grandfathered in if they could prove they had live music for a certain number of years. Thus Snug Harbor was home free, but Cafés Brasil and Istanbul were not. In January 1992, both clubs were cited for illegal live performances. The usual finger pointing ensued, along with the usual professions of ignorance about permits from the owners and contentions from the district's council representative, Jackie Clarkson, that no regulatory activity had happened up to that point.[56] After a neighborhood meeting, where both support for the clubs and complaints about their effect on the Triangle were aired, temporary permits were granted.[57] But the truce proved short. In July of that year, the city decided to have a massive sweep of bars, looking for underage drinking, narcotics, and required permits. Café Istanbul's owner was arrested due to the presence of three underage drinkers, and a musician was roughed up by the police.[58]

At the dawn of the twenty-first century, two clubs, d/b/a/ in the old Theater Marigny space at 616 and the Spotted Cat at 623, opened close by Snug Harbor. The d/b/a club had music from its opening. Demand from the fans and a plentitude of bands looking for gigs led the Spotted Cat to follow suit and feature live music. The Frenchmen strip's musical party scene shifted to a higher gear of synergy.[59]

The continuous pitched battle over permitting, the catch-as-catch-can enforcement, and the complaints of residents led to the 2004 creation of the Frenchmen Street Arts and Culture Overlay District.[60] The district includes the 400–600 blocks of the Frenchmen strip, the 1400 block of Decatur, and the odd numbers of the 400 block and 501 Esplanade. The non-Frenchmen lots recognized the growth of the entertainment constellation to include such venues as Checkpoint Charlie's lounge and laundry at 501 Esplanade, which wraps around to the very short 1400 block of Decatur, which includes Dragon's Den.[61] The district specifies that no more than four thousand square feet, including storage and other nonrevenue space of the interior, be devoted to performance in any one venue. It further specifies a ratio of 20 percent cocktail lounges and 80 percent other uses for the district. Restaurants can have no more than a three-piece unamplified band.[62]

As approved, the district's detailed provisos are believed to have been driven by the FMIA, in an attempt to rein in the growth of bars.[63] New Orleans preservationists know from bitter experience that despite nearly ninety years of zoning, amendments, commissions, and laws, businesses will still stretch the restrictions beyond the breaking point, like the burlesque queen who busts her brassiere and neglects to cover up because the audience loves it. The business argument is cogent. The public wants more and more entertainment; the city usually turns its head at violations; sales and tax money comes in and everyone gets something. Besides, the argument continues, the city has tacitly abandoned any hopes for new industry and placed all its economic bets on tourism. Because of the numerous grandfather clauses, the zoning ordinances are sometimes perceived as an effort to keep non-native investors out, while favoring long-established venues. By 2007, bars and restaurants were the predominant businesses of the strip.

The overlay district compromise neither suited all parties nor prevented all conflicts.[64] The so-called 80/20 rule quickly became farcical. A 2012 survey found that about 50 percent of the street's entertainment places and restaurants were de facto cocktail lounges.[65] In other words, a place would be permitted as a restaurant and obtain a liquor license and then operate more or less as a bar while using amplified music and seating customers on the sidewalk just outside of open doors and windows.[66] The overlay district worked in favor of existing businesses, some of which were in that 50 percent. Newcomers had to abide by the regulations verbatim and had to contend with the neighborhood association's stance of "not one more bar."

One of the newcomers was Bamboula's, which in 2012 sought to open a club in the vacant former Laborde Printing building at 514. The owner averred that he had attempted to lease the building for some time without any offers and, going with the flow of the modern strip, decided to operate a nightclub.[67] The owners started work twice without permits, and the city shut them down each time.[68] Apparently the applicants did not do their homework, since their application to the City Planning Commission proposed a venue far outside the limits the overlay district imposes.[69] The first revision was also in excess of the four-thousand-square-foot performance space limit. Bamboula's spokesperson stated that they did not want to create "a giant music club."[70] Strenuous opposition from neighbors, including other bars,[71] and from the FMIA[72] caused the City Planning Commission to reject the first application[73] and forced a severe scaling back of the plans.[74] The downscaled Bamboula's opened as a "restaurant-theater" in October 2013 and earned the ire of its commercial and residential neighbors by using street barkers and large to-go drinks.[75] Not even two years later, Bamboula's went back to the City Planning Commission asking to be permitted as a cocktail lounge with live entertainment, while exceeding the four-thousand-square-foot rule.[76]

Here is a classic example of the tension between limits on commercial expansion in formerly residential areas and those who espouse expansion. Hearings are held, compromises reached, ordinances passed, and platitudes offered. Then club developers flow under and around the regulations, consider fines part of the cost of doing business, and after getting a foot in the door, disregard the limits of their permits, hopefully long enough to become grandfathered in. Meanwhile, the city pleads lack of resources to enforce all these noble ordinances while encouraging the arrival of more and more tourists.

The Marigny is all too well versed in the Quarter's struggles with commercialization of formerly residential subneighborhoods and the cynical games that rolled over Quarter residents' objections. So it is not surprising that neighborhood associations, and some individuals, wary after so many rounds of this charade, reflexively oppose *any* development or redevelopment, even if the new business would benefit otherwise unloved blocks and save abandoned old buildings.

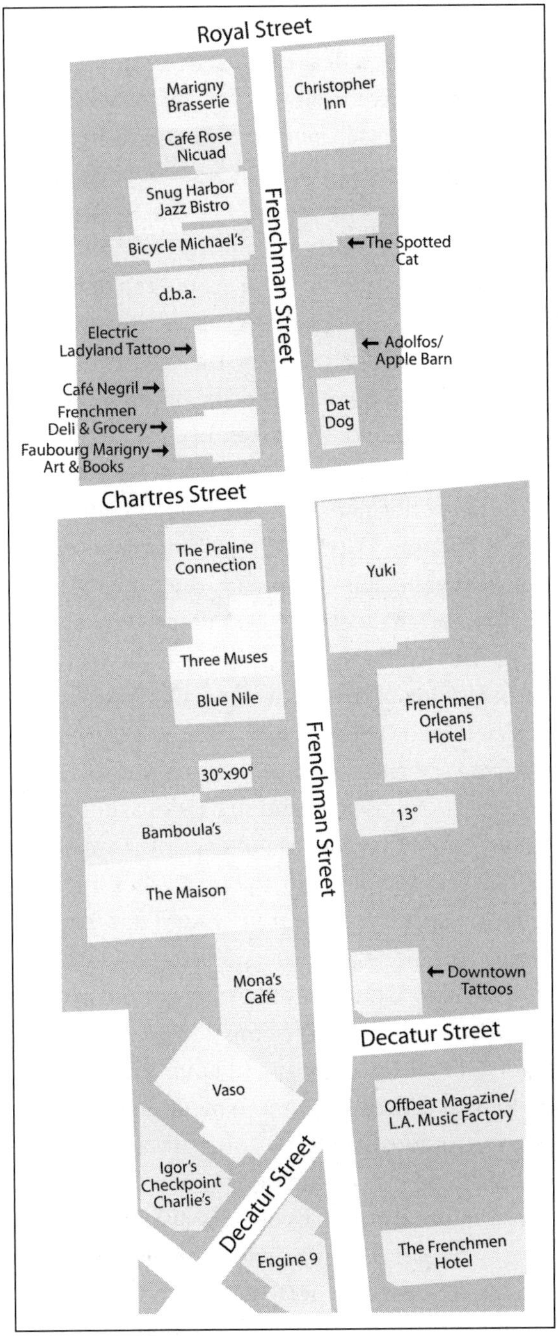

The Frenchmen Strip, 2016. Illustration by Amanda Glenn.

The city's love of street performers, who sang, tapped, mimed, and juggled, rarely ran smooth either. In the 1960s, street musicians were officially banned in the Quarter but were allowed to play in Jackson Square on Sunday afternoon, occupying certain benches near the cathedral.[77] The city now specifies licenses for performers and forbids street performers in the Quarter and especially on Bourbon between Canal and St. Ann.[78]

In reality, street buskers continue to ply their trade, district or license be damned.[79] Children who should be in school tap dance for money, and drifters strum and sing with open guitar cases on the tourist thoroughfares. In all the dealings with street performers, the city's evolving approach was that everything in the *tout ensemble* should be reviewed, regulated, licensed, and in any way possible, taxed through fees. In effect, it promoted the equivalent of a Vieux Carré Commission for the nonarchitectural aspects of the tourist landscape. No performer should be too loud, too scruffy, or heaven forbid, not "family friendly." No "legitimate" business should be impeded or annoyed in any way. Insofar as possible, the tourists' street experience would be via "legitimate" channels and their perceptions shaped by the tourist authorities. In the two decades that bridged the end of the twentieth century and the beginning of the twenty-first, this viewpoint was applied to "legitimate" musicians and venues as well. Getting a gig in a club was a comfortable step up from the curb of Royal or a doorstep on Decatur Street. If it didn't offer riches, it promised an end to hassles about permits and being told to "move along" until the law was out of sight. As more clubs sought to offer "authentic" New Orleans music, the market for live performers blossomed. As the live music played, the tourists and new residents drank and tapped and tipped.

One might think New Orleans would treasure and even coddle its musicians, especially those who represent the unbroken chain of jazz lineage, from Buddy Bolden, to Jellyroll Morton, to Louis Armstrong, to Pete Fountain, to Deacon John and Tuba Fats, not to mention the thousands of other talents that keep the famous jazz scene going, decade after decade. But the city and its musical children have traditionally had a rough relationship. The black jazzmen entertained the patrons of Storyville, brought the middle-class tourists to the big clubs of the Quarter, and miraculously preserved their traditions long enough for connoisseurs like William Russell and Larry Borenstein to create some institutional memory.[80] But until the mid-1960s blacks could not perform with whites, nor could they drink with a white admirer.[81]

Black jazzmen were suspected of dealing drugs, seducing white women, and tempting white teenagers into rebellion; and sometimes, yes, these things happened. White jazz musicians had a somewhat easier time, due to the passport of their skin. However, they still carried the old actors' and troubadours' stigma of sexual license and defiance of bourgeois convention.

In New Orleans' official revulsion against "beatniks and hippies," white rock 'n' rollers were only grudgingly welcomed. Famous out-of-town acts were not immune to hassles, as the Grateful Dead discovered in a well-publicized bust in 1971.[82] Even as social and official attitudes began to soften toward the end of the twentieth century, New Orleans musicians, of all colors and genres, still struggled. In the all-encompassing view of "official tourism," musicians are a commodity like the low-wage club workers of the Quarter.[83]

The dynamics of the Frenchmen Street club scene and the regulatory framework meant that some clubs left doors open and charged no cover fee, letting music wash out to be enjoyed for free by strolling tourists. Other clubs kept their doors closed and charged covers. In many cases, musicians received a portion of the bar sales (the "bar ring") plus tips.[84] Few musicians were satisfied with this arrangement, and most perceived that tourists thought that all New Orleans music was "free" for the taking, like a shared file downloaded from the Internet. After all, tourists could buy drinks at one bar, take them on the street in go-cups, and stand outside another club, listening to music in which they had no investment. The band's share of the bar ring is rarely, if ever, as much as a set fee funded by a cover charge. Many clubs are reluctant to charge a cover, for fear of driving tourists to other, no-cover clubs just down the street. Observers realize that musicians find it hard to take any collective action, when hungrier players, desperate for any gig, will step up to play for the bar ring or even just for tips. Judging from experience with the zoning overlay and other flaccid city regulations, government intervention does not seem to be an answer.[85]

Beyond the debate over music and noise, other attempted crackdowns created New Orleans' own version of a culture war. Over the centuries, city hall was always persecuting some social group, be it ambitious Américains, free people of color, Germans and Irish, freed slaves, gays, or "hippies." Now, post-Katrina, with the town again standing proudly on its own feet, was the messy, chaotic gumbo of native culture going to be pasteurized by regulation? It was proposed that vendors at second line parades would need permits and the colorful and clever street wallpaper of flyers announcing music gigs and happenings would be forbidden. In short, the city establishment attempted to rein in the exploding music scene not by actually enforcing zoning, with its attendant political consequences, but by schoolmarming the musicians and vendors, who had few resources. Fortunately, these nanny regulations were withdrawn. A loud, angry parade of brass musicians invaded city hall to make it clear that they were not going to be regulated off the streets.[86]

In an ironic turn of events, it was soon the Frenchmen strip club owners who were complaining about "noise." There are various programs to give young musicians band instruments. New Orleans always needs marching bands for every occasion, and raising up new crops of marching musicians is a high priority in a city with few opportunities for young African Americans. One of these bands, the Young Fellaz, gathered in front of the vacant former Café Brasil and began to beat and blow, rivaling the volume of the music pouring out of the clubs. The band could be heard on the other side of Elysian Fields and over in the lower Quarter. The club owners were furious at the unlicensed, uninvited, and uncontrolled competition. A restaurant in the old Judy's Collage space gave up after negotiations with the band over volume and hours went nowhere. A conference brokered by the Music and Culture Coalition of New Orleans (MaCCNO) with the Young Fellaz was fruitless.[87] The frustrated businessmen realized that calling the police was futile since the spectacle of the police arresting the band for merely playing music on the banquette was too much to stomach.[88] An uneasy tolerance prevailed, and the band played on.

Frenchmen Street was the first Marigny flashpoint of commercial versus residential development in New Orleans' tourist-centric economy. Like a flare ascending to the heavens for all to see, it foreshadowed similar struggles across the entire neighborhood.

15

On and On and On

The New Year of the New Orleans' calendar begins with the start of Carnival season, Twelfth Night, on January 6. Varying with the date of Easter and, hence, Mardi Gras, Carnival season can be long or short. The year 2000 saw a long Carnival season, ending on a warm March 7, with brilliant sunshine.

The turnover of the calendar was welcomed as a fresh start for a town weary from its long slide down into poverty, crime, and endless self-delusion. Most of the Society of St. Anne, always noted for inventive costumes, adopted—whether by agreement or coincidence—the theme of flowers, and a fantastic garden blossomed along Royal Street. Other clever costumes included a human sink with a string of pearls for water, astronomical bodies, and an endless variety of other designs.

The 2000 census showed a very slight drop in the Marigny's population from 1990. However, nearly a third of the black population of 1990 was gone, with that group's numbers lower than those in any census since 1950. The Triangle lost 11 percent of its population, but the Rectangle gained a little over 3 percent. This is contrasted with the city at large, which lost about 2.5 percent of its population in the preceding decade and was about 67 percent black, 27 percent white, and about 7 percent other ethnicities.[1]

Society of St. Anne Parade, 2016. Courtesy of Scott Deweese.

A Last Bell Tolling

Across New Orleans, Catholic congregations were declining. The faithful of Sts. Peter and Paul, on Burgundy at Marigny, were dwindling and getting on in years. The church school closed in 1993. The same story was true of the Annunciation Church, once the Marigny plantation chapel, at Marais and Mandeville Streets in New Marigny; St. Cecilia, at France and North Rampart at the downriver edge of Bywater; and St. Vincent De Paul, on Dauphine Street in upper Bywater. In early 2001 the archdiocese closed all but St. Vincent de Paul and consolidated the remaining congregations into that church, renaming it Blessed Francis X. Seelos. The parishioners of the closing churches, many elderly and no longer drivers, were outraged, but the decision stood.[2] The churches that saw so many baptisms, first communions, weddings, and funerals down the generations were no more. Sts. Peter and Paul stood empty, brooding and graffiti-scarred, for nearly two decades.

The Future Begins Now

The twenty-first century did not arrive in New Orleans until August 28, 2005. On that day, the first outliers of Hurricane Katrina were felt in New Orleans. A mandatory evacuation was ordered, but many people in the Quarter, Marigny, and Bywater—all on the "Sliver by the River"—elected to stay. After the initial windstorm, the city sighed with relief. The damage was no worse than it had been in other storms across time. Then the levees on the canals broke, flooding low-lying parts of the city and displacing thousands in a tsunami of misery, compounded by official ineptitude.

Many in the Marigny evacuated after the magnitude of the disaster became evident. A few stayed, without electrical power. Some who had left returned in secret, evading roadblocks and hiding from the National Guard, who might drag them off to the Superdome, the shelter of last resort.[3]

Those who did stay lived a bizarre waking dream of hot sunshine in the day and utter darkness at night as the moon waned at month's end. A few had generators, with carefully rationed gasoline, to power tools and radios during the day and air conditioners at night. The complete darkness meant that people could stand next to each other without realizing it until their presence was betrayed by sound or smell.[4] The remaining Marigny residents were concerned about roving bands from the flooded areas, who might be looking simply for food and water or seeking to loot, particularly guns.[5]

A Red Cross station was set up at the vacant site of the St. Aloysius School on Esplanade at North Rampart to hand out food and bottled water. Although city water was running, it was deemed unusable except for flushing toilets, so every drop of potable water, included melted ice, was precious.[6]

Most of the Marigny's physical damage consisted of the usual dislodged roof slates, downed trees, and a few shattered windows. A few Marigny buildings sustained serious damage. A three-story house at Port and North Rampart took a direct hit from a toppling tree. Unknown to the owner, an interior load-bearing wall had been removed in years past, and the shock wave from the impact knocked the brick wall off the Port Street side.

By late October, power had been restored to the Marigny, and the work of repair began in earnest as tools and air conditioners whirred to life. One of the buildings that sustained serious damage was Robert's Fresh Market on St. Claude, formerly the original Schwegmann's supermarket. The store was heavily damaged by the storm and looted.

One of the Marigny's enduring strengths was its walkability. Nearly everything could be obtained with short strolls. Even as the retail venues of Frenchmen and St. Claude vanished, Schwegmann's and later Robert's were always there for residents to "make their groceries." The store's departure worked a serious hardship on residents without cars, who now had to depend on the kindness of friends or buses to take them to stores farther afield.

Years passed as Robert's, the insurer, and the Schwegmanns fought a three-ring battle royal over insurance proceeds and responsibility. In 2013 Robert's finally prevailed in court.[7] The supermarket reopened at the end of 2017.

The St. Anne parade of Fat Tuesday 2006 reflected sorrow over the storm and anger at governmental ineptitude. Many costumes featured portions of the ubiquitous blue tarps that covered leaking roofs for months after the hurricane. "Has any one gotten your Road Home Money yet?" asked one of the parade leaders. "No!" dozens chorused back.

The fact that nearly all housing on the Sliver had survived spurred a brief but intense period of realty speculation. The reasoning went that people who had lost houses in the flooded parts of town would be eager—and able—to buy Quarter, Marigny, and Bywater properties. Real estate agents glibly told owners to spruce up their houses and they could easily get $200 or more a square foot from buyers desperate to stay in New Orleans at almost any price. For a year after the storm, this was pretty much true, as premiums of 20 to 30 percent were asked—and sometimes received.

By 2007 the bubble burst. Some insurance companies compounded the suffering by refusing to pay claims or canceling policies on houses that had been repaired.[8] Insurance rates all across the Gulf Coast went up as some companies left the market, forcing the highest-risk properties and poorest owners into state-run programs. The state-administered Road Home program got off to a slow start and then was hindered by the Bush administration's political meddling.[9] Slowly, house prices came down, albeit not to their prestorm levels.[10] Rents did shoot up and, with some neighborhood variation, have remained higher than before the storm.[11]

Reeling from the abrupt changes, the background hum of New Orleans' anxiety got louder. It was hushed, to a degree, by the town's old handmaiden, liquor, by prescription antidepressants, and for some middle-age residents, by a renewed use of cannabis, once put away as parenthood and careers replaced youthful revelry. Not all the shock and stress could be tamed with Mother's Little Helpers, as a series of horrific poststorm crimes showed.

Waking Nightmares

The concept of God is in all of us, and so is the concept of Satan. The Old Deceiver, Old Scratch, the Dark Angel is in our cells, occasionally coalescing into one easily recognizable monster in a Third Reich or slipping out of a milquetoast in a moment of rage only to draw back and disappear.

The careless have always been easy victims in the Crescent City, and for many years it was chiefly due to alcohol dulling the senses, making the illusion of freedom seem limitless until one dropped off the edge. Then sometimes the Dark Angel would appear. The Dark Angel could be a fellow partier, a professional mugger awaiting the drunks around Sanctity Row, or a repressed psychopath who suddenly found an outlet.

A tragically more enduring visitation takes the forms of young black men who prey on each other for turf, respect, and control over the drug trade. Over and over the scene repeats. The teenagers lying in the street, covered in sheets; the detectives setting out bullet markers; and the mothers, grandmothers, and aunts wailing in grief and disbelief. In these cases, the easy, facile explanations of gang wars seemed obvious.

Once in a while, the Dark Angel made a New Orleans visit whose cause was unexplainable by handy stereotypes and clichés. These inexplicable moments struck even more fear into people simply trying to survive.

In the early years of the 1900s, the Axman hacked Crescent City citizenry into a panic with grisly murders and assaults but was never apprehended.[12] The Hammer Murderer killed three gay men in the 1980s and also vanished out of the reach of justice.[13]

Just after Katrina, a deliveryman for a Quarter grocery killed and partially ate his girlfriend in their apartment on North Rampart. After a subsequent night of drugs, booze, and hookers, he jumped from a high roof, taking his reasons with him.[14] In the waning days of 2006, Dinerral Shavers, a popular musician and teacher, was shot in a dispute concerning his stepson.[15] Twenty-four hours of January 4–5, 2007, saw six murders in the city. One of these touched the very core of the Marigny ethos.

That Thursday morning, a black man forced the front door of a guesthouse on North Rampart Street and tried to get into a guestroom. The guests barricaded themselves in the room, and the intruder fled. As the innkeeper and the rattled visitors spoke with police, gunshots rang out from the end of the block. The assailant had forced his way into the home of a white filmmaker and her physician husband. Saying nothing, he shot the woman to death and wounded the doctor, who was protecting the couple's young child.[16] Then the gunman vanished, never to be identified.

The shock the Marigny felt is hard to portray in words. Ink on a page does no justice to the stabbing mixture of surprise, sorrow, and anger the neighborhood felt. Helen Hill was an experimental filmmaker and taught the craft. Her husband, Paul Gailiunas, worked in clinics doctoring the poor. They were, as many friends said, the kind of people that the Marigny should attract and retain.

As a historian, I am supposed to, and I can, portray events dispassionately. But I was pierced also by this terrible event. The now-former innkeepers are my close friends; I have stayed in that guestroom often and considered that place my home in the Marigny. I had walked by the scene of the murder many times, seeing the family come and go, and that block was my center of New Orleans' gravity.

As with the Louisiana Pizza Kitchen murders in the French Quarter in 1996,[17] the bloody days of early 2007 sparked a large rally at city hall. Mayor Nagin, who had worn out his welcome with poststorm gaffes, was not allowed to speak.[18]

A small memorial appeared on the stoop of the little house where Hill and Gailiunas had lived. Signs, ribbons, and candles expressed sorrow for the family, father and child having fled out of state. In time, only the stubs of the candles remained, waxy disks slowly washed away as the tears of the angels fell.

Clawing for rationales, the press dared not publish the currents of thought circulating in the white community. The old accommodation of shared working-class life, bridging most racial divides, has almost evaporated in New Orleans. The tide of gentrification now brought middle-class whites, some from out of town and thus unequipped with native knowledge, into neighborhoods with a residual black poor and working-class cadre. The explanation for these nonrobbery, black-on-white crimes is simmering black rage. Fury surged from the loss of African Americans' three-decade grip on city government, regret at the diaspora of so many blacks displaced by Katrina, never to return, and barely muted anger at white incursions into neighborhoods majority black for many decades. The slowly gentrifying St. Roch area saw assaults by groups of young blacks on whites who lived and worked in the neighborhood.[19] The old economic divisions of the town, with each stratum "in its place," were jumbled as formerly worthless properties were snapped up and rehabilitated into marketability. "In New Orleans, wealth is right up in the face of poverty," observes a native friend.

The 2010 Census

Perhaps no census has been so eagerly awaited as the first post-Katrina count. As expected, it showed a nearly 30 percent drop in New Orleans' population since 2000. The Marigny showed a loss of 162 people, or about 5.7 percent, compared to 2000's numbers. African Americans made up 5 percent less of the neighborhood's numbers, while Asians, Native Americans, and Hispanics all registered small gains. There were about 3 percent fewer households and an increase in vacant housing units of almost 4 percent. There was a slight decrease in people living in officially defined poverty, and about 6 percent less than discovered for New Orleans itself. This makes an interesting contrast with the wages earned per month by Marigny residents, which were less than those of the city as a whole in the two lowest bands, but over 16 percent higher in the highest category, $3,333 a month or more.[20]

Brian Godfrey, in his landmark 1984 study of San Francisco's "nonconformist communities,"[21] identified three stages of the life cycles of these enclaves. As draped over the Faubourg Marigny:

The first stage, a "bohemian influx," occurred in the 1970s, thanks to Eugene Cizek, Lloyd Sensat, aggressive real estate agents, gay men longing to be homeowners, and counterculturists escaping the scrutiny of the French Quarter.

The second stage, a "middle-class transition," appeared unevenly as the city's economy sputtered and the scythe of AIDS swung in the mid- and late 1980s.

The third stage, "bourgeois consolidation," was well underway at the turn of the century. Outside investors arrived to bid on properties, Katrina drove up rents with probable permanency, and the Marigny's population was shifting from New Orleans' austere vision of the petit bourgeois to the national scale of upper middle-class strata. The first wave of Marigny gentrifiers had been mainly gay men whose children were surrogates with four paws and tails. Some of the millennial new arrivals had human children and displayed parental sensibilities not seen in the Marigny for a generation.

The Marigny meanwhile was benefiting, or suffering, depending on your point of view, from national exposure. It was touted as a new hipster destination, which attracted out-of-towners, some with serious money or personal sweat to invest, some to buy pieds-à-terre, and some who just drifted in to live on the streets. Some of the Marigny's older residents, survivors of the first wave of revival, mistrusted the arriviste hipsters and despised the street people. They called the hipsters the "fedora brigade," after the headgear then in fashion. Some of the new hipster investors turned into buyers, owners, and neighbors. Some turned into absentee landlords and part-timers. Just as in the Quarter, remotely owned properties became unwelcome, with strangers coming and going, absorbing scarce parking and leaving trash behind.

Several former commercial buildings and churches waited to be roused from slumber and reanimated. "What a shame," muttered neighbors as they walked past moldering, silent churches and factories. Then people arrived with plans and money for these places, and the neighbors were stunned.

Part of the opposition to renovation of old commercial and church buildings stemmed from the "romance of ruins," which formed the basis of early Quarter tourism[22] and the loathsome post-Katrina disaster sightseeing tours. Impressionistic, noble, and sad in their dishabille, the old factories and churches lent an antique patina to the Marigny's *tout ensemble* that some found fascinating. That these could be repurposed as homes, performance venues, stores, or condos seemed an insult, like stripping the yellowed glaze off an Old Master. This romantic swoon did not allow opportunities for other people, and it ignored the many squatters who roosted in these properties year after year. In fact, these romancers of ruins had no plans or resources of their own and usually were galvanized into action by someone else's concepts for the buildings. Of course, there is the ever-present fear, from experience in the Quarter, that a business could be permitted as something benign and then morph into a loud nightclub in the middle of a residential neighborhood. The city might issue injunctions, but these could be countered with lawsuits, and the process would drag on for years, making a mockery of the entire zoning and permitting process, as we have seen on Frenchmen Street.

Flashpoints sparked where residents had thus grown comfortable with the abandoned, silent buildings. No neighbors were the best kind of neighbors, so the reasoning went. Now strangers showed up, investing heavily to restore the buildings. Some of the early gentrifiers forgot that, once, *they* had been the interlopers in a Marigny much more populous than it is today.

Holy Trinity Catholic Church needed major repairs by the mid-1990s, and attendance had declined markedly. It was deconsecrated and sold off in 1997.[23] The larger stained glass windows were removed, but the rosette windows high up still bore the names of the old German families who worshiped there, including the Gross family of bakers. The owner let the building fall into further disrepair, and the lawn often grew so high as to hide a group of statues. In 2011 two men from San Francisco bought the place and began the long journey of fixing it up.

On the next block sits the Mardi Gras Zone, an always-open store that offers groceries, Carnival goods, and a kitchen with hot food. Some of the Zone's neighbors didn't like it because, for one, it was not a full-service discount grocery like the long-lost Schwegmann's/Robert's, and two, young people hung around. Young adults of no apparent means, as all middle-aged bourgeois busybodies know, are intrinsically dangerous and must be discouraged from frequenting "nice neighborhoods." The rebirth of the old church concerned these neighbors, who feared it would create a new nexus for young street people in symbiosis with the Mardi Gras Zone. A few circulated a petition urging the FMIA to intervene; a counterpetition drew far more supporting signatures.[24]

The Marigny Opera House was finally licensed as a nondenominational church of the arts and features its own ballet company and performances by choirs and chamber musicians.

Although it seemed that peace would prevail with the Opera House's neighbors, in reality, a faction was just waiting to pounce. The New Orleans Fringe Festival of 2014 featured fifty performances at various venues, and one was the Opera House. On November 16, 2014, singer Solange Knowles, sister of superstar Beyoncé Knowles, was married at the Opera House. The neighbors were perturbed by the crowds and traffic, and probably by the presence of so many people of color. The city was tipped off, and a misunderstanding arose about the validity of permitting for the event. Just before Fringe Fest, the city issued an injunction closing the Opera House. A team of twelve inspectors swarmed over the building looking for code violations, a safety theater performance to which major tourist venues in the Quarter are never subject. Only minor issues, like exit signing, were found, and the Opera House reopened.[25]

Not every rehabilitation was greeted with resistance. The old Sts. Peter and Paul Church is currently being reconstructed into condos and a performance space. In general, its neighbors heartily approve the rescue of the old monument, especially with its ample off-street parking.

Another historic church was Second Methodist at 2525 Burgundy. The neo-Gothic, crenelated structure dating from 1907 ceased to be a church in 1984.[26] It was a private residence for several years and in 2016 became the Sanctuary Cultural Arts Center. The center features yoga, circus arts, performances, and visual arts.[27]

The New Orleans Triumph Baptist Church anchored the corner of St. Anthony ("St. Anntiny") and North Rampart from 1960 to 2014, when the building was sold and the congregation moved on. At this writing, it is being remodeled into a bakery and apartment.[28]

Not all Marigny churches have folded. The Spain Street Church of God in Christ (COGIC), on Spain between North Rampart and St. Claude, was established in 1964 on the site of a former Pentecostal church.[29] The Thompson Methodist Church on St. Roch between St. Claude and North Rampart has conducted services since 1867.

A Towering Rage

These one-block redevelopment tiffs were overshadowed—literally—by the largest and perhaps most ominous notion of gentrification. The Marigny's riverfront had been cut off from the public for decades. Unless you worked on the wharves, you probably knew little about the narrow strip on the other side of the levee wall. Passing down the river at night, the east bank of lower New Orleans looked less like a city than dark, almost empty country with ghostly trees outlined by streetlights, peeking over the wall.

As the docks saw less and less traffic, developers looked at the old wharf land covetously. Much was adjacent to abandoned industrial areas and had the immensely valuable asset of an unobstructed river view. The Marigny and Bywater have a large swath of this disused riverfront. In 2006 the Nagin administration, partnering with local developers and a team of design agents, launched the Reinventing the Crescent initiative. This reinvention included the Port of New Orleans' cession of maritime servitude from inactive wharves. The reinvented Crescent would include a number of public accesses, parks, and venues, and of course, commercial development. One of the stated purposes was to "show a 21st century design face" to the world, with conceptual sketches portraying buildings much like those of the London and Shanghai waterfronts.[30]

Redeveloping the riverfront became an obsession with developers and their political allies. At the same time, the city wrestled with a comprehensive zoning ordinance (CZO) that, it was hoped, would yield consistently appropriate zoning and an end to spot zoning born of cronyism. In 2012, ahead of the CZO's adoption, local developer Sean Cummings proposed a three-building complex, the Elisio Lofts, on Decatur Street and Elysian Fields, on the site of the former Dickey's Potato Chip factory, across from the power substation. One of these buildings was a seventy-four-foot tower, which the developer's website averred would be monumental, asserting that the three buildings together averaged forty-eight feet in height.[31]

Cummings had previously redeveloped the seventy-five-foot-high Rice Mill, built in 1892, on Montegut Street at the upriver edge of Bywater. Compared to traditional New Orleans rates, the Rice Mill rents are high, but the in-house amenities defray much of the sticker shock, and fetishized, lease-protected graffiti from squatter days adorns many units.[32] Now, Cummings sought to create another expensive enclave.

The height of the tower immediately became the bête noire of the piece. Cummings defended the height by citing nearby buildings that were similarly tall: the ugly substation across the street; the redeveloped Alden Mills building at 511 Marigny, at about fifty feet; and the 1984 Hotel de la Monnaie on Esplanade, at sixty-five feet. Another building cited in defense was the Christopher Inn, the nine-story senior citizen and low-income residence, built in 1972 on the sites of a library and a church wrecked by Hurricane Betsy.

The hulking Christopher Inn overlooking Royal Street and Washington Park never gets much love from Marigny preservationists, but it was built at the first glimmers of a revived Marigny consciousness, before the Historic District designation. The building may irritate, but its mission protects it from both hungry condo developers and revanchist aesthetes who would just as soon see it demolished and replaced with nothing, so as not to jostle their sensibilities. So, the Christopher Inn, protected by its human shield, is sui generis, and citing it as a precedent can't have helped Cummings's case.

The Vieux Carré's struggles with development, out-of-control tourism, political spot zoning, and unenforced regulations inform the stances of other neighborhood groups. Although the dynamics are not the same in each part of town, every neighborhood association tends to mimic the reflexive "not no, but hell no" mantra of Quarter groups.

Setting a precedent for a tall building was deemed doubly risky; the tower could have been cited in defense of even taller future buildings, and the unsigned CZO might have suddenly included height allowances matching the Elisio tower. A common fear was that the riverfront would soon be lined with a screen of tall buildings of trendy or bizarre designs, creating a dissonant backdrop to the old streetscape.

One supporting argument was that more rentals on the riverfront would reduce rental prices in the interior of the neighborhood. This argument was countered by the assertion that the very high rents of the proposed complex would have no impact on rents paid by working-class folks a few blocks away and that such a lux compound would attract more people of greater means who would drive the demand for even more grandiose developments.[33]

FMIA started a campaign, "Size Matters," to counter Elisio. Posters showing the tower looming over a typical Marigny skyline appeared. The City Planning Commission cheerfully acquiesced to the project, granting five variances, including one for height,[34] while the Historic District Landmarks Commission narrowly refused to give conceptual approval.[35]

The city council usually accedes to the wishes of each council member in matters of his or her district, and this comity ruled the fate of the Elisio Lofts. Councilperson Kristin Gielson Palmer asked the council to reject the height variance, and it did so. Cummings declined to accept a fifty-foot tower, and the proposal uttered its death rattle.[36]

However, as a group the developers had the last laugh, because the CZO as adopted in the spring of 2015 allowed for height bonuses of twenty-five feet in the Riverfront Overlay district in exchange for certain on-site amenities. This meant that new buildings in the district could build to eighty feet. The height bonus provision was not subject to public input, and a particular precedent was cited—the Rice Mills Lofts.[37]

The old Dickey's site, which is not included in the bonus plan, was bought by a hotel developer to build a four-story Hampton Inn, and the wary eyes of Marigny's home guard again turned to the riverfront.[38]

This controversy presented an interesting contrast. The Marigny, having been revived first by urban pioneers now verging on retirement, was deemed more resistant to change, while the Bywater, renovated by a younger generation, seemed more open to nontraditional development.

New Foodways and Folkways

Long before Katrina, most New Orleanians, raised for generations on supermarket food, ate a fairly typical American cuisine, with the city's signature dishes like red beans and rice, gumbo, crawfish, and the fancier Creole entrées reserved for special occasions. Yet when desired, all these foods were right at hand, in humble neighborhood eateries, famous restaurants, or just "ya mama's" kitchen.

Hubig's Pies at 2419 Dauphine survived the storm, although the damage forced it to concentrate on its fried, folded-over pies. These pies, the best-remembered product, were similar to offerings by nationwide companies, but their cachet of being created "at home" was another part of New Orleans' illusion of an independent ecosystem. The pies were heavy, with thick glazed crusts and gooey sweet filling. Lunchbox partners for generations, they were also perfect fodder for devotees of cannabis with the munchies or drunks looking to ballast liquor before taking to bed. There were defined styles of consumption. One was to nibble the fluted crust around the seam until the filling was exposed, like opening an "erster." Another style was to open the top of the package and eat the pie downward, so that the envelope, with founder Savory Simon's fulsome image, would protect the hand.

On July 27, 2012, New Orleans suffered another tear in the tattered cloakk of hometown sustenance when Hubig's bakery burned down.[39] Despite being offered space by the New Orleans Center for the Creative Arts (NOCCA) at 2800 Chartres and having the support of the neighborhood, Hubig's foundered due to indecision and did not return. The bakery's site was filled by condos.

Marigny's neighborhood bars served as gathering places for generations. New Orleans' tradition of round-the-clock taverns meant that you could get hot, if indifferent, coffee from your corner watering hole at 8:00 a.m., and many times it was free because the bartender needed it too and besides, he saw you every day at various hours. The bars didn't serve breakfast fare.

Coffeehouses had been plentiful in the city's past, but the pace of modern life had pushed them to the edge of extinction. The most famous, Café du Monde and the Morning Call, became tourist venues. The modern coffee shop era began in the city with PJ's Coffeeshop, founded in the Carrollton neighborhood in 1978. Community Coffee's CC's chain debuted in 1995, including a store on Royal in the Quarter. Coffeehouses as cool places to roost in the long summer heat, to recharge devices, to use WiFi, and to ballast caffeine with light food really emerged in the 1990s in the Marigny. One of the oldest was Flora's, across Royal Street from 2601. Flora's attracted a young, roadwise clientele, who could play chess or checkers, huddle on the narrow sidewalk, smoke, and socialize by the hour.

The Orange Couch, on Royal at Mandeville, a favorite of teleworking folk, is frequently visited by a free-range rooster. The Who Dat at Mandeville and Burgundy morphed from an elemental coffee shop to a full-service restaurant. Sidewalk tables draw a regular crowd each morning and afternoon, observing the renovation of the former Sts. Peter and Paul Church. The Cake Café on Chartres has a devoted following.

The coffee shops and the always-connected Internet life synergized each other. In a town famed for gregariousness, the shops allowed absorption in a screen or meeting the neighbors as one desired, outside of the customary bars and attendant all-day drinking and, until recently, smoking.

Tentacles of the outside world were felt in the decline of traditional New Orleans restaurants. No longer offering the customary red beans and rice on Mondays and fish on Fridays, with the usual menu suspects in between, these now catered to trendy national tastes. A perfect example was Schiro's, which still had a vestigial grocery from its heyday. For years its restaurant fare was dependable for New Orleans mainstays.[40] Then it went Indian/Thai as Silk Road, and its old laundromat, a valuable neighborhood resource, was converted to more dining space. Marie's Lounge on Burgundy, a favorite with mid-Marigny tipplers, featured pop-up restaurants. The old Gross bakery on Elysian Fields was occupied by an expanded Sukhoi Thai and endeared itself by remaining open on Fat Tuesday evening, when most restaurants don't want to deal with the bedraggled, staggering masses.

The storm had many surprising effects. One was the blurring of lines, long thought indelible, between cultures. Gays and straights have long co-existed in the Marigny, with generally cordial relations. With the exceptions I have already noted, these groups tended to stay in bars catering to their respective preferences. After Katrina, for reasons that are not entirely clear, straight people, and especially women, started frequenting bars traditionally the preserve of gay men. Perhaps, for women, the appeal was in a feeling of safety and the absence of straight men making sexual overtures.

The legal inability to exclude women clashed with some bar patrons' unease at sharing the formerly all-male cruising space with the other gender. This unease tended to be generational. Older men, who had come of age in a time of strict divisions between gay, lesbian, and straight bars, found women in gay bars hard to accept. Younger men, who had come out in a more liberal society, had no problem hanging out with a multisexual crowd. Both generations agreed that gawking, giggling, drunk bachelorettes on "zoo tours" were especially obnoxious and let the intruders know they were unwelcome, law be damned.

Charlene's closed in 1999, and a follow-on women's bar there folded soon after. A women's bar on Frenchmen, Rubyfruit Jungle, had a run of ten years.[41] As their bars evaporated, some lesbians also started coming to gay bars.

The drag world found new wings with more media attention and acceptance. The former Charlene's became JohnPauls (later, Mag's), a mixed show bar featuring drag revues nearly every weekend. The drag divas now often arrived with siblings and mothers—but rarely fathers—in tow, forming a cheering section for their lip-syncing sons as they took the stage in their other personas.

While no one wants a return to the balkanization of the Great Oppression, Marigny gays and lesbians have mixed feelings about straights cheek by jowl with them in bars, clubs, and other formerly all-gay settings. As these lines are written, there is an undercurrent of wanting to retain the hard-won "gay identity" of the Marigny, so it should not become submerged in a tide of heterosexual investors, hipsters, and nuclear families, however gay friendly.

Don't Tell Nobody

Renovators fixing up a double needed a revenue stream to make the gambit work, and after fixing up one side, would live in it while fixing up the other, then rent that side out. Some rentals were still let on the basis of friendship and tended to be priced below, and sometimes far below, market rates. These lucky few renters, not asked for credit reports or about criminal records, got to experience the traditional genteel poverty of "bohemia" that had been almost wiped out decades before. One old friend of mine lived at first on Marigny Street in half a house. As he skidded downward, he moved to an apartment next to the laundry on lower Elysian Fields, and finally to a friend's garage in the Rectangle, where he may have paid no rent at all before giving up and going home to Mississippi. *Requiesce in pace,* Joe.

As New Orleans' tourist trade shifted into high gear in the 1990s, property owners realized that their units need not sit empty for lack of a tenant. Real estate agents frequently mentioned the bed-and-breakfast (B&B) gambit as a way to help pay the mortgage. Those who earnestly sought licensing for a guesthouse were often stymied by the city bureaucracy and gave up trying to be legitimate, not to mention balking at fees the city demanded for bed-and-breakfasts, starting at $200 per year. Just as with apartments let to friends, some guestrooms were let to cronies for special events, with only cash or a dinner out in payment. Everything was kept on the quietus to avoid inflaming the neighbors or alerting the otherwise uninterested city government. The French Quarter was most notorious for illegal guesthouses, with some longtime lessees kicked out in favor of the overnight trade.[42] Before the Internet, these rooms were found by asking friends, real estate agents, or bartenders. As the Internet blossomed in the early 1990s, B&Bs could be found while sitting in one's hometown, be that Boise or Beijing. However, this meant that the B&B was visible to one's neighbors as well. Web services for B&B operators, like Airbnb and HomeAway, exploded.

A 2016 study of the city's short-term rental market showed that the Marigny/Bywater area had more Airbnb listings than any other studied neighborhood, more than double those of either the lower Garden District or the French Quarter. Of these listings, the great majority were for whole homes or apartments. A review of the study's data showed that as of April 2016, 148 Marigny short-term rentals were hosted by Airbnb and HomeAway. Additionally, 56 licensed B&Bs operated in the neighborhood, for a total of 204 short-term rental venues. Although these were well dispersed across the Marigny, the largest concentration was in the Triangle, with another large constellation in the Rectangle between Burgundy and Chartres.[43]

Even if Airbnb and its ilk vanished, Marigny apartments would be too pricey for all but the city's pinched middle class. In November 2017, Zillow listed fourteen Marigny apartments for rent, averaging about $1,460 per month,[44] out of the reach of most working-class people. Formerly, the high and low tides of the local economy dictated rents, whether it was the speculative prices just before the World's Fair of 1984 or the more realistic rents after the fair imploded. Global money is now a driving factor, as wealthy buyers from other states and countries bid for properties to buy and lease.[45]

The idea of the "hustle," gambits that bring in money outside of laws and regulations, is an ancient New Orleans tradition. At the government level, it is called corruption. Whether committed high or low, it is defended under the limitless aegis of New Orleans "exceptionalism." Governor Kerlerec and his erstwhile cronies did it in 1759. Kids tap-dancing on Bourbon Street, street people "flying signs" on upper Decatur, city officials crafting contracts for personal gain all do the New Orleans hustle. The short-term rental (STR) was now the middle-class turn at the dance. The repugnant post-Katrina "disaster tourism" that brought busloads of gawkers past canal breaches and ruined homes even had a part in the short-term rental hustle, allowing tourists to stay in "seedy, dangerous," but oh-so-"authentic" neighborhoods and then safely escape when the vacation is over.[46]

Their neighbors, those who were not in on the hustle themselves, despised the strangers coming and going, generating noise and trash. They especially hated the whole-house rentals operated by remote owners who had no stake in the neighborhood.[47] Owners of the legitimate B&Bs who paid their city fees gnashed their teeth at the perceived free rein of the unlicensed rentals.

The city was roused to interest, if not action, by a coalition of housing advocates and neighborhood watchdog groups and, above all, by the tantalizing prospect of more revenue. By the time city hall energized on the issue, thousands of unblessed B&Bs were in town, with the legal staff of big corporations like Airbnb to assist them.

The unlicensed B&B owners made countervailing points. First, with soaring mortgage and insurance costs, they needed the money. If the city has abandoned everything but a tourist economy, why should homeowners be denied their share of the tourism revenue? What was the difference, at least in economic legitimacy, between a musician working the curb of Royal Street and a homeowner peddling his wares on Airbnb? How else could homeowners hang on as insurance and property taxes escalated?

The question was asked, "Are homeowners responsible for creating or funding 'affordable' housing?" and by extension, "Are short-term rental operators guilty of gutting the supply of affordable housing?"

The answer to the first half of this contention is no. The city loudly claims to drive the availability of affordable housing through permitting of large projects that require some percentage to be "affordable," whatever that may mean. Yet the city has protected slumlordism for centuries, and tenants have little recourse in cases of lack of upkeep or flatly dangerous conditions. So *affordable* may not know *comfortable* or *safe* as companion adjectives.

The extended question is especially accurate in a city that has no renter protections of any kind and one where, anecdotally at least, longtime tenants have frequently been evicted in the name of greater profits. Therefore, the supply of "affordable" and desirable housing for long-term residents only slowly increases, while STRs eat away at the supply, which may never result in any balance.

The city was roused to act in late 2016. The City Planning Commission recommended against whole-house rentals as espoused by Mayor Landrieu. The city council, on October 20, 2016, voted with only one "nay" to legalize short-term rentals, with various restrictions to be codified, and enforcement specified, at a later date.[48]

After the council acted, the city cracked down, with varying success, on short-term rentals in the Quarter. The legalized (and some still illegal) rentals spread out over the rest of the city. In the Marigny, as of late 2017, one in ten residences was registered as a short-term rental through Airbnb, the highest ratio in the city. The competition for properties that could be rented drove assessed values, and therefore taxes, skyward even for people who simply wanted to stay in their homes. The sound of luggage wheels on the rippled old sidewalks now became a familiar part of the Marigny soundscape.[49]

Not long after the city formalized the short-term rental process, it became evident that those benefiting were not just homeowners trying to pay a mortgage. A March 2018 report by the Jane Place Sustainability Initiative found that slightly over 18 percent of STR operators controlled almost half the legal short-term rentals in New Orleans. Thus, corporate entities have essentially converted many apartments into hotel rooms.[50]

Condo development in the Marigny and Bywater was also spurred by the short-term rental boom. Some developers touted their new condos as "Airbnb compliant." The accelerating costs of the now-trendy central city area made downriver properties more desirable, and depicted them as affordable, compared to ultra lux properties upriver.[51]

Sounds and Furies

Just seventy years ago, the Marigny was awash in sound: children calling up and down the banquette, street vendors crying out their wares, mothers hollering at offspring, spouses and lovers quarreling through open windows, and musicians practicing their craft. Add to this the rumble and clang of the streetcars and the snorts of automobiles.

The innovations of television and air conditioning changed not only the indoor climate but the outdoor. Air conditioning demands shut windows and lays a blanket of white noise over the soundscape, drowning out awareness of the outer world. The streets became lonelier.

After Katrina, two distinct trends converged in the Marigny. New arrivals came to embrace their next frontier of urban living, and clubs wanted live music to entertain their clientele.

As more people came to central New Orleans from other cities, they moved for many reasons, often citing the "vibes," "authenticity," "funky culture," and other tokens of hipster discourse. They also brought their past domicile experience, often air conditioned and suburban, with them. When they moved into old buildings with hard plaster walls and no insulation, they were surprised that the "funky vibes" and "authenticity" could be heard indoors, even over the A/C. Also, perhaps the inside of people's heads got noisier as much of social life moved online.

After Katrina in 2005, New Orleans, amid its other struggles, wrestled with the issue of live music in clubs that either had never had it before or had simply professed ignorance of the need for the appropriate permit. Even before the storm, the city's bureaucracy had applied its historic lack of consistency to the issue, leading to live and recorded music playing for years without permits or a murmur from city hall and sudden, heavy-handed crackdowns on a few nightclubs that left owners and observers bewildered.[52]

Since the city's founding, police raids for any nominal reason normally indicated a lack of payoffs or that someone of influence had complained. The twilight of "no permits but no bust, this time" allowed clubs to operate at the sufferance of police and inspectors, creating a perfect opportunity for the collection of bribes. Now the NOPD glibly explained the raids as a fruit of "quality-of-life policing." But whose "quality of life"? Cosimo Matassa, one of the godfathers of modern New Orleans music, had this to say in 2004: "We [Matassa's Grocery in the Quarter] put a sign out about two years ago—one of those A-frame type of things—and two policemen, not one, two policemen show up—the 'quality of life' police. That was their title, and that's what they were doing. Telling us we can't put that sign up there. I asked them, I said, 'How many little old ladies are getting mugged while you two fools are here telling us to get rid of this sign?'"[53]

Post-Katrina, many clubs wanted to host live music, to cater to the throngs of young music lovers who had taken up residence and the jazz fans who considered New Orleans the Bethlehem of that genre. Jukeboxes and music videos were no longer much of a draw. The storm-tossed musicians were happy to have any gigs. The club owners felt, and rightfully, that they were contributing to the city's revival as it rose out of the muck and struggled to stand upright again.

Out-of-towners who moved in near new or long-established bars and clubs were dismayed to hear these places inside their homes. The clubs also brought cars to compete for scarce on-street parking and intoxicated ramblers who battered the *tout ensemble* with trash and petty vandalism. Thus, the prized "ambience" and "authenticity" were things the new homeowners wanted to leave outside, like a dog tied up in the yard because he is not trusted indoors.

Complaints not grounded in lack of bribes or offense of the powerful began to flow soon after the city reopened. On North Rampart, King Bolden's jazz club opened on the site of a former gay strip club that had used loud recorded music for years. King Bolden's liquor license was not grandfathered in and no live music permit could be had, so they were shut down. The president of a Quarter civic group stated that art galleries, not jazz clubs, were wanted on North Rampart.[54] These self-appointed keepers of taste—mainly white and wealthy—wanted businesses that would only attract "their kind" of people. Apparently, "their kind" might be found sipping wine while listening to a gallery owner extol the virtues of a costly painting. Blasts of music, now labeled "noise" from an open door or window, were averred to attract "undesirables," just as guitar strumming was deemed a threat to public order in Jackson Square in the 1960s.

Frenchmen Street was the original Marigny flashpoint of this conflict. Although the "strip" stopped at Royal Street, inebriated patrons still lurched, often boisterously, up Frenchmen to parking spots on Dauphine, Burgundy, and St. Claude or down Chartres to Elysian Fields.[55] Neighbors on the surrounding blocks, particularly longtime residents, were not amused by this parade. After all, they were the urban pioneers who had kept their blocks from decay during the lean years of the 1970s and 1980s and the city's decline in the 1990s. Throngs of noisy drunks leaving the Frenchmen strip reminded the residents all too much of upper Bourbon, with its loud mobs of soused youngsters.

The former 2601 club at Royal and Franklin, a bar since at least 1970,[56] became Mimi's in 2002.[57] The gay neighbors who had sustained 2601 for years dwindled, from the economy, from AIDS, and from sheer fatigue from putting up with New Orleans. The personalities of bars and their clienteles evolve, and Mimi's now attracted a younger, straighter, more music-oriented crowd, replacing the former patrons who used it as a gay socializing and cruising ground just steps from their homes.

The change of the bar's personality brought unlicensed loud live music, drunks spilling out onto the banquette, profane screams, and vandalism of adjacent residential property.[58] Mimi's had been twice denied live music permits, in 2004 and 2005, but continued. Like several other clubs, Mimi's was cited by the city in a 2012 crackdown on unpermitted music venues. In April 2013 five neighbors filed suit to stop the performances and abate the noise.[59] The club was granted a live music permit in September 2013,[60] but the suit pressed on, until the bar signed a consent judgment in July 2015. That judgment specified that Mimi's surrender its live music permit but may host live performances nine times a year, provided it receives special events permits.

The music community of New Orleans spun these crackdowns as capricious by the city and selfish and culturally ignorant by the complaining neighbors. Music, it was asserted, as New Orleans' vox populi, should be utterly free of restraint, regulation, and interference. Here is the shear point: the residents of the Marigny are getting older, and more have families. At the same time, it seems every neighborhood bar down through history, in turn having offered prizefights on radio, football on television, and gay anthems on the jukebox, now wants to be a nightclub. A younger culture is trying to nest in the middle of a graying, more conservative one. The neighbors of Mimi's believed, with ample justification, that Franklin might become another Frenchmen Street and wanted to take preemptive action to arrest uncontrolled change.

St. Claude and St. Roch

In the days when it was called Good Children, St. Claude served first as a common street of Bernard's original faubourg and the border with his Nouveau Marigny. Over the years, it had morphed from important commercial artery to tense dividing line between the gentrifying Marigny and its decaying younger cousin. The commercial scene changed from retailers to auto repair and beauty shops as stores fled to New Orleans East and other suburbs. St. Claude remained an important east-west highway, running from its origin as North Rampart Street in the Modern Creole Tremé to largely white "Yat" St. Bernard Parish: a voyage between cultures.

Yet the old buildings of St. Claude have good bones and were not forgotten. The Universal Furniture building at St. Claude and St. Roch had been closed for years when Katrina hit. The Fifth District police precinct, its headquarters destroyed, stayed there from late 2007 to the spring of 2011.[61]

Developer Pres Kabacoff, his companion, Sallie Ann Glassman, and their friends conducted a salon after Katrina to discuss recovery initiatives. The Universal Furniture store, which Kabacoff had rehabilitated for the police, was selected for a community-centered multipurpose offering, the New Orleans Healing Center (NOHC). As Kabacoff explained, "The mission of NOHC is to lead revitalization of a downtown corridor [St. Claude Avenue], provide healing services, products and services, and assure they are available to the diverse economic populations on either side of the corridor."[62]

The Healing Center opened in the spring of 2011.[63] It offered a yoga studio, a credit union, art gallery space, classrooms, a bookstore, the Fatoush restaurant, a food co-op, and a music venue, Café Istanbul, transplanted from Frenchmen Street. The St. Roch Market, after years of decay, was being renovated across St. Claude.

Even before the St. Roch Market was renovated, sitting in the Fatoush restaurant at sunset, watching the amber light caress the battered old market, it was easy to see revival on the street. People came and went, walking along casually, unlike the wary skulking of three decades before when I first visited the Marigny borderlands.

The Healing Center, like the Marigny Opera House, aroused the immune system of ruins romancers, who finger the worry beads of parking, noise, and crime at each new development. Café Istanbul in particular, as a performance space, fanned the usual fears. The FMIA and Café Istanbul signed a community benefits agreement (CBA) just before its opening in November 2011. The CBA included stipulations about noise, sales of alcohol, and especially, behavior in the parking lot, which nestles between an apartment building (the old Temperance Hall) and houses facing North Rampart.[64]

The alcohol clause decreed that the café could only open and sell beverages during performances, which meant that about 150 people entered and then left as a herd. Naturally, many socialized in the parking lot, creating the kind of late-night noise and litter the CBA was crafted to avoid. In September 2015 the café was cited as a public nuisance. The city tried to strangle Café Istanbul for five months,[65] as regulators required that music be inaudible outside the café, even at the outer door, and that the café fire employees who violated the rules. Café Istanbul and the city signed a consent decree in April 2016 without these onerous provisos, but it mandated the hiring of private security guards and recognition that performers loading or unloading and patrons entering or leaving were not loitering.[66]

The rest of the immediate St. Claude strip began to regrow businesses. Taking St. Claude to St. Bernard at night in the early 2000s, one saw block after dark block of shuttered stores and abandoned homes. Now the nighttime streetscape sparkled with brightly lit restaurants and galleries.

The neighborhood called New Marigny was beginning to see this revival, albeit in smaller increments. Crossing St. Claude, like crossing North Rampart from the Quarter, was deemed risky for many years. Currently, lakeward from St. Claude, crime, and the perception of danger, increases markedly. The desire to gentrify "uncharted territory" is tempered with the

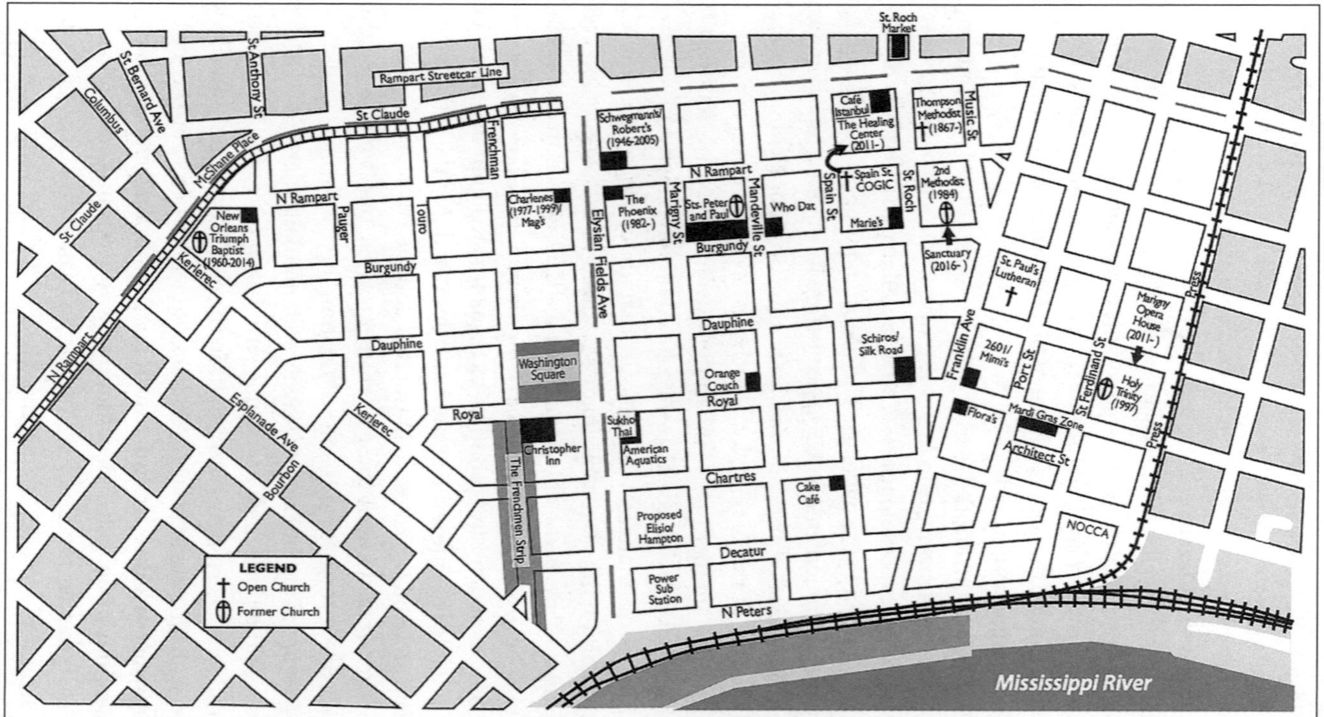

The Faubourg Marigny in the Twenty-First Century. Map by Amanda Glenn.

knowledge that the farther toward the lake side of the St. Roch/St. Claude nexus, the more the gain-to-pain ratio decreases.

A Coda and An Overture

The Faubourg Marigny, near the end of the second decade of the twenty-first century, is no longer on the front lines of traditional gentrification. That tide has passed on to other neighborhoods nearby. The factors attending the Marigny's rebirth in the 1970s—the gay artistic and commercial leadership, emigration from the costly and cranky Vieux Carré, and a pioneering generation of male couples—are unlikely to coalesce in any other New Orleans neighborhood again.

The Marigny is most definitely on the front lines of reuse of commercial and ecclesiastical buildings, and an interesting and sometime fractious relationship with older gentrification is evolving.

New Orleans' traditionally glacial changes often mislead to give the impression of no change at all, especially compared with the lifetimes of human beings. Katrina forced the town into a time machine, propelling the city's consciousness forward along the calendar. It was no longer the long daydream of white rule, nor was it the thirty-two-year run of the black city hall "franchise." Now it was possible to openly discuss long-standing issues, such as what role the ethnic majority—and economic minority—would play as the sands of the economy washed out from under it. How "outsiders" and the global economy would shape the "new New Orleans." If exceptionalism is still an excuse for lassitude and corruption. And, most sensitively, the real feelings the city's blacks and whites had for each other, stripped of code words and polite obfuscation.

A significant part of the city wants to go backward. To return to the day before the chain of disasters, to forget the old questions that demand new and urgent answers. To return to the collective illusion that bound the city into "exceptional" complacency. Even as some people try to claw backward in time and oppose any disruption of civic and social mythology, there is no going back. All the noblesse oblige and veiled power of the old-line Carnival organizations, all the earnest imprecations of the "reverends" vying for civic influence, all the federal funds and much-appreciated help from the outside world could not, and more importantly, *should not,* thrust the city backward into the long slide down of the two decades before the storm.

Every generation of New Orleanians has its own nostalgia, and the most celebrated is that for the "bohemian" life of the 1920s through the 1960s. The romantic mist of New Orleans, the comfortable decay just a notch above decrepitude, the easy living for young artists, writers, and poets, the creative synergy all derive from James Nolan's formula: "Three ingredients are essential for a bohemian community to take root and flourish—creative misfits, magic and cheap rent."[67]

This formula still holds true: New Orleans still hosts creative misfits, some native and some imported; magic is still to be found, though of a less overt kind than the tourist industry would suggest. The final part of the recipe—cheap rent—is rarely to be had. That omission means that the romanticized boho life of years past, as sampled by Faulkner, Williams, and countless other enchanteés, is slipping away. Gone, unless another economic collapse à la 1929 comes along and depresses all activity. That might help a small group of nostalgia-driven young whites, but it would push the black population of New Orleans even further, if that is possible, into poverty.

The Reinventing the Crescent initiative was inevitable, given the vast fallow land at river's edge, which will doubtless see high-rises, some palatable for local tastes and some not. If it is any comfort to the doubters, like most grand schemes hatched in New Orleans, the complete "reinvention" will probably never arrive intact. History predicts that only bits and pieces will survive feast-and-famine funding, changes of political will, legal challenges, and the eventual and inevitable public and commercial fatigue with the matter. As a point of reference, it took the city eighteen years to arrive at a contract to repurpose Clay Shaw's cenotaph, the old World Trade Center at 2 Canal Street.

Short-term rentals are probably the most significant agent of change the Marigny has seen since the onslaught of AIDS in the mid-1980s. The regulatory edicts are, like most high-sounding New Orleans ordinances, enforced with neither effectiveness nor consistency.

City hall's desire for control and revenue is colliding with fast-changing, web-enabled entrepreneurship and expertise, informed by global thinking. Everything the city can't, or won't, do is being done by people who can, and who are willing to ride out the reactionary process of fines and lawsuits long enough to bend the city to their will, or simply ignore ordinances and play "catch me if you can." The return of the streetcar to North Rampart, at least as far as Elysian Fields, heralds new opportunities—but for what?

Connecting the residential, reviving inner-city areas with the business district is favorable for commuters but also links tourists with the Marigny and beyond, bringing influences not yet fully understood.

Beyond the elaborate initiatives and the much-welcomed streetcar, the Marigny needs a full-service, mainstream grocery store at the old Robert's/Schwegmann's location. The other neighborhood grocery offerings are all very well, but there must be a means for people to buy basic food without paying the tariff for "organic" or designer foodstuffs. At this writing, the new Robert's is finally open.

The current buyers and renters of the Marigny's old houses hopefully feel some twinge of history, even absent spectral visitations. The rooms freshly painted by new owners may have witnessed a free black family, walking the fine line between the abyss of slavery and the toleration of white society. Perhaps a German entrepreneur, prosperous from baking or undertaking, had pride of place. An Italian widow may have marked the passage of a husband, children flown, and the frequent shuffling off to mass. Those rooms may have sheltered hungry barbacks banking on peanut butter and canned soup to take them to payday. Pioneering male couples may have nested, creating evanescent pastel architectural confections, doing a lot of living and some dying.

The Marigny is a rich kaleidoscope, whirling with changes. Every resident and, yes, every visitor, has a duty of stewardship to keep the kaleidoscope twirling and ensure that communal feeling does not slip away in a tide of absentee speculation and overnight guests.

I walk through the Marigny frequently, and I'm always pleased to see the decorations owners place outside. Like the row of foam mannequin heads stuck on fence pinnacles, the beads woven into alley gates, the doors painted to resemble openings to other lands, and recently the sidewalks stenciled in gay pride rainbows. These external ornaments manifest the almost five decades of stewardship since the start of revival. Hopefully, the neighborhood will retain its core of long-term resident conservators. It is to them we must hopefully and watchfully entrust the Faubourg Marigny.

Decorated Gate in the Marigny. Photo by author.

APPENDIX

Street Names of the Faubourg Marigny

Current Name	Former Name(s), in Order	Year Changed	Notes
Architect	None	N/A	
Bourbon	Bagatelle (Trifle)	1852	*Trifle* was the anglicized form of Bagatelle. See also Pauger.
Burgundy	Craps	1852	
Chartres	Moreau	1852	
Columbus	Mystérieuse	1852	
Dauphine	Grand Hommes	1852	
Decatur	De la Victorie/Levee	1852	
Elysian Fields	Champs-Élysées	N/A	
Franklin	Enghein/Lafayette	1852/c. 1917	
Frenchmen	des Français	N/A	Anglicized
Kerlerec	de L'Historie	1852	Above Dauphine to St. Claude
Kerlerec	Paix (Peace)	>1883	Below Dauphine to Chartres
Mandeville	None		
Marigny	None	N/A	
Music	La Musique	N/A	
Pauger	Bagatelle/Bourbon	1852/1924	
N. Peters	Public Road/Levee	1852/1855	
Port	None	N/A	

Current Name	Former Name(s), in Order	Year Changed	Notes
Press	Cotton Press		No record of change; shortened name
N. Rampart	Amour	1852	
Royal	Casa Calvo	1852	Last Spanish governor
St. Anthony	St. Antoine	N/A	
St. Claude	Bons Enfants (Good Children)	1852	
St. Ferdinand	None		
St. Roch	Poètes/Washington	1852/1894	
Spain	Espagne		
Touro	l'Union	1894	Judah Touro

SOURCE: Amos B. Gray, comp., *Corrected—Index, Alphabetical and Numerical, of Changes in Street Names and Numbers, Old and New, 1852 to Current Date* (New Orleans: Works Progress Administration, 1938).

NOTES

1. The Father of Waters and the Fathers of the Marignys

1. Ervin G. Otvos Jr., "New Orleans–South Hancock Holocene Barrier Trends and Origins of Lake Pontchartrain," *Transactions of Gulf Coast Associations of Geological Societies* 28 (1987): 337–55.

2. U.S. Geologic Survey, "Environmental Overview–Regional Description of the Lake Pontchartrain Basin," in *Environmental Atlas of the Lake Pontchartrain Basin,* accessed March 1, 2015, http://pubs.usgs.gov/of/2002/of02-206/env-overview/geologic-history.html.

3. *Sieur* (sir) was a knightly rank just above chevalier. The Le Moyne brothers are today remembered by these titles; their legal names, if rendered in English usage, would be Sir Pierre Le Moyne of Iberville and Sir Jean-Baptiste Le Moyne of Bienville.

4. Charles Gayarré, *History of Louisiana,* vol. 1, *The French Domination* (New York: Redfield, 1854), 101.

5. M. Floriana Spalek, "Bernard Xavier Philippe de Marigny de Mandeville and the Americanization of New Orleans" (MA thesis, Catholic University of America, 1959), 15.

6. Jean Baptiste Louis Franquelin, *Carte de l'Amerique Septentrionnale: Depuis le 25, jusqu'au 650 deg. de latt. & environ 140, & 235 deg. de longitude* (Quebec: 1688), Library of Congress copy of 1909–10, http://hdl.loc.gov/loc.gmd/g3300.ct000668; LePage du Pratz, *History of Louisiana* (London: T. Beckett, 1774), Project Gutenberg, www.gutenberg.org/ebooks/9153, 38. Du Pratz lodged in one of huts.

7. Baron Marc de Villiers, "A History of the Foundation of New Orleans (1717–1722)," trans. Warrington Dawson, *Louisiana Historical Quarterly* 3, no. 2 (April 1920): 179.

8. *Heirs of Villars v. J. M. Kennedy et al.,* Supreme Court of Louisiana, December 1850, in *Reports of Cases Argued and Determined in the Supreme Court of Louisiana*, vol. 5, William W. King, reporter (New Orleans: T. Rea, 1851).

9. François-Xavier Martin, *The History of Louisiana from the Earliest Period* (New Orleans: Lyman and Beardslee, 1827), 1:234.

10. John Fortier, "Philippe De Hautmesnil De Mandeville, François," in *Dictionary of Canadian Biography*, vol. 2 (University of Toronto/Université Laval, 2003), http://www.biographi.ca/en/bio/philippe_de_hautmesnil_de_mandeville_François.

11. William de Marigny Hyland, "A Reminiscence of Bernard de Marigny, Founder of Mandeville," speech before Mandeville Horizons, Inc., May 26, 1984, Mandeville, LA.

12. 410–414 Chartres St., Square 28, Lot No. 11075-01, C. Diboll Collins Vieux Carré Digital

Survey, Williams Research Center, Historic New Orleans Collection, accessed October 22, 2016, http://www.hnoc.org/vcs/property_info.php?lot=11075-01.

13. Fortier, "Philippe De Hautmesnil De Mandeville, François."

14. "The 'Code Noir' (1685)," reprinted from *Le Code Noir, ou récueil des réglements rendus jusqu' à présent* (Paris: Pault, 1767), trans. John Garrigus, reproduced by the Societé d'Histoire de la Guadeloupe, 1980, https://labs.wsu.edu/sue-peabody/wp-content/uploads/sites/1205/2016/02/code-noir.pdf.

15. Louis Billouart, Chevalier de Kerlerec, to Minister de Marine, April 24, 1759, in *Report Concerning Canadian Archives for the Year 1905, in Three Volumes, Being an Appendix to the Report of the Minister of Agriculture,* vol. 1 (Ottawa: S.E. Dawson, 1906).

16. This pamphlet was attributed to Jean-Philippe Grondel, one of those who plotted against Kerlerec. Grondel, *A Letter from a Louisiana Officer to the Commissioner of the Marine* (New Orleans, 1764), cited in *Adventures in Americana, 1492–1897,* vol. 2 (New York: Cooper Square, 1964). Eames, who wrote the preface to this collection, believes the pamphlet was actually published in Holland.

17. Marc de Villiers du Terrage, *The Last Years of French Louisiana,* trans. Hosea Phillips, ed. Carl A. Brasseaux and Glenn R. Conrad (Lafayette: Center for Louisiana Studies, University of Southwestern Louisiana, 1982), 335.

18. François Ravaisson-Mollien, ed., *Archives de la Bastille: Documents inédits* (Paris: G. Pedone, 1904), 141.

19. Du Terrage, *Last Years of French Louisiana,* 386.

20. Ravaisson-Mollien, *Archives de la Bastille,* 128.

21. The claimed damages totaled 1,444,500 livres, or roughly $14.6 billion in current American money. Du Terrage, *Last Years of French Louisiana,* 394–95, 400. One livre equaled eight ounces of gold; the U.S. price of gold was $1,262.70 per ounce on June 24, 2017.

22. Du Terrage, *Last Years of French Louisiana,* 404–5.

23. Ibid., 395.

24. Carl A. Brasseaux, *Denis-Nicolas Foucault and the New Orleans Rebellion of 1768* (Ruston, LA: McGinty Publications, 1987), 66.

25. "Report Describing the Expulsion of Antonio de Ulloa from Louisiana, 1768," trans. Andrejz Raczynski, February 16, 1769, Historic New Orleans Collection, 2011.0209.

26. Brasseaux, *Denis-Nicolas Foucault,* 72–83.

27. Martin, *History of Louisiana,* 202–9.

28. Ibid., 43–44.

29. Jack D. L. Holmes, *Gayoso: The Life of a Spanish Governor in the Mississippi Valley, 1789–1799* (Baton Rouge: Louisiana State University Press for the Louisiana Historical Association, 1965), 255.

30. New Orleans Notarial Archives, Acts of Andre Almonaster y Roxas, vol. 1, April 29, 1779.

31. St. Bernard Parish is named for the patron saint of Governor Bernardo de Gálvez and not, as some sources suggest, for the as-yet-unborn Bernard Marigny. It is very possible, however, that Bernard was named in honor of Pierre's good friend the governor.

32. John Walton Caughey, *Bernardo de Gálvez in Louisiana, 1776–1783* (Gretna, LA: Pelican Publishing, 1972), 79.

33. Baptismal certificate of Antonio Xavier Bernardo de Marigny de Mandeville, Archives of the Archdiocese of New Orleans, folio 601, no. 1267, February 6, 1786.

34. Martin, *History of Louisiana,* 256.

35. Ibid., 256.

36. Carlos Trudeau, copy and translation from *The Original Spanish Plan Showing the City of New Orleans, Its Fortifications and Environs by Carlos Trudeau, 1798,* copied April 1875, Historic New Orleans Collection, Williams Research Center, 1953.42.

37. "Contract of Marriage between Bernard Marigny and Marie Jones, May 19, 1808," trans. Andrejz Raczynski, ed. Scott S. Ellis, Pedro Pedesclaux Indexes, vol. 47, 1784–1886, New Orleans Notarial Archives, http://www.notarialarchives.org/pedesclaux.htm. Article 3 reads, "The possessions of the future couple include one house, located near Fort Charles, seven arpents facing the river, eighty deep, one side joining the city's fortifications." The stated size was 560 arpents; the colonial arpent was approximately 0.84 of a current U.S. acre. However, Roulhac Toledano, Sally K. Evans, Mary Louise Christovich, and Samuel Wilson Jr. mention in *The Creole Faubourgs,* vol. 4 of *New Orleans Architecture* (Gretna, LA: Pelican Publishing, 1996), 8, a later claim by Bernard Marigny of 1,372 arpents, bounded by Gayoso's Line and the property of Nicholas Daunoy. This would be approximately 1,161 American acres. This claim was confirmed. My theory is that the land claimed in the marriage contract, including the erroneous mention of "joining the city's fortifications," was the land specifically put under the marriage contract, and not the full extent of the Marigny property.

38. *Heirs of Villars v. J. M. Kennedy.*

39. Toledano et al., *Creole Faubourgs,* 18.

40. *Carte particuliere du flevue St. Louis dix lieües au dessus de la Nouvelle Orleans: Ou sont marqué les habitations et les terrains concedés à plusiers particuliers au Mississipy,* ca. 1723, Cartes Marines Manuscript Map Collection, Edward E. Ayer Manuscript Map Collection, Newberry Library.

41. Toledano et al., *Creole Faubourgs,* 3, 4.

42. Carlos Trudeau, *Plano figurativo del medimiento y repartimiento de la tierra commun con Dn. Nicolas Daunoy y la success[io]n de Mr. Favre Daunoy,* 1787, Louisiana State Museum, T0055.1997.0273. On the Web, this map is frequently misdated as 1728.

43. "The Sugar Cane in Louisiana," *DeBow's Review* 22, no. 6 (June 1857): 616.

44. Toledano et al., *Creole Faubourgs,* 4.

45. Ibid., 6.

46. It is uncertain who built this house. Coleman believed that the house existed when the property was owned by Gilbert de St. Maxent from 1776 to 1789. De St Maxent sold the property to Sigur in 1789, not 1777, as Coleman states. James Julian Coleman Jr., *Gilbert Antoine de St Maxent, the Spanish-Frenchman of New Orleans* (New Orleans: Pelican Publishing, 1968).

47. Herman de Bachelle Seebold, *Old Louisiana Plantation Homes and Family Trees* (Gretna, LA: Pelican Press 2004), 54–55.

48. Holmes, *Gayoso,* 212.

49. Karl Bernhard, Duke of Saxe-Weimar-Eisenach, *Travels through North America, during the Years 1825 and 1826* (Philadelphia: Carey, Lea and Carey, 1828), 76.

50. Louis-Philippe, King of France, *Diary of My Travels in America,* trans. Stephen Becker

(New York: Delacorte Press, 1977), 145. Interestingly, Pierre Marigny's succession makes no mention of this as an account receivable. Spanish Government of Louisiana, "Succession of Pedro Phelipe [*sic*] de Marigny, May 24, 1800," file 99, document 3906, Colonial Black Book No. 149, Louisiana Historical Center, Louisiana State Museum.

51. Penny Johnson, "Eulalie de Mandeville: An Ethnohistorical Investigation Challenging Notions of Plaçage in New Orleans as Revealed through the Lived Experiences of a Free Woman of Color" (MS thesis, University of New Orleans, 2010), 11–13, http://scholarworks.uno.edu/td/1285.

2. Bernard and the Stars and Stripes Ascend

1. Spanish Government of Louisiana, "Succession of Pedro Phelipe [*sic*] de Marigny, May 24, 1800," file 99, document 3906, Colonial Black Book No. 149, Louisiana Historical Center, Louisiana State Museum.

2. J. W. Cruzat, "Biographical and Genealogical Notes Concerning the Family of Philippe de Mandeville, Sieur de Marigny, 1709–1910," *Louisiana Historical Quarterly* 5, no. 1 (1911): 43; Grace King, *Creole Families of New Orleans* (New York: Macmillan, 1921), 24–27. Both of these sources have factual errors. Cruzat's genealogy is wrong and King dates a letter Delino wrote about Marigny's allowance to 1808, which is impossible since Marigny was already emancipated by that time. Also, the Panton-Leslie Collection at the University of West Florida has no mention of Marigny, an interesting gap in the record. Dean DeBolt to Scott Ellis, "Re: Inquiry about Panton-Leslie Collection," March 17, 2015.

3. Cruzat, "Biographical and Genealogical Notes," 42–50.

4. "Don Ignacio Delino, Curator of Minor Don Bernardo De Marigny, Presented a Detailed Account to the New Curator, Don Francisco Delille Dupard," trans. Elizabeth Elmwood and Deicy Jimenez, August 3, 1801, Spanish Colonial Documents, no. 1801080301, Louisiana Historical Center, Louisiana State Museum.

5. "Information Requested by Don Ignacio Delino, Guardian of the Minor, Don Bernardo de Marigny, and His Property," trans. Elizabeth Elmwood, May 27, 1801, Spanish Colonial Documents, no. 1801052704, Louisiana Historical Center, Louisiana State Museum.

6. M. Floriana Spalek, "Bernard Xavier Philippe de Marigny de Mandeville and the Americanization of New Orleans" (MA thesis, Catholic University of America, 1959), 35.

7. Orleans Parish Civil Courts Collection, Index to the Suit Records, 1813–1835, New Orleans Public Library, City Archives and Special Collections, http://neworleanspubliclibrary.org/inv/vcp/parish1.htm; Orleans Parish Civil Courts Collection, First Judicial District Court Suit Records, 1813–1835, New Orleans Public Library, City Archives and Special Collections, http://neworleanspubliclibrary.org/inv/1jdc/m1jdc.htm.

8. Thomas Jefferson to Thomas Mann Randolph Jr., Washington City, May 14, 1801, Thomas Jefferson Papers, Manuscript Division, Library of Congress, https://www.loc.gov/resource/mtj1.023_0808_0809/?sp=1&q=thomasrandolph.

9. Bernard Marigny, *À ses concitoyens,* trans. Howard Margot (New Orleans, 1853), 1, in University of New Orleans Library, F374.M32 A3.

10. Pierre Clement Laussat, *Memoirs of My Life to My Son during the Years 1803 and After . . . ,*

trans. Agnes-Josephine Pastwa, ed. Robert D. Bush (Baton Rouge: Louisiana State University Press, 1978), 17.

11. Ibid., 88–89.

12. Campbell Gibson, "Population of the 100 Largest Cities and Other Urban Places in the United States: 1790 To 1990," (working paper no. 27, Population Division, U.S. Bureau of the Census, June 1998).

13. Certificate of Marriage, Bernardo de Marigny and Maria Jones, May 28, 1804, Marriages, vol. 2, 1795–1806, Archdiocese of New Orleans, Sacramental Records.

14. "Contract of Marriage between Bernard Marigny and Marie Jones, May 19, 1808," trans. Andrejz Raczynski, ed. Scott S. Ellis, Pedro Pedesclaux Indexes, 47:534–36, New Orleans Notarial Archives.

15. The current value of this 100,000 *piastres* is difficult to calculate (*piastre* was French and Spanish slang for "dollar"). The mansion, dependencies, and land (soon to be the Faubourg Marigny) amounted to 80 percent of this figure. The twenty-eight slaves were valued at $15,000 and cash amounted to $5,000. Thus we see that although the inheritance probably represented the single-greatest individual wealth in the territory of Louisiana, most of it was not liquid, and Bernard the young heir cannot be considered a millionaire by the standards of his day.

16. Archdiocese of New Orleans, Sacramental Records, vol. 8, 1804–1806, 96, cited in "Clemente de Marigny de Mandeville," Stewart-deJaham Genealogy Pages, accessed May 8, 2016, http://www.raymondjohnson.net/genealogy/getperson.php?personID=I2700&tree=stewart.

17. C. L. R. James, *The Black Jacobins,* 2nd ed. (New York: Vintage Books 1963), 45.

18. Ibid., 85–117.

19. Roulhac Toledano, Sally K. Evans, Mary Louise Christovich, and Samuel Wilson Jr., *The Creole Faubourgs,* vol. 4 of *New Orleans Architecture* (Gretna, LA: Pelican Publishing, 1996), 26.

20. Paul F. Lachance, "The 1809 Immigration of Saint-Domingue Refugees to New Orleans: Reception, Integration and Impact," *Louisiana History* 29, no. 2 (1988): 258.

21. Nathalie Dessens, *From Saint-Domingue to New Orleans: Migration and Influences* (Gainesville: University Press of Florida, 2007), 27.

22. Joseph Tregle, *Louisiana in the Age of Jackson: A Clash of Cultures and Personalities* (Baton Rouge: Louisiana State University Press, 1999), 31–33.

23. Louisiana Territorial Legislature, "An Act Authorizing the Guardian of Bernard Marigny to Effect the Afore-Mentioned Sales," April 19, 1805, record group 335, T025.2003.125 1726–231, Louisiana Historical Center, Louisiana State Museum.

24. *Heirs of Villars v. J. M. Kennedy et al.,* Supreme Court of Louisiana, December 1850, in *Reports of Cases Argued and Determined in the Supreme Court of Louisiana,* vol. 5, William W. King, reporter (New Orleans: T. Rea, 1851).

25. City of New Orleans, Conseil de Ville, "Report of the Committee to Inform the Town, at the Request of Mr. Bernard Marigny, of the Limits of His Family Land," May 15, 1805, AB300, 1803–36, New Orleans City Archives.

26. Toledano et al., *Creole Faubourgs,* 12.

27. Ibid., 12–13.

28. Louisiana Territorial Legislature, "Agreement between Bernard Marigny and Jacques Pitot, Mayor of New Orleans, for Dividing Marigny Plantation into a Suburb," June 17, 1805,

record group 335, T025.2003.125 1726–1830, Louisiana Historical Center; Barthélémy Lafon, *Plan du Faubourg Marigny conforme au trace fait par Bm. Lafon Ingr. geog. et arpenteur du Compte d'Orleans, 1807* (New Orleans, 1807), Williams Research Center, Historic New Orleans Collection, 1966.34.5.

29. Toledano et al., *Creole Faubourgs,* 17.

30. Charles F. Zimpel, *Topographical Map of New Orleans and Its Vicinity, Embracing a Distance of Twelve Miles Up and Eight and Three-Quarters Miles Down the Mississippi,* 1834, Williams Research Center, Historic New Orleans Collection, 1945.13 i–xix.

31. Toledano et al., *Creole Faubourgs,* 19.

32. Acts before notary Narcissus Broutin, vol. 9, January 16–May 30, 1805, New Orleans Notarial Archives.

33. Lafon, *Plan du Faubourg Marigny,* copy by Claude Jules Allou d'Hémécourt, ca. 1870, Williams Research Center, Historic New Orleans Collection, 1966.33.1.

34. Acts of the Louisiana Territorial Legislature, 1806–7, first session, chap. 27.

35. Paul Lachance to Scott Ellis, September 11, 2011.

36. Dessens, *From Saint-Domingue to New Orleans,* 64.

37. Toledano et al., *Creole Faubourgs,* 27.

38. Jonathan Fricker, Donna Fricker, and Patricia L. Duncan, *Louisiana Architecture: A Handbook on Styles* (Lafayette: University of Louisiana at Lafayette Press, 2011), 7.

39. Toledano et al., *Creole Faubourgs,* 10.

40. James Tanesse, *Plan of the City and Suburbs of New Orleans from an Actual Survey Made in 1815 by J. Tanesse, City Surveyor,* Williams Research Center, Historic New Orleans Collection, 1971.4.

41. Toledano et al., *Creole Faubourgs,* 32–33.

42. Ibid., 117.

43. Elizabeth C. Neidenbach, "'*Mes dernières volontés*': Testaments to the Life of Marie Couvent, a Former Slave in New Orleans," *Transatlantica,* 2 (2012), published online May 17, 2013, http://transatlantica.revues.org/6186.

44. Certificate of Baptism, Prospero Francisco Antiono Pedro Phelipe de Marigny, April 18, 1806, Baptisms, vol. 5, 1806–1809, p. 36, act 519, and Certificate of Baptism, Gustavo Adolpho Eduardo de Marigny, April 18, 1807, Baptisms, vol. 15, p. 36, act 520, Archdiocese of New Orleans, Sacramental Records.

45. Marigny, *À ses concitoyens,* 1.

46. Certificate of Burial, Maria Jones, Funerals, p. 27b, act 137, Archdiocese of New Orleans, Sacramental Records.

47. "History of Annunciation Catholic Church, New Orleans, LA," New Orleans Churches.com, accessed October 31, 2015, http://www.neworleanschurches.com/annunciation/history.html.

48. Toledano et al., *Creole Faubourgs,* 11.

49. Clarence L. Johnson, "The Family of Marigny de Mandeville and the Fontainebleau Plantation, 1700–1938," pt. 2, *Louisiana Conservation Review* 7, no. 4 (Winter 1938–39): 50.

50. *Louisiana Courier,* September 22, 1809, p. 3, col. 1; Marigny, *À ses concitoyens,* 2.

51. Marigny, *À ses concitoyens,* 1.

52. Certificate of Baptism, Antonio Santiago de Marigny y Morales, July 30, 1813, Archdiocese of New Orleans, Sacramental Records.

53. Donald R. Hickey, *Glorious Victory: Andrew Jackson and the Battle of New Orleans* (Baltimore: Johns Hopkins University Press, 2015), 93.

54. Bernard Marigny, "Reflections on the Campaign of General Andrew Jackson in Louisiana, 1814 and 1815," trans. Grace King, *Louisiana Historical Quarterly* 6, no. 1 (1923): 65.

55. Ibid., 83.

56. Lachance, "1809 Immigration of Saint-Domingue Refugees," 138.

57. Toledano et al., *Creole Faubourgs,* 32.

3. Princes and Municipalities

1. Noah Miller Ludlow, *Dramatic Life as I Found It* (St. Louis: G. I. Jones, 1880), 143–45.

2. J. S. Buckingham, *The Slave States of America* (London: Fisher & Son, 1842), 1:344.

3. George Washington Cable, *The Creoles of Louisiana* (New York: Charles Scribner's Sons, 1884), 39.

4. "Contract of Marriage between Bernard Marigny and Marie Jones, May 19, 1808," trans. Andrejz Raczynski, ed. Scott S. Ellis, Pedro Pedesclaux Indexes, vol. 47, 1784–1886, New Orleans Notarial Archives.

5. A. Oakey Hall, *The Manhattaner in New Orleans* (New Orleans: J. C. Morgan, 1851), 87. The militia parades are mentioned in Buckingham's *Slave States of America,* 1:355.

6. Bernard Marigny, *À ses concitoyens,* trans. Howard Margo (New Orleans, 1853); Louisiana State Legislature, "An Act Concerning Deliberations of Family Meetings and Meetings of Creditors, Awards of Arbiters, and for Other Purposes," March 16, 1822.

7. Joseph Tregle, *Louisiana in the Age of Jackson: A Clash of Cultures and Personalities* (Baton Rouge: Louisiana State University Press, 1999), 114.

8. *Louisiana Gazette,* June 27, 1824.

9. *Courrier de la Louisiane,* June 28, 1824.

10. American Antiquarian Society and Tufts University Digital Collections, "Louisiana 1824 Governor," in *A New Nation Votes: American Election Returns, 1787–1825,* accessed November 1, 2015, http://elections.lib.tufts.edu/catalog/tufts:la.governor.1824.

11. Karl Bernhard, Duke of Saxe-Weimar-Eisenach, *Travels through North America, during the Years 1825 and 1826* (Philadelphia: Carey, Lea and Carey, 1828), 84.

12. Dumont de Montigny, *Plan de la Nouvelle Orleans, ville capitalle de la Louisianne et ses environs,* 1747, Ministère de la Guerre, Archives Historiques, 7C 216, Louis C. Karpinski Map Collection, Newberry Library.

13. Golda Mary McArdle, "The Pontchartrain Railroad, Pioneer in the South" (MA thesis, Tulane University, 1931), 6–7.

14. Earl F. Niehaus, *The Irish in New Orleans, 1800–1860* (Baton Rouge: Louisiana State University Press, 1965), 44–46. The cited estimates of Irish deaths in digging the canal range from three thousand to thirty thousand.

15. Vols. 26–30. "Assignment of Rights by Mr. Bernard Marigny to the Pontchartrain Railroad Company," February 23, 1830, book 18, folio 326, Louisiana Historical Center, record group 335, T025.2003.125, 1726–1830.

16. McArdle, "Pontchartrain Railroad," 52, 55–56.

17. Joseph Ingraham, *The South-West, by a Yankee* (New York: Harper Brothers, 1835), 1:172–73.

18. McArdle, "Pontchartrain Railroad," 57.

19. Jean Boze to Henri de Ste-Gême, June 6–July 7, p. 8, Ste-Gême Family Papers, MSS 100, folder 240, Williams Research Center, Historic New Orleans Collection.

20. Ingraham, *The South-West, by a Yankee,* 1:172–73.

21. James P. Baughman, "A Southern Spa: Ante-bellum Lake Pontchartrain," *Louisiana History* 3, no. 1 (Winter 1962): 5–8.

22. Clarence L. Johnson, "The Family of Marigny de Mandeville and the Fontainebleau Plantation, 1700–1938," pt. 3, *Louisiana Conservation Review* 8, no. 1 (Spring 1939): 21–26. This article also has a list of errors regarding Marigny family history in works by Grace King and J. W. Cruzat.

23. Clarence L. Johnson, "The Family of Marigny de Mandeville and the Fontainebleau Plantation, 1700–1938," pt. 4, *Louisiana Conservation Review* 8, no. 2 (Summer 1939): 40–42.

24. Henry C. Castellanos, *New Orleans as It Was* (Gretna, LA: Pelican Press, 1990), 252–53.

25. Ludlow, *Dramatic Life,* 140–42, 521.

26. George C. H. Kernion, "Samuel Jarvis Peters, the Man Who Made New Orleans of To-Day and Became a National Personality," *Louisiana Historical Quarterly* 7, no. 1 (1913): 69–83. Kernion quotes extensively from a rediscovered alleged autobiography by Peters, which is also silent on the matter.

27. Ludlow, *Dramatic Life,* 140–42.

28. William H. Sparks, *The Memories of Fifty Years* (Philadelphia: Claxton, Remsen & Haffelinger, 1870), 449.

29. Grace King, *Creole Families of New Orleans* (New York: Macmillan, 1921), 44–45.

30. John S. Kendall, *History of New Orleans* (Chicago: Lewis Publishing, 1922), 7:125.

31. Rita Katherine Carey, "Samuel Jarvis Peters," *Louisiana Historical Quarterly* 30, no. 2 (1947): 445.

32. Castellanos, *New Orleans as It Was,* 251–52.

33. Henry C. Castellanos obituary, *Daily Picayune,* August 8, 1896.

34. "Act of Sale, a Portion of a Block and Buildings, the Company of Architects of the City of New Orleans from Bernard Marigny, April 12, 1832," Felix de Armas, notary, vol. 36, no. 239, New Orleans Notarial Archives; "Act of Sale, a Portion of a Block and Buildings, the Company of Architects of the City of New Orleans from Bernard Marigny, April 12, 1832," Felix de Armas, notary, vol. 36, no. 240, New Orleans Notarial Archives.

35. The *gourde* is the official currency of Haiti. Boze cited the transaction in *gourdes* since he and St. Gême were both refugees from Saint-Domingue, the predecessor of Haiti. In the act, the amount is stated to be $50,000.

36. "Nouvelles Diverses," Jean Boze, New Orleans, to Henri Ste-Gême, St. Gaudins, France, May 1–31, 1832, trans. Howard Margot, Ste-Gême Family Papers, MSS 100, folder 204, Williams Research Center, Historic New Orleans Collection.

37. Rebecca Smith, Williams Research Center, Historic New Orleans Collection, to Scott Ellis, November 19, 2015.

38. Marigny, *À ses concitoyens*, 3.

39. King, *Creole Families,* 45.

40. "Nouvelles Diverses," Jean Boze, New Orleans, to Henri Ste-Gême, St. Gaudins, France, December 1, 1828, folder 134, 76, and September 3–October 29, 1829, folder 148, 9, Ste-Gême Family Papers, MSS 100, Williams Research Center, Historic New Orleans Collection.

41. Orleans Parish, Court of Probate, Receipt of Taxes, p. 27, June 1830–February 1834.

42. "Act of Sale, Bernard Marigny to Louis Muh, May 24, 1864," Adolphe Boudousquie, notary, vol. 22, no. 97, New Orleans Notarial Archives.

43. Kernion, "Samuel Jarvis Peters," 70–72.

44. Editorial by John Gibson, *Louisiana Advertiser,* February 28, 1835.

45. Kernion, "Samuel Jarvis Peters," 75–76.

46. *New Orleans Bee,* October 19, 1835.

47. *New Orleans Bee,* October 28, 1835.

48. Sparks, *Memories of Fifty Years,* 449.

49. "An Act to Amend an 'Act to Incorporate the City of New Orleans' Approved February the Seventeenth, Eighteen Hundred and Five, and Other Acts Amending the Same," in *Acts Passed at the Second Session of the Twelfth Legislature of the State of Louisiana* (New Orleans: Jerome Bayon, 1836), 28–37.

50. *Wards de la Nouvelle Orleans* (New Orleans: Bureau of Governmental Research, 1961), Williams Research Center, Historic New Orleans Collection, JK1982.B8.

51. "The Census," *Daily Picayune,* November 3, 1850. The figures have been rounded due to a poor original image; calculations by the author.

52. *Daily Picayune,* August 19, 1837.

53. *Soards' New Orleans City Directory*, 1841.

54. The 1811, 1822, 1832, 1842, 1851, and 1861 New Orleans directories have been transcribed and published online by the USGenWeb Archives Project at www.usgwarchives.net/la/orleans/directry.htm. Every New Orleans historian owes these transcribers an enormous debt of gratitude. The 1811 directory, James R. Hills Jr., based on a transcription by Colleen Fitzpatrick, September 2002; 1822 directory, James R. Hills Jr., based on a transcription by Colleen Fitzpatrick, September 2002; 1832 directory, James R. Hills Jr., based on a transcription by Colleen Fitzpatrick, September 2002; 1842 directory, James R. Hills Jr., based on transcriptions by Colleen Fitzpatrick, Louis Lavedan, Cheramie Breaux, Frankie Palisi, and Janice Worthen, September 2002; 1851 directory, Colleen Fitzpatrick, Linda Dean, and Louis Lavedan, January 2002; 1861 directory, Colleen Fitzpatrick, Kathy Sharp, Julie Moritz, Susan Billet Kost, Beverly Benoit, and Betty Ware, July 2004. Hereafter referred to as "New Orleans Directory for [year]." It must be remembered that the directories reported only the heads of households and are not substitutes for the census. I have considered only the responses from addresses that are contained within the present-day boundaries of the Marigny. Because of the vagaries of street naming and numbering over time, some of these addresses may well have been located slightly outside the present-day bounds. Such variation is small and still reflects the Third Municipality and the district as a whole. I am responsible for the correlations and mathematical analysis presented here.

55. "The Census," *Daily Picayune,* December 3, 1850.

56. "Death of Andreas Hansen," *Daily Picayune,* January 16, 1900.

57. "Charles Burkenstock," *Daily Picayune,* July 23, 1900.

58. "Death of John Lange," *Daily Picayune,* June 27, 1900.

59. Hodding Carter, *The Past as Prelude: New Orleans, 1718–1968* (New Orleans: Tulane University, 1968), 128.

60. "Annual Examination," *Daily Orleanian,* May 17, 1856.

61. *Daily Picayune,* September 14, 1838.

62. "Thomas B. O'Brien's Academy," *Daily Orleanian,* January 6, 1852.

63. "New Orleans, Her Commerce and Her Duties: Condition of the Three Municipalities," *DeBow's Review* 3, no. 4 (April 1847): 346.

64. "Mayor's Message, Mayoralty of New Orleans, February 15, 1847," *Louisiana Courier,* February 24, 1847.

65. "Third Municipality," *Louisiana Courier,* June 6, 1845; "Third Municipality Meeting," *Louisiana Courier,* June 9, 1845.

66. "Council of Municipality No. 3," *Daily Orleanian,* September 19, 1849.

67. "Licenses in New Orleans," *Daily Orleanian,* March 10, 1852.

68. "The Wharves," *Daily Picayune,* September 22, 1850.

69. "The Third Municipality," *Daily Crescent,* June 4, 1850.

70. Robert C. Reinders, *End of an Era: New Orleans, 1850–1860* (New Orleans: Pelican Publishing, 1964), 231.

71. "The Immigrants," *Daily Orleanian,* April 13, 1849.

72. Reinders, *End of an Era,* 231.

73. Frederick Law Olmstead, *Journeys and Explorations in the Cotton Kingdom* (London: Sampson, Low & Son, 1861), 1:331.

74. Ibid., 1:329.

75. Malcolm Heard, *French Quarter Manual: An Architectural Guide to the Vieux Carré* (New Orleans: Tulane School of Architecture, 1997), 110–15.

76. Richard C. Wade, *Slavery in the Cities* (New York: Oxford University Press, 1964), 127–28.

77. Ibid., 36.

78. Ibid., 152.

79. Niehaus, *Irish in New Orleans,* 54.

80. Kenneth Aslakson, "Making Race: The Role of Free Blacks in the Development of New Orleans' Three-Caste Society, 1791–1812" (PhD diss., University of Texas, Austin, 2007), 141–42.

81. 1825 Civil Code of Louisiana, art. 174, p. 27; art. 1775, p. 269; own emancipation, art. 1783, p. 272, cited in Bill Quigly and Maha Zaki, "The Significance of Race: Legislative Racial Discrimination in Louisiana, 1803–1865," *Southern University Law Review,* Spring 1997, 10n186.

82. Erin Greenwald, Historic New Orleans Collection, to Scott S. Ellis, March 12, 2015.

83. "Negroes for Sale!!!" *Daily Picayune,* August 21, 1838, November 30, 1854.

84. *New Orleans as it is, its manners and customs—morals—fashionable life—profanation of the Sabbath—prostitution—licentiousness—slave markets and slavery, &c., &c., &c.* ([New Orleans?], 1850), 75.

85. Solomon Northup, *Twelve Years a Slave* (Los Angeles: Graymalkin Media, 2014), 48–49.

86. Documentation package for Solomon Northup historical marker, Louisiana Office of Tourism, 2016.

87. Richard Campanella, "On The Structural Basis of Social Memory: Cityscapes of the New Orleans Slave Trade," pt. 2, *Preservation in Print,* April 2013.

88. "Table 8. Population of 100 Largest Urban Places: 1850," U.S. Bureau of the Census, June 15, 1998, https://www.census.gov/population/www/documentation/twps0027/tab08.txt; "Table 9. Population of the 100 Largest Urban Places: 1860," U.S. Bureau of the Census, June 15, 1998, ttps://www.census.gov/population/www/documentation/twps0027/tab09.txt.

89. Wade, *Slavery in the Cities,* 263–64.

90. Carl Brasseaux, "The Moral Climate of French Colonial Louisiana, 1699–1763," *Louisiana History* 27, No. 1 (Winter 1986): 39.

91. Thomas O'Connor, ed., *History of the Fire Department of New Orleans* (New Orleans, 1895), 71–72.

92. Ibid., 153–54.

93. Ibid., 159.

94. Richard Tansey, "Southern Expansionism: Urban Interests in the Cuban Filibuster," *Plantation Society* 1, no. 2 (June 1979): 227–51.

95. O'Connor, *History of the Fire Department,* 53.

96. Ibid., 69–70.

4. Disorder Is Our Order

1. Dale A. Somers, *The Rise of Sports in New Orleans, 1850–1900* (Baton Rouge: Louisiana State University Press, 1972), 52–53.

2. Joseph Ingraham, *The South-West, by a Yankee* (New York: Harper Brothers, 1835), 1:157–58.

3. J. S. McFarlane, *The Epidemic Summer: List of Interments in the Cemeteries of New Orleans, from the First of May to the First of November 1853* (New Orleans: Proprietor of the *True Delta,* 1853), viii.

4. "N.B.," *Daily Orleanian,* May 12, 1850, lists twenty-three hundred "licensed coffee houses and cabarets," and the 1850 census listed 116,375 residents. Calculation by the author.

5. *New Orleans Daily Crescent,* December 27, 1858.

6. Somers, *Rise of Sports,* 71–72.

7. "The City Racket," *Daily Picayune,* September 14, 1858.

8. "Nouvelles Diverses," Jean Boze to Henri de Ste-Gême, May 12–June 1, 1830, Ste-Gême Family Papers, MSS 100, folder 166, Williams Research Center, Historic New Orleans Collection.

9. "Our Municipality," *Daily Orleanian,* February 13, 1852.

10. Ingraham, *The South-West, by a Yankee,* 1:127–35.

11. Herbert Asbury, *The French Quarter* (New York: Garden City Publishing, 1936), 325.

12. "Brutal Assault," *Daily Picayune,* March 7, 1853.

13. "City Intelligence, Bad Set," *Daily Picayune,* March 10, 1853.

14. "A Hundred Years Ago" *Times-Picayune,* May 24, 1953.

15. "City Intelligence, Charge and Countercharge," *Daily Picayune,* August 21, 1852.

16. Judith Kelleher Schafer, *Brothels, Depravity, and Abandoned Women: Illegal Sex in Antebellum New Orleans* (Baton Rouge: Louisiana State University Press, 2009), 5. Schafer lists 132 homicide inquests in these years. "Table 9: Population of the 100 Largest Urban Places: 1860," in Campbell Gibson, "Population of the 100 Largest Cities and Other Urban Places in the United States: 1790 to 1990," (working paper no. 27, Population Division, U.S. Bureau of the Census, Washington, D.C., June 1998) lists New Orleans as having 168,375 people in 1860. U.S. Census, State and County Quick Facts, "New Orleans (city) Louisiana, 2015" estimates New Orleans' 2014 population at 384,320. Reported murders in New Orleans totaled 150 in 2014. Naomi Martin. "New Orleans Murders Down in 2014, but Violent Crime on the Rise," *Times-Picayune,* January 7, 2015. Therefore the 2014 murder rate per one thousand residents was 2.56, versus 2.55 for 1860. Calculation by the author.

17. Schafer, *Brothels, Depravity, and Abandoned Women,* 3.

18. Richard Tansey, "Prostitution and Politics in Antebellum New Orleans," *Southern Studies* 18, no. 4 (Winter 1979): 449–79, reprinted in Nancy F. Cott, ed., *History of Women in the United States: Historical Articles on Women's Lives and Activities,* vol. 9, *Prostitution* (Munich: K. G. Saur, 1993), 51.

19. *Daily Orleanian,* April 25, 1862.

20. Earl F. Niehaus, *The Irish in New Orleans, 1800–1860* (Baton Rouge: Louisiana State University Press, 1965), 54.

21. Schafer, *Brothels, Depravity, and Abandoned Women,* 137, 183.

22. "Terpsichore in the Old Third," *Daily Picayune,* October 6, 1855.

23. "Another Murder in the Third," *Daily Picayune,* February 19, 1849.

24. "City Intelligence: He Was a Stranger and They Fleeced Him," *Daily Picayune,* October 13, 1849.

25. Schafer, *Brothels, Depravity, and Abandoned Women,* 79.

26. Tansey, "Prostitution and Politics," 56, 61.

27. "To the Honorable President and Members of the Council of Municipality No. 3," *Daily Orleanian,* June 21, 1849.

28. "Council of Municipality No. 3," *Daily Orleanian,* July 6, 1849.

29. Tansey, "Prostitution and Politics," 62.

30. Ibid., 48.

31. "The Supreme Bench and the Public Balls," *Daily Orleanian,* March 26, 1851.

32. Tansey, "Prostitution and Politics," 49.

33. "The Mayor and the Ballrooms," *Daily Orleanian,* October 16, 1850.

34. Schafer, *Brothels, Depravity, and Abandoned Women,* 80.

35. Tansey, "Prostitution and Politics," 64–65n36.

36. Schafer, *Brothels, Depravity, and Abandoned Women,* 128.

37. Ibid., 138.

38. "The City, Third District, Bearding the Lion in His Den," *Daily Picayune,* October 18, 1854.

39. Tansey, "Prostitution and Politics," 64.

40. Ibid., 50, 65.

41. Ibid., 65–66.

42. Ibid., 66–73.

43. Al Rose, *Storyville, New Orleans* (Tuscaloosa: University of Alabama Press, 1974), 190; Ordinance No. 3267, O.S., March 10, 1857.

44. Rose, *Storyville*, 8–9.

5. The Marquis Marigny in Midlife

1. William de Marigny Hyland, interview by Scott Ellis, New Orleans, May 14, 2011.

2. "Nouvelles Diverses," Jean Boze to Henri de Ste-Gême, September 3–October 3, 1829, trans. Elizabeth Elmwood, Ste-Gême Family Papers, MSS 100, folder 148, 11–12, Williams Research Center, Historic New Orleans Collection.

3. Penny Johnson, "Eulalie de Mandeville: An Ethnohistorical Investigation Challenging Notions of Plaçage in New Orleans as Revealed through the Lived Experiences of a Free Woman of Color" (MS thesis, University of New Orleans, 2010), 13, http://scholarworks.uno.edu/td/1285.

4. "Nouvelles Diverses," Jean Boze to Henri de Ste-Gême, July–November 25, 1830, Ste-Gême Family Papers, MSS 100, folder 174, Williams Research Center, Historic New Orleans Collection.

5. Grace King, *Creole Families of New Orleans* (New York: Macmillan, 1921), 30.

6. William H. Sparks, *The Memories of Fifty Years* (Philadelphia: Claxton, Remsen & Haffelinger, 1870), 450.

7. King, *Creole Families,* 34.

8. Jean Boze to Henri de Ste-Gême, June 3–11, 1832, Ste-Gême Family Papers, MSS 100, folder 205, Williams Research Center, Historic New Orleans Collection.

9. P. F. de Gournay, "The F.M.C.s of Louisiana," *Lippincott's Monthly Magazine* 53 (1894): 513.

10. Nathalie Dessens, *From Saint-Domingue to New Orleans: Migration and Influences* (Gainesville: University Press of Florida, 2007), 120.

11. 716–724 Governor Nicholls St., Square: 55, Lot Number: 22892, in Collins C. Diboll, Vieux Carré Digital Survey, Williams Research Center, Historic New Orleans Collection, http://www.hnoc.org/vcs/property_info.php?lot=22892#sthash.jFAuJoVs.dpuf.

12. Steven Fauré, "200 Years of History: The Cabildo in New Orleans," *Inside Northshore,* March–April 2012, 2.

13. *Courrier de la Louisiane,* July 19, 1826.

14. Louisiana State Legislature, "An Act to Dispense Prosper and Gustave Marigny with the Time Prescribed by Law Respecting Age of Majority," January 12, 1827.

15. "Nouvelles Diverses," Jean Boze to Henri de Ste-Gême, September 3–October 29, 1829, Ste-Gême Family Papers, MSS 100, folder 148, 12, Williams Research Center, Historic New Orleans Collection.

16. "Nouvelles Diverses," Jean Boze to Henri de Ste-Gême, December 1828–June 1829, Ste-Gême Family Papers, MSS 100, folder 143, 19–20, Williams Research Center, Historic New Orleans Collection.

17. "Nouvelles Diverses," Jean Boze to Henri Ste-Gême, July–November 25, 1830, Ste-Gême Family Papers, MSS 100, folder 174, 17–18, Williams Research Center, Historic New Orleans Collection.

18. "Association against Duels," *L'Abeille* (New Orleans), September 19, 1834, trans. P. J. Stakelum Jr. in *New Orleans Genesis* 37, no. 145 (January 1998).

19. James Kimmens Greer, "Louisiana Politics, 1845–1861," *Louisiana Historical Quarterly* 12, no. 3 (July 1929): 415.

20. Certificate of Baptism, Antonio Santiago de Marigny y Morales, July 30, 1813, Archdiocese of New Orleans, Sacramental Records. The birth date is recorded as November 21, 1811.

21. "Col. Mandeville Marigny," *New York Times,* June 4, 1890.

22. William Keyse Rudolph, *Vaudechamp in New Orleans* (New Orleans: Historic New Orleans Collection, 2007), 80–81, n34. Rudolph was unable to find any record of Mandeville's attendance at Saint-Cyr. My speculation is that his name was expunged from the academy's rolls after his dueling faux pas. I do not believe Mandeville lied about his education, which, given the frequent traffic between Louisiana and France, would have been very easy for his contemporaries to check.

23. Ibid., 77.

24. James Lide, "Report on the Citizens Bank of Louisiana and the New Orleans Canal and Banking Company" (Rockville MD: History Associates, February 8, 2005).

25. Ibid.

26. George D. Green, "The Citizens Bank of Louisiana: Property Banking in Troubled Times, 1833–1842," *Business and Economic History,* 1st ser., 4 (1968): 59.

27. Ibid., 59.

28. Bernard Marigny, *À ses concitoyens,* trans. Howard Margot (New Orleans, 1853), 10, in University of New Orleans Library, F374.M32 A3.

29. Green, "Citizens Bank of Louisiana," 67.

30. Marigny, *À ses concitoyens,* 10.

31. John Smith Whitaker (attributed), "A Member of the New Orleans Bar," *Sketches of Life and Character in Louisiana* (New Orleans: Ferguson and Crosby, 1847), 82–85.

32. Cyprien Dufour, "Bernard Marigny," *Louisiana Courier,* March 8, 1847, trans. R. W. Colomb in *Louisiana Historical Quarterly* 14, no. 3 (October 1931): 396–98.

33. Marigny, *À ses concitoyens,* 11.

34. Lide, "Report on the Citizens Bank of Louisiana."

35. Marigny, *À ses concitoyens,* 12.

36. Ibid.

37. Ibid., 11–12.

38. "Died," *Daily Picayune,* August 3, 1859.

39. U.S. Census of 1860, "Barnard [*sic*] Marigny," 8th Ward, New Orleans, Louisiana, United States, p. 60, Household ID 517, U.S. National Archives and Records Administration (NARA), Publication M653 GS, Film 803421, Digital Folder: 004231232, Image 00312.

6. The Wet Grave

1. Leonard V. Huber, "New Orleans Cemeteries: A Brief History," in *New Orleans Architecture,* vol. 3, *The Cemeteries,* by Leonard V. Huber, Peggy McDowell, and Mary Louise Christovich (Gretna, LA: Pelican Publishing, 2004), 4; Peggy McDowell, "Influences on 19th-Century Funerary Architecture," ibid., 3:73–74.

2. Herbert Asbury, *The French Quarter* (New York: Garden City Publishing, 1938), 71.

3. John Duffy, *Sword of Pestilence: The New Orleans Yellow Fever Epidemic of 1853* (Baton Rouge: Louisiana State University Press, 1966), 24.

4. Bernard Lemann, *The Vieux Carré: A General Statement* (New Orleans: Tulane University School of Architecture, 1966), 24.

5. Duffy, *Sword of Pestilence,* 19.

6. Louisiana State Legislature, *Annual Report of the Board of Health of the State of Louisiana to the General Assembly for the Year 1880* (New Orleans: J. S. Rivers, 1881), 257.

7. Duffy, *Sword of Pestilence,* 49.

8. Benjamin H. Trask, *Fearful Ravages: Yellow Fever in New Orleans, 1796–1905* (Lafayette: Center for Louisiana Studies, University of Louisiana at Lafayette, 2005), 48–49.

9. Peggy Bassett Hildreth, "Early Red Cross: The Howard Association of New Orleans, 1837–1878," *Louisiana History* 20, no. 1 (Winter 1979): 54.

10. Ibid.

11. J. S. Buckingham, *The Slave States of America* (London: Fisher & Son, 1842), 1:383–84. The author quotes Dr. Charles Luzenberg, one of the leading physicians of New Orleans at the time.

12. Centers for Disease Control, "Yellow Fever," accessed February 20, 2017, https://www cdc.gov/yellowfever/.

13. Bennet Dowler, *Tableaux of New Orleans* (New Orleans: *Daily Delta,* 1853), 19–21.

14. Trask, *Fearful Ravages,* 32.

15. John F. Nau, *The German People of New Orleans, 1850–1900* (Hattiesburg: University of Southern Mississippi, 1974), 18, 19.

16. "The Howard Association—The Fever," *Daily Orleanian,* September 23, 1854.

17. Ibid.

18. William Robinson (attributed), *The Diary of a Samaritan, by a Member of the Howard Association of New Orleans* (New York: Harper Brothers, 1860), 281.

19. Editorial, *Daily Picayune,* August 19, 1837.

20. Robinson, *Diary of a Samaritan,* 18.

21. Hildreth, "Early Red Cross," 51, 52.

22. *New York Times,* March 3, 1854.

23. Robinson, *Diary of a Samaritan,* 22.

24. "The Howard Association—The Fever," *Daily Orleanian,* September 23, 1854.

25. Ellen C. Merrill, *Germans of Louisiana* (Gretna, LA: Pelican Publishing, 2005), 65.

26. Jo Ann Carrigan, *The Saffron Scourge: A History of Yellow Fever in Louisiana, 1796–1905* (Lafayette: Center for Louisiana Studies, University of Southwestern Louisiana, 1994), 60.

27. *New York Times,* March 3, 1854.

28. Robinson, *Diary of a Samaritan,* 123.

29. Auguste Hoppe survived his bout of yellow fever and died in 1862. "Obituary of Auguste Hoppe," *Deutsche Zeitung,* February 19, 1862.

30. Louis Voss, *History of the German Society of New Orleans* (New Orleans: Sendkar Printing Service, 1927), 80.

31. Duffy, *Sword of Pestilence,* 84. The totals are 269 officially recorded, 28 in St. Patrick's Cemetery without certificates, another 18 in "Hebrew graveyards."

32. Ibid., 65.

33. Robinson, *Diary of a Samaritan,* 159, 160.

34. *Daily Picayune,* August 4, 1853.

35. *Daily Delta,* August 21, 1853.

36. Ibid.

37. Campbell Gibson, "Population of the 100 Largest Cities and Other Urban Places in the United States: 1790 to 1990" (working paper no. 27, Population Division, U.S. Bureau of the Census, Washington, D.C., June 1998).

38. "Statistical Recapitulation," in J. S. McFarlane, *The Epidemic Summer: List of Interments in the Cemeteries of New Orleans, from the First of May to the First of November, 1853* (New Orleans: Proprietor of the *True Delta*, 1853), following xiii. The percentage of German deaths is calculated by dividing McFarlane's figure of 2,344 into the median of the 1850 and 1860 census figures (15,653), as depicted in table II.6, "Germans in New Orleans, La., 1850–1870," in Andrea Mehrlander, *The Germans of Charleston, Richmond and New Orleans during the Civil War Period, 1850–1870* (Berlin: de Gruyter, 2011), 60. The calculation returns 14.97 percent. Mehrlander (51) cites 25 percent of the German population as fatalities.

39. Robinson, *Diary of a Samaritan,* appendix.

40. Hildreth, "Early Red Cross," 75.

41. Trask, *Fearful Ravages,* 105–22.

7. The Germans and the Irish

1. Ellen C. Merrill, *Germans of Louisiana* (Gretna, LA: Pelican Publishing, 2005), 21.

2. Reinhardt Kondert, "German Immigration to French Colonial Louisiana: A Reevaluation," in *Proceedings of the Fourth Meeting of the French Colonial Historical Society, April 6–8, 1978, University of Mississippi, Oxford, Mississippi,* ed. Alf Andrew Heggoy and James J. Cooke (Washington, D.C.: University Press of America, 1979), 73–75.

3. J. Hanno Deiler, "The System of Redemption in the State of Louisiana," trans. Louis Voss, *Louisiana Historical Quarterly* 12, no. 3 (July 1929): 446.

4. Louisiana Territorial Legislature, "An Act for the Regulation of the Rights and Duties of Apprentices and Indentured Servants," May 21, 1806, in *Acts Passed at the First Session of the First Legislature of the Territory of Orleans* (New Orleans: Bradford & Anderson, 1807), 44–56, cited in Paul Lachance, "Index to New Orleans Indentures, 1809–1843," New Orleans Public Library, accessed June 24, 2013, http://nutrias.org/~nopl/inv/indentures/ind-intr.htm.

5. John F. Nau, *The German People of New Orleans, 1850–1900* (Hattiesburg: University of Southern Mississippi, 1974), 2.

6. Deiler, "System of Redemption," 446.

7. Ibid., 432.

8. Ibid., 446.

9. Louis Voss, *History of the German Society of New Orleans* (New Orleans: Sendkar Printing Service, 1927), 76.

10. John Duffy, *Sword of Pestilence: The New Orleans Yellow Fever Epidemic of 1853* (Baton Rouge: Louisiana State University Press, 1966), 52.

11. Deiler, "System of Redemption," 440–41. One of the children who arrived via the 1818

voyage was Salome Müller, better known as Sally Miller. Sally was sold and owned as a slave until a celebrated court case freed her. See John Bailey, *The Lost German Slave Girl* (New York: Grove Press, 2006).

12. Louisiana State Legislature, "An Act for the Relief and Protection of Persons Brought into This State as Redemptioners," approved March 20, 1818, in Moreau Lislet, ed., *A General Digest of the Acts of the Legislature of Louisiana: Passed from the Year 1804 to 1827, Inclusive, and in Force at This Last Period* (New Orleans: Benjamin Levy, 1828), 2:297–302.

13. Paul Lachance, "Information on Persons Named in Indentures," New Orleans Public Library, 1998, http://nutrias.org/~nopl/inv/indentures/bioginfo.htm.

14. Frederick Law Olmstead, *Journeys and Explorations in the Cotton Kingdom* (London: Sampson, Low & Son, 1861), 1:89.

15. Earl F. Niehaus, *The Irish in New Orleans, 1800–1860* (Baton Rouge: Louisiana State University Press, 1965), 139.

16. Ibid., 30–31.

17. Saints Peter and Paul Church, *Centennial of the Church of Sts. Peter and Paul, 1860–1960* (New Orleans, 1960).

18. Michael Doorley, "Irish Catholics and French Creoles: Ethnic Struggles within the Catholic Church in New Orleans, 1835–1920," in *New Orleans and Urban Louisiana,* pt. A, *Settlement to 1860,* ed. Samuel C. Shepherd Jr. (Lafayette: Center for Louisiana Studies, University of Louisiana at Lafayette, 2005), 394. Calculations by the author using U.S. census figures.

19. Nau, *German People of New Orleans,* 21.

20. "Immigrant Societies," *Daily Orleanian,* March 1, 1849.

21. Niehaus, *Irish in New Orleans,* 140–42.

22. "To The Humane," *Daily Orleanian,* March 29, 1849.

23. "Immigrants" *Daily Orleanian,* November 27, 1849.

24. "A Stroll," *Daily Picayune,* April 1, 1853.

25. "Sailor Boarding-House Runners," *Daily Picayune,* February 6, 1848.

26. Wilford Hill LeCheminant, *Peter and Sarah Farr LeCheminant and the 1854 Mormon Immigration from Europe to the Great Salt Lake Valley* (Bountiful, UT, 1979), 15.

27. Voss, *History of the German Society of New Orleans,* 77.

28. Merrill, *Germans of Louisiana,* 60.

29. Ibid.

30. Voss, *History of the German Society of New Orleans,* 77–78.

31. Ella Lonn, *Foreigners in the Confederacy* (Gloucester, MA: Peter Smith, 1965), 26. Lonn avers that the so-called Dutch were also considered a lower caste by their own countrymen for transacting with slaves, especially in the illegal sale of liquor.

32. "German Association Life in New Orleans," *Tägliche Deutsche Zeitung,* December 6, 1859; trans. William Black.

33. Merrill, *Germans of Louisiana,* 268–69.

34. Ibid., 272.

35. Ibid., 285.

36. "Death of John Lange," *Daily Picayune,* June 27, 1900.

37. "Louis Leonhard Dies of Paralysis," *Daily Picayune,* September 16, 1901.

38. "Historical Note," Jacob Schoen and Son Collection, MSS 307, Earl Long Library, University of New Orleans, accessed October 28, 2016, http://library.uno.edu/specialcollections/inventories/307.htm.

39. William Robinson Konrad, "The Diminishing Influences of German Culture in New Orleans Life since 1865," *Louisiana Historical Quarterly* 24, no. 1 (January 1941): 6.

40. Nau, *German People of New Orleans,* 17; Merrill, *Germans of Louisiana,* 83.

41. J. Hanno Deiler, *Geschichte der New Orleanser Deutschen Presse,* trans. William Black (New Orleans: Paul J. Sendker, 1901), 11.

42. Richard Campanella, *Geographies of New Orleans: Urban Fabrics before the Storm* (Lafayette: Center of Louisiana Studies, University of Louisiana at Lafayette, 2006), 255–56. A search of the *Daily Picayune* and its successor, the *Times-Picayune,* reveals no mention of "Little Saxony" before 1987. Campanella's account should be read closely for his careful parsing of the sobriquet "Little Saxony."

43. Andrea Mehrlander, *The Germans of Charleston, Richmond and New Orleans during the Civil War Period, 1850–1870* (Berlin: de Gruyter, 2011), 71.

44. *Journal of the Proceedings of the Convention of the State of Louisiana, Begun and Held in the City of New Orleans, on the 14th Day of January, 1845* (New Orleans: Besançon, Ferguson, 1845), 19–24.

45. Louisiana State Constitution of 1845, article 5, http://en.wikisource.org/wiki/Louisiana_State_Constitution_of_1845.

46. Ibid., article 10.

47. *Proceedings and Debates of the Convention of Louisiana Which Assembled at the City of New Orleans, January 14, 1844* (New Orleans: Besançon, Ferguson, 1845), 835–36.

48. Medal presented to Bernard de Marigny by the Naturalized Citizens of Louisiana. Williams Research Center, Historic New Orleans Collection, 1972.32.

49. Antonius Holtmann, "Emigration to America in the Context of an (Unsuccessful) Revolution, 1848/49: Scenario of a Misjudged Interconnection," in *Schöne Neue Welt: Rheinländer erobern Amerika,* ed. Rheinisches Freilicht- und Landesmuseum für Volkskunde (Wiehl: Martina Galunder Verlag, 2001), 2:329–38, http://www.nausa.uni-oldenburg.de/1848/1848holten.html.

50. "Commercial," *Daily Picayune,* November 9, 1845; "Arrival of Steamship Acadia," *Daily Picayune,* November 26, 1846.

51. Nau, *German People of New Orleans,* 5, 6.

52. Voss, *History of the German Society of New Orleans,* 78.

53. Robert T. Clark Jr., "The German Liberals in New Orleans (1840–1860)," *Louisiana Historical Quarterly* 20, no 1 (January 1937): 6.

54. Voss, *History of the German Society of New Orleans,* 79.

55. Patricia Heminghouse, "The German Secrets of New Orleans," *German Studies Review* 27, no. 1 (February 2004): 3.

56. "Mrs. E. M. Gross: Death of the Margaret of the Lower District," *Daily Picayune,* April 16, 1906.

57. Roulhac Toledano, Sally K. Evans, Mary Louise Christovich, and Samuel Wilson Jr., *The Creole Faubourgs,* vol. 4 of *New Orleans Architecture* (Gretna, LA: Pelican Publishing, 1996), 130.

58. Doorley, "Irish Catholics and French Creoles," 394.

59. Rail times are taken from Charles O. Paullin and John K. Wright, *Rates of Travel, 1857,* in *Atlas of the Historical Geography of the United States* (Washington, D.C.: Carnegie Institute of Washington and the American Geographical Society of New York, 1932), 138c, reproduced in *Railroads and the Making of Modern America*, University of Nebraska–Lincoln, http://railroads.unl.edu/documents/view_document.php?id=rail.str.0241.

60. Voss, *History of the German Society of New Orleans,* 77.

61. Konrad, "Diminishing Influences," 6.

62. Merrill, *Germans of Louisiana,* 125–26.

63. Hilary S. Irvin, "The Impact of German Immigration on New Orleans Architecture," in *New Orleans and Urban Louisiana,* pt. A, *Settlement to 1860,* ed. Samuel C. Shepherd Jr. (Lafayette: Center for Louisiana Studies, University of Louisiana at Lafayette, 2005), 426.

64. Nau, *German People of New Orleans,* 84–85.

65. Kevin Bozant, *Port and Burgundy, 1840–1990: A Pictorial History St. Paul Lutheran Church New Orleans* (New Orleans: St. Paul's Lutheran Church, 1990), 4.

66. Ibid., 6.

67. Ibid., 5, citing *Lafayette City Advertiser,* January 29, 1842.

68. Ibid., 5; Grace Powers Thomas, ed., *Where to Educate, 1898–1899* (Boston: Brown, 1898), 102.

69. Konrad, "Diminishing Influences," 24.

70. "Historical Perspective on Holy Trinity Parish," accessed November 16, 2013, neworleanschurches.com/holytrinity/history.htm.

71. John Kendall, *History of New Orleans* (Chicago: Lewis Publishing, 1922), 717, transcribed by Bill Thayer, http://penelope.uchicago.edu/Thayer/E/Gazetteer/Places/America/United_States/Louisiana/New_Orleans/_Texts/KENHNO/44*.html.

8. Reconsolidation and Repression

1. "New Orleans, Her Commerce and Her Duties: Condition of the Three Municipalities," *DeBow's Review* 3, no. 4 (April 1847).

First Municipality (Vieux Carré)
Debt: $919, 611; percentage past due: 2.8
Receipts: $382,469
Disbursements: $338,619
Ratio of debt to disbursement: 2.4

Second Municipality ("American")
Debt: $2,700,000; percentage past due: 16.7
Receipts: $519,321
Disbursements: $591,713
Ratio of debt to disbursement: 5.2

Third Municipality (Faubourg Marigny and Outlying Eastern Wards)
Debt: $845,342; percentage past due: 31.8

Receipts: $115,777
Disbursements: $127,374
Ratio of debt to disbursement: 7.3

Calculations by the author, rounded to the nearest tenth of a percent.

2. Richard Tansey, "Southern Expansionism: Urban Interests in the Cuban Filibuster," *Plantation Society* 1, no. 2 (June 1979): 227–51.

3. Merl E. Reed, "The New Orleans Short Lines," in *New Orleans and Urban Louisiana,* pt. A, *Settlement to 1860,* ed. Samuel C. Shepherd Jr. (Lafayette: Center for Louisiana Studies, University of Louisiana at Lafayette), 2005, 473.

4. Louisiana State Legislature, *Report of the Special Committee on the Mexican Gulf Railroad* (New Orleans: J. O. Nixon, 1866).

5. Map by William K. Hubbell in Robert C. Black, *The Railroads in the Confederacy* (Chapel Hill: University of North Carolina Press, 1952), reproduced in Bell Irvin Wiley, *Embattled Confederates* (New York: Harper and Row, 1964), 130–31.

6. "Speech of James Robb, Esq. Delivered at the South-Western Railroad Convention, Held in the Municipal Hall (Second Municipality), New Orleans, January 7, 1852," *DeBow's Review* 12, no. 5 (May 1852): 543–45.

7. Leon Cyprian Soulé, *The Know Nothing Party in New Orleans: A Reappraisal* (Baton Rouge: Louisiana Historical Association, 1961), 20.

8. B. M. Norman, *Norman's Map of New Orleans & Environs* (New Orleans, 1849), Williams Research Center, Historic New Orleans Collection, 1952.29.

9. Louisiana Legislature, Act No. 71, February 23, 1852.

10. Arnold R. Hirsch and Joseph Logsdon, eds., *Creole New Orleans: Race and Americanization* (Baton Rouge: Louisiana State University Press, 1992), 207.

11. Rodolphe Lucien Desdunes, *Our People and Our History,* trans. and ed. Sr. Dorothea Olga McCants (Baton Rouge: Louisiana State University Press, 1973), 111.

12. Louisiana State Constitution of 1852, article 10, http://en.wikisource.org/wiki/Louisiana_State_Constitution_of_1852.

13. Soulé, *Know Nothing Party,* 36.

14. New Orleans City Council, Ordinance 395, Common Council Series, November 20, 1852.

15. Soulé, *Know Nothing Party,* 36.

16. Editorial, *Daily Orleanian,* January 5, 1855.

17. Soulé, *Know Nothing Party,* 27.

18. Ibid., 36.

19. Ibid., 31.

20. Ibid., 42.

21. "The Election," *Daily Picayune,* November 10, 1853.

22. Soulé, *Know Nothing Party,* 49.

23. Ibid., 47–48.

24. Edith Challin Follette, "The History of the Know-Nothing Party in Louisiana" (MA thesis, Tulane University, 1910), 55.

25. *Louisiana Courier,* March 25, 1854.

26. *Daily Orleanian,* September 13, 1854.

27. Follette, "History of the Know-Nothing Party," 23.

28. "Police Officials," *Daily Orleanian,* September 22, 1854.

29. Soulé, *Know Nothing Party,* 64.

30. "Financial Mismanagement," *Louisiana Courier,* June 26, 1855.

31. "Municipal Elections, June 2nd," *Daily Orleanian,* May 17, 1856; Ancestry.com, "Woods Family History: (Pierre Achille) François Seuzeneau," accessed May 4, 2014, http://wc.rootsweb.ancestry.com/cgi-bin/igm.cgi?op=GET&db=beebeewood&id=I1922. Seuzeneau died in Matamoros, Mexico, in 1858.

32. Soulé, *Know Nothing Party,* 68.

33. "Thibodaux Barbecue," *Daily Picayune,* August 10, 1855.

34. "American Mass Meeting," *Daily Picayune,* August 16, 1855.

35. Bernard Marigny, *À ses concitoyens,* trans. Howard Margot (New Orleans: 1853), 1.

36. Soulé, *Know Nothing Party,* 70.

37. Ibid., 72–73.

38. Follette, "History of the Know-Nothing Party," 47.

39. Ibid., 103.

40. "A Brilliant Prospect," *Daily True Delta,* October 31, 1855; "Local Matters, Terrible Doings," *Daily Orleanian,* November 5, 1857; "The Game Begun," *Louisiana Courier,* October 29, 1857.

41. "Know-Nothing Protection! Scenes at the Polls," *Louisiana Courier,* November 7, 1856.

42. Follette, "History of the Know-Nothing Party," 83.

43. Soulé, *Know Nothing Party,* 91.

44. Ibid., 110–11.

45. Follette, "History of the Know-Nothing Party," 103–4.

46. Soulé, *Know Nothing Party,* 112.

9. The *Gens de Couleur Libres*

1. David C. Rankin, "The Impact of the Civil War on the Free Colored Community of New Orleans," *Perspectives in American History* 11 (1977–78): 380.

2. Ibid., 385.

3. Emily Epstein Landau, *Spectacular Wickedness: Sex, Race, and Memory in Storyville, New Orleans* (Baton Rouge: Louisiana State University Press, 2013), 32–34.

4. Kimberly S. Hanger, *Bounded Lives, Bounded Places: Free Black Society in Colonial New Orleans, 1769–1803* (Durham, NC: Duke University Press, 1997), 18, 22.

5. Richard C. Wade, *Slavery in the Cities* (New York: Oxford University Press, 1964), 269.

6. Ibid., 267.

7. Judith Kelleher Schafer, *Becoming Free, Remaining Free: Manumission and Enslavement in New Orleans, 1846–1862* (Baton Rouge: Louisiana State University Press, 2003), 97–114.

8. Ibid., 115–28.

9. Louisiana Territorial Legislature, "An Act to Prescribe Certain Formalities Respecting Free Persons of Color," 1st sess., 2nd Leg., March 31, 1808, 138–40.

10. P. F. de Gournay, "The F.M.C.s of Louisiana," *Lippincott's Monthly Magazine* 53 (1894): 513.

11. Some of the information presented here was furnished to the author by the late Don G. Richmond, curator of the Rochon house at 1515 Pauger, which is now owned by the Southern Food and Beverage Museum. A summary of extant information is found at Frenchcreoles.com, accessed October 29, 2016, http://www.frenchcreoles.com/CreoleCulture/famouscreoles/rosette%20rochon/rosetterochon.htm.

12. Elizabeth C. Neidenbach, "'*Mes dernières volontés*': Testaments to the Life of Marie Couvent, a Former Slave in New Orleans," *Transatlantica* 2 (2012): 8, 9, published online May 17, 2013, http://transatlantica.revues.org/6186.

13. Ibid., 11.

14. Ibid., 6.

15. Elizabeth Neidenbach to Scott Ellis, August 27, 2015.

16. Neidenbach, "*Mes dernières volontés,*" 11.

17. Ibid., 16.

18. Ibid., 8.

19. Wayne Everard and Irene Wainwright, "The World of François Lacroix," 1, New Orleans Public Library, City Archives and Special Collections, 2002, http://nutrias.org/exhibits/lacroix/title.htm.

20. *New Orleans Annual and Commercial Register of 1846* (New Orleans: E. A. Michel, 1846), 177.

21. "Romance of a Tax Bill," *Daily Picayune,* September 9, 1874.

22. *New Orleans Annual and Commercial Register*, 350.

23. Everard and Wainwright, "World of François Lacroix," 24–25.

24. Shirley Elizabeth Thompson, *Exiles at Home: The Struggle to Become American in Creole New Orleans* (Cambridge, MA: Harvard University Press, 2009), 136–37.

25. Roulhac Toledano, Sally K. Evans, Mary Louise Christovich, and Samuel Wilson Jr., *The Creole Faubourgs,* vol. 4 of *New Orleans Architecture* (Gretna, LA: Pelican Publishing, 1996), 35.

26. Ibid., 34.

27. Thompson, *Exiles at Home,* 137.

28. "Romance of a Tax Bill," *Daily Picayune,* September 9, 1874.

29. Rankin, "Impact of the Civil War," 402.

30. Toledano et al., *Creole Faubourgs,* 27.

31. "An Act to Punish the Crimes Therein Mentioned, and for Other Purposes," Acts of January 4, 1830, Ninth Legislature of Louisiana, March 16, 1830, 2nd sess., section 3, at 96 1830, cited in Bill Quigley and Maha Zaki, "The Significance of Race: Legislative Racial Discrimination in Louisiana, 1803–1865," *Southern University Law Review,* Spring 1997.

32. Wade, *Slavery in the Cities,* 271.

33. Ibid., 326.

34. Annie Lee West Stahl, "The Free Negro in Ante-bellum Louisiana," *Louisiana Historical Quarterly* 25, no. 2 (April 1942): 381.

35. Frank Lovato to Scott Ellis, August 27, 2015.

36. Frank Joseph Lovato, "Households and Neighborhoods among Free People of Color in New Orleans: A View from the Census, 1850–1860" (MA thesis, University of New Orleans, 2010), 16, http://scholarworks.uno.edu/td/1174.

37. Loren Schweninger, "Antebellum Free Persons of Color in Postbellum Louisiana," *Louisiana History* 30 (Fall 1989): 345–64, appendices 1 and 2.

38. Penny Johnson, "Eulalie de Mandeville: An Ethnohistorical Investigation Challenging Notions of Plaçage in New Orleans as Revealed through the Lived Experiences of a Free Woman of Color" (MS thesis, University of New Orleans, 2010), 17, http://scholarworks.uno.edu/td/1285.

39. Caryn Cossé Bell, *Revolution, Romanticism, and the Afro-Creole Protest Tradition in Louisiana, 1718–1868* (Baton Rouge: Louisiana State University Press, 1997), 86; Rodolphe Lucien Desdunes, *Our People and Our History,* trans. and ed. Sr. Dorothea Olga McCants (Baton Rouge: Louisiana State University Press, 1973), 112–13.

40. de Gournay, "The F.M.C.s of Louisiana," 517.

41. "The City, Free Black Emigration," *Daily Picayune,* June 23, 1859.

42. Mary Niall Mitchell, "A Good and Delicious Country: Free Children of Color and How They Learned to Imagine the Atlantic World in Nineteenth-Century Louisiana," in *Chartered Schools: Two Hundred Years of Independent Academies in the United States, 1727–1925,* ed. Nancy Beadie and Kim Tolley (New York: Routledge Falmer, 2002), 140.

43. At least four legislative acts, from 1830 through 1860, placed restrictions on free blacks from other states from working on vessels traveling in Louisiana:

- "An Act to Prevent Free Persons of Colour from Entering into This State," 1830 Acts, 2nd sess., 9th leg., January 4, 1830, sections 1–17. See Quigley and Zaki, "Significance of Race," 90–94n282.
- Acts of January 19, 1852, Fourth Legislature of Louisiana (effective March 18, 1852), Act No. 279, sections 1–3. See Quigley and Zaki, "Significance of Race, "193–94n269.
- Acts of January 17, 1859, Fourth Legislature of Louisiana (effective March 17, 1859), 2nd sess., Act No. 219, section 1. See Quigley and Zaki, "Significance of Race," 172n268.
- Acts of January 16, 1860, Fifth Legislature of Louisiana (effective March 7, 1860), 1st sess., Act No. 100, section 1. See Quigley and Zaki, "Significance of Race," 172n268.

44. Act 214, Third Legislature, Session at Baton Rouge, March 20, 1850, Quigley and Zaki, "Significance of Race," 179n305.

45. Acts of January 17, 1859, Fourth Legislature of Louisiana (effective March 17, 1859), 2nd sess., Act No. 275, sections1–4, Quigley and Zaki, "Significance of Race," 214n312.

46. Schafer, *Becoming Free, Remaining Free,* 150–52.

47. "Hayti and Immigration Thither," *Daily Picayune,* July 16, 1859.

48. New Orleans Directory for 1842.

49. Neidenbach, "*Mes dernières volontés,*" 33–35; used by permission.

50. Elizabeth Neidenbach to Scott Ellis, August 27, 2015.

51. Desdunes, *Our People and Our History,* 102–8.

52. Stephen J. Ochs, *A Black Patriot and a White Priest: André Cailloux and Claude Paschal Maistre in Civil War New Orleans* (Baton Rouge: Louisiana State University Press, 2000), 53–54; Desdunes, *Our People and Our History,* 104.

53. Maitre Desarzant, *Prospectus de l'institution Catholique des orphelins indigents* (New Orleans: Maitre Desarzant, 1847), 4, Louisiana Research Collection, Tulane University, 976.31 (362.7) P966.

54. Desdunes, *Our People and Our History,* 105.

55. Ibid., 14n4.

56. Ochs, *A Black Patriot and a White Priest,* 56.

57. Ibid., 62–63.

58. Ibid., 51–52.

59. Schafer, *Becoming Free, Remaining Free,* 145–46.

60. "Idolatry and Quackery," *Louisiana Gazette,* August 16, 1820. Contemporary newspapers usually used *voudou* when referring to the practice within New Orleans. Today a distinction is made between American *voodoo* and Caribbean *voudou.*

61. "A Mystery of the Old Third," *Daily Crescent,* June 29, 1850.

62. "The Rites of Voudou," *Daily Crescent,* July 31, 1850; "Unlawful Assemblies," *Daily Picayune,* July 31, 1850; "Police Matters, before Recorder Solomon," *Daily Picayune,* November 7, 1857.

63. "The Voudous vs. Municipality No. 3," *Daily Delta,* July 14, 1850.

64. Melissa Daggett to Scott Ellis, August 21, 2015; used by permission.

65. Desdunes, *Our People and Our History,* 114.

66. Melissa Daggett, "Spiritualism among Creoles of Color in Nineteenth-Century New Orleans: The Life and Times of Henry Louis Rey," *Louisiana History* 55, no. 4 (Fall 2014): 409–31.

10. Waiting for Farragut

1. Jerry L. Tarver, "The Political Clubs of New Orleans in the Presidential Election of 1860," *Louisiana History* 4, no. 2 (Spring 1963): 121.

2. David T. Gleeson, *The Green and the Gray: The Irish in the Confederate States of America* (Chapel Hill: University of North Carolina Press, 2013), 33.

3. Tarver, "Political Clubs of New Orleans," 124.

4. John Smith Kendall, *History of New Orleans* (Chicago: Lewis Publishing, 1922), 232–34, transcribed by Bill Thayer, http://penelope.uchicago.edu/Thayer/E/Gazetteer/Places/America/United_States/ Louisiana/New_Orleans/_Texts/KENHNO/home.html.

5. "The City: The Meeting on Canal Street," *Daily Picayune,* October 30, 1860.

6. Kendall, *History of New Orleans,* 232.

7. Ibid., 232–34.

8. Louisiana State Legislature, "An Ordinance to Dissolve the Union between the State of Louisiana and Other States, United with Her under the Compact Entitled 'The Constitution of the United States of America,'" January 26, 1861.

9. "City Intelligence: The Martial Spirit," *New Orleans Bee,* April 9, 1861.

10. "The City: Jackson Guards," *Daily Picayune,* May 3, 1862.

11. "The Irish Contingent," *Daily True Delta,* March 9, 1862.

12. "The Blücher Guards," *Daily Picayune,* May 3, 1861.

13. "Meeting of the Colored Population," *Daily Picayune,* April 22, 1861.

14. Stephen J. Ochs, *A Black Patriot and a White Priest: André Cailloux and Claude Paschal Maistre in Civil War New Orleans* (Baton Rouge: Louisiana State University Press, 2000), 78.

15. Melissa Daggett, "Spiritualism among Creoles of Color in Nineteenth-Century New Orleans: The Life and Times of Henry Louis Rey," *Louisiana History* 55, no. 4 (Fall 2014): 416.

16. Thomas O'Connor, ed., *History of the Fire Department of New Orleans* (New Orleans, 1895), 140.

17. Arthur W. Bergeron Jr., *Guide to Louisiana Confederate Military Units, 1861–1865* (Baton Rouge: Louisiana State University Press, 1989), 187.

18. "Military Fair," *Daily Picayune,* July 2, 1861.

19. "Ladies' Aid Society, Third District," *Daily Picayune,* August 8, 1861.

20. "Col. Mandeville Marigny in the Field," *Daily Picayune,* April 27, 1861.

21. Bergeron, *Guide to Louisiana Confederate Military Units,* 96–97.

22. Ella Lonn, *Foreigners in the Confederacy* (Gloucester, MA: Peter Smith 1965), 113–15; "European Brigade," *Daily Picayune,* February 15, 1862.

23. Marion Southwood, *Beauty and Booty, the Watchword of New Orleans* (New York: M. Doolady, 1867), 18.

24. Michael D. Pierson, *Mutiny at Fort Jackson* (Chapel Hill: University of North Carolina Press, 2008), 100–101; Confederate States of America, War Department, *Proceedings of the Court of Inquiry Relative to the Fall of New Orleans* (Richmond, VA: R. M. Smith, 1864), 16.

25. George Washington Cable, "New Orleans before the Capture," *Century Illustrated Monthly Magazine* 29, no. 7 (July 1886): 919.

26. Kendall, *History of New Orleans,* 242–43.

27. Julia LeGrand, *Journal of Julia LeGrand, New Orleans, 1862–1863,* ed. Kate Mason Rowland and Mrs. Morris L. Croxall (Richmond, VA: Everrett Waddey, 1911), 37.

28. "The City: Mayor's Office Besieged," *Daily Picayune,* August 1, 1861.

29. Committee of the Free Market of New Orleans, *Report of the Committee of the Free Market of New Orleans* (New Orleans: Bulletin Book and Job Office, 1862), 66.

30. Cable, "New Orleans before the Capture," 918.

31. Pierson, *Mutiny at Fort Jackson,* 53.

32. "Vigilance of Mayor Monroe," *Daily Picayune,* September 27, 1861.

33. Pierson, *Mutiny at Fort Jackson,* 7.

34. Ibid., 16.

35. Ibid., 43.

36. Ibid., 120.

37. Confederate States of America, War Department, *Proceedings of the Court of Inquiry,* 19.

38. William Howard Russell, *My Diary North and South* (London: Bradbury and Evans, 1862), 1:361–62.

39. Kendall, *History of New Orleans,* 261.

40. Lonn, *Foreigners in the Confederacy,* 481.

41. Pierson, *Mutiny at Fort Jackson,* 70.

42. Confederate States of America, War Department, *Proceedings of the Court of Inquiry,* 11–13.

43. Pierson, *Mutiny at Fort Jackson,* 114.

44. Ibid., 117.

45. Ibid., 130–31.

46. Confederate States of America, War Department, *Proceedings of the Court of Inquiry,* 102.

47. Southwood, *Beauty and Booty,* 21.

48. Kendall, *History of New Orleans,* 260–62; "The City," *Daily Picayune,* April 26, 1862.

49. Kendall, *History of New Orleans,* 260–62.

50. Confederate States of America, War Department, *Proceedings of the Court of Inquiry,* 158.

51. Pierson. *Mutiny at Fort Jackson,* 101–3.

52. "The Reign of Terror in New-Orleans," *New York Times,* May 25, 1862.

53. Pierson, *Mutiny at Fort Jackson,* 3–4.

54. Kendall, *History of New Orleans,* 263–69.

55. Pierson, *Mutiny at Fort Jackson,* 134–35.

56. Robert S. Holzman, *Stormy Ben Butler* (New York: Macmillan, 1954), 34.

57. Benjamin F. Butler, *Autobiography and Personal Reminiscences of Major-General Benj. F. Butler: Butler's Book* (Boston: A.M. Thayer, 1892), 438.

58. Ibid., 417–19.

59. Kendall, *History of New Orleans,* 278–80.

60. Southwood, *Beauty and Booty,* 270–72. Monroe was released by Department of the Gulf, General Order 115, December 23, 1862.

61. Butler, *Autobiography,* 449.

62. LeGrand, *Journal,* 120–24.

63. Edward McPherson, *The Political History of the United States of America during the Great Rebellion* (Washington, D.C.: Phillips & Solomon, 1864), 543–45.

64. Gerald M. Capers, *Occupied City: New Orleans under the Federals, 1862–1865* (Lexington: University of Kentucky Press, 1965), 189.

65. John F. Nau, *The German People of New Orleans, 1850–1900* (Hattiesburg: University of Southern Mississippi, 1974), 88.

66. O'Connor, *History of the Fire Department,* 169–72.

67. "Names of Persons Taking the Oath of Allegiance Index and Registered Enemies Record"; includes "Copy of Index to Five Books. Containing the Names of Persons Taking the Oath of Allegiance in 1862," and "Copy of a Record of Registered Enemies," Williams Research Center, Historic New Orleans Collection, MSS 143.1, MSS 143.2; U.S. Army, "List of Receipts, Special Supply Agent, Rebel Property. New Orleans, U.S. Army," by Benjamin F. Flanders, September 5, 1863, Williams Research Center, Historic New Orleans Collection, MSS 281, F.2.

68. Bergeron, *Guide to Louisiana Confederate Military Units,* 95.

69. U.S. Army, Department of the Gulf, General Order No. 55, August 4, 1862, *Daily Picayune,* August 6, 1862.

70. Butler, *Autobiography,* 395, 406.

71. Jo Ann Carrigan, *The Saffron Scourge: A History of Yellow Fever in Louisiana, 1796–1905* (Lafayette: Center for Louisiana Studies, University of Southwestern Louisiana 1994).

72. Benn Trask to Scott Ellis, July 27, 2011.

73. Butler, *Autobiography,* 491.

74. Ochs, *A Black Patriot and a White Priest,* 76.

75. Ibid., 116–17.

76. Anthony Del Rosario, "Historic Structures Report for Schwegmann Family Tomb in St. Roch Cemetery No. 1 New Orleans," unpublished report for Studio in Building Preserva-

tion, Master in Preservation Studies, Tulane School of Architecture, February 12, 2010, http://docslide.us/documents/schwegmann-family-tomb-report.html.

77. Holzman, *Stormy Ben Butler,* 79–82.

78. Butler, *Autobiography,* 522–26.

79. Ochs, *A Black Patriot and a White Priest,* 144.

80. "The City: Negro Funeral," *Daily Picayune,* July 30, 1863.

81. David C. Rankin, "The Impact of the Civil War on the Free Colored Community of New Orleans," *Perspectives in American History* 11 (1977–78): 402.

82. Eric Foner, *Reconstruction: America's Unfinished Revolution, 1863–1877,* 2nd ed. (New York: Harper Perennial, 2014), 35–37.

83. John C. Rodrigue, *Lincoln and Reconstruction* (Carbondale: Southern Illinois University Press, 2013), 51–53.

84. Foner, *Reconstruction,* 200–201.

85. Kendall, *History of New Orleans,* 241.

86. Butler, *Autobiography,* 426.

87. James G. Hollandsworth, *An Absolute Massacre: The New Orleans Race Riot of July 30, 1866* (Baton Rouge: Louisiana State University Press, 2001), 135, map facing introduction.

88. Loren Schweninger, "Antebellum Free Persons of Color in Postbellum Louisiana," *Louisiana History* 30 (Fall 1989): 353–54.

89. Rankin, "Impact of the Civil War," 402.

90. *Gardner's New Orleans Directory for 1866* (New Orleans: C. Gardner, 1866).

91. "The City Election," *Daily Picayune,* March 13, 1866.

92. Giles Vandal, *The New Orleans Riot of 1866: Anatomy of a Tragedy* (Lafayette: Center for Louisiana Studies, University of Southwestern Louisiana, 1983), 204–7.

93. Hollandsworth, *Absolute Massacre,* 44–45.

94. Vandal, *New Orleans Riot,* 128–34.

95. Ibid., 171–80.

96. Ibid., 180–82.

97. Rankin, "Impact of the Civil War," 402–3.

98. Hollandsworth, *Absolute Massacre,* 151–52.

99. Rankin, "Impact of the Civil War," 399–400.

100. Justin A. Nystrom, "Redeemer's Carnival: The Urban Drama of Reconstruction in New Orleans" (PhD diss., University of Georgia, 2004), 7.

101. Daggett, "Spiritualism among Creoles of Color," 409–31.

102. Second German Presbyterian Church, "Resolution of the Board of Trustees of the Second German Presbyterian Church, June 17, 1867," in *Claiborne Avenue Presbyterian Church (New Orleans, LA.) Records, 1863–1955* (Montreat, NC: Historical Foundation of the Presbyterian and Reformed Churches, 1983); Second German Presbyterian Church, *Fiftieth Anniversary of the German Presbyterian Church* (New Orleans: Second German Presbyterian Church, 1913).

103. William de Marigny Hyland, interview by Scott Ellis, New Orleans, May 14, 2011.

104. Grace King, *Creole Families of New Orleans* (New York: Macmillan, 1921), 55–56.

105. "Death of Mr. Bernard Marigny," *New Orleans Daily Bee,* February 4, 1868.

106. "Funeral of Mr. Bernard Marigny," *New Orleans Bee,* February 6, 1868. Lloyd Sensat,

partner of Eugene Cizek, portrayed Marigny in several reenactments. He is also buried in the Marigny tomb.

107. The sum of the two inventories was $15,454. "Succession of Mrs. Bernard de Marigny," State Library of Louisiana. Bernard's succession of February 7 and 8, 1868, is cataloged under that of his second wife, and appears as pp. 3–12 of the online exhibit, http://cdm16313.contentdm.oclc.org/cdm/compoundobject/collection/LWP/id/1446/rec/1, accessed November 21, 2016.

11. A Restless Sleep

1. Charles Nordhoff, *The Cotton States in the Spring and Summer of 1875* (New York: D. Appleton, 1876), 57–60.

2. John Smith Kendall, *History of New Orleans* (Chicago: Lewis Publishing, 1922), 597, transcribed by Bill Thayer, http://penelope.uchicago.edu/Thayer/E/Gazetteer/Places/America/United_States/Louisiana/New_Orleans/_Texts/KENHNO/home.html.

3. Louisiana State Legislature, *Annual Report of the Auditor of Public Accounts to the General Assembly of the State of Louisiana, 1877* (New Orleans: Office of the *Democrat*, 1877), 146–49.

4. *Daily Picayune*, March 15, 1870; "The Third District," *Daily Picayune*, July 29, 1870; "The Suburbs: A Sentimental Journey through the Old Third," *Daily Picayune*, May 17, 1874.

5. "Appeal to the Citizens of the Third District," *Daily Picayune*, August 22, 1881; "Washington Square," *Daily Picayune*, September 2, 1881.

6. Kendall, *History of New Orleans*, 359–75, 376–80.

7. Ibid., 400–406.

8. This and all subsequent census figures are from the U.S. censuses of the given dates.

9. Daniel Rosenberg, *New Orleans Dockworkers: Race, Labor and Unionism, 1892–1923* (Albany: State University of New York Press, 1988), 18.

10. John G. Schwegmann, "Just Like Meeting an Old Friend," *Times-Picayune*, June 28, 1978.

11. Joseph Jones, *Quarantine and Sanitary Operations of the Board of Health of the State of Louisiana during 1880, 1881, 1882 and 1883* (Baton Rouge: Leon Jastremski, 1884), 185–86.

12. Joy Jackson, *New Orleans in the Gilded Age: Politics and Urban Progress, 1880–1896*, 2nd ed. (Lafayette: Louisiana Historical Association, in cooperation with the Center for Louisiana Studies of the University of Southwestern Louisiana, 1997), 95, 103.

13. Louisiana Cotton Manufactory, "Report to the Stockholders of the Louisiana Cotton Manufactory," February 8, 1872, and "Report of the Superintendent to the Board of Directors of the Louisiana Cotton Manufactory," January 31, 1872, Tulane University Library, 976.3 (633.5) N932.

14. "By Master in Chancery, Auction Sale by Order of Court, Louisiana Cotton Manufactory and Batture," *Daily Picayune*, March 22, 1877.

15. "100 Years Ago," *Times-Picayune*, April 15, 1987.

16. Richard Campanella, *Geographies of New Orleans: Urban Fabrics before the Storm* (Lafayette: Center for Louisiana Studies, University of Louisiana at Lafayette, 2006), 256.

17. Records of Saints Peter and Paul and Holy Trinity Catholic Churches, Archdiocese of New Orleans, Sacramental Records.

18. Jeremy Labadie and Argyle Wolf-Knapp, *New Orleans Beer: A Hoppy History of Big Easy Brewing* (Charleston, SC: American Palate/History Press, 2014), 37–39.

19. "Columbia Brewery Taps First Kegs," *Daily Picayune,* June 23, 1899.

20. "Spinning Yarns," *Daily Picayune,* September 8, 1890.

21. G. J. Wegener, *A Brief Story of My Life* (New Orleans, 1943), 46.

22. William Robinson Konrad, "The Diminishing Influences of German Culture in New Orleans Life since 1865," *Louisiana Historical Quarterly* 24, no. 1 (January 1941): 23.

23. "The City Council," *Daily Picayune,* May 21, 1884.

24. L. W. Brown, "Protection of Cities against Encroachment of the Mississippi," in *Riparian Lands of the Mississippi River, Past–Present–Prospective,* ed. Frank Tompkins (Chicago: A. L. Swift, 1901), 258–66.

25. Rosenberg, *New Orleans Dockworkers,* 47.

26. Ibid., 1–2.

27. Eric Arnesen, "New Orleans Dock Workers Struggle for Control, 1902–1903," in *New Orleans and Urban Louisiana,* pt. B, *1860 to World War I,* ed. Samuel C. Shepherd Jr. (Lafayette: Center for Louisiana Studies, University of Louisiana at Lafayette, 2005), 532, 534.

28. Certificate of Burial, Mandeville de Marigny, June 4, 1890, Archdiocese of New Orleans, Sacramental Records.

29. New Orleans Public Service, Inc., "Did You Know?," *Riders' Digest,* March 11, 1957.

30. *Soards' New Orleans City Directory,* 1870, 1880, 1890, and 1900.

31. "Wanted: Male Help," *Daily Picayune,* December 8, 1905; "Wanted: Female Help," *Daily Picayune,* October 22, 1903.

32. Underwriters Inspection Bureau of New Orleans street rate slips, 1897, New Orleans Public Library, City Archives and Special Collections, http://nutrias.org/~nopl/info/louinfo/1897/dauphiner.htm.

33. Jackson, *New Orleans in the Gilded Age,* 161.

34. Ibid., 101–2.

35. Pascal Calogero, interview by Scott Ellis, New Orleans, May 12, 2011.

36. Konrad, "Diminishing Influences," 16–21.

37. "Death of John Lange," *Daily Picayune,* June 27, 1900; "Charles Burkenstock," *Daily Picayune,* July 23, 1900; "Louis Leonhard Dies of Paralysis," *Daily Picayune,* September 16, 1901.

38. "The Last Days of the Ueber School," *Daily Picayune,* September 22, 1901.

39. "Ask Julia Street," *New Orleans Magazine,* March 2010.

40. "Opening of the Elysium Theater," *Freeman* (Indianapolis), December 1, 1906.

41. "Twenty Four Enter for C.A.A. Stag," *Times-Picayune,* November 24, 1915.

42. "Girl Not Guilty in Theater Fire, Relative Claims," *Times-Picayune,* March 15, 1919.

43. Theater listings, *Times-Picayune,* June 16, 1945.

44. Jackson, *New Orleans in the Gilded Age,* 200–201.

12. The Workers' Paradise

1. Pascal Calogero, interview by Scott Ellis, New Orleans, May 12, 2011.

2. "Italian Opera," *Daily Picayune,* November 10, 1860.

3. A. V. Margavio and Jerome J. Salomone, *Bread and Respect: The Italians of Louisiana* (Gretna, LA: Pelican Publishing, 2002), 36, 37.

4. Louise Edwards, "Yellow Fever and the Sicilian Community in New Orleans" (unpublished manuscript, University of Minnesota, May 30, 1989), 12.

5. Louise Reynes Edwards-Simpson, "Sicilians Come to New Orleans: The Making of Little Palermo," in *New Orleans and Urban Louisiana,* pt. B, *1860 to World War I,* ed. Samuel C. Shepherd Jr. (Lafayette: Center for Louisiana Studies, University of Louisiana at Lafayette, 2005), 387.

6. Eleanor McMain, "Behind the Yellow Fever in Little Palermo," *Charities,* November 4, 1905, 12, transcribed by Bill Thayer, http://penelope.uchicago.edu/Thayer/E/Gazetteer/Places/America/United_States/Louisiana/New_Orleans/_Texts/Yellow_Fever_in_Little_Palermo*.html.

7. Margavio and Salomone, *Bread and Respect,* 66.

8. Dino Cinelli, "Estratto," *Cintro Studi Emigrazione* (Rome), no. 97 (March 1990): 66.

9. Thomas Fiehrer, "From Quadrille to Stomp: The Creole Origin of Jazz," in *New Orleans and Urban Louisiana,* pt. B, *1860 to World War I,* ed. Samuel C. Shepherd Jr. (Lafayette: Center for Louisiana Studies, University of Louisiana at Lafayette, 2005), 463.

10. "Heavy Damage Done by Storm on River Front," *Times-Picayune,* September 30, 1915.

11. "Poland St. Barn Wrecked by Wind; Three Men Hurt," *Times-Picayune,* September 30, 1915.

12. "Vieux Carré in Direct Path of Hurricane; Weathers Storm with Very Little Damage," *Times-Picayune,* September 30, 1915.

13. "Negro Orphanage Gone," *Times-Picayune,* October 3, 1915.

14. CreoleGen.org, "Couvent School Board of Directors, 1917," July 21, 2012, http://www.creolegen.org/2012/07/21/couvent-school-board-of-directors-1917/.

15. "Third District Building Association," *Times-Picayune,* May 4, 1917.

16. The formal name of the Industrial Canal is the Inner Harbor Navigation Canal. Frederick Dobney, David Moore, Jeffrey Teffinger, R. Christopher Goodwin, Mark Catin, Paul C. Armstrong, James Cripps, and Carol Poplin, *Evaluation of the National Register Eligibility of the Inner Harbor Navigation Canal Lock in Orleans Parish, Louisiana* (New Orleans: R. Christopher Goodwin and Associates, 1987), 90–116.

17. Juliette Landphair, "'The Forgotten People of New Orleans': Community, Vulnerability, and the Lower Ninth Ward," *Journal of American History* 94 (December 2007): 837–45.

18. "Church Dedicated Sunday," *Times-Picayune,* January 10, 1920.

19. New Orleans City Council, Ordinance C.C.S. 7842, "An Ordinance Providing for the Opening, Widening and Extension of North Rampart Street, St. Bernard Street, Annette Street and St. Claude Avenue or Street," April 19, 1924.

20. "Women's Meetings," *Times-Picayune,* August 25, 1914.

21. Lolita C. Cherrie, "Seventh Ward Civic League, Its History and Accomplishments," accessed July 15, 2016, http://www.creolegen.org/2013/06/08/seventhward-civic-league-its-history-and-accomplishments.

22. Roman Heleniak, "Local Reaction to the Great Depression in New Orleans, 1929–1933," *Louisiana History* 10, no. 4 (Fall 1969): 304–6.

23. "Up and Down the Street, Baptist Rescue," *Times-Picayune,* February 16, 1940.

24. Kenneth Holditch, interview by Scott Ellis, New Orleans, June 21, 2014.

25. U.S. Federal Housing Administration, *Underwriting Manual: Underwriting and Valuation Procedure under Title II of the National Housing Act* (Washington, D.C.: Federal Housing

Administration, April 1936), section 232, Urban Oasis, http://www.urbanoasis.org/projects/fha/FHAUnderwritingManualPtII.html#201 (site discontinued.

26. U.S. Federal Housing Administration, Federal Home Loan Bank Board, Home Owners' Loan Corporation, "New Orleans Residential Security Map," ca. 1935, National Archives and Records Administration, 6082413, Urban Oasis, http://www.urbanoasis.org/projects/holc-fha/digital-holc-maps/ (site discontinued).

27. Benjamin Alexander-Bloch, "Domino Sugar's Chalmette Refinery's History and Production Recognized," *Times-Picayune,* December 13, 2012. The sugar refinery has operated since 1909.

28. Elizabeth Ellison-Frost, "Chalmette Refining, LLC Celebrates 100 Years in St. Bernard Parish, Louisiana," September 23, 2015, http://www.chalmetterefining.com/go/doc/5707/2451122/Brief_History_for_The_Lamp.docx (page no longer available). The oil refinery has operated since 1915.

29. Richard Campanella, "When St. Bernard Made Cars: Arabi Assembly Plant Represented a Little Bit of the Motor City in the Crescent City," *Times-Picayune,* November 5, 2014. The Ford plant was active from 1923 to 1971.

30. George J. Binczewski, "The Energy Crisis and the Aluminum Industry: Can We Learn from History?," *Member Journal of the Minerals, Metals & Materials Society (JOM),* February 2002, http://www.tms.org/pubs/journals/JOM/0202/Binczewski-0202.html.

31. Contributing Writer, "Hubig's Pies: 'Simon the Pieman' Was Major Player," *Times-Picayune,* May 26, 2011.

32. "Stoblers Play Mysterious Nine; Continue to Win," *Times-Picayune,* July 12, 1924.

33. "Black Golds Win over Hubigs 7–6," *Times-Picayune,* October 29, 1924.

34. Evelyn Broders, interview by Scott Ellis, New Orleans, December 21, 2013.

35. Joan and Laura Guiccione, interview by Scott Ellis, New Orleans, August 2, 2014.

36. Calogero interview; Chris and Marilyn Hankel, interview by Scott Ellis, New Orleans, November 16, 2011; Joan and Laura Guiccione interview.

37. Amy Ferrara Smith, "The New Orleans Grocery Man: Ferrara Supermarket's Mr. Merrill" (MA thesis, University of New Orleans Theses and Dissertations, 2007), http://scholarworks.uno.edu/td/1059.

38. Calogero interview.

39. "1875 St. Roch Market," *Makin' Groceries in New Orleans,* accessed April 19, 2016, http://www.websitesneworleans.com/makingroceriesinneworleans/id197.html.

40. "Three Markets Will Be Rebuilt as WPA Project," *Times-Picayune,* November 30, 1938.

41. Hankel interview.

42. Joan and Laura Guiccione interview.

43. Ibid.

44. *Directory of St. Paul's Evangelical Lutheran Church* (New Orleans: St. Paul's Lutheran Evangelical Church, 1920), ttp://freepages.religions.rootsweb.ancestry.com/~neworleans/st_paul_records/.

45. "Catholics Begin Enrolling Pupils for New Session," *Times-Picayune,* September 7, 1938.

46. Calogero interview.

47. Edward F. Haas, *DeLesseps S. Morrison and the Image of Reform* (Baton Rouge: Louisiana State University Press, 1974), 52–53.

48. Hankel interview.

49. "The Last of the Maltese," *Daily Picayune,* June 12, 1881.

50. Calogero interview.

51. "Battle Field to Play Ground," *Times-Picayune Dixie Roto Magazine,* February 11, 1951, 12–13.

52. Hankel interview.

53. "Downtown Gym Has an Outdoor Swimming Pool," *Times-Picayune,* November 20, 1916.

54. Eve Abrams, "Along Saint Claude," accessed September 4, 2015, http://eveabrams.com/audiodocs.html.

55. Hankel interview; used by permission.

56. Abrams, "Along Saint Claude."

57. Joan and Laura Guiccione interview.

58. Jack Haney, "Lagniappe, Odds and Ends of the Town, Here and There," *Times-Picayune,* December 9, 1925.

59. Carolyn Kolb, "Steppin' Back: The Golden Days of Dance Halls," *New Orleans Magazine,* April 2011, http://www.myneworleans.com/New-Orleans-Magazine/April-2011/STEPPIN-rsquo-BACK/.

60. Michael Hurly, "Paris Theatre in New Orleans, LA," Cinema Treasures, accessed March 24, 2016, http://cinematreasures.org/theaters/22787.

61. Cinema Tour, "Piety Theatre," accessed March 24, 2016, http://www.cinematour.com/tour/us/40322.html.

62. Cinema Tour, "Bijou Theatre," accessed March 24, 2016, http://www.cinematour.com/tour/us/40311.html.

63. "Up and Down the Street," *Times-Picayune,* June 11, 1941.

64. "Toasts to Three Queens Offered by King Thirdist," *Times-Picayune,* February 22, 1939.

65. "When Carnival Hit Home," *Times-Picayune,* February 25, 2001.

66. "Carnival Balls, Parades Called Off for Season," *Times-Picayune,* December 13, 1941.

67. R. J. Henson, "Big Slot Syndicate Is Operating Openly," *Times-Picayune,* October 3, 1945.

68. "Court Upholds Slots' Smashing," *Times-Picayune,* November 28, 1947.

69. "Smokey Mary Makes Last Run to Milneburg, Crowds Jam Coaches of Old Train," *Times-Picayune,* March 16, 1932.

70. Catherine Mieri, "53 in Marigny," *Faubourg Marigny News* 9, nos. 1 and 2 (January–February 1980).

71. "Pontchartrain Tracks, First Laid in United States, to Be Taken Up," *Times-Picayune,* March 29, 1935.

72. Clarence John Laughlin Photograph Collection, Williams Research Center, Historic New Orleans Collection, http://cdm16313.contentdm.oclc.org/cdm/landingpage/collection/p16313coll21.

73. Abrams, "Along Saint Claude"; Hankel interview.

74. "1944: Higgins Industries in New Orleans Contributes to War Effort," *Times-Picayune,* November 17, 2011; U.S. Merchant Marines at War, "American Merchant Marine at War," accessed July 6, 2016, www.usmm.org.

75. John G. Schwegmann Jr., "Just Like Meeting an Old Friend: The Impossible Dream," *Times-Picayune,* September 6, 1978.

76. U.S. Department of the Interior, National Parks Service, National Register of Historic Places, "Schwegmann Bros. Giant Supermarket No. 1," Registration Form, National Register Information System ID Number 14000314, June 11, 2014.

77. Catharine Mieri, "Historic Businesses of Faubourg Marigny," *Preservation in Print* 10, no. 6 (August 1983): 10.

78. Amy Ferrara Smith to Scott Ellis, January 13, 2016.

79. U.S. Congress, "Servicemen's Readjustment Act of 1944," S. 1767, Public Law 346, 78th Cong., 2nd sess.

80. Liva Baker, *The Second Battle of New Orleans* (New York: Harper Collins, 1996), 2, 3.

81. John Smestad Jr., "The Role of Archbishop Joseph F. Rummel in the Desegregation of Catholic Schools in New Orleans," *Student Historical Journal* (Loyola University History Department) 25 (1993–94).

82. Justin Nystrom, "The Vanished World of the New Orleans Longshoreman," *Southern Spaces,* March 5, 2014, 3, 7, http://southernspaces.org/2014/vanished-world-new-orleans-longshoreman.

83. Scott S. Ellis, *Madame Vieux Carré: The French Quarter in the Twentieth Century* (Jackson: University Press of Mississippi, 2009), 79–80.

84. 716 Dauphine St., Lot 18755, Square: 73, Collins C. Diboll Vieux Carré Digital Survey, Williams Research Center, Historic New Orleans Collection, accessed November 5, 2016, http://www.hnoc.org/vcs/property_info.php?lot=18755.

85. Eugene Cizek to Scott Ellis, July 21, 2014.

86. Martha Ann Samuel, "Renovation Brings Beauty," *Times-Picayune Dixie Roto Magazine,* September 27, 1964, 18–19.

87. Eugene Cizek and Lloyd Sensat, interview by Scott Ellis, New Orleans, February 8, 2011.

88. Holditch interview.

89. Cizek and Sensat interview.

90. "Public Notice, Expressway Protest Meeting," *Times-Picayune,* June 13, 1965.

91. Ellis, *Madame Vieux Carré,* 96–101.

92. "Factions Agree on Legislature," *Times-Picayune,* April 14, 1956.

93. Lawrence M. Knopp Jr., "Gentrification and Gay Community Development in a New Orleans Neighborhood" (PhD diss., University of Iowa, 1989), 65.

94. Paul Atkinson, "Survey Lists Landmarks and Areas Worth Saving," *Times-Picayune,* June 7, 1967.

95. Darlene Fife, *Portraits from Memory: New Orleans in the Sixties* (New Orleans: Surregional Press, 2000), 1.

96. *The Quorum* (Manhattan, KS: Doorknob Films & Such-A-Much Productions, 2004), DVD.

97. "Pastor Resigns Post with Club; Other Duties, Possible Transfer Cited," *Times-Picayune,* May 20, 1965.

98. *The Quorum.*

99. "Four Plead Guilty in Quarter Raid," *Times-Picayune,* July 31, 1964.

100. Christine Wiltz, *The Last Madam* (New York: Da Capo Press, 2001), 151–81.

101. Soulé quoted in "Four Plead Guilty in Quarter Raid," *Times-Picayune,* July 31, 1964.

102. "Gettys Enters Suit over Bribe Money," *Times-Picayune,* January 25, 1975.

103. Lee Meitzen Grue, interview by Scott Ellis, New Orleans, November 22, 2014.

104. Ellis, *Madame Vieux Carré,* 87.

105. *The Quorum.*

106. "Quorum Club Cases Dropped; Charges against 68 are Nol Prossed," *Times-Picayune,* September 23, 1964.

107. The last newspaper mention of the club appears in "N.O. Anti-Viet War Group Plans Film," *Times-Picayune,* January 25, 1967; Grue interview.

108. Ellis, *Madame Vieux Carré,* 88–90.

13. Rebirth and Reclaiming

1. All population figures are from the U.S. Census of the stated year. These population figures are derived from census tracts 18 (the Triangle) and 26 (the majority of the Rectangle). Calculations by the author. Tract 26 ends at Franklin, so part of the Rectangle is missing from these figures. Other cited sources, such as Knopp and Roesel, derive certain statistics from the Franklin to Press portion of the Marigny.

2. Lawrence M. Knopp Jr., "Gentrification and Gay Community Development in a New Orleans Neighborhood" (PhD diss., University of Iowa, 1989), 50, table 1.

3. Ibid., table 2.

4. Ibid., 51, table 4.

5. Ibid., 56, table 7.

6. Ibid., 52, fig. 6.

7. Jeffrey W. Roesel, "A Sense of Place: Residential Perceptions of Waterfront Land Use Changes in the Vieux Carré and Marigny" (MA thesis, University of New Orleans, 1992), 45, table 3–8.

8. Knopp, "Gentrification and Gay Community," 57, table 8.

9. "Apartments below Canal, Unfurnished," *Times-Picayune,* May and June 1970.

10. Knopp, "Gentrification and Gay Community," 60, fig. 11, 61, fig. 13.

11. "Houses for Sale, below Canal," *Times-Picayune,* January, May, and November, 1970.

12. Bill Rushton, "The Faubourg Marigny: Straddling the Centuries," *New Orleans Magazine,* March 1970, 56; used by permission of *New Orleans Magazine.*

13. Frank Gagnard, "On The Square, Stage Notes," *Times-Picayune,* January 21, 1969.

14. James Nolan, interview by Scott Ellis, New Orleans, October 13, 2007.

15. Cinema Tour, "Paris Theatre," accessed March 24, 2016, http://www.cinematour.com/tour/us/25587.html.

16. Eugene Cizek and Lloyd Sensat, interview by Scott Ellis, New Orleans, February 8, 2011; used by permission.

17. Knopp, "Gentrification and Gay Community," 70.

18. "Building Watchers," *Preservation Press* (New Orleans), 1, no. 1 (August 1975): 5.

19. Cizek and Sensat interview.

20. Faubourg Marigny Improvement Association, "Restated Articles of Incorporation of the Faubourg Marigny Improvement Association, Inc.," September 20, 2007.

21. Alex Vialou, interview by Scott Ellis, New Orleans, November 10, 2012.

22. U.S. Department of the Interior, National Park Service, National Register of Historic

Places, "Faubourg Marigny Historic District," National Register Information System ID Number 74000930, December 31, 1974.

23. Historic Tax Credit Coalition, *First Annual Report on the Economic Impact of the Federal Historic Tax Credit* (Washington, D.C., March 2010), 6.

24. "Historic Districts Body Created Here," *Times-Picayune,* February 28, 1975.

25. City of New Orleans, Historic District Landmarks Commission Guidelines, Introduction, April 2015, http://www.nola.gov/hdlc/documents/01_introduction-2015–04–24/.

26. Robyn Halvorsen, interview by Scott Ellis, New Orleans, May 23, 2013.

27. Cizek and Sensat interview; used by permission.

28. Loren R. Brooks, "Insured Homesteads Set Up Central Appraisal Bureau," *Times-Picayune,* March 8, 1936.

29. "Appraising Appraisals," *Times-Picayune,* October 2, 1976.

30. Charles B. Goslee Jr., "Appraisal-Housing Problem," *Preservation Press* (Preservation Resource Center, New Orleans) 1, no. 2 (October 1975).

31. Cizek and Sensat interview.

32. Frank L. Schneider, "S&Ls Revamping Central Appraisal Bureau," *Times Picayune,* March 26, 1976.

33. "Appraisal Bureau Use No Longer Mandatory," *Times-Picayune,* March 9, 1979.

34. J. Douglas Murphy, "Loan Institutions Also Bilked," *Times-Picayune,* May 5, 1979.

35. *Times Picayune,* December 9, 1968.

36. "Realty Board Accepts Two," *Times-Picayune,* October 8, 1972.

37. "Business Charters Listed by La. Secretary of State," *Times-Picayune,* March 5, 1973.

38. Halvorsen interview.

39. Halvorsen interview; Dorian Bennett, interview by Scott Ellis, New Orleans, September 29, 2013.

40. Kenneth Holditch, interview by Scott Ellis, New Orleans, June 21, 2014; used by permission.

41. Gordon Gsell, "Took Payoffs, Appraiser Says," *Times-Picayune,* May 15, 1979.

42. Gordon Gsell, "Property Appraiser Guilty," *Times-Picayune,* May 18, 1979.

43. "Hudson Fined Total of $10,000," *Times-Picayune,* September 7, 1979. Hudson died circa 1988.

44. Knopp, "Gentrification and Gay Community," 75.

45. Joan and Laura Guiccione, interview by Scott Ellis, New Orleans, August 2, 2014; used by permission.

46. Bennett interview.

47. "Aaron" (pseud), email interview by Scott Ellis, January 20, 2011; used by permission.

48. Jamie Temple, interview by Scott Ellis, Bay St. Louis, MS, October 18, 2014.

49. Susan Finch, "Gay Community Losing Charlene's, Lesbians Felt Safe since '77," *Times-Picayune,* February 19, 1999.

50. Temple interview, October 18, 2014.

51. Ibid.

52. Jamie Temple, interview by Scott Ellis, Pass Christian, MS, April 23, 2016.

53. "100 Years Ago" (advertisement), *Times-Picayune,* April 15, 1987.

54. "Homestead to Become Factory," *Times-Picayune,* October 16, 1938; legal notices, Jason's Bar, *Times-Picayune,* January 1, 1986.

55. Nancy Weldon, "Gay Crisis Line Lending an Ear to Homosexuals," *Times-Picayune,* March 6, 1977.

56. Paul Atkinson, "Gay Fest Gets Beer OK," *Times-Picayune,* June 22, 1979.

57. Rich Magill, *Exposing Hatred: A Report on the Victimization of Lesbian and Gay People in New Orleans, Louisiana* (New Orleans: Louisiana Lesbian and Gay Political Action Caucus, 1991), 34.

58. Scott S. Ellis, *Madame Vieux Carré: The French Quarter in the Twentieth Century* (Jackson: University Press of Mississippi, 2009), 164–68.

59. Patrick O'Rourke, interview by Scott Ellis, New Orleans, March 20, 2005.

60. Ibid., 158.

61. Historic Tax Credit Coalition, *First Annual Report on the Economic Impact of the Federal Historic Tax Credit* (Washington, D.C., March 2010), 6.

62. Bennett interview.

63. John Pope, "Killer's Trail Has Left Few Clues to Cure," *Times-Picayune,* August 11, 1985.

64. John Pope, "AIDS Fears among N.O. Gays Are Growing," *Times-Picayune,* May 27, 1985.

65. Temple interview, April 23, 2016; David Leser, "N.O.'s Gay Chorus Finds Something to Sing About," *Times-Picayune,* September 7, 1983.

66. John Pope, "Charity Cradles the Dying," *Times-Picayune,* August 13, 1985.

67. Temple interview, April 23, 2016.

68. John Pope, "Catholics Plan AIDS Residence," *Times-Picayune,* June 21, 1985.

69. Kevin Bozant, interview by Scott Ellis, New Orleans, November 11, 2012.

70. Howard Smith to Scott Ellis, email, August 1, 2016.

71. Elizabeth Mullener, "Exodus Leaves City with Empty Feeling," *Times-Picayune,* January 16, 1994.

72. Robyn Halvorsen, "Making the City More Livable" (letter to the editor), *Times-Picayune,* February 2, 1994.

73. "Grocery Pioneer Dies at 83; Schwegmann Built Empire," *Times-Picayune,* March 7, 1995.

74. Ronnette King, "Grocery Buyout a Costly Venture; Schwegmann Goes into Debt," *Times-Picayune,* March 31, 1996.

75. Ronnette King, "Food Fight: Schwegmann's Exit from the Grocery Store Scene Left a Hole in the New Orleans Area Market and Competitors Are Eager to Fill the Void," *Times-Picayune,* October 3, 1999.

76. Polk directories' responses for St. Claude and Elysian Field from 1978 to 2010 were analyzed for retail and residential activity. Every address listed as residential, even if a multi-family unit, was counted as one residence. Although government and nonprofit offices were also noted, their numbers were too small to be significant.

77. Robert Tallant, *Mardi Gras . . . as It Was* (Gretna, LA: Pelican Publishing, 2000), 144–45.

78. Constance Adler, "Drawing from the Past," *Gambit,* February 25, 2003, http://www.bestofneworleans.com/gambit/drawing-from-the-past/Content?oid=1241234.

79. "Second Line" was written and recorded by Bill Sinegal in 1964. David Kunian, "Obituary: Bill Sinegal," *Offbeat,* April 14, 2014.

14. The Many Lives of Frenchmen Street

1. John Churchill Chase, *Frenchmen, Desire, Goodchildren, and Other Streets of New Orleans*, 3rd ed. (New York: Touchstone Books, 1997), 57.

2. Barthélémy Lafon, *Plan du Faubourg Marigny conforme au trace fait par Bm. Lafon, ingens. geogr. et arpenteur du Compte d' Orleans* (New Orleans, 1807), Williams Research Center, Historic New Orleans Collection, 1966.34.5.

3. New Orleans Directory for 1811.

4. New Orleans Directories for 1822, 1832, and 1842.

5. "Amusements, Louisiana Ball-Room, American Style," *Daily Picayune*, September 15, 1849.

6. "City Intelligence: A Ball Room Row," *Daily Picayune*, January 12, 1849.

7. "City Intelligence: Another Murder in the Third," *Daily Picayune*, February 19, 1849.

8. "Keeping a Disorderly House," *New Orleans Bee*, March 29, 1849.

9. New Orleans Directory for 1851.

10. "Confectionary for Sale and Store for Rent," *Daily Picayune*, November 19, 1874.

11. "Third District Schools," *Daily Picayune*, June 25, 1853.

12. "Fire Department," New Orleans Public Library, Image of the Month, March 1997, http://nutrias.org/monthly/mar97/march.htm.

13. "Charles Burkenstock: Death of One of the Third District's Solid Citizens," *Daily Picayune*, July 8, 1900.

14. William de Marigny Hyland, interview by Scott Ellis, New Orleans, May 14, 2011.

15. "The Names of Our Streets," *Daily Picayune*, May 15, 1870.

16. Richard Campanella, *Geographies of New Orleans: Urban Fabrics before the Storm* (Lafayette: Center for Louisiana Studies, University of Louisiana at Lafayette, 2006), 258.

17. Wayne Everard and Irene Wainwright, "The World of François Lacroix," 2002, p. 1, New Orleans Public Library, City Archives and Special Collections, http://www.neworleanspubliclibrary.org/~nopl/exhibits/lacroix/title.htm.

18. Sidney Benjamin Rougelot IV, "Rougelot's Department Store," *New Orleans Historical*, accessed January 3, 2015, http://neworleanshistorical.org/items/show/630.

19. "Branch, New Orleans Public Library, Frenchmen and Royal Streets (July 1907)," New Orleans Public Library, Image of the Month, July 2007, http://nutrias.org/~nopl/monthly/july2007/july200707.htm.

20. *Daily Picayune*, October 10, 1907.

21. "Contests Prove Big Magnets for Merry Maskers," *Times-Picayune*, February 17, 1915.

22. This section about Frenchmen's retail life between 1905 and the 1930s is drawn from advertisements and articles in the *Daily Picayune* and the *Times-Picayune* from 1905 to 1933. The mention of Reboul's coffee roasting is from Christopher Cooper, "Frenchmen's Mystique Is Rediscovered by Locals," *Times-Picayune*, April 14, 1991.

23. Joan Guiccione, interview by Scott Ellis, New Orleans, August 2, 2014.

24. Louis C. Hennick and E. Harper Charlton, *The Streetcars of New Orleans* (Gretna, LA: Firebird Press, 2000), 66. The famous Desire streetcar ended its service in 1949.

25. "Up and Down the Street, Frenchmen Fascination," *Times-Picayune*, July 3, 1940.

26. "Up and Down the Street, Baptist Rescue," *Times-Picayune*, February 16, 1940. This

shelter seems to have been called both the Baptist Emergency Home and the Baptist Rescue Mission.

27. *Polk's New Orleans City Directory, 1938* (Detroit: R. L. Polk, 1938).

28. Jason Patterson, interview by Scott Ellis, New Orleans, April 2, 2013.

29. Steve Keith, interview by Scott Ellis, by telephone, November 2, 2014.

30. John Swenson, *New Atlantis: Musicians Battle for the Survival of New Orleans* (New York: Oxford University Press, 2011), 172.

31. James Nolan, interview by Scott Ellis, New Orleans, October 13, 2007; quote used by permission.

32. Nolan interview; Keith interview. Mr. Nolan's sojourn on Frenchmen Street preceded that of Mr. Keith.

33. "Branch, New Orleans Public Library,"

34. "Holy Redeemer Church Shattered by Betsy's Winds," *Times-Picayune,* September 11, 1965.

35. "Senior Citizens Home to Open," *Times-Picayune,* April 25, 1972.

36. Scott S. Ellis, *Madame Vieux Carré: The French Quarter in the Twentieth Century* (Jackson: University Press of Mississippi, 2009), 120.

37. Darlene Fife, *Portraits from Memory: New Orleans in the Sixties* (New Orleans: Surregional Press, 2000), 44.

38. Ellis, *Madame Vieux Carré,* 120.

39. Christopher Cooper, "Frenchmen's Mystique Is Rediscovered by Locals," *Times-Picayune,* April 14, 1999.

40. "Go-Go Girls Wanted," Help Wanted, Female, Miscellaneous, *Times-Picayune,* June 18, 1969.

41. "Four Arrested by Vice Squad," *Times-Picayune,* December 7, 1964; James H. Gillis, "Special NOPSI Runs Dropped," *Times Picayune,* October 20, 1967.

42. "Explosion, Fire, Destroy N.O. Bar," *Times-Picayune,* July 21, 1976.

43. "Former Bar Owner Fined for Explosive," *Times-Picayune,* August 8, 1979; Keith Spera, "Construction Is Changing Landscape of Frenchmen Street," *Times-Picayune,* March 21, 2014.

44. "Notice of Application for Liquor License," Business Personals, *Times-Picayune,* September 23, 1976.

45. Sally Tunmer, "Hear the Pulse of New Orleans on Frenchmen Street," *GoNOLA Radio,* February 15, 2012, http://www.gonola.com/2012/02/15/hear-the-pulse-of-new-orleans-on-frenchmen-street.html.

46. Swenson, *New Atlantis,* 173.

47. Richard Dodds, "Chalking Up a 10 on the Boards," *Times-Picayune,* December 30, 1990.

48. Jason Patterson to Scott Ellis, February 21, 2015.

49. Betty Guillaud, "Some Sound Reasons for Paying a Visit to Audubon Zoo Bandstand," *Times-Picayune,* July 27, 1983.

50. Vanessa Smith-Torres, "Café Brasil," *Media Nola,* Tulane University, accessed June 29, 2014, http://medianola.org/discover/place/858/Cafe-Brasil.

51. Keith Spera, "Dream Palace Site Becomes a Dream Home for Trad Jazz," *Times-Picayune,* December 17, 1999; Jill T. Anding, "Serving Up a Turkish Blend at Café Istanbul," *Times-Picayune,* August 7, 1992.

52. Patterson interview.

53. Timothy White, "Diverse Club Scene Spills onto Sidewalks in the Land of Dreams," *Billboard,* June 8, 1996.

54. Frank Gagnard, "New Orleans' Newest Bohemia," *Times-Picayune,* January 3, 1992.

55. Praline Connection Restaurant, "A History of the Praline Connection Restaurant," accessed January 4, 2015, http://www.pralineconnection.com/history-praline-connection-restaurant.

56. Christopher Cooper and Scott Aigles, "Stop the Music: Stage Acts Banned at Two Clubs," *Times-Picayune,* January 31, 1992.

57. Christopher Cooper, "Music Comes Back to Life at Two Clubs on Frenchmen Street," *Times-Picayune,* February 8, 1992.

58. Susan Finch, "Fifteen Bars Closed in Police Sweep," *Times Picayune,* July 29, 1992.

59. Patterson interview.

60. Bruce Eggler, "Zoning Plan Taking Note of Music Clubs," *Times-Picayune,* September 3, 2003; Bruce Eggler, "City Gives Nod to Marigny Arts District," *Times-Picayune,* September 18, 2004.

61. New Orleans City Planning Commission, Zoning Docket 002/13, January 28, 2013, 16.

62. New Orleans Code of Ordinances, section 10.13, AC Arts and Cultural Overlay District, accessed January 4, 2015, municode.com.

63. Patterson interview.

64. John Swenson, "Another Troubled Street," *Offbeat,* April 2009.

65. New Orleans City Planning Commission, Zoning Docket 002/13, 16.

66. Casey Ferrand, "Crackdown on Frenchmen Street Flusters Businesses," November 25, 2013, WDSU TV, New Orleans, http://www.wdsu.com/news/local-news/new-orleans/crackdown-on-frenchman-street-rules-strikes-chord-with-businesses/23139864.

67. Richard A. Webster, "Frenchmen Street's Nightclub Limit Challenged by Bamboula's," *Times-Picayune,* January 15, 2015.

68. Richard A. Webster, "Frenchmen Street Proposal Ignites Worries," *Times-Picayune,* December 16, 2012.

69. New Orleans City Planning Commission, Zoning Docket 002/13, January 28, 2013, 16.

70. Webster, "Frenchmen Street Proposal Ignites Worries."

71. Ibid.

72. Bruce Eggler, "Plan for New Club on Frenchmen Runs into Opposition," *Times-Picayune,* January 13, 2013.

73. Bruce Eggler, "Planning Commission Rejects Frenchmen Club Proposal," *Times-Picayune,* January 23, 2013.

74. Webster, "Frenchmen Street's Nightclub Limit Challenged."

75. Gwendolyn Knapp, "Apparently Only Bamboula's Wants Bamboula's to Become a Nightclub," *NOLA Eater,* January 15, 2015, http://nola.eater.com/2015/1/15/7553721/apparently-only-bamboulas-wants-bamboulas-to-become-a-nightclub.

76. Ibid.

77. Keith interview.

78. New Orleans Code of Ordinances, Article XX, Street Entertainer, Sections 30-1451–30-1464, accessed August 8, 2016, municode.com.

79. Jim Flynn, *Sidewalk Saints: Life Portraits of the New Orleans Street Performer Family* (Detroit: Curbside Media, 2009).

80. William Carter, *Preservation Hall* (New York: W. W. Norton, 1991), 8, 110–36.

81. "Zachary Scott Booked in Raid, Nine Held for Drinking in Negro Establishment," *Times-Picayune,* November 17, 1952.

82. Dennis McNally, *Long Strange Trip: The Inside History of the Grateful Dead and the Making of Modern America* (London: Corgi Books, 2003), 477–79.

83. Keith interview.

84. Chelsea Brasted, "Are Frenchmen Street Musicians Being Fairly Paid?," *Times-Picayune,* June 6, 2017.

85. Jan Ramsey, "Why Are Frenchmen Street Musicians Undervalued?," *Offbeat,* June 7, 2017.

86. "Now Hear This," *Times-Picayune,* January 19, 2014.

87. Jan V. Ramsey, "Frenchmen Street Brass Band Controversy," *Offbeat,* April 16, 2014.

88. Shelby Hartman, "Frenchmen Street Discord: With Noise Ordinances Up in the Air, Brass Bands and Businesses Are Forced to Work Out Their Differences," *Times-Picayune,* May 30, 2014.

15. On and On and On

1. U.S. Census 2000, tracts 18 and 26; Greater New Orleans Community Data Center, "Orleans Parish: People and Household Characteristics, 2000," accessed February 5, 2017. www.datacenterresearch.org/pre-katrina/orleans/people.html. The totals exceed 100 percent due to rounding.

2. Bruce Nolan, "Archdiocese Closing 3 Historic Churches," *Times-Picayune,* March 5, 2001.

3. Jim Grigsby and Barnie Williams, interview by Scott Ellis, New Orleans, April 2, 2013.

4. Matt Easley, interview by Scott Ellis, New Orleans, April 3, 2013.

5. Grigsby and Williams interview.

6. Ibid.

7. Richard Webster, "Robert Takes Over St. Claude Location; Grocery, Landlord Settle Dispute," *Times-Picayune,* April 12, 2013.

8. Rebecca Mowbray, "Homeowners Dumbfounded by Allstate's Cancellations," *Times-Picayune,* February 24, 2007.

9. David Hammer, "Examining Post-Katrina Road Home Program: 'It's More than the Money. It's the Hoops We Had to Jump through to Do It,'" *Baton Rouge Advocate,* August 23, 2015.

10. Greg Thomas, "Glut of Houses Sends Prices Plummeting," *Times-Picayune,* June 23, 2007.

11. Associated Press, "New Orleans' Post-Katrina Funk," January 18, 2007.

12. Gary Krist, *Empire of Sin: A Story of Sex, Jazz, Murder, and the Battle for Modern New Orleans* (New York: Broadway Books, 2014), 259–98.

13. Scott S. Ellis, *Madame Vieux Carré: The French Quarter in the Twentieth Century* (Jackson: University Press of Mississippi, 2009), 169.

14. Ethan Brown, *Shake the Devil Off: A True Story of the Murder That Rocked New Orleans* (New York: St. Martins Griffin, 2010).

15. Brendan McCarthy and Laura Maggi, "Killings Bring the City to Its Bloodied Knees; Husband, Wife Just Two of 6 Shot in 24 Hours," *Times-Picayune,* January 5, 2007.

16. Brendan McCarthy, "Marigny Victims Worked to Leave Mark on City," *Times-Picayune,* January 6, 2007.

17. Ellis, *Madame Vieux Carré,* 213.

18. Laura Maggi and Gwen Filosa, "Enough! Thousands March to Protest City's Alarming Murder Rate," *Times-Picayune,* January 12, 2007.

19. Mason Miller, "New Orleans Middle Schoolers Are Beating the Shit Out of Artists and Gays," *Vice,* August 21, 2014, http://www.vice.com/read/new-orleans-middle-schoolers-are-beating-the-shit-out-of-its-artists-and-gays-820.

20. Data Center, "Marigny Statistical Area," accessed October 10, 2016, http://www.datacenterresearch.org/data-resources/neighborhood-data/district-7/Marigny/. The numbers for each of the listed statements are:

Population	*2000*	*2010*
Orleans Parish*	484,674	343,829
Faubourg Marigny	3,145	2,973

Ethnicity in the Marigny	*2000*	*2010*
Black or African American	17.7%	12.7%
Asian	1.0%	1.6%
American Indian	0.5%	0.8%
Hispanic (any race)	6.0%	6.8%

Other (Marigny)	*2000*	*2010*
Total households	1,960	1,881
Vacant housing units	16.6%	20.3%

*Coterminous with the city of New Orleans

Source: Data Center analysis of data from U.S. Census 2000 Summary File 1 (SF1) and U.S. Census 2010 Summary File 1 (SF1).

People living in poverty in the Marigny: 24.1% in 2000; 21.4% in 2010 (Data Center analysis of data from U.S. Census 2000 Summary File 3 [SF3] and 2010–14 American Community Survey). Workers living in the neighborhood by wage level: 25.3%, more than $3,333 per month in 2004; 41.6% in 2013 (Data Center analysis of Local Employment Dynamics, U.S. Census Bureau).

21. Brian Godfrey, *Neighborhoods in Transition: The Making of San Francisco's Ethnic and Nonconformist Communities* (Berkeley: University of California Press, 1988), 48–49. Based on a 1984 thesis.

22. Ellis, *Madame Vieux Carré,* 133–34.

23. Bruce Nolan, "Holy Trinity's Doors Shut after Last Mass, 400 Come Back to Say Goodbye," *Times-Picayune,* March 23, 1997.

24. Dave Hulbert, interview by Scott Ellis, New Orleans, April 8, 2012.

25. Doug McCash, "Solange Wedding Permit Problem Led to Temporary Marigny Opera House Closure, According to Owner," *Times-Picayune,* November 21, 2014.

26. Dylan Landis, "Dissection of Church Organ Reveals Symphonic Secrets," *Times-Picayune,* June 18, 1984.

27. Sanctuary Cultural Arts Center, accessed October 14, 2016, http://www.sanctuarynola.org/.

28. Kathy Reckdahl, "How Members of Triumph Baptist Church in New Orleans Confronted Pastor over Theft Allegations," *New Orleans Advocate,* October 9, 2016.

29. Rev. and Mrs. Johnnie Montgomery, interview by Scott Ellis, New Orleans, November 15, 2015.

30. Reinventing the Crescent, "New Orleans Riverfront: Reinventing the Crescent, Development Plan," 18, accessed September 25, 2016, http://www.reinventingthecrescent.org/about/.

31. Ekistics, Inc. "Elisio Lofts/About/Height," accessed September 24, 2016, http://www.elisiolofts.com/index.php?/about/height/.

32. Mimi Read, "Where the Walls Do Talk," *New York Times,* June 6, 2012.

33. Alex Vialou, interview by Scott Ellis, New Orleans, November 10, 2012. At the time of the interview, Vialou was president of the Faubourg Marigny Improvement Association.

34. Charles Maldonado, "The Marigny and the Lofts," *Gambit,* August 21, 2012.

35. Bruce Eggler, "Council Rejects Marigny Project," *Times-Picayune,* September 7, 2012.

36. Ibid.

37. Robert McClendon, "Judge Clears Tall Buildings for Faubourg Marigny Waterfront, but Criticizes 'Abhorrent' Process," *Times-Picayune,* August 27, 2015.

38. Lauren Laborde, "Marigny Warehouse, Once Planned for Sean Cummings' Elisio Lofts, Sells to Hotel Developer," *Curbed New Orleans,* September 22, 2016, http://nola.curbed.com/2016/9/22/13020760/elisio-lofts-marigny-new-orleans-warehouse-sold.

39. Danny Monteverde, "Hubig's Pies Bakery Destroyed by Fire in Faubourg Marigny," *Times-Picayune,* July 27, 2015.

40. Schiro's Café, "Welcome to Schiro's Café" [menu], accessed December 31, 2013, schiroscafe.com.

41. New Orleans Dyke Bar History Project, "The Way They Go," *Last Call Stories,* podcast episode 5, June 10, 2016, http://www.lastcallnola.org/podcast/2016/6/10/episode-5-the-way-they-go.

42. Ellis, *Madame Vieux Carré,* 207–8.

43. New Orleans Short Term Rental Report, accessed September 25, 2016, http://nolarentalreport.com/#/#about Data current as of April 21, 2016; Marigny-specific counts by the author.

44. Zillow, "Marigny New Orleans Apartments," accessed November 12, 2017, https://www.zillow.com/homes/for_rent/Marigny-New-Orleans-LA/condo,apartment_duplex_type/269714_rid/featured_sort/29.970425,-90.044315,29.959345,-90.05969_rect/16_zm/; calculations by the author.

45. Aboubacar Ndiaye, "Eight Reasons Why the Rent Is Too Damn High," National Public Radio, January 7, 2014, http://www.npr.org/sections/codeswitch/2014/01/06/260282186/eight-reasons-why-the-rent-is-too-damn-high.

46. Dorian Commode and Jules Bentley, "UnfairBNB: What Unlicensed Short-Term

Rentals Mean for New Orleans," *Antigravity,* March 2014, http://www.antigravitymagazine.com/2014/03/unfairbnb-what-unlicensed-short-term-rentals-mean-for-new-orleans/.

47. Joan and Laura Guiccione, interview by Scott Ellis, August 2, 2014, New Orleans.

48. Jeff Adelson, "City Council Approves New Short-Term Rental Rules," *New Orleans Advocate,* October 20, 2016.

49. Emily Peck and Charles Maldonado, "How Airbnb Is Pushing Locals Out of New Orleans' Coolest Neighborhoods," *Lens,* October 30, 2017, http://thelensnola.org/2017/10/30/how-airbnb-is-pushing-locals-out-of-new-orleans-coolest-neighborhoods.

50. Kevin Litten, "New Orleans Short-Term Rental Rules Aren't Discouraging Investors, Housing Group Finds," *Times-Picayune,* March 28, 2018.

51. Kathy Finn, "Surging Condo Development Spreads Downriver to Marigny and Bywater, "*New Orleans Advocate,* November 5, 2017, http://www.theadvocate.com/new_orleans/news/article_d889e0b2-c1dc-11e7-958e-27b55c136dfa.html.

52. Keith Spera, "Police Raids Anger N.O. Music Club Owners; City Hall Displays Disdain, They Say," *Times-Picayune,* November 27, 1998.

53. Cosimo Matassa, interview by Scott Ellis, New Orleans, April 24, 2004.

54. Ellis, *Madame Vieux Carré,* 190.

55. Kenneth Holditch, interview by Scott Ellis, New Orleans, June 21, 2014.

56. Business Personals, *Times-Picayune,* February 6, 1970.

57. New Orleans Real Estate Transfers, *Times-Picayune,* December 14, 2002.

58. Lorelei Cropley, interview by Scott Ellis, New Orleans, April 4, 2013.

59. Orleans Parish, Civil District Court, "Lorelei Cropley, Jeanne F. Turnipseed, Daniel Harris, Diane Lease, and Kenneth S. Witkowski v. Royal Franklin LLC, Royal Franklin Bar, LLC, and 2601 Royal Street Bar, LLC," No. 13-3509, April 11, 2013.

60. Alison Fensterstock, "Crescent City Culture Clash," *Times-Picayune,* September 13, 2013.

61. Brendan McCarthy, "5th District Police Getting New Home," *Times-Picayune,* October 9, 2007.

62. Pres Kabacoff to Scott Ellis, email, November 30, 2016; used by permission.

63. Stephanie Bruno, "Building Reborn as Healing Center," *Times-Picayune,* April 11, 2011.

64. "Community Benefit Agreement by and between Café Istanbul and the Faubourg Marigny Improvement Association," November 22, 2011, Act 2012-02473, New Orleans Notarial Archives.

65. Richard A. Webster, "Cafe Istanbul Trial: Resident Rights, Economic Growth, Culture," *Times-Picayune,* April 18, 2016.

66. Richard A. Webster, "Cafe Istanbul, Landrieu Administration Reach Agreement," *Times-Picayune,* April 18, 2016.

67. James Nolan, "Remembering Kamas: The Square Round Is Also Round," *New Laurel Review* 16 (1988): 72; used by permission.

BIBLIOGRAPHY

PRIMARY SOURCES

ARCHIVES

Archdiocese of New Orleans, Sacramental Records

Certificates of Baptism. 1773–1813.

Certificates of Burial. 1799, 1800, 1808, 1890.

Certificates of Marriage. Marriages, vol. 2, 1795–1806.

Completed Genealogical Research Reports. Jean Philippe de Marigny de Mandeville, May 15, 2015. Antoine Philippe de Marigny, May 15, 2015. Armand Marigny de Mandeville, December 5, 2016.

Records of Saints Peter and Paul, and Holy Trinity Catholic Churches.

Sacramental Records, vol. 8 (1804–1806), 96. Cited in "Clemente de Marigny de Mandeville." Stewart-deJaham Genealogy Pages. Accessed May 8, 2016. http://www.raymondjohnson.net/genealogy/getperson.php?personID=I2700&tree=stewart.

Historic New Orleans Collection, Williams Research Center

Collins, C. Diboll. Vieux Carré Digital Survey.

410–414 Chartres Street. Square 28, Lot No. 11075-01, http://www.hnoc.org/vcs/property_info.php?lot=11075-01.

716–724 Governor Nicholls Street. Square 55, Lot No. 22892, http://www.hnoc.org/vcs/property_info.php?lot=22892#sthash.jFAuJoVs.dpuf .

716 Dauphine Street. Square 73, Lot No. 18755, http://www.hnoc.org/vcs/property_info.php?lot=18755.

Laughlin, Clarence John. Photograph Collection.

Medal presented to Bernard de Marigny by the Naturalized Citizens of Louisiana. 1972.32.

"Report Describing the Expulsion of Antonio de Ulloa from Louisiana, 1768." Translated by Andrejz Raczynski. February 16, 1769. 2011.0209.

Ste-Gême Family Papers. Jean Boze to Henri de Ste-Gême, various dates. MSS 100, folders 134, 143, 148, 166, 174, 204, 205.
Wards de la Nouvelle Orleans. New Orleans: Bureau of Governmental Research, 1961. JK1982.B8, 90-482-RL.
U.S. Army. "List of Receipts, Special Supply Agent, Rebel Property. New Orleans, U.S. Army." By Benjamin F. Flanders. September 5, 1863. MSS 281, F.2.

Library of Congress

Jefferson, Thomas. Letter to Thomas Mann Randolph Jr., Washington City, May 14, 1801. Thomas Jefferson Papers. Manuscripts Division.

Louisiana Historical Center, Louisiana State Museum

Delino, Don Ignacio. "Don Ignacio Delino, Curator of Minor Don Bernardo De Marigny, Presented a Detailed Account to the New Curator, Don Francisco Defile Depart." August 3, 1801. Spanish Colonial Documents, no. 1801080301.
"Information Requested by Don Ignacio Delino, Guardian of the Minor, Don Bernardo de Marigny, and His Property." May 27, 1801. Spanish Colonial Documents, no. 1801052704.
"Succession of Pedro Phelipe [*sic*] de Marigny, May 24, 1800." File 99, document 3906, Colonial Black Book No. 149.

Louisiana Research Collection, Tulane University

Desarzant, Maitre. *Prospectus de l'institution Catholique des orphelins indigents.* New Orleans: Maitre Desarzant, 1847. 976.31 (362.7) P966.

New Orleans Notarial Archives

"Act of Sale, a Portion of a Block and Buildings, the Company of Architects of the City of New Orleans from Bernard Marigny, April 12, 1832." Felix de Armas, notary, vol. 36, no. 239.
"Act of Sale, a Portion of a Block and Buildings, the Company of Architects of the City of New Orleans from Bernard Marigny, April 12, 1832." Felix de Armas, notary, vol. 36, no. 240.
"Act of Sale, Bernard Marigny to Louis Muh, May 24, 1864." Adolphe Boudousquie, notary, vol. 22, no. 97.
Acts before notary Narcissus Broutin, vol. 9, January 16–May 30, 1805.
Acts of Andre Almonaster y Roxas, vol. 1, April 29, 1779.

"Assignment of Rights by Mr. Bernard Marigny to the Pontchartrain Railroad Company." February 23, 1830. No. 129. Felix Armas, notary. Book 18, folio 326. Louisiana Historical Center, record group 335, T025.2003.125. 1726–1830.
"Community Benefit Agreement by and between Café Istanbul and the Faubourg Marigny Improvement Association." November 22, 2011. Act 2012-02473.
"Contract of Marriage between Bernard Marigny and Marie Jones, May 19, 1808." Translated by Andrejz Raczynski. Edited by Scott S. Ellis. Pedro Pedesclaux Indexes, vol. 47, 1784–1886.

New Orleans Public Library, City Archives and Special Collections

Everard, Wayne, and Irene Wainwright. "The World of François Lacroix." 2002. http://nutrias.org/exhibits/lacroix/title.htm.
Image of the Month. "Fire Department." March 1997. Accessed December 16, 2014. http://nutrias.org/monthly/mar97/march.htm.
Image of the Month. "Branch, New Orleans Public Library, Frenchmen and Royal Streets (July 1907)." July 2007. Accessed December 16, 2014. http://nutrias.org/~nopl/monthly/july2007/july200707.htm.
Orleans Parish Civil Courts Collection. First Judicial District Court Suit Records, 1813–1835. http://nutrias.org/inv/1jdc/1jdcind.htm.
———. Index to the Suit Records, 1813–1835. http://nutrias.org/~nopl/inv/vcp/parish1.htm.
Underwriters Inspection Bureau of New Orleans street rate slips. 1897. http://nutrias.org/~nopl/info/louinfo/1897/dauphiner.htm.

State Library of Louisiana

Succession of Mrs. Bernard de Marigny. Accessed November 21, 2016. http://cdm16313.contentdm.oclc.org/cdm/compoundobject/collection/LWP/id/1446/rec/1. (URL no longer available.) [Bernard's succession of February 7 and 8, 1868, is cataloged under that of his wife and appears as pp. 3–12of the online exhibit.]

University of New Orleans

"Historical Note." Jacob Schoen and Son Collection. Earl Long Library. MSS307. Accessed October 28, 2016. http://library.uno.edu/specialcollections/inventories/307.htm.

Committee of the Free Market of New Orleans. *Report of the Committee of the Free Market of New Orleans.* New Orleans: Bulletin Book and Job Office, 1862.

Data Center. "Marigny Statistical Area." Accessed October 10, 2016. http://www.datacenterresearch.org/data-resources/neighborhood-data/district-7/Marigny/.

Directory of the St. Paul's Lutheran Evangelical Church. New Orleans: St. Paul's Lutheran Evangelical Church, 1920. http://freepages.religions.rootsweb.ancestry.com/~neworleans/st_paul_records/.

Dobney, Frederick, David Moore, Jeffrey Teffinger, R. Christopher Goodwin, Mark Catin, Paul C. Armstrong, James Cripps, and Carol Poplin. *Evaluation of the National Register Eligibility of the Inner Harbor Navigation Canal Lock in Orleans Parish, Louisiana.* New Orleans: R. Christopher Goodwin and Associates, 1987.

Ekistics, Inc. "Elisio Lofts/About/Height." Accessed September 24, 2016. www.elisiolofts.com/index.php?/about/height.

Ellison-Frost, Elizabeth. "Chalmette Refining, LLC Celebrates 100 Years in St. Bernard Parish, Louisiana." September 23, 2015. http://www.chalmetterefining.com/go/doc/5707/2451122/Brief_History_for_The_Lamp.docx. (Page no longer available.)

Faubourg Marigny Improvement Association. "Restated Articles of Incorporation of the Faubourg Marigny Improvement Association, Inc." September 20, 2007.

German Society of New Orleans. "Notice to Captains of Emigrant Vessels Entering the Mississippi River." July 1, 1849.

Historic Tax Credit Coalition. *First Annual Report on the Economic Impact of the Federal Historic Tax Credit.* Washington, D.C., March 2010.

Lide, James. "Report on the Citizens Bank of Louisiana and the New Orleans Canal and Banking Company." Rockville MD: History Associates, February 8, 2005.

Louisiana Cotton Manufactory. "Report to the Stockholders of the Louisiana Cotton Manufactory," February 8, 1872, and "Report of the Superintendent to the Board of Directors of the Louisiana Cotton Manufactory," January 31, 1872. Tulane University Library. 976.3 (633.5) N932.

Magill, Rich. *Exposing Hatred: A Report on the Victimization of Lesbian and Gay People in New Orleans, Louisiana.* New Orleans: Louisiana Lesbian and Gay Political Action Caucus, 1991.

New Orleans Public Service, Inc. "Did You Know?" *Riders' Digest,* March 11, 1957.

Praline Connection Restaurant. "A History of the Praline Connection Restaurant." Accessed January 4, 2015. http://www.pralineconnection.com/history-praline-connection-restaurant.

Reinventing the Crescent. "New Orleans Riverfront: Reinventing the Crescent,

Development Plan." Accessed September 25, 2016. http://www.reinventingthecrescent.org/about/.
Saints Peter and Paul Church. *Centennial of the Church of Sts. Peter and Paul, 1860–1960.* New Orleans, 1960.
Second German Presbyterian Church. *Fiftieth Anniversary of the Second German Presbyterian Church.* New Orleans: Second German Presbyterian Church, 1913.
———. "Resolution of the Board of Trustees of the Second German Presbyterian Church, June 17, 1867." In *Claiborne Avenue Presbyterian Church (New Orleans, LA) Records, 1863–1955.* Montreat, NC: Historical Foundation of the Presbyterian and Reformed Churches, 1983.

AUTOBIOGRAPHIES, REMINISCENCES, AND MEMOIRS

Bernhard, Karl, Duke of Saxe-Weimar-Eisenach. *Travels through North America, during the Years 1825 and 1826.* Philadelphia: Carey, Lea and Carey, 1828.
Buckingham, J. S. *The Slave States of America.* Vol. 1. London: Fisher & Son, 1842.
Butler, Benjamin F. *Autobiography and Personal Reminiscences of Major-General Benj. F. Butler: Butler's Book.* Boston: A. M. Thayer, 1892.
Fife, Darlene. *Portraits from Memory: New Orleans in the Sixties.* New Orleans: Surregional Press, 2000.
Grondel, Jean-Philippe (attributed). *A Letter from a Louisiana Officer to the Commissioner of the Marine.* New Orleans, 1764. Cited in *Adventures in Americana, 1492–1897.* Vol. 2. New York: Cooper Square, 1964.
Hall, A. Oakey. *The Manhattaner in New Orleans.* New Orleans: J. C. Morgan, 1851.
Hyland, William de Marigny. "A Reminiscence of Bernard de Marigny, Founder of Mandeville." Speech before Mandeville Horizons, Inc., May 26, 1984, Mandeville, LA.
Ingraham, Joseph. *The South-West, by a Yankee.* New York: Harper Brothers, 1835.
Laussat, Pierre Clement. *Memoirs of My Life to My Son during the Years 1803 and After . . .* Translated by Agnes-Josephine Pastwa. Edited by Robert D. Bush. Baton Rouge: Louisiana State University Press, 1978.
LeGrand, Julia. *Journal of Julia LeGrand, New Orleans, 1862–1863.* Edited by Kate Mason Rowland and Mrs. Morris L. Croxall. Richmond, VA: Everrett Waddey, 1911.
Louis-Philippe, King of France. *Diary of My Travels in America.* Translated by Stephen Becker. New York: Delacorte Press, 1977.
Ludlow, Noah Miller. *Dramatic Life as I Found It.* St. Louis: G. I. Jones, 1880.
Marigny, Bernard. *À ses concitoyens.* Translated by Howard Margot. New Orleans, 1853. University of New Orleans Library, F374.M32 A3.

Mieri, Catherine. "53 in the Marigny." *Faubourg Marigny News* 9, nos. 1 & 2 (January–February 1980).

Nolan, James. *Flight Risk: Memoirs of a New Orleans Bad Boy.* Jackson: University Press of Mississippi, 2017.

———. "Remembering Kamas: The Square Round Is Also Round." *New Laurel Review* 16 (1988): 72.

Nordhoff, Charles. *The Cotton States in the Spring and Summer of 1875.* New York: D. Appleton, 1876.

Northup, Solomon. *Twelve Years a Slave.* Los Angeles: Graymalkin Media, 2014.

Olmstead, Frederick Law. *Journeys and Explorations in the Cotton Kingdom.* Vol. 1. London: Sampson, Low & Son, 1861.

Robinson, William (attributed). *The Diary of a Samaritan, by a Member of the Howard Association of New Orleans.* New York: HarperBrothers, 1860.

Russell, William Howard. *My Diary North and South.* London: Bradbury and Evans, 1862.

Sparks, William H. *The Memories of Fifty Years.* Philadelphia: Claxton, Remsen & Haffelinger, 1870.

Wegener, G. J. *A Brief Story of My Life.* New Orleans, 1943.

Whitaker, John Smith (attributed). *Sketches of Life and Character in Louisiana.* New Orleans: Ferguson & Crosby, 1847.

DIRECTORIES

Gardner's New Orleans Directory for 1866. New Orleans: C. Gardner, 1866.

New Orleans Annual and Commercial Register of 1846. New Orleans: E. A. Michel, 1846.

Polk's New Orleans City Directory, 1938. Detroit: R. L. Polk, 1938.

Soards' New Orleans City Directory. 1841, 1870, 1880, 1890, 1900.

USGenWeb Archives Project. New Orleans City Directories. www.usgwarchives.net/la/orleans/directry.htm.

1811. James R. Hills Jr., based on a transcription by Colleen Fitzpatrick. September 2002.

1822. James R. Hills Jr., based on a transcription by Colleen Fitzpatrick. September 2002.

1832. James R. Hills Jr., based on a transcription by Colleen Fitzpatrick. September 2002.

1842. James R. Hills Jr., based on transcriptions by Colleen Fitzpatrick, Louis Lavedan, Cheramie Breaux, Frankie Palisi, and Janice Worthen. September 2002.

1851. Colleen Fitzpatrick, Linda Dean, and Louis Lavedan. January 2002.

1861. Colleen Fitzpatrick, Kathy Sharp, Julie Moritz, Susan Billet Kost, Beverly Benoit, and Betty Ware. July 2004.

GOVERNMENT DOCUMENTS

Billouart, Louis, Chevalier de Kerlerec. To Minister de Marine, April 24, 1759. In *Report Concerning Canadian Archives for the Year 1905, in Three Volumes, Being an Appendix to the Report of the Minister of Agriculture,* vol. 1 Ottawa: S. E. Dawson, 1906.

City of New Orleans. Conseil de Ville. "Report of the Committee to Inform the Town, at the Request of Mr. Bernard Marigny, of the Limits of His Family Land." May 15, 1805. New Orleans City Archives, AB300, 1803–36.

"The 'Code Noir' (1685)." Reprinted from *Le Code Noir, ou récueil des reglements rendus jusqu'à présent.* Paris: Pault, 1788. Translated by John Garrigus. Reproduced by the Societé d'Histoire de la Guadeloupe, 1980. https://labs.wsu.edu/sue-peabody/wp-content/uploads/sites/1205/2016/02/code-noir.pdf.

Confederate States of America. War Department. *Proceedings of the Court of Inquiry Relative to the Fall of New Orleans.* Richmond, VA: R.M. Smith, 1864.

Gibson, Campbell. "Population of the 100 Largest Cities and Other Urban Places in the United States: 1790 to 1990." Working Paper No. 27, Population Division, U.S. Bureau of the Census, Washington, D.C., June 1998.

Louisiana Office of Tourism. Documentation package for Solomon Northup historical marker, 2016.

Louisiana State Legislature. "An Act Concerning Deliberations of Family Meetings and Meetings of Creditors, Awards of Arbiters, and for Other Purposes." March 16, 1822.

———. "An Act for the Relief and Protection of Persons Brought into This State as Redemptioners." Approved March 20, 1818. In *A General Digest of the Acts of the Legislature of Louisiana: Passed from the Year 1804 to 1827, Inclusive, and in Force at This Last Period,* vol. 2, edited by Louis Moreau Lislet. New Orleans: Benjamin Levy, 1828.

———. "An Act to Amend an 'Act to Incorporate the City of New Orleans' Approved February the Seventeenth, Eighteen Hundred and Five, and Other Acts Amending the Same." In *Acts Passed at the Second Session of the Twelfth Legislature of the State of Louisiana,* 28–37. New Orleans: Jerome Bayon, 1836.

———. "An Act to Dispense Prosper and Gustave Marigny with the Time Prescribed by Law Respecting Age of Majority." January 12, 1827.

———. *Annual Report of the Auditor of Public Accounts to the General Assembly of the State of Louisiana, 1877.* New Orleans: Office of the *Democrat,* 1877.

———. *Annual Report of the Board of Health to the Legislature of the State of Louisiana, January 1861.* Baton Rouge: John M. Taylor, 1861.

———. *Annual Report of the Board of Health of the State of Louisiana to the General Assembly for the Year 1871.* New Orleans, 1872.

———. *Annual Report of the Board of Health of the State of Louisiana to the General Assembly for the Year 1880.* New Orleans: J. S. Rivers, 1881.

———. *Journal of the Proceedings of the Convention of the State of Louisiana, Begun and Held in the City of New Orleans, on the 14th Day of January, 1845.* New Orleans: Besançon, Ferguson, 1845.

———. Louisiana State Constitution of 1845. http://en.wikisource.org/wiki/Louisiana_State_Constitution_of_1845.

———. Louisiana State Constitution of 1852. http://en.wikisource.org/wiki/Louisiana_State_Constitution_of_1852.

———. "Names of Persons Taking the Oath of Allegiance, Index and Registered Enemies Record." Includes "Copy of Index to Five Books. Containing the Names of Persons Taking the Oath of Allegiance in 1862" and "Copy of a Record of Registered Enemies." Williams Research Center, Historic New Orleans Collection, MSS 143.1 and MSS 143.2.

———. "An Ordinance to Dissolve the Union between the State of Louisiana and Other States, United with Her under the Compact Entitled 'The Constitution of the United States of America.'" January 26, 1861.

———. *Proceedings and Debates of the Convention of Louisiana Which Assembled at the City of New Orleans, January 14, 1844.* New Orleans: Besançon, Ferguson, 1845.

———. *Report of the Special Committee on the Mexican Gulf Railroad.* New Orleans: J. O. Nixon, 1866.

Louisiana Territorial Legislature. "An Act for the Regulation of the Rights and Duties of Apprentices and Indentured Servants." May 21, 1806. In *Acts Passed at the First Session of the First Legislature of the Territory of Orleans,* 44–56. New Orleans: Bradford & Anderson, 1807. Cited in Paul Lachance, "Index to New Orleans Indentures, 1809–1843," New Orleans Public Library. Accessed June 24, 2013. http://nutrias.org/~nopl/inv/indentures/ind-intr.htm.

———. "An Act to Prescribe Certain Formalities Respecting Free Persons of Color." 1st sess., 2nd Leg., March 31, 1808.

———. "Agreement between Bernard Marigny and Jacques Pitot, Mayor of New Orleans, for Dividing Marigny Plantation into a Suburb." June 17, 1805. Louisiana Historical Center, Louisiana State Museum, record group 335, T025.2003.125. 1726–1830.

———. "An Act Authorizing the Guardian of Bernard Marigny to Effect the Afore-Mentioned Sales." April 19, 1805. Louisiana Historical Center, Louisiana State Museum, record group 335, T025.2003.125. 1726–1830.

New Orleans City Council. Code of Ordinances through September 30, 2016.

———. Introduction. Historic District Landmarks Commission Guidelines. Accessed July 24, 2016. http://www.nola.gov/hdlc/documents/01_introduction-2015-04-24/.
———. New Orleans Comprehensive Zoning Ordinance. August 12, 2015. http://czo.nola.gov/home/.
———. Ordinance 395, Common Council Series (CCS). 1852.
———. Ordinance C.C.S. 7842. "An Ordinance Providing for the Opening, Widening and Extension of North Rampart Street, St. Bernard Street, Annette Street and St. Claude Avenue or Street." April 19, 1924.
———. Zoning Docket 002/13. January 28, 2013.
Orleans Parish. Civil District Court. "Lorelei Cropley, Jeanne F. Turnipseed, Daniel Harris, Diane Lease and Kenneth Witkowski v. Royal Franklin, LLC, Royal Franklin Bar, LLC and 2601 Royal Street Bar, LLC." No. 13-3509. April 11, 2013.
———. Court of Probate. Receipt of Taxes in Probate Court. June 1830–February 1834.
Ravaisson-Mollien, Francois, ed. *Archives de la Bastille: Documents inédits.* Paris: G. Pedone, 1904.
Supreme Court of Louisiana. *Heirs of Villars v. J. M. Kennedy et al.* December 1850. In *Reports of Cases Argued and Determined in the Supreme Court of Louisiana*, vol. 5, William W. King, reporter. New Orleans: T. Rea, 1851.
U.S. Army, Department of the Gulf. General Order No. 55. August 4, 1862.
U.S. Congress. "Servicemen's Readjustment Act of 1944." S. 1767, Public Law 346, 78th Cong., 2nd sess.
U.S. Department of Commerce, Bureau of the Census. Census of 1850, 2nd District of the 3rd Municipality, in Parish of Orleans.
———. Census of 1860. "Barnard [*sic*] Marigny," 8th Ward, New Orleans, Louisiana, United States. P. 60. Household ID 517. U.S. National Archives and Records Administration (NARA). Publication M653 GS, Film 803421, Digital Folder 004231232, Image 00312.
U.S. Department of the Interior, National Park Service, National Register of Historic Places. "Faubourg Marigny Historic District." National Register Information System ID Number 74000930. December 31, 1974.
———. "Schwegmann Bros. Giant Supermarket No. 1." National Register Information System ID Number 14000314. June 11, 2014.
U.S. Federal Housing Administration. *Underwriting Manual: Underwriting and Valuation Procedure under Title II of the National Housing Act.* Washington, D.C.: Federal Housing Administration, April 1936. Urban Oasis. http.//www.urbanoasis.org/projects/fha/FHAUnderwritingManualPtII.html#201. (Site discontinued.)
U.S. Federal Housing Administration. Federal Home Loan Bank Board. Home

Owners' Loan Corporation. "New Orleans Residential Security Map." Ca. 1935. National Archives and Records Administration, 6082413. Urban Oasis. http://www.urbanoasis.org/projects/holc-FHA/digital-holc-maps/. (Site discontinued.)

U.S. Geologic Survey. *Environmental Atlas of the Lake Pontchartrain Basin.* Accessed June 12, 2011. http://pubs.usgs.gov/of/2002/of02-206/index.html.

Works Progress Administration. "Corrected—Index, Alphabetical and Numerical, of Changes in Street Names and Numbers, Old and New, 1852 to Current Date." 1938. New Orleans, 1938.

INTERVIEWS

All interviews were conducted by the author.

Aaron (pseud.) by email, January 20, 2011.

Bennett, Dorian. New Orleans, September 28, 2013.

Berg, Chuck. New Orleans, April 6, 2012.

Bozant, Helen. Covington, LA, July 22, 2012.

Bozant, Kevin. New Orleans, November 11, 2012.

Broders, Evelyn. New Orleans, December 21, 2013.

Calogero, Pascal. New Orleans, May 12, 2011.

Cizek, Eugene, and Lloyd Sensat. New Orleans, February 8, 2011.

Cropley, Lorelei. New Orleans, April 4, 2013.

Easley, Matt. New Orleans, April 3, 2013.

Grigsby, Jim, and Barnie Williams. New Orleans, April 2, 2013.

Grue, Lee Meitzen. New Orleans, November 22, 2014.

Guiccione, Ann and Laura. New Orleans, June 22, 2014.

Guiccione, Joan and Laura. New Orleans, August 2, 2014.

Halvorson, Robyn. New Orleans, May 23, 2013.

Hankel, Chris and Marilyn. New Orleans, November 16, 2011.

Holditch, Kenneth. New Orleans, June 21, 2014, August 3, 2014.

Hulbert, Dave. New Orleans, April 8, 2012.

Hyland, William deMarigny. New Orleans, May 14, 2011.

Irvin, Dale. New Orleans, April 5, 2012.

Johnson, David. New Orleans, April 8, 2012.

Kabacoff, Pres. New Orleans, April 3, 2013.

Keith, Steve. by telephone, November 2, 2014.

Matassa, Cosimo. New Orleans, April 24, 2004.

Meyer, Richard. New Orleans, August 13, 2011.

Montgomery, Rev. and Mrs. Johnnie. New Orleans, November 15, 2015.

Mutter, Julian Doerr. New Orleans, March 5, 2011.
Nolan, James. New Orleans, October 13, 2007.
O'Rourke, Patrick. New Orleans, March 20, 2005.
Patterson, Jason. New Orleans, April 2, 2013.
Temple, Jamie. Bay St. Louis, MS, October 18, 2014. Pass Christian, MS, April 23, 2016.
Vialou, Alex. New Orleans, November 10, 2012.

MAPS

Carte particuliere du flevue St. Louis dix lieües au dessus de la Nouvelle Orleans: Ou sont marqué les habitations et les terrains concedes à plusiers particuliers au Mississipy. Ca. 1723. Cartes Marines Manuscript Map Collection, Edward E. Ayer Manuscript Map Collection, Newberry Library, Chicago.

Franquelin, Jean-Baptiste Louis. *Carte de l'Amerique Septentrionnale: Depuis le 25, jusqu'au 650 deg. de latt. & environ 140, & 235 deg. de longitude.* Quebec, 1688. Library of Congress copy of 1909–10. http://hdl.loc.gov/loc.gmd/g3300.ct000668.

Lafon, Barthélémy. *Plan du Faubourg Marigny conforme au trace fait par Bm. Lafon ingens. geogr. et arpenteur du Compte d'Orleans.* New Orleans, 1807. Williams Research Center, Historic New Orleans Collection, 1966.34.5.

———. Copy by Claude Jules Allou d'Hémécourt. Ca. 1870. Williams Research Center, Historic New Orleans Collection, 1966.33.1.

Montigny, Dumont de. *Plan de la Nouvelle Orleans, ville capitalle de la Louisianne et ses environs.* 1747. Ministère de la Guerre, Archives Historiques. 7C 216. Louis C. Karpinski Map Collection, Newberry Library, Chicago.

Norman, B. M. *Norman's Map of New Orleans & Environs.* New Orleans, 1849. Williams Research Center, Historic New Orleans Collection, 1952.29.

Paullin, Charles O., and John K. Wright. *Railroads 1850 and 1860; Overland Mail, 1850–1869.* In *Atlas of the Historical Geography of the United States,* by Charles O. Paullin and John K. Wright, 139. Washington, D.C.: Carnegie Institute of Washington and the American Geographical Society of New York, 1932. Reproduced in *Railroads and the Making of Modern America*, University of Nebraska–Lincoln. http://railroads.unl.edu/documents/view_document.php?id=rail.str.0243.

———. *Rates of Travel, 1857.* In *Atlas of the Historical Geography of the United States,* by Charles O. Paullin and John K. Wright, 138c. Washington, D.C.: Carnegie Institute of Washington and the American Geographical Society of New York, 1932. Reproduced in *Railroads and the Making of Modern America*, University of Nebraska–Lincoln, http://railroads.unl.edu/documents/view_document.php?id=rail.str.0241.

Pilié, Gilbert Joseph. *Plan d'e l'ancien Faubourg Marigny. New Orleans: 1811.* Historic New Orleans Collection, Williams Research Center, 1985.39.

Robinson, Elisha, and Rodger Pidgeon. *Robinson's Atlas of the City of New Orleans, Louisiana.* New York, 1883. New Orleans Notarial Archives. http://www.orleanscivilclerk.com/robinson/index.htm.

Tanesse, James. *Plan dressé en éxécution de l'arrête du conseil de ville de la Nlle. Orleans, approuvé par le maire le 15 juin 1807.* New Orleans, 1809. Louisiana Historical Center, 1975.115.2.14.

———. *Plan of the City and Suburbs of New Orleans from an Actual Survey Made in 1815 by J. Tanesse, City Surveyor.* Williams Research Center, Historic New Orleans Collection, 1971.4.

Trudeau, Carlos. Copy and translation from *The Original Spanish Plan Showing the City of New Orleans, Its Fortifications and Environs by Carlos Trudeau, 1798.* Copied April 1875. Williams Research Center, Historic New Orleans Collection, 1953.42.

———. *Plano figurativo del medimiento y repartimiento de la tierra commun con Dn. Nicolas Daunoy y la success[io]n de Mr. Favre Daunoy.* 1787. Louisiana State Museum, T0055.1997.0273.

Zimpel, Charles F. *Topographical Map of New Orleans and Its Vicinity, Embracing a Distance of Twelve Miles Up and Eight and Three-Quarters Miles Down the Mississippi.* New Orleans, 1834. Williams Research Center, Historic New Orleans Collection, 1945.13 i–xix.

NEWSPAPERS

L'Abeille, 1834/*New Orleans Bee,* 1835–68
Courrier de la Louisiane, 1824
Daily Crescent, 1858
Daily Delta, 1850
Daily Orleanian, 1849–56
Daily Picayune, 1837–1907
Daily True Delta, 1862
The Freeman (Indianapolis), 1906
Louisiana Advertiser, 1835
Louisiana Courier, 1809–57
New Orleans Advocate, 2015–17
New York Times, 1854–90
Tägliche Deutsche Zeitung 1854–62
Times-Picayune, 1914–2017

Abrams, Eve. "Along Saint Claude." Accessed September 4, 2015. http://eveabrams.com/audiodocs.html.

Ancestry.com. "Woods Family History: (Pierre Achille) François Seuzeneau." Accessed May 4, 2014. http://wc.rootsweb.ancestry.com/cgi-bin/igm.cgi?op=GET&db=beebeewood&id=I1922.

Cherrie, Lolita C. "Seventh Ward Civic League, Its History and Accomplishments." Accessed July 15, 2016. http://www.creolegen.org/2013/06/08/seventh-ward-civic-league-its-history-and-accomplishments.

CreoleGen.org. "Couvent School Board of Directors, 1917." July 21, 2012. http://www.creolegen.org/2012/07/21/couvent-school-board-of-directors-1917/.

Greater New Orleans Community Data Center. "Orleans Parish: People and Household Characteristics, 2000." Accessed February 5, 2017, www.datacenter-research.org/pre-katrina/orleans/people.html.

Lachance, Paul. "Information on Persons Named in Indentures." New Orleans Public Library, 1998. http://nutrias.org/~nopl/inv/indentures/bioginfo.htm.

Neworleanschurches.com. "History of Annunciation Catholic Church, New Orleans, LA." Accessed October 31, 2015. http://www.neworleanschurches.com/annunciation/history.htm.

———. "Perspective on Holy Trinity Catholic Church." Accessed November 16, 2013. http://www.neworleanschurches.com/holytrinity/holytrin.htm.

New Orleans Dyke Bar History Project. "The Way They Go." *Last Call Stories*. Podcast episode 5. June 10, 2016. http://www.lastcallnola.org/podcast/2016/6/10/episode-5-the-way-they-go.

New Orleans Short Term Rental Report. Accessed September 25, 2016. http://nola-rentalreport.com/#/#about.

NOLA City Museum. "Rougelot's Department Store." Accessed January 8, 2015. http://www.nolacitymuseum.org/items/show/984. (Site discontinued.)

Nystrom, Justin A. "The Vanished World of the New Orleans Longshoreman." *Southern Spaces.* March 5, 2014. http://southernspaces.org/2014/vanished-world-new-orleans-longshoreman.

The Quorum. Manhattan, KS: Doorknob Films & Such-A-Much Productions, 2004. DVD.

"1875 St. Roch Market." *Makin' Groceries in New Orleans.* Accessed April 19, 2016. http://www.websitesneworleans.com/makingroceriesinneworleans/id197.html.

Richmond, Don. "The Story of Rosette Rochon." Musée Rosette Rochon. Accessed March 5, 2014. http://www.rosetterochon.com/rosette-r2.html. (Site discontinued.)

Rougelot, Sidney Benjamin, IV. "Rougelot's Department Store." *New Orleans Historical.* Accessed January 3, 2015. http://neworleanshistorical.org/items/show/630.

Sanctuary Cultural Arts Center. Accessed October 14, 2016. http://www.sanctuarynola.org/.

Smith-Torres, Vanessa. "Café Brasil." *Media Nola.* Tulane University. Accessed June 29, 2014. http://medianola.org/discover/place/858/Cafe-Brasil.

Tunmer, Sally. "Hear the Pulse of New Orleans on Frenchmen Street." *GoNOLA Radio.* February 15, 2012. http://www.gonola.com/2012/02/15/hear-the-pulse-of-new-orleans-on-frenchmen-street.html.

U.S. Merchant Marine at War. "American Merchant Marine at War." Accessed July 6, 2016. http://www.usmm.org.

Zillow. "Marigny New Orleans Apartments." Accessed November 12, 2017. https://www.zillow.com/homes/for_rent/Marigny-New-Orleans-LA/condo,apartment_duplex_type/269714_rid/featured_sort/29.970425,-90.044315,29.959345,-90.05969_rect/16_zm/

SECONDARY SOURCES

BOOKS AND ESSAYS

Arnesen, Eric. "New Orleans Dock Workers Struggle for Control, 1902–1903." In *New Orleans and Urban Louisiana*, pt. B, *1860 to World War I,* edited by Samuel C. Shepherd Jr. Lafayette: Center for Louisiana Studies, University of Louisiana at Lafayette, 2005.

Asbury, Herbert. *The French Quarter.* New York: Garden City Publishing, 1936.

Bailey, John. *The Lost German Slave Girl.* New York: Grove Press, 2006.

Baker, Liva. *The Second Battle of New Orleans.* New York: Harper Collins, 1996.

Bell, Caryn Cossé. *Revolution, Romanticism, and the Afro-Creole Protest Tradition in Louisiana, 1718–1868.* Baton Rouge: Louisiana State University Press, 1997.

Bergeron, Arthur W., Jr. *Guide to Louisiana Confederate Military Units, 1861–1865.* Baton Rouge: Louisiana State University Press, 1989.

Berlin, Ira. *Slaves without Masters: The Free Negro in the Antebellum South.* New York: Pantheon, 1975.

Bozant, Kevin. *Port and Burgundy: A Pictorial History of St. Paul's Lutheran Church, New Orleans.* New Orleans: St. Paul's Lutheran Church, 1990.

Brasseaux, Carl A. *Denis-Nicolas Foucault and the New Orleans Rebellion of 1768.* Ruston, LA: McGinty Publications, 1987.

Brown, Ethan. *Shake the Devil Off: A True Story of the Murder That Rocked New Orleans.* New York: St. Martins Griffin, 2010.

Brown, L. W. "Protection of Cities against Encroachment of the Mississippi." In *Riparian Lands of the Mississippi Delta, Past–Present–Prospective,* edited by Frank Tompkins. Chicago: A. L. Swift, 1901.

Cable, George Washington. *The Creoles of Louisiana.* New York: Charles Scribner's Sons, 1884.

Campanella, Richard. *Geographies of New Orleans: Urban Fabrics before the Storm.* Lafayette: Center for Louisiana Studies, University of Louisiana at Lafayette, 2006.

Capers, Gerald M. *Occupied City: New Orleans under the Federals, 1862–1865.* Lexington: University of Kentucky Press, 1965.

Carrigan, Jo Ann. *The Saffron Scourge: A History of Yellow Fever in Louisiana, 1796–1905.* Lafayette: Center for Louisiana Studies, University of Southwestern Louisiana, 1994.

Carter, Hodding. *The Past as Prelude: New Orleans, 1718–1968.* New Orleans: Tulane University, 1968.

Carter, William. *Preservation Hall.* New York: W. W. Norton, 1991.

Castellanos, Henry C. *New Orleans as It Was.* Reprint, Gretna, LA: Pelican Press, 1990.

Caughey, John Walton. *Bernardo de Gálvez in Louisiana, 1776–1783.* Gretna, LA: Pelican Publishing, 1972.

Chase, John Churchill. *Frenchmen, Desire, Good Children, and Other Streets of New Orleans.* 3rd ed. New York: Touchstone Books, 1997.

Coleman, James Julian, Jr. *Gilbert Antoine de St Maxent, the Spanish-Frenchman of New Orleans.* New Orleans: Pelican Publishing, 1968.

Corrigan, Jo Ann. *The Saffron Scourge: A History of Yellow Fever in Louisiana, 1796–1905.* Lafayette: Center for Louisiana Studies, University of Southwestern Louisiana, 1994.

Crété, Liliane. *Daily Life in Louisiana, 1815–1830.* Translated by Patrick Gregory. Baton Rouge: Louisiana State University Press, 1981.

Deiler, J. Hanno. *Geschichte der New Orleanser Deutschen Presse.* Translated by William Black. New Orleans: Paul J. Sendker, 1901.

Desdunes, Rodolphe Lucien. *Our People and Our History.* Translated and edited by Sr. Dorothea Olga McCants. Baton Rouge: Louisiana State University Press, 1973.

Dessens, Nathalie. *From Saint-Domingue to New Orleans: Migration and Influences.* Gainesville: University Press of Florida, 2007.

Doorley, Michael. "Irish Catholics and French Creoles: Ethnic Struggles within the Catholic Church in New Orleans, 1835–1920." In *New Orleans and Urban Louisiana,* pt. A, *Settlement to 1860,* edited by Samuel C. Shepherd Jr. Lafayette: Center for Louisiana Studies, University of Louisiana at Lafayette, 2005.

Dowler, Bennet. *Tableaux of New Orleans.* New Orleans: *Daily Delta,* 1853.

Duffy, John. *Sword of Pestilence: The New Orleans Yellow Fever Epidemic of 1853.* Baton Rouge: Louisiana State University Press, 1966.

Edwards-Simpson, Louise Reynes. "Sicilians Come to New Orleans: The Making of Little Palermo." In *New Orleans and Urban Louisiana,* pt. B, *1860 to World War I,* edited by Samuel C. Shepherd Jr. Lafayette: Center for Louisiana Studies, University of Louisiana at Lafayette, 2005.

Ellis, Scott S. *Madame Vieux Carré: The French Quarter in the Twentieth Century.* Jackson: University Press of Mississippi, 2009.

Fiehrer, Thomas. "From Quadrille to Stomp: The Creole Origin of Jazz." In *New Orleans and Urban Louisiana,* pt. B, *1860 to World War I,* edited by Samuel C. Shepherd Jr. Lafayette: Center for Louisiana Studies, University of Louisiana at Lafayette, 2005.

Flynn, Jim. *Sidewalk Saints: Life Portraits of the New Orleans Street Performer Family.* Detroit: Curbside Media, 2009.

Foner, Eric. *Reconstruction: America's Unfinished Revolution, 1863–1877.* 2nd ed. New York: Harper Perennial, 2014.

Fortier, John. "Philippe De Hautmesnil De Mandeville, François." In *Dictionary of Canadian Biography.* Vol. 2. Toronto: University of Toronto/Université Laval, 2003–. http://www.biographi.ca/en/bio/philippe_de_hautmesnil_de_mandeville_francois_2E.html.

Fricker, Jonathan, Donna Fricker, and Patricia Duncan. *Louisiana Architecture: A Handbook of Styles.* Lafayette: University of Louisiana at Lafayette Press, 1998.

Gayarré, Charles. *History of Louisiana,* vol. 1, *The French Domination.* New York: Redfield, 1854.

Gleeson, David T. *The Green and the Gray: The Irish in the Confederate States of America.* Chapel Hill: University of North Carolina Press, 2013.

Godfrey, Brian. *Neighborhoods in Transition: The Making of San Francisco's Ethnic and Nonconformist Communities.* Berkeley: University of California Press, 1988.

Haas, Edward F. *DeLesseps S. Morrison and the Image of Reform.* Baton Rouge: Louisiana State University Press, 1974.

Hanger, Kimberly S. *Bounded Lives, Bounded Places: Free Black Society in Colonial New Orleans, 1769–1803.* Durham, NC: Duke University Press, 1997.

Heard, Malcolm. *French Quarter Manual: An Architectural Guide to the Vieux Carré.* New Orleans: Tulane School of Architecture, 1997.

Hennick, Louis C., and E. Harper Charlton. *The Streetcars of New Orleans.* Gretna, LA: Firebird Press, 2000.

Hickey, Donald R. *Glorious Victory: Andrew Jackson and the Battle of New Orleans.* Baltimore: Johns Hopkins University Press, 2015.

Hirsch, Arnold R., and Joseph Logsdon, eds. *Creole New Orleans: Race and Americanization.* Baton Rouge: Louisiana State University Press, 1992.

Hollandsworth, James G. *An Absolute Massacre: The New Orleans Race Riot of July 30, 1866.* Baton Rouge: Louisiana State University Press, 2001.

Holzman, Robert S. *Stormy Ben Butler.* New York: Macmillan, 1954.

Holmes, Jack D. L. *Gayoso: The Life of a Spanish Governor in the Mississippi Valley, 1789–1799.* Baton Rouge: Louisiana State University Press for the Louisiana Historical Association, 1965.

Huber, Leonard V., Peggy McDowell, and Mary Louise Christovich. *New Orleans Architecture,* vol. 3, *The Cemeteries.* Gretna, LA: Pelican Publishing, 2004.

Irvin, Hillary S. "The Impact of German Immigration on New Orleans Architecture." In *New Orleans and Urban Louisiana,* pt. A, *Settlement to 1860,* edited by Samuel C. Shepherd Jr. Lafayette: Center for Louisiana Studies, University of Louisiana at Lafayette, 2005.

Jackson, Joy. *New Orleans in the Gilded Age: Politics and Urban Progress, 1880–1896.* 2nd ed. Lafayette: Louisiana Historical Association, in cooperation with the Center for Louisiana Studies of the University of Southwestern Louisiana, 1997.

James, C. L. R. *The Black Jacobins.* 2nd ed. New York: Vintage Books, 1963.

Jones, Joseph. *Quarantine and Sanitary Operations of the Board of Health of the State of Louisiana during 1880, 1881, 1882 and 1883.* Baton Rouge: Leon Jastremski, 1884.

Kendall, John Smith. *History of New Orleans.* Chicago: Lewis Publishing, 1922. Transcribed by Bill Thayer at http://penelope.uchicago.edu/Thayer/E/Gazetteer/Places/America/United_States/Louisiana/New_Orleans/_Texts/KENHNO/home.html.

King, Grace. *Creole Families of New Orleans.* New York: Macmillan, 1921.

Kondert, Reinhart. "German Immigration to French Colonial Louisiana: A Reevaluation." In *Proceedings of the Fourth Meeting of the French Colonial Historical Society, April 6–8, 1978, University of Mississippi, Oxford, Mississippi,* edited by Alf Andrew Heggoy and James J. Cooke. Washington, D.C.: University Press of America, 1979.

Krist, Gary. *Empire of Sin: A Story of Sex, Jazz, Murder, and the Battle for Modern New Orleans.* New York: Broadway Books, 2014.

Labadie, Jeremy, and Argyle Wolf-Knapp. *New Orleans Beer: A Hoppy History of Big Easy Brewing.* Charleston, SC: American Palate/History Press, 2014.

Landau, Emily Epstein. *Spectacular Wickedness: Sex, Race, and Memory in Storyville, New Orleans.* Baton Rouge: Louisiana State University Press, 2013.

LeCheminant, Wilford Hill. *Peter and Sarah Farr LeCheminant and the 1854 Mormon Immigration from Europe to the Great Salt Lake Valley.* Bountiful, UT, 1979.

Lemann, Bernard. *The Vieux Carré: A General Statement.* New Orleans: Tulane University School of Architecture, 1966.

Lonn, Ella. *Foreigners in the Confederacy.* Gloucester, MA: Peter Smith, 1965.

Margavio, A. V., and Jerome J. Salomone. *Bread and Respect: The Italians of Louisiana.* Gretna, LA: Pelican Publishing, 2002.

Martin, Francois-Xavier. *The History of Louisiana from the Earliest Period.* Vol. 1. New Orleans: Lyman and Beardslee, 1827.

McFarlane, J. S. *The Epidemic Summer: List of Interments in the Cemeteries of New Orleans, from the First of May to the First of November, 1853.* New Orleans: Proprietor of the *True Delta*, 1853.

McNally, Dennis. *Long Strange Trip: The Inside History of the Grateful Dead and the Making of Modern America.* London: Corgi Books, 2003.

McPherson, Edward. *The Political History of the United States of America during the Great Rebellion.* Washington, D.C.: Phillips & Solomon, 1864.

Mehrlander, Andrea. *The Germans of Charleston, Richmond and New Orleans during the Civil War Period, 1850–1870.* Berlin: de Gruyter, 2011.

Merrill, Ellen C. *Germans of Louisiana.* Gretna, LA: Pelican Publishing, 2005.

Mitchell, Mary Niall. "A Good and Delicious Country: Free Children of Color and How They Learned to Imagine the Atlantic World in Nineteenth-Century Louisiana." In *Chartered Schools: Two Hundred Years of Independent Academies in the United States, 1727–1925,* edited by Nancy Beadie and Kim Tolley. New York: Routledge Falmer, 2002.

Nau, John F. *The German People of New Orleans, 1850–1900.* Hattiesburg: University of Southern Mississippi, 1974.

New Orleans as it is, its manners and customs—morals—fashionable life—profanation of the Sabbath—prostitution—licentiousness—slave markets and slavery, &c., &c., &c. [New Orleans?], 1850.

Niehaus, Earl F. *The Irish in New Orleans, 1800–1860.* Baton Rouge: Louisiana State University Press, 1965.

Ochs, Stephen J. *A Black Patriot and a White Priest: André Cailloux and Claude Paschal Maistre in Civil War New Orleans.* Baton Rouge: Louisiana State University Press, 2000.

O'Connor, Thomas, ed. *History of the Fire Department of New Orleans.* New Orleans, 1895.

Pierson, Michael D. *Mutiny at Fort Jackson.* Chapel Hill: University of North Carolina Press, 2008.

du Pratz, Le Page. *History of Louisiana.* London: T. Beckett, 1774. Project Gutenberg, www.gutenberg.org/ebooks/9153.

Reed, Merl E. "The New Orleans Short Lines." In *New Orleans and Urban Louisiana,* pt. A, *Settlement to 1860,* edited by Samuel C. Shepherd Jr. Lafayette: Center for Louisiana Studies, University of Louisiana at Lafayette, 2005.

Reinders, Robert C. *End of an Era: New Orleans, 1850–1860.* New Orleans: Pelican Publishing, 1964.

Rodrigue, John C. *Lincoln and Reconstruction.* Carbondale: Southern Illinois University Press, 2013.

Rose, Al. *Storyville, New Orleans.* Tuscaloosa: University of Alabama Press, 1974.

Rosenberg, Daniel. *New Orleans Dockworkers: Race, Labor and Unionism, 1892–1923.* Albany: State University of New York Press, 1988.

Rudolph, William Keyse. *Vaudechamp in New Orleans.* New Orleans: Historic New Orleans Collection, 2007.

Schafer, Judith Kelleher. *Becoming Free, Remaining Free: Manumission and Enslavement in New Orleans, 1846–1862.* Baton Rouge: Louisiana State University Press, 2003.

———. *Brothels, Depravity, and Abandoned Women: Illegal Sex in Antebellum New Orleans.* Baton Rouge: Louisiana State University Press, 2009.

Seebold, Herman de Bachelle. *Old Louisiana Plantation Homes and Family Trees.* Gretna, LA: Pelican Press 2004.

Somers, Dale A. *The Rise of Sports in New Orleans, 1850–1900.* Baton Rouge: Louisiana State University Press, 1972.

Soulé, Leon Cyprian. *The Know Nothing Party in New Orleans: A Reappraisal.* Baton Rouge: Louisiana Historical Association, 1961.

Southwood, Marion. *Beauty and Booty, the Watchword of New Orleans.* New York: M. Doolady, 1867.

Swenson, John. *New Atlantis: Musicians Battle for the Survival of New Orleans.* New York: Oxford University Press, 2011.

Tallant, Robert. *Mardi Gras . . . as It Was.* Gretna, LA: Pelican Publishing, 2000.

Tansey, Richard. "Prostitution and Politics in Antebellum New Orleans." *Southern Studies* 18, no. 4 (Winter 1979), reprinted in *History of Women in the United States: Historical Articles on Women's Lives and Activities,* vol. 9, *Prostitution,* edited by Nancy F. Cott. Munich: K. G. Saur, 1993.

Terrage, Marc de Villiers du. *The Last Years of French Louisiana.* Translated by Hosea Phillips. Edited by Carl A. Brasseaux and Glenn R. Conrad. Lafayette: Center for Louisiana Studies, University of Southwestern Louisiana, 1982.

Thomas, Grace Powers, ed. *Where to Educate, 1898–1899.* Boston: Brown, 1898.

Thompson, Shirley Elizabeth. *Exiles at Home: The Struggle to Become American in Creole New Orleans.* Cambridge, MA: Harvard University Press, 2009.

Tinker, Edward Larocque. *The Palingenesis of Craps.* New York: Press of the Woolly Whale, 1933.

Toledano, Roulhac, Sally K. Evans, Mary Louise Christovich, and Samuel Wilson Jr. *The Creole Faubourgs.* Vol. 4 of *New Orleans Architecture.* Gretna, LA: Pelican Publishing, 1996.

Trask, Benjamin H. *Fearful Ravages: Yellow Fever in New Orleans, 1796–1905.* Lafayette: Center for Louisiana Studies, University of Louisiana at Lafayette, 2005.

Tregle, Joseph. *Louisiana in the Age of Jackson: A Clash of Cultures and Personalities.* Baton Rouge: Louisiana State University Press, 1999.

Vandal, Giles. *The New Orleans Riot of 1866: Anatomy of a Tragedy.* Lafayette: Center for Louisiana Studies, University of Southwestern Louisiana, 1983.

Voss, Louis. *History of the German Society of New Orleans.* New Orleans: Sendkar Printing Service, 1927.
Wade, Richard C. *Slavery in the Cities.* New York: Oxford University Press, 1964.
Wiley, Bell Irvin. *Embattled Confederates.* New York: Harper & Row, 1964.
Wiltz, Christine. *The Last Madam.* New York: Da Capo Press, 2001.

DISSERTATIONS, THESES, AND UNPUBLISHED PAPERS

Aslakson, Kenneth. "Making Race: The Role of Free Blacks in the Development of New Orleans' Three-Caste Society, 1791–1812." PhD diss., University of Texas, Austin, 2007.
Babb, Winston C. "French Refugees from Saint Domingue to the Southern United States, 1791–1810." PhD diss., University of Virginia, 1954.
Edwards, Louise. "Yellow Fever and the Sicilian Community in New Orleans." Unpublished manuscript, University of Minnesota, May 30, 1989.
Follette, Edith Challin. "The History of the Know-Nothing Party in Louisiana." MA thesis, Tulane University, 1910.
Johnson, Penny. "Eulalie de Mandeville: An Ethnohistorical Investigation Challenging Notions of Plaçage in New Orleans as Revealed through the Lived Experiences of a Free Woman of Color." MS thesis, University of New Orleans, 2010. http://scholarworks.uno.edu/td/1285.
Knopp, Lawrence M., Jr. "Gentrification and Gay Community Development in a New Orleans Neighborhood." PhD diss., University of Iowa, 1989.
Lovato, Frank Joseph. "Households and Neighborhoods among Free People of Color in New Orleans: A View from the Census, 1850–1860." MA thesis, University of New Orleans, 2010. http://scholarworks.uno.edu/td/1174.
McArdle, Golda Mary. "The Pontchartrain Railroad, Pioneer in the South." MA thesis, Tulane University, 1931.
Nystrom, Justin A. "Redeemer's Carnival: The Urban Drama of Reconstruction in New Orleans." PhD diss., University of Georgia, 2004.
Rosario, Anthony Del. "Historic Structures Report for Schwegmann Family Tomb in St. Roch Cemetery No. 1. New Orleans." Unpublished report for Studio in Building Preservation, Master in Preservation Studies, Tulane School of Architecture, February 12, 2010. http://docslide.us/documents/schwegmann-family-tomb-report.html.
Roesel, Jeffrey W. "A Sense of Place: Residential Perceptions of Waterfront Land Use Changes in the Vieux Carré and Marigny." MA thesis, University of New Orleans, 1992.
Smestad, John, Jr. "The Role of Archbishop Joseph F. Rummel in the Desegrega-

tion of Catholic Schools in New Orleans." *Student Historical Journal* (Loyola University History Department) 25 (1993–94).

Smith, Amy Ferrara. "The New Orleans Grocery Man: Ferrara Supermarket's Mr. Merrill." MA thesis, University of New Orleans, 2007. http://scholarworks.uno.edu/td/1059.

Spalek, M. Floriana. "Bernard Xavier Philippe de Marigny de Mandeville and the Americanization of New Orleans." MA thesis, Catholic University of America, 1959.

PERIODICAL ARTICLES

Adler, Constance. "Drawing from the Past," *Gambit,* February 25, 2003, http://www.bestofneworleans.com/gambit/drawing-from-the-past/Content?oid=1241234.

Alexander-Bloch, Benjamin. "Domino Sugar's Chalmette Refinery's History and Production Recognized." *Times-Picayune,* December 13, 2012.

Allman, Kevin, Jeanie Reiss, Missy Wilkinson, and Alex Woodward. "One Night on Frenchmen." *Gambit* 35, no. 31 (August 11, 2014).

"Ask Julia Street." *New Orleans Magazine.* March 2010.

Baughman, James P. "A Southern Spa: Ante-bellum Lake Pontchartrain." *Louisiana History* 3, no. 1 (1962): 5–32.

Binczewski, G. J. "The Energy Crisis and the Aluminum Industry: Can We Learn from History?" *Member Journal of the Minerals, Metals, & Materials Society,* February 2002. http://www.tms.org/pubs/journals/JOM/0202/Binczewski-0202.html.

Brasseaux, Carl. "The Moral Climate of French Colonial Louisiana, 1699–1763." *Louisiana History* 27, no. 1 (Winter 1986).

"Building Watchers." *Preservation Press* 1, no. 1 (August 1975).

Cable, George Washington. "New Orleans before the Capture." *Century Illustrated Monthly Magazine* 29, no. 7 (July 1886): 918–22.

Campanella, Richard. "On The Structural Basis of Social Memory: Cityscapes of the New Orleans Slave Trade." Pt. 2. *Preservation in Print* (Preservation Resource Center, New Orleans), April 2013.

Carey, Rita Katherine, "Samuel Jarvis Peters." *Louisiana Historical Quarterly* 30, no. 2 (1947).

Cinelli, Dino "Estratto." *Cintro Studi Emigrazione* (Rome), no. 97 (March 1990).

Clark, Robert T., Jr. "The German Liberals in New Orleans (1840–1860)." *Louisiana Historical Quarterly* 20, no. 1 (January 1937).

Cruzat, J. W. "Biographical and Genealogical Notes Concerning the Family of Phillipe de Mandeville, Sieur de Marigny, 1709–1910." *Louisiana Historical Quarterly* 5, no. 1 (1911): 42–50.

Daggett, Melissa. "Spiritualism among Creoles of Color in Nineteenth-Century New Orleans: The Life and Times of Henry Louis Rey." *Louisiana History* 55, no. 4 (Fall 2014): 409–31.

Deiler, J. Hanno. "The System of Redemption in the State of Louisiana." Translated by Louis Voss in *Louisiana Historical Quarterly* 12, no. 3 (July 1929).

Dufour, Cyprien. "Bernard Marigny." *Louisiana Courier,* March 8, 1847. Translated by R. W. Colomb in *Louisiana Historical Quarterly* 14, no. 3 (October 1931): 396–98.

Fauré, Steven. "200 Years of History: The Cabildo in New Orleans." *Inside Northshore,* March–April 2012, 2.

Goslee, Charles B., Jr. "Appraisal-Housing Problem." *Preservation Press* (Preservation Resource Center, New Orleans) 1, no. 2 (October 1975).

de Gournay, P. F. "The F.M.C.s of Louisiana." *Lippincott's Monthly Magazine* 53 (1894).

Green, George D. "The Citizens Bank of Louisiana: Property Banking in Troubled Times, 1833–1842." *Business and Economic History,* 1st ser., 4 (1968).

Greer, James Kimmens. "Louisiana Politics, 1845–1861." *Louisiana Historical Quarterly* 12, no. 3 (July 1929).

Heleniak, Roman. "Local Reaction to the Great Depression in New Orleans, 1929–1933." *Louisiana History* 10, no. 4 (Fall 1969).

Heminghouse, Patricia. "The German Secrets of New Orleans." *German Studies Review* 27, no. 1 (February 2004): 1–16.

Hildreth, Peggy Bassett. "Early Red Cross: The Howard Association of New Orleans, 1837–1878." *Louisiana History* 20, no. 1 (Winter 1979): 49–75.

Holtmann, Antonius. "Emigration to America in the Context of an (Unsuccessful) Revolution, 1848/49: Scenario of a Misjudged Interconnection." In *Schöne Neue Welt: Rheinländer erobern Amerika,* vol. 2, edited by Rheinisches Freilicht- und Landesmuseum für Volkskunde, 329–38. Wiehl: Martina Galunder Verlag 2001. http://www.nausa.uni-oldenburg.de/1848/1848holten.html.

Johnson, Clarence L. "The Family of Marigny de Mandeville and the Fontainebleau Plantation, 1700–1938." Pts. 2–4. *Louisiana Conservation Review* 7, no. 4 (Winter 1938–39): 47–51; 8, no. 1 (Spring 1939): 21–26; 8, no. 2 (Summer 1939) 40–42.

Kernion, George C. H. "Samuel Jarvis Peters, the Man Who Made New Orleans To-Day and Became a National Personality." *Louisiana Historical Quarterly* 7, no. 1 (1913): 69–83.

Kolb, Carolyn. "Steppin' Back: The Golden Days of Dance Halls." *New Orleans Magazine,* April 2011. http://www.myneworleans.com/New-Orleans-Magazine/April-2011/STEPPIN-rsquo-BACK/.

Konrad, William Robinson. "The Diminishing Influences of German Culture in New Orleans Life since 1865." *Louisiana Historical Quarterly* 24, no. 1 (January 1941).

Kunian, David. "Obituary: Bill Sinegal." *Offbeat,* April 14, 2014.

Lachance, Paul. "The 1809 Immigration of Saint-Domingue Refugees to New Orleans: Reception, Integration and Impact" *Louisiana History* 29, no. 2 (1988).

Landphair, Juliette. "'The Forgotten People of New Orleans': Community, Vulnerability, and the Lower Ninth Ward." *Journal of American History* 94 (December 2007): 837–45.

Maldonado, Charles. "The Marigny and the Lofts." *Gambit,* August 21, 2012.

Marigny, Bernard. "Reflections on the Campaign of General Andrew Jackson in Louisiana, 1814 and 1815." Translated by Grace King. *Louisiana Historical Quarterly* 6, no. 1 (1923).

Martin, Naomi. "New Orleans Murders Down in 2014, but Violent Crime on the Rise." *Times-Picayune,* January 7, 2015.

McMain, Eleanor. "Behind the Yellow Fever in Little Palermo." *Charities,* November 4, 1905. Transcribed by Bill Thayer at http://penelope.uchicago.edu/Thayer/E/Gazetteer/Places/America/United_States/Louisiana/New_Orleans/_Texts/Yellow_Fever_in_Little_Palermo*.html.

Mieri, Catharine. "Historic Businesses of Faubourg Marigny." *Preservation in Print* 10, no. 6 (August 1983).

"New Orleans, Her Commerce and Her Duties: Condition of the Three Municipalities." *DeBow's Review* 3, no. 4 (April 1847).

Otvos, Ervin G., Jr. "New Orleans–South Hancock Holocene Barrier Trends and Origins of Lake Pontchartrain." *Transactions of Gulf Coast Associations of Geological Societies* 28 (1987): 337–55.

Quigley, Bill, and Maha Zaki. "The Significance of Race: Legislative Racial Discrimination in Louisiana, 1803–1865." *Southern University Law Review,* Spring 1997.

Ramsey, Jan V. "Frenchmen Street Brass Band Controversy." *Offbeat,* April 16, 2014.

———. "Why Are Frenchmen Street Musicians Undervalued?" *Offbeat,* June 7, 2017.

Rankin, David C. "The Impact of the Civil War on the Free Colored Community of New Orleans." *Perspectives in American History* 11 (1977–78): 380.

Rushton, Bill. "The Faubourg Marigny: Straddling the Centuries." *New Orleans Magazine,* March 1970.

Schweninger, Loren. "Antebellum Free Persons of Color in Postbellum Louisiana." *Louisiana History* 30 (Fall 1989).

"Speech of James Robb, Esq. Delivered at the South-Western Railroad Convention, Held in the Municipal Hall (Second Municipality), New Orleans, January 7, 1852." *DeBow's Review* 12, no. 5 (May 1852).

Stahl, Annie Lee West. "The Free Negro in Ante-bellum Louisiana." *Louisiana Historical Quarterly* 25, no. 2 (April 1942).

"The Sugar Cane in Louisiana." *DeBow's Review* 22, no. 6 (June 1857): 616.

Swenson, John. "Another Troubled Street." *Offbeat*, April 2009.

Tansey, Richard. "Southern Expansionism: Urban Interests in the Cuban Filibuster." *Plantation Society* 1, no. 2 (June 1979): 227–51.

Tarver, Jerry L. "The Political Clubs of New Orleans in the Presidential Election of 1860." *Louisiana History* 4, no. 2 (Spring 1963).

de Villiers, Baron Marc. "A History of the Foundation of New Orleans (1717–1722)." Translated by Warrington Dawson. *Louisiana Historical Quarterly* 3, no. 2 (April 1920).

White, Timothy. "Diverse Club Scene Spills onto Sidewalks in the Land of Dreams." *Billboard,* June 8, 1996.

ONLINE ARTICLES

American Antiquarian Society and Tufts University Digital Collections. "Louisiana 1824 Governor." In *A New Nation Votes: American Election Returns, 1787–1825.* Accessed November 1, 2015. http://elections.lib.tufts.edu/catalog/tufts:la.governor.1824.

Cinema Tour. "Bijou Theatre." Accessed March 24, 2016. http://www.cinematour.com/tour/us/40311.html.

———. "Paris Theatre." Accessed March 24, 2016. http://www.cinematour.com/tour/us/25587.html.

———. "Piety Theatre." Accessed March 24, 2016. http://www.cinematour.com/tour/us/40322.html.

Commode, Dorian, and Jules Bentley. "UnfairBNB: What Unlicensed Short-Term Rentals Mean for New Orleans." *Antigravity,* March 2014. http://www.antigravitymagazine.com/2014/03/unfairbnb-what-unlicensed-short-term-rentals-mean-for-new-orleans/.

Delaup, Rick. "Gallery of Eccentrics." Accessed November 2, 2006. http://www.eccentricneworleans.com/gallery_of_eccentrics.htm (site discontinued).

Ferrand, Casey. "Crackdown on Frenchmen Street Flusters Businesses." WDSU TV, New Orleans, November 25, 2013. http://www.wdsu.com/news/local-news/new-orleans/crackdown-on-frenchman-street-rules-strikes-chord-with-businesses/23139864.

Hurley, Michael. "Paris Theatre in New Orleans, LA." Cinema Treasures. Accessed October 24, 2014. http://cinematreasures.org/theaters/22787.

Knapp, Gwendolyn. "Apparently Only Bamboula's Wants Bamboula's to Become a Nightclub." *NOLA Eater.* January 15, 2015. http://nola.eater.com/2015/1/15/7553721/apparently-only-bamboulas-wants-bamboulas-to-become-a-nightclub.

Laborde, Lauren. "Marigny Warehouse, Once Planned for Sean Cummings' Elisio Lofts, Sells to Hotel Developer." *Curbed New Orleans,* September 22, 2016.

http://nola.curbed.com/2016/9/22/13020760/elisio-lofts-marigny-new-orleans-warehouse-sold.
Miller, Mason. "New Orleans Middle Schoolers Are Beating the Shit Out of Artists and Gays." *Vice,* August 21, 2014. http://www.vice.com/read/new-orleans-middle-schoolers-are-beating-the-shit-out-of-its-artists-and-gays-820.
Ndiaye, Aboubacar. "Eight Reasons Why the Rent Is Too Damn High." National Public Radio, January 7, 2014. http://www.npr.org/sections/codeswitch/2014/01/06/260282186/eight-reasons-why-the-rent-is-too-damn-high.
Neidenbach, Elizabeth C. "'*Mes dernières volontés*': Testaments to the Life of Marie Couvent, a Former Slave in New Orleans." *Transatlantica* 2 (2012). Published online May 17, 2013. http://transatlantica.revues.org/6186.
Peck, Emily, and Charles Maldonado. "How Airbnb Is Pushing Locals Out of New Orleans' Coolest Neighborhoods." *Lens,* October 30, 2017. http://thelensnola.org/2017/10/30/how-airbnb-is-pushing-locals-out-of-new-orleans-coolest-neighborhoods.
Schiro's Café. "Welcome to Schiro's Café" [menu]. Accessed December 31, 2013. schiroscafe.com (site discontinued).

INDEX

Numbers in italic denote illustrations.